The text of this book is composed in Garamond with the display set in
Caslon Open Face and Cochin italic.
Composition and manufacturing by the Maple–Vail Book Manufacturing
Group.
Book design by Charlotte Staub

Library of Congress Cataloging-in-Publication Data

Darnton, Robert,
    The forbidden bestsellers of pre-revolutionary France / Robert
Darnton.
      p. cm.
    1. French literature—18th century—History and criticism.
2. Popular literature—France—History and criticism. 3. Books and
reading—France—History—18th century. 4. Best sellers—France—
History—18th century. I. Title.
PQ265.D37   1995
840.9′005—dc20   94-24180
ISBN 0-393-03720-7

W. W. Norton & Company, Inc.,
500 Fifth Avenue, New York, N.Y. 10110
W. W. Norton & Company Ltd.,
10 Coptic Street, London WC1A 1PU
1 2 3 4 5 6 7 8 9 0

To Harry Pitt,
tutor and friend

*The companion volume
to this book is*

The Corpus of
Clandestine Literature
in France,

1769–1789,

*also published by
W. W. Norton & Company*

꧁꧂

Contents

CONTENTS

IV.
"PHILOSOPHICAL BOOKS": A SHORT ANTHOLOGY

List of Tables, Maps, and Figures

List of Illustrations

xv

Introduction

THE BIG QUESTIONS IN HISTORY often seem unmanageable. What causes revolutions? Why do value systems change? How does public opinion influence events? This book is meant to address those questions by beginning with a query of a different order, one that can be answered: What did the French read in the eighteenth century?

How that small question can open up the big ones should become clear in the course of this study. At this point, I would merely like to pose it and to note that it, too, has a history. It was first raised eighty-three years by Daniel Mornet, who made it the starting point for a vast inquiry into the intellectual origins of the French Revolution. Whatever the French read in the eighteenth century, Mornet argued, it was not what we commonly take to be eighteenth-century French literature. We envisage the literature of every century as a corpus of works grouped around a core of classics; and we derive our notion of the classics from our professors, who took it from their professors, who got it from theirs, and so on, back to some disappearing point in the early nineteenth century. Literary history is an artifice, pieced together over many generations, shortened here and lengthened there, worn thin in some places, patched over in others, and laced through everywhere with anachronism. It bears little relation to the actual experience of literature in the past.

Mornet set out to capture that experience, *la littérature vécue,* by finding out what people read under the Old Regime. He began by counting books, a great many of them: 20,000 in all, which he compiled from auction catalogues of eighteenth-century private libraries. After accumulating a mountain of index cards, he decided to determine how many copies of Rousseau's *Social Contract* had been unearthed. Answer: one. One copy in a mass of 20,000 works! It looked as though the greatest political treatise of the century, the bible of the French Revolution, went unread before 1789. The connecting links between the Enlightenment and the Revolution seemed to dissolve. Instead of pondering arguments about popular sovereignty and the General Will, the French appear to have amused themselves with the sentimental novels of Mme Riccoboni and the adventure stories of Thémiseul de Saint-Hyacinthe. The Revolution was not "la faute à Rousseau," and probably not "la faute à Voltaire," either.[1]

That was 1910. We know now that Mornet made several false steps. He ended his inquiry in 1780, just when the first of many editions of Rousseau's works, *Du Contrat Social* included, began to appear. He neglected popularized versions of the *Social Contract,* notably the one in Book V of Rousseau's *Emile,* which was incontestably a best-seller before the Revolution. And his source was flawed. Libraries important enough to be sold in public auctions hardly represented a common variety of book ownership, not to mention reading. And the catalogues printed for those auctions had to pass through the censorship. So the ideological element was excluded from the very source where Mornet hoped to find it.

Whatever the adequacy of his answer, Mornet's question remains valid. It has provoked a succession of attempts, in research projects scattered over three quarters of a century, to identify the literature that French people actually read under the Old Regime. Each attempt has strengths and weaknesses of its own. Each has added to our knowledge. But cumulatively they tend to cancel one another out, or to contain so many contradictions that no general pattern can be identified. Mornet's question continues to hang over literary history, as tantalizing as ever.

It can easily become a *question mal posée,* because it is far less simple than it seems. In order to trim it down to manageable proportions, I would like to limit my inquiry to the element that Mornet left out of his: illegal literature. That eliminates a vast amount, I know. I simply cannot circumnavigate all of French literature in the eighteenth century, but I think I can map the forbidden sector, and that sector was enormous. In fact, it contained almost the entire Enlightenment and everything that Mornet was later to identify with the intellectual origins of the French Revolution. To French readers in the eighteenth century, illegal literature was virtually the same as modern literature. The official in charge of suppressing it, C.-G. de Lamoignon de Malesherbes, found the task impossible. Indeed, he refused to do it: "A man who had read only books that originally appeared with the formal approval of the government," he wrote, "would be behind his contemporaries by nearly a century."[2]

Instead of attempting to confiscate everything published outside the law, Malesherbes opened loopholes in his administration, which left room for unofficial but inoffensive works to circulate without receiving legal recognition by the state. This practice went back to the seventeenth century, when the state tried to control the printed word by subjecting it to institutions that typified the absolutism of Louis XIV: censorship (*censeurs royaux* attached to the Direction de la librairie or book trade administration); police (specialized *inspecteurs de la librairie* under the lieutenant general of police in Paris); and a monopolistic guild (provincial corporations and especially the Communauté des libraires et des imprimeurs de Paris, which owned most book privileges and enforced them by inspecting domestic shipments). In order to be published legally, a book had to clear all sorts of hurdles within this system and to appear with a royal privilege printed out in full. Like a modern copyright, the privilege gave its owner the exclusive right to reproduce the text. But it also served as a royal stamp of approval. It guaranteed the quality as well as the orthodoxy of the text, and so did the approbations of the censors, which usually accompanied it at the beginning or end of the book. To be fully legal, a book had to conform to elaborate standards set by the state.

Anything that deviated from those standards was usually printed outside France and smuggled into the kingdom. Dozens of publishing houses sprang up all around France's borders. Hundreds of agents operated an underground system, which brought the books to readers. But this enormous industry drained a great deal of wealth from the kingdom, while spreading a great many unorthodox ideas inside it. Finding itself unable to destroy the competition that it had helped create, the French administration devised categories to permit the trade in books that could not be given a royal privilege but did not attack the Church, the state, or conventional morality. By 1750, book inspectors distinguished graduated nuances of legality in a wide spectrum, which extended from *privilèges* to *permissions tacites, permissions simples, permission de police,* and *simples tolérances.* Legality shaded off into illegality by almost imperceptible degrees. But meanwhile, a libertine literature had grown up, which undercut all the orthodox values of the Old Regime. So the regime replied with renewed repression, this time against books that existed at the far end of the spectrum, in a category of unalloyed illegality, beyond the pale, far outside the law. Those are the books I propose to study.

Easier said than done. The irredeemably illegal element in eighteenth-century literature does not stand out to the twentieth-century eye. Some title pages flaunt their forbidden character by gross language—*Le Cul d'Iris (Iris's Ass)*—or by provocative false addresses: "printed in Philadelphia," or "at the sign of liberty," or "at a hundred leagues from the Bastille." But many look anodyne, or at least not perceptively more illegal than the quasi-legal works that were tolerated by the government. How can one identify the truly "bad books" *(mauvais livres),* as they were known to the police? The police kept a few lists. The king's council issued individual condemnations. Bishops fulminated from pulpits. And the public hangman lacerated and burned forbidden books in great ceremony at the foot of the grand staircase before the Parlement of Paris. But none of those activities generated enough documentation for one to be able to study the entire body of forbidden literature.

The only way to track down all of the "bad" books is to follow them through the channels of the underground book trade, and the only access to those channels is through the papers of the professionals who utilized them. But the only papers that have survived come from a single source: the Société typographique de Neuchâtel, a major publisher and wholesaler that supplied the French market from the principality of Neuchâtel in French-speaking Switzerland. Those archives contain enough material—50,000 letters and several shelves of account books—for one to reconstruct the entire trade in France. But they have certain limitations, so they must be supplemented by research in the vast Parisian archives concerning the administration and policing of the book trade. Having worked through all this material, I want to report my findings here.

Actually, the subject is too large to be compressed within the covers of a single volume. This book (along with its companion, *The Corpus of Clandestine Literature*) is the second of what will be a trilogy. The first was a publishing history of Diderot's *Encyclopédie,* and the third will be a study of publishing and bookselling in general.[3] This work is devoted to the books themselves—their identification, their diffusion, and their texts.

Although I find this research so intriguing that I have kept at it for twenty-five years, I realize that it may look like sheer antiquarianism to some of my readers. Why bother to identify a corpus of literature that has been forgotten for two hundred years, they may ask. Why pore over the texts of best-sellers from the eighteenth century when the best-sellers of our own day often seem so trivial? What is at stake in all this scholarship?

I would answer, first, that the history of books as a new discipline within the "human sciences" makes it possible to gain a broader view of literature and of cultural history in general. By discovering what books reached readers throughout an entire society and (at least to a certain extent) how readers made sense of them, one can study literature as part of a general cultural system. This view makes it necessary to abandon preconceptions about great books by famous authors. But it does not mean that literature must be swallowed up in sociology. On the contrary, many of the forgotten best-sellers still make excellent reading today. By analyzing some of them in detail, I hope to show how textual study belongs to the core of book history as a discipline. And by producing a bibliography of the entire corpus of forbidden books in pre-Revolutionary France, with information about their geographical distribution and the relative strength of the demand for each of them, I hope to provide a basic guide for further research.

A great deal remains to be done, because most of this literature has never been investigated. In order to bring some of it within the range of English readers, I have included a short anthology of translated excerpts from three of the most important works. By sampling them, the reader will be able to form his or her own impressions of the world of illegal literature. It may seem surprising, shocking, naughty, or comic; but it certainly will look different from the world made familiar by the great-man, great-book variety of literary history.

Second, I hope to show how the history of books opens onto the larger field of the history of communication. Literature itself can be understood as a communications system, which extends from authors and publishers through printers and booksellers to readers. It also belongs to a general culture, where media of all sorts—printed, written, oral, and visual—crisscross and interconnect. In eighteenth-century France, books did not compete with radio and television, but they circulated in a society that overflowed with gossip, rumors, jokes, songs, graffiti, posters, pasquinades, broadsides, letters, and journals. Many of these media left their imprint on the books themselves, just as the books affected them. The process of transmission and amplification flooded France with words and images. But how did it operate, and how did it threaten the stability of the Old Regime?

Those questions concern a third area I wish to investigate: the articulation of ideologies and the formation of public opinion. This is speculative territory, because we have only a vague notion of what the public was—if in fact we can speak of a single public—and of how it formed opinions in the eighteenth century. But the forbidden books contain so much information about what they refer to as "public opinion" that I have not resisted the temptation to speculate.

The speculations lead back to a fourth area of study, which is more familiar and concrete: political history and the origins of the French Revolution. Here I can only sketch an argument that I hope to fill out with further research; but I believe it deserves a place in the discussion of forbidden books, because those books conveyed a political message and a general view of politics. To be sure, they did not correspond to the actual practice of powerbrokering in Versailles. On the contrary, they had so little to do with political reality that they represent what I have called a "folklore." But in doing so, they shaped reality itself and helped determine the course of events.

I may be promising more than I can deliver, however, so I had better return to the point of departure, Mornet's question about what the French read before 1789. It is a leading question, one of history's happiest, because the pursuit of it takes one deep into unfamiliar territory. This book explores that territory. It is meant to open up new questions while chasing after old ones, and to suggest some general implications in a field of research that no longer needs to be recognized but now must prove itself worthy of its promise: the study of the printed word as a force in history.

In publishing the results of this research after so many years of labor, I must record my debt to the Society of Fellows of Harvard University, which helped me get a start on it in 1964 and to the MacArthur Foundation, which helped me keep it going in the final stretch. I completed writing in the congenial surroundings of the Wissenschaftskolleg zu Berlin. And along the way I benefited from the criticism of many friends and colleagues, notably Raymond Birn, Peter Brown, Roger Chartier, Steven Forman, Carlos Forment, Anthony Grafton, Christian Jouhaud, Jeffrey Merrick, Pierre Rétat, François Rigolot, and Dale Van Kley. Cynthia Gessele provided invaluable help in calculating the statistics, Marjorie Asbury in typing the bibliography, and Susan Darnton in translating the French texts. The bibliography also benefited from the expert advice of Robert Dawson, and of Vivienne Mylne, whose death deprived eighteenth-century scholars of one of their finest colleagues.

Forbidden Literature and the Literary Market

PART ONE

Chapter 1

Philosophy
Under the Cloak

WHEN THE PUBLIC HANGMAN lacerated and burned forbidden books in the courtyard of the Palais de Justice in Paris, he paid tribute to the power of the printed word. But he often destroyed dummy copies, while the magistrates kept the originals—and they were less profligate with their autos-da-fé than is generally believed. Knowing that nothing promoted sales better than a good bonfire, they preferred to impound books and imprison booksellers with as little fuss as possible. According to one estimate, the authorities condemned only 4.5 books and pamphlets on average per year during the 1770s and 1780s, and publicly burned only 19 of them.[1]

While those works went up in flames, however, thousands of others circulated secretly through the channels of the underground book trade. They provided the basic diet of illegal literature for hungry readers throughout the kingdom. Yet no one knows what they were.

What was the size and shape of this huge body of literature, the ordinary variety sold "under the cloak" *(sous le manteau)* by peddlers everywhere? The regime itself had no idea. Despite some attempts at bibliographical police work, it kept no record of all the books that could be considered illegal even though they had never been formally condemned.[2] The very notion of legality in literature remained fuzzy, because the authorities in

3

charge of the book trade constantly fudged the line that separated the licit from the illicit. On the legal side, they not only issued various kinds of privileges and permissions but also casual authorizations that went without a name or appeared in registers with circumlocutions such as "permitted only for persons who are very well known."[3] On the illegal side, they confiscated pirated editions of legal books (contrefaçons), legal books that were imported by an individual who did not go through an official bookseller, books that were not offensive but that lacked any kind of permission (often imports of books authorized in other countries), and books that caused offense in the three standard ways specified by royal edicts and censors' reports: by undermining the authority of the king, the Church, or conventional morality.

One could not even determine the degree of iniquity among the "bad books" (as the police called them) in the last category—and such distinctions mattered, because some books, if confiscated, might be returned to the bookseller and some might be grounds for sending him to the Bastille. Between 1771 and 1789, officials of the booksellers' guild in Paris filled a series of registers with the titles of all the books confiscated in the Paris Customs. At first they classified them under three general rubrics: "prohibited books" (to be sequestered or destroyed), "not permitted books" (to be returned in some cases to the sender), and "pirated books" (to be sold for the profit of the bookseller who owned the original privilege). But as the entries accumulated, the distinctions disintegrated into a confusion of overlapping, inconsistent terms; and in the end the classification system collapsed into an undifferentiated mass of 3,544 entries with only one characteristic in common: they all smelled somehow of illegality.[4]

When it came to fine distinctions, the officials could not trust their sense of smell. For who could keep up with the literature pouring off the presses? Who could tell the difference between a quasi-legal book and a moderately illegal one? Shipping agents were supposed to have this ability, because they could be fined for forwarding illegal literature. Yet Jean-François Pion, an agent in Pontarlier, confessed himself incapable of recognizing forbidden books. And when he asked for guidance from an officer in the customs bureau at the Swiss border, he received the following reply:

> I cannot tell M. Pion positively which books are prohibited. In general, everything that is opposed to religion, the state, and good morals cannot enter. There are specific proscriptions against some books, such as a pirated history of France, the *Encyclopédie,* and others. But the quality of books doesn't much concern the customs office. It is a matter for the booksellers' guilds.[5]

Booksellers, of course, were better informed. They ordered the shipments, and the syndics of their guilds inspected them, accompanied in principle by a royal *inspecteur de la librairie.* But most booksellers had only an approximate idea of what books were actually in circulation, especially those that traveled through the underground. Literary journals were censored and were not supposed to review such works, though they sometimes did so. One could not even judge a book by its title. Of course, title pages gave off many clues. Anything with the standard formula—"with approbation and privilege from the king"—printed at the bottom was likely to be legal, though it might be pirated. Anything with a flagrantly false address— "printed at the expense of the Vatican," "at the printing shop of Priapus," "chez William Tell"—made no pretense of respect for the law. But there was plenty of room for confusion between those extremes. Booksellers often ordered from catalogues or even from rumors passed through the trade grapevine, and they often got the titles wrong. Some of them could hardly spell. When Poinçot of Versailles asked for twenty-five "nouvelles des couvertes des ruse," his Swiss supplier realized that he wanted a travel book, *Nouvelles découvertes des russes.* The Swiss also correctly read his remark on "la bes Raynalle" as a reference to the abbé Raynal's *Histoire philosophique et politique des établissements et du commerce des européens dans les deux Indes.*[6] But they badly bungled an order from Veuve Baritel of Lyon, which seemed to concern some innocent-sounding "Portraits des Chartreux" and in fact referred to the pornographic and anticlerical *Histoire de dom B . . . , portier des Chartreux.*[7]

Such mistakes could have serious consequences. A book-seller caught with *Histoire de dom B . . .* in his shop could be imprisoned or disbarred from the trade. A wagoner trans-porting it could be fined and forced to surrender everything on his cart. A peddler selling it could be branded with the letters GAL (for *galérien* or galley convict) and shipped off in chains to row in the galleys. Those punishments actually occurred.[8] The Old Regime in its last years was not the jolly, tolerant, laissez-faire sort of world imagined by some historians, and the Bastille was no three-star hotel. Although it should not be confused with the torture house invented by pre-revolutionary propagan-dists, it ruined the lives of many people engaged in literature—not authors so much as publishers and booksellers, the profes-sionals who made literature happen even if they did not create it. Such persons had to distinguish between legal and illegal books every day in the course of their ordinary business. By studying the way they coped with that difficulty in the eigh-teenth century, one can move toward a solution of a problem that has plagued historians two centuries later—the problem of identifying the dangerous element in the literature that actually circulated in France on the eve of the Revolution. This proce-dure provides a way around the dangers of anachronism. Instead of beginning with modern notions of what should have threatened the orthodoxies of the Old Regime, it offers the possibility of identifying forbidden books by examining the practices of eighteenth-century bookmen—the way they talked about it in the jargon of their trade, exchanged it among them-selves, marketed, ordered, packaged, shipped, and sold it throughout a vast system for getting books to readers outside the limits of the law.

Trade Jargon

The problem of demarcating forbidden literature appears at first as a question of language. When the police interrogated one of their prisoners in the Bastille, a bookseller named Hubert Cazin who had been caught with all kinds of forbidden books and compromising papers in his shop in Reims, they asked him to explain a puzzling term that cropped up often in his correspondence: "philosophical articles." Cazin defined it as a "conventional expression in the book trade to characterize everything that is forbidden."[9] The police had heard other terms: "clandestine books," "drugs," "miseries." As already mentioned, they had a favorite expression of their own: *mauvais livres,* "bad books." Printers used another one in their craft slang: *marron*—"chestnut" (a forbidden book); *marronner*—"to chestnut" (to work on a clandestine job).[10] But publishers and booksellers preferred a more elevated term, *livres philosophiques*—"philosophical books." It served as a signal in their commercial code to designate books that could get them in trouble, books that had to be handled with care.

The terminology of the trade can be studied best in the papers of the Société typographique de Neuchâtel (STN), a major publisher and wholesaler located in the principality of Neuchâtel on France's eastern border with Switzerland. Like dozens of similar houses, the STN faced the daily problem of matching supply and demand, and that involved coping with formidable problems of communication. Aside from the difficulties of getting heavy crates of easily damaged, unbound sheets over primitive roads to the right person in the right place at the right time, the publishers had to make sense of the letters they received; and their customers had to get the message straight when they sent in their orders. The directors of the STN received letters from booksellers they did not know in places they had never seen requesting works they had never heard of. The titles were often inaccurate, misspelled, or illegible. And the books were frequently dangerous. To send the wrong work through the wrong channel was to court disaster. But how could one tell right from wrong in the unbound ocean of French literature and the confusion of the daily mail?

The publishers relied on their code. "Philosophy" signaled danger. When the directors of the STN first went into business, they did not stock many forbidden books and did not favor the jargon of the trade: "From time to time there appear some new works that are called quite improperly *philosophical,*" they wrote to a bookseller. "We don't carry any, but we know where to find them and can supply them when we are asked to."[11] But they soon realized that the term "philosophical" designated a vital sector of the trade for many of their customers. P.-J. Duplain in Lyon informed them that he was eager to do business, "especially in the philosophical genre, which seems to be the one favored in our century." Manoury wrote from Caen: "N.B. Would you have any philosophical things? It's my main line." Letters from every corner of the kingdom contained variations on the same theme: "philosophical merchandise" (Le Lièvre of Belfort), "philosophical works" (Blouet of Rennes), "books of philosophy" (Audéart of Lunéville), "philosophical books of all kinds" (Billault of Tours).[12]

Because the code was shared by everyone in the trade, the booksellers assumed their supplier would know what they were talking about when, as in the case of Patras in Bar-sur-Aube, they issued blank orders for "three copies of all your newest philosophical works." The same assumption underlay their requests for information. Thus Rouyer of Langres: "If you have something good, something new, something curious, something interesting, and some good philosophical books, please let me know"; and Regnault le jeune of Lyon: "My line is all philosophical, so I want almost nothing except that kind." The supplier was expected to know what books belonged to that category, and in any case the orders often made the point clear. In an order for eighteen titles, Regnault marked all the "philosophical" books with a cross, explaining that they should be carefully hidden in the crate. There were six: *Le Compère Matthieu, Dom B*****, Portier des Chartreux, La Fille de joie, L'Académie des dames, De l'Esprit,* and *L'An 2440*—a typical selection, which ranged from pornography to philosophy as we know it today.[13]

Exchanges

"Philosophical books" could not be handled in the same way as legal works or even mildly illegal ones, the kind that were merely pirated or uncensored but not offensive enough to run much risk of confiscation. Instead of printing dangerous works itself, the STN preferred to procure them by means of exchanges with specialists in underground publishing, marginal entrepreneurs who were willing to take risks, like Jean-Samuel Cailler in Geneva, Gabriel Décombaz in Lausanne, and Samuel Fauche in Neuchâtel itself. Exchanges were common in all kinds of eighteenth-century publishing. By swapping the works he printed against assortments from the stock of other houses, a publisher could diffuse his editions rapidly, thereby reducing the risk of piracy or counterpiracy while increasing the variety of his own list. Publishers balanced their exchange accounts *(comptes de changes)* by calculating the number of sheets that changed hands. Except in the case of unusual formats or illustrated editions, a sheet of one book would be taken as the equivalent of a sheet in another. But *livres philosophiques* were worth more than ordinary books. They fetched more on the market and cost more to produce, or at least involved greater risks, for even in the relative liberty of Swiss towns, local authorities prodded by Calvinist pastors sometimes impounded editions and imposed fines. Exchanges involving prohibited works therefore required special ratios: two sheets of a "philosophical book" for three of an ordinary pirated edition, or one sheet for two, or three sheets for four, depending on the bargaining power on either side.

The STN got the best terms and the most audacious books from Geneva, where a cluster of small, marginal publishers had grown up in the shadow of the great houses like Cramer and de Tournes. In April 1777, two of the STN's directors received the following reminder from the home office while on a business trip to Geneva: "Until now Geneva has been our main source of philosophical books, which, in accordance with the taste of this century, make up an essential part of our stock. Cailler, G. Grasset, and Gallay have supplied them to us in exchanges at two sheets against three of our own: see what you can arrange with them."[14] The archives do not reveal what happened at that particular bargaining session, but the general nature of the bargaining is clear from the STN's correspondence with two of its most important suppliers in Geneva, Jacques-Benjamin Téron and Gabriel Grasset.

Téron scraped together a living by tutoring in mathematics, selling books, running a *cabinet littéraire* (commercial library), and doing any intellectual odd job that would fetch a penny.

Between bankruptcies in 1773 and 1779, he established a small publishing business. He selected a few forbidden books that seemed to be most in demand and, with some capital advanced by a friend, hired local printers to produce clandestine editions. These he sold under the counter for cash and traded for legal works that could be offered above the board in his bookshop, which was nothing more than a room on the second floor of a house in Geneva's Grand'rue. Sensing a potentially important new source of supply, the STN wrote to Téron in April 1774: "We are also often asked for the kind of books called *philosophical*. Let us know whether you might be in a position to furnish us with them. We would gladly take our supplies from you, and our trade would certainly be worth your while." Téron replied by return of post: "I will give you three sheets of the philosophical books you want for every four that I choose from your stock." Generous terms, but the STN was a valuable customer; and Téron needed to win its good will, because he had failed to pay the bills for some of his earlier speculations. Three weeks later, he sent off its first order: "8 *Histoire critique de Jésus-Christ*, 6 *Lettres de Bolingbroke*, 3 *Traité des trois imposteurs*, 6 *Théologie portative*, 12 *Catéchumène*, 2 *Choses utiles et agréables*, 6 *Saul*"—533 ½ sheets in all, or 711 sheets credited to Téron's *compte de change* at the agreed ratio of 3:4. Téron specialized somewhat in Voltaire's works, because he tapped the literature that came coursing out of Ferney, where Voltaire directed the campaign against *l'infâme* (essentially, the Catholic Church). But he also carried the odd pornographic volume and some political tracts, notably an edition of the *Journal historique de la révolution opérée dans la constitution de la monarchie française par M. de Maupeou, chancelier de France*. In return, the STN sent him the relatively innocent products of its own presses. "I especially need a great many novels, travel books, and historical works," he explained. And so the swapping continued, with ups and downs, for five years, until Téron's business collapsed.[15]

Gabriel Grasset supervised the printing shop of the Cramers for several years before establishing his own printing and bookselling business. Despite some sub rosa patronage by Voltaire, it never amounted to much, because Grasset was more of a printer than a businessman. He ran two presses and handled all the billing and correspondence by himself, scrambling accounts and falling constantly farther behind in his payments. Things got so bad by April 1770 that he offered to sell all his material to the STN and to come and work as its foreman. But he kept afloat by printing forbidden books and selling them under the cloak.

Grasset's exchanges with the STN began in 1772 at the prevailing rate of two sheets to one, for he insisted that he would accept nothing less: "As all the other booksellers give me two sheets for every one of the philosophical kind, I propose the same exchange to you." He selected works from the STN's catalogue, and it chose what it wanted from lists that he sent of the books he kept in stock. Soon it was trading its edition of the Bible for *La Profession de foi des théistes* and the *Traité des trois imposteurs.* It acquired many other clandestine classics—*Thérèse philosophe, Le Compère Matthieu, L'An 2440*—in this way; and while the books traveled back and forth, it attempted to extract more favorable terms. In April 1774, the STN tried to get Grasset to accept three instead of four of its sheets for every two of his. But he dug in his heels: "As for your proposition of exchanging three for two sheets, that certainly goes against our old arrangement. Surely you would agree that the costs and risks in the philosophical sector warrant a rate that is greater than two-to-one. In order to continue doing business with you, I will exchange [at the rate of two-to-one] all the philosophical works whose prices have been entered on the enclosed list." Grasset kept up his exchange rate, but he lowered his guard. In January 1780, the Genevan Petit Conseil fined and imprisoned him for printing obscene and irreligious works. When he got out of jail he had to sell off his printing shop, but he hung on to his secret stock of books. He offered to swap 100 *Histoire critique de Jésus-Christ* in August 1780, and seems to have continued his under-the-cloak trade until his death in February 1782.[16]

Marketing and Pricing

Grasset's remark about a list enclosed within his letter illustrates another way in which *livres philosophiques* received special treatment. They were listed in separate, clandestine catalogues.

Grasset printed his on a small sheet of paper headed "Note de Livres Philosophiques." It included seventy-five titles arranged in alphabetical order with no indication of the source where they might be procured. Publishers always kept compromising information off these catalogues, in contrast to the catalogues of their legal list, which carried their names and addresses and circulated openly. For example, when the two Genevan publishers, J.-L. Chappuis and J.-E. Didier, joined businesses in 1780, they announced the merger in a printed circular accompanied by two printed catalogues. The first covered the bulk of their stock: 106 titles of books on standard subjects—history, travel, law, religion, belles-lettres, all of them held "in large quantity" and perfectly legal. The second, entitled "Note Séparée," included twenty-five works, all extremely illegal, from *L'Académie des dames* to *Vénus dans le cloître,* with plenty of Voltaire, d'Holbach, and political libel in between.[17]

Catalogues of this kind seem to have circulated everywhere in the underground book trade, although they have escaped the attention of modern bibliographers. The STN's papers contain five of them from its suppliers in Geneva and Lausanne and two that it drew up itself: a handwritten list of 110 works headed "Livres philosophiques," probably from 1775, and a printed list of sixteen titles under the heading "Note séparée," dated 1781. The catalogues served two purposes: to publishers and wholesalers, they showed the stock from which exchanges could be selected; to retailers, they indicated what works could be acquired through clandestine channels. But they were dangerous in themselves, so they, too, circulated under the cloak. One of the most incriminating pieces of evidence in the papers seized by the police when they raided the bookshop of the widow Stockdorf in Strasbourg in March 1773 was a printed "Catalogue de livres français / à Berne 1772." It included 182 titles, and gave the police a splendid view of the stock of a Swiss supplier and his trade with a French customer. Jeremy Wittel, a Swiss publisher on a sales trip to Paris in 1781, was arrested merely for having distributed "a printed catalogue of bad books." When booksellers exchanged such catalogues within France, they employed a certain amount of hugger-mugger: letters written in code, with names and addresses expunged, and imprecations such as, "Keep mum about my catalogue." The police knew all about these maneuvers. Hoping to ingratiate itself with a key official in the Book Trade Department (Direction de la librairie), the STN sent one of its biggest customers, Poinçot of Versailles, to argue its case, armed with its legal catalogue. "He was satisfied," Poinçot reported. "But he said to me, 'They have another one for their bad books.'"[18]

Despite the danger, the catalogues were essential for marketing, and the publishers sent them through the regular mail. In August 1776, the STN tried to attract new customers by a circular letter sent to 156 booksellers scattered throughout Europe. While recording their names in its letterbook, a clerk wrote "with phil. books" after some, "without phil. books" after others. The former—reliable veterans like Bouchard in Metz, Babin in Nancy, and Chambeau in Avignon—might be interested in illegal literature and entrusted with the clandestine catalogue. The latter—Molin in Valencia, Bouardel et Simon in Barcelona, Borel in Lisbon, Hermil in Naples—lived in dangerously Catholic countries, where such things were best left out of letters.[19]

The French booksellers seemed to have little fear of compromising mail. Despite the occasional use of cryptograms and remarks about seals broken in the secret chambers of the police, they had no inhibitions about asking for philosophical books. When the STN sent him its standard, legal catalogue, Laisney of Beauvais protested. He did not want the standard fare; he wanted "several philosophical works that are not in your catalogue and that I believe nonetheless to be in your warehouse." Prévost of Melun sent in the same complaint: "Your catalogue contains nothing but ordinary books." His customers required "the other sort, philosophical books"; and after the STN sent its clandestine catalogue, they got them. The same message arrived, loud and clear, from Malassis of Nantes: "Send me as quickly as you can—that is, by return mail—a catalogue of all your philosophical books, and I will sell a great many for you." Wherever booksellers dealt in forbidden books, they assumed their suppliers kept a special stock and drew up special catalogues. To set the system in motion, they sent a standard signal: "philosophical books."[20]

The same signal went out from the suppliers, carrying additional messages about marketing and pricing. Sometimes, as mentioned, the STN conducted mail campaigns. But every day it sent letters to its customers, adding strategically placed notes about the newest titles in its stock. Thus a typical aside in a letter to Bergeret of Bordeaux: "As for philosophical books, we don't print any, but we know where to get them. Here is a short list taken from our catalogue of philosophical books." Bergeret replied with an order full of works like *Thérèse philosophe* and *Théologie portative*. Before embarking on an important clandestine operation, however, the STN thought it wise to send a warning about the prices in this sector:

> Among the works you have ordered we notice that there are a great many from the genre that is called philosophical. We don't keep these in stock, but we can supply them, thanks to our contacts with other houses. We should warn you, however, that these books cost more than others for reasons that are easy to imagine. We cannot supply them at the same price as the others in our catalogue, because we have to buy them ourselves at a higher price. Still, we will try to get them for you on the best possible terms. Books of this kind are now proliferating all around us.[21]

The prices of philosophical books did not behave like those of other books. They began at a higher level—usually twice that of a comparable pirated work—and then dipped and soared erratically, depending on condemnations (always good for business), police raids (a stimulus for demand among readers but a deterrent for customers among booksellers), and the vagaries of supply (the market could be flooded by a half dozen editions produced secretly and simultaneously by competing houses). In general, the STN fixed the wholesale price of its ordinary books at 1 sous per sheet and that of its forbidden books at 2 sous per sheet. It often traded two sheets of a legal work for one of a philosophical book. But, as in its exchanges with Téron and Grasset, the ratio changed whenever someone got the upper hand in the bargaining. And everyone expected the price of a brand-new work to skyrocket if it was sufficiently scandalous and fresh on the market.[22]

The volatility in pricing left its mark on the clandestine catalogues—literally, for the suppliers often added the current prices by hand. Gabriel Grasset printed his "Note de livres philosophiques" without prices. After agreeing to exchange his works against those of the STN at a rate of two sheets to one, he wrote in prices according to the number of sheets in each book. As the STN charged 1 sous per sheet, he charged 2. Thus he set the price of *Théologie portative,* a book of twenty sheets, at 2 livres (40 sous). But he would exchange only thirty-three of the seventy-five titles on his list at that rate. He expected to get more for the others, which included some classics like *La Fille de joie* and *L'Espion chinois,* and so they appeared without prices. Grasset also insisted on special pricing for his two most recent productions, *Le Taureau blanc* and *Dialogue de Pégase et du vieillard,* just turned out by Voltaire's satanic assemblyline in Ferney: "As for the *Taureau blanc* and *Pégase,* which contains six sheets, I sell them for one livre [i.e., 20 sous] in cash to all our Genevan booksellers, because they are both printed on blue tinted paper. But my desire to do business with you has made me resolve to offer you a special price of 18 sous."[23]

Newness, notoriety, special paper, illustrations, revised and augmented editions—many factors made the prices of forbidden books fluctuate erratically. The same work often appeared in different forms and at different prices in different catalogues. *L'Académie des dames,* a pornographic best-seller that had gone through several metamorphoses since it first appeared on the market in 1680, turned up in three of the clandestine catalogues. In 1772, the Société typographique de Berne listed it without any bibliographical details at a price of 24 livres. In 1776, Gabriel Décombaz of Lausanne offered it, "corrected, improved, and enlarged, two volumes octavo with illustrations, 1775, 12 livres." And in 1780, Chappuis et Didier of Geneva proposed two very different editions: "large octavo, a handsome edition from Holland adorned with 37 illustrations, 13 livres," and "2 volumes with illustrations, duodecimo, 3 livres."[24]

At 2 or 3 livres a volume, forbidden books fell within the purchasing power of many French readers. Skilled workmen made as much or more money in a day. But the catalogues gave wholesale prices, and the books had to pass through many hands—smugglers, shipping agents, wagoners, retailers—before they reached the readers. The difficulties of distribution magnified the variations in pricing, so a consumer might pay twice or ten times what the producer had charged. Competition produced some leveling out at the retail level, but not in remote areas plied by peddlers. They sold philosophical books along with chapbooks, for whatever price they could get. Paul Malherbe, who supplied a whole army of peddlers from his secret warehouse in Loudun, noted, "Peddlers are extremely eager to get books of this kind. They make more on them than on others, because they charge whatever they fancy and get whatever a book will fetch, depending on the general desire for it."[25]

The art of marketing was especially hazardous in such an unpredictable marketplace. In order to be informed about sudden changes and to stay in touch with demand, publishers generally relied on their commercial correspondence. But they also sent special agents on sales trips and received detailed reports on the state of the underground trade. In 1776, the STN dispatched its trusted clerk, Jean-François Favarger, on a swing through Switzerland, Savoy, Lyonnais, Burgundy, and Franche-Comté. He loaded his horse with a supply of sample books, title pages, and catalogues, both kinds. Then, town by town and bookseller by bookseller, he reported on his transactions. Thus after leaving the shop of Brette in Grenoble, he wrote: "Despite his links with the Société typographique de Lausanne, which was a step ahead of me everywhere along my route, he is inclined to order any Swiss editions he may need from us. I gave him a philosophical catalogue. He told me he already had almost everything on it." And after negotiating with Capel in Dijon: "M. Capel is first-rate, or at least his shop is very well stocked. He deals a lot in philosophical books. I gave him a list [of philosophical books] and a catalogue with a prospectus. He will see about placing an order with us. He is the book trade inspector. All of the crates that we shipped [by smugglers] through Jougne passed through his hands. He isn't scrupulous about that sort of thing." At every stage in the journey, as at every point in the process of producing, stockpiling, pricing, and marketing, it was clear that philosophical books required special treatment and received it.[26]

Ordering and Shipping

The same tendency stood out at the other end of the diffusion process, in the way illegal books were ordered and shipped. Sometimes, in writing orders, booksellers scrambled legal, illegal, and quasi-legal works of all varieties. But when they sensed danger, they took precautions to isolate the philosophical books. They occasionally listed the inoffensive parts of their order in the main body of their letter and then wrote the titles of the forbidden books on a scrap of paper *(papier volant)* that they slipped inside. The scrap did not carry their signature and was to be discarded after the letter arrived, although several of them can still be found in the papers of the STN.[27] More commonly, booksellers used various devices to set off the most dangerous titles in their orders. Manoury of Caen grouped them in one section of his list; Desbordes of La Rochelle placed them at the end; Malassis of Nantes arranged them in separate columns; Baritel of Lyon marked them with a cross; Billault of Tours, Charmet of Besançon, and Sombert of Châlons-sur-Marne listed the legal works first, then drew a line and listed the prohibited ones.[28]

All these techniques served the same purpose: to alert the supplier to books that required special handling in order to escape detection if the crates should be inspected. After listing sixty works that he wanted, Bergeret of Bordeaux marked off eleven, all hard-core philosophical books, with an x, and explained, "Please marry all the x books with the others." To "marry" books was to stuff the sheets of one into those of the other, a fairly simple procedure, as books were usually shipped unbound. Booksellers also called this practice "larding." Charmet of Besançon ordered six copies of the obscene and irreligious *La Chandelle d'Arras,* along with three copies of the innocent but pirated works of Mme Riccoboni. "Put another title on the bill of lading and lard this work *{La Chandelle d'Arras}* in the Riccoboni," he instructed. "I show the bills of lading in the intendant's office so that they don't open certain crates. That's why it is crucial to put the philosophical works under other names." The clerks of the STN copied such instructions into its order book, presumably with a straight face, though it is hard to believe that they did not get a few laughs from entries like the following:

Ecole des filles
Cruautés religieuses ⎫ in *Liturgie des Protestants en France*
Parnasse libertin ⎭
Fille de joie in *Nouveau Testament*[29]

They had been instructed to marry Fanny Hill with the Gospel.

In any case, the way the books were ordered bore directly on the way they were packed and shipped. Regnault le jeune wanted everything that he marked with an x hidden in the bottom of the crate so he could maneuver it past the inspectors in Lyon. Nubla of Dijon wanted all the illegal books placed in a bundle at the top so that he could remove them surreptitiously before the crate was inspected in his guild house. Jacquenod of Lyon favored the bottom of the crates along with doctored bills of lading for his philosophical books. And Barrois of Paris wanted his hidden in the packing material *(maculature)*. The techniques varied enormously, but all depended on drawing a clear distinction between books that were relatively safe and books that were likely to be confiscated.[30]

If a bookseller wanted to avoid risks altogether, he did not attempt to sneak illegal works through the legal channels of the trade; he hired smugglers—or "insurers" *(assureurs)*, as they were known in the business. The shipper often arranged for this service, but the customer paid for it, usually on receipt of the goods. The insurers hired teams of porters who lugged the books along secret trails past customs houses at the borders and inspection stations inside the kingdom. If caught, the porters might be condemned to the galleys, the books would be confiscated, and the insurer would refund the loss. The system was cumbersome and expensive (a border crossing near Geneva cost 16 percent of the value of the merchandise in 1773), but it provided what some booksellers wanted most: security. Blouet, a pillar of the book trade in Rennes, ordered prohibited works only when he knew he could sell them safely and at a price that covered his costs: "You wrote that you have made an arrangement with insurers to get shipments into the kingdom without passing through guild halls or being subject to any inspection," he wrote to the STN. "I think it best for you to use this channel for my philosophical books, which, I believe, will not get through Lyon without being confiscated. As for the other works, you can send them to me through the normal Lyon route. . . . I am quite ready to pay for all costs, but I don't want to run any risk of confiscation."[31]

For a bookseller like Blouet, the distinction between mildly illegal and downright "philosophical" books involved calculations of costs, risks, and routes. For the smugglers, it was virtually a matter of life and death. In April 1773, Guillon l'aîné, an insurer in the Franche-Comté, reported that two of his porters had been captured with a load of Mercier's *L'An 2440* and Voltaire's *Questions sur l'Encyclopédie*. They seemed certain to be shipped off to the galleys, because the bishop of Saint-Claude had taken an interest in the case. Although they were eventually released, the other porters stopped work. To get them back, Guillon tried to persuade the STN to pack its most dangerous books in separate crates so that the men could drop them and run if they came across a flying patrol of the customs. The STN replied that anything shipped through him was bound to be way outside the law: that was the whole point of using the insurance system instead of the packing tricks and sleight of hand that propelled the less illegal books through the normal channels of the trade.[32]

When things calmed down, the porters resumed work. But a conflict of interest continued to oppose them to their employers, and it ran along the line that divided the truly "bad" from the merely reprehensible elements in the book trade. Men who backpacked eighty-pound crates over tortuous mountain trails could not be expected to have a fine eye for literature. Most of them on the French-Swiss border had picked up their trade by hauling calicoes (*indiennes*) past the customs barrier designed to protect French silks. They were quite ready to strap anything counterfeit on their backs. But they balked at the prospect of carrying anything so illegal that it could expose them to an agonizing death as a galley slave. Hence the advice of another STN agent, who organized "insurance" along the route from Neuchâtel to Pontarlier:

> Your business is particularly tricky, because the porters are afraid that if they get caught they will be held responsible for works that attack religion or that slander certain public figures—a danger that does not exist when they are merely smuggling goods to avoid paying tariffs. If you want to smuggle books that are irreproachable in their contents [i.e., pirated versions of legal works], then the porters will ask you to guarantee that that is the case, and you will find some in our area who will get them to Pontarlier for you for 12 livres a hundredweight.[33]

The practices of smuggling confirm those of stocking, exchanging, pricing, advertising, selling, ordering, packing, shipping, and even talking about forbidden books. At every stage in the production and diffusion process, the men who worked in the obscure territory dividing legal from illegal literature knew that a certain class of books had to be handled in a certain way. To do otherwise was to invite catastrophe.

Catastrophe struck the whole system of government in 1789. Was ideological erosion from the "philosophical" sector of the publishing industry a necessary condition for the general collapse? Before we can tackle that question, we need to identify the entire corpus of forbidden books, to examine its contents, and to study its reception. But even at this stage in the investigation, it seems clear that the "philosophy" circulating through the channels of the underground book trade differed considerably from the set of ideas commonly associated with the Enlightenment. In fact, after watching the professionals of the trade go about their business, day in and day out, for twenty years, from 1769 to 1789, one begins to doubt many of the common associations built up in standard histories of the eighteenth century.

The classic question—What was the relation of the Enlightenment to the Revolution?—begins to look like a *question mal posée.* For if we put the issue that way, we are likely to distort it, first by reifying the Enlightenment as if it could be separated from everything else in eighteenth-century culture; then by injecting it into an analysis of the Revolution, as if it could be traced through the events of 1789–1800 like a substance being monitored in the bloodstream.

The world of the printed word in eighteenth-century France was too complex to be sorted into categories like "Enlightened" and "Revolutionary." But the individuals who transmitted literature to the reading public before 1789 devised a very workable category for distinguishing the truly dangerous element in the books they handled. If we take their experience seriously, we must rethink some basic distinctions of literary history—including the notions of danger and of literature itself. We consider *Du Contrat social* political theory and *Histoire de Dom B . . .* pornography, perhaps even as something too crude to be treated as literature. But the bookmen of the eighteenth century lumped them together as "philosophical books." If we try to look at their material in their way, the seemingly self-evident distinction between pornography and philosophy begins to break down. We are ready to perceive a philosophical element in the prurient—from *Thérèse philosophe* to *Philosophie dans le boudoir*—and to reexamine the erotic works of the *philosophes:* Montesquieu's *Lettres persanes,* Voltaire's *Pucelle d'Orléans,* Diderot's *Bijoux indiscrets.* It no longer seems so puzzling that Mirabeau, the embodiment of the spirit of 1789, should have written the rawest pornography and the boldest political tracts of the previous decade. Liberty and libertinism appear to be linked, and we can find affinities among all the best-sellers in the clandestine catalogues. For once we learn to look for philosophy under the cloak, anything seems possible, even the French Revolution.

Chapter 2

Best-Sellers

THIS EXCURSION INTO THE FOLKWAYS of eighteenth-century publishing has led to a preliminary conclusion: illegal literature was a world of its own, a special sector of the book trade, marked off by well-established practices and organized around a working notion of the "philosophical." Having reached that point, we now can set off on a more ambitious inquiry: an attempt to determine precisely which books flowed through the channels of the underground trade. By following publishers and booksellers on their daily rounds, we can identify the "philosophical" element in their commerce. They made it their business to mediate between supply and demand. So by analyzing their businesses, we can see how the taste for the taboo became translated into books and how those books actually reached readers. In the end, it should be possible to construct a best-seller list of the most wanted forbidden books in France during the twenty years before the Revolution.

Those are large claims, and the reader may well feel beset by doubts: how can one possibly measure literary demand in the hidden sector of the book trade two centuries ago, before the existence of reliable data on almost anything, including death and taxes?[1] I must plead for a temporary suspension of disbelief while I discuss some case studies, which illustrate the basic character of the clandestine book business. They come from the archives of the Société-typographique de Neuchâtel, the only complete set of papers from a publisher-wholesaler to have survived from the eighteenth century. The STN occupied an ideal site just across the French border for producing illegal French books and for shipping them down the Rhône or the Rhine or across the Jura Mountains. Its stock included a vast assortment of all kinds of current literature in addition to its own publications, and its customers, mostly retail booksellers, came from all the major cities and most of the sizeable towns in France—as well as dealers who sold French books throughout the rest of Europe, from St. Petersburg to Naples and from Budapest to Dublin.

Every day the booksellers' orders arrived in the offices of the STN, accompanied in many cases by comments on the state of the market and directions for smuggling. A typical order from a French retailer contained a dozen or so titles, including an admixture of forbidden books if he dealt in the "philosophical" sector. But he would usually ask for only a few copies per title. Trade practices did not permit the return of unsold books; so he would limit himself to books that his own customers had already requested, or that he felt confident of selling, sometimes stretching things in order to get the free thirteenth copy when the STN offered him a chance at a baker's dozen. Of course, some booksellers took greater risks than others, both in the size of their orders and in their willingness to venture into the illegal branches of the trade. But the lack of a provision for returns—a publisher's dream today—meant that all orders stayed close to the dealer's perception of demand.

Once an order had arrived in Neuchâtel, a clerk copied it into the left-hand column of an account book called a "livre de commissions." And after it was shipped out, he entered the corresponding number of copies per title in the right-hand column of the register. Demand and supply therefore stand out vividly in the accounts. They usually matched, because the STN procured anything it did not have in stock from allied publisher-wholesalers by means of exchanges. So the papers of the STN—the correspondence of the booksellers supplemented by the "livres de commissions" and by other account books (daily ledgers called *brouillons* and *journaux*)—provide an exceptional opportunity to follow the flow of literary demand, title by title, and to trace the supply of books to local markets everywhere in France. The papers also make it possible to identify the forbidden books, because as explained above the "philosophical" items were singled out for special handling at each stage of the system. By tracing all the signals of the "philosophical," one can build up a bibliography of the entire corpus of forbidden literature that circulated in France from 1769 to 1789—that is, of books considered to be truly dangerous as opposed to those that could be sold safely even though they lacked privileges or permissions. And by compiling data from an adequate sample of orders, one can discover which books sold best.[2]

But the numbers will not speak for themselves. In order to make sense of them, one needs to understand how booksellers conducted their businesses and how their businesses fitted into the surrounding society. Case studies provide the best way of blending quantitative and qualitative analysis. They could be strung out indefinitely, thanks to the inexhaustible richness of the material in Neuchâtel and Paris. I have limited myself to four: first, two booksellers who typify the occasional customers of the STN, then two of its regular customers. The first pair provide glimpses of trade patterns built up from small-scale transactions improvised as occasions arose from time to time and place to place. The second reveal the full profiles of important businesses that drew a large proportion of their stock from Neuchâtel.

Snapshots of the Marketplace

Matthieu of Nancy epitomized the rough-and-ready book trade of Lorraine. He began as a peddler in 1754, before the province's absorption into France in 1766, when the easygoing regime of Stanislas Leszczynski allowed virtually anyone to speculate on forbidden books. The trade was still booming in 1767, according to a police report:

Everyone is free to sell and import books in Nancy. Second-hand furniture dealers buy up private libraries and sell them off from their homes or in public squares. They also buy from children and others. Peddlers swarm through the province, bringing in everything they like. They show up at all the small-town fairs and in the gatherings of spas at Plombières and Bains-les-Bains. They are the most dangerous of all, owing to their complete liberty and the favorable terms given them by printers.[3]

By 1764, Matthieu had accumulated enough in the rag-and-bone branch of the trade to set up shop in Nancy. But it was a modest affair, according to the police: he had less than two hundred volumes in stock, and he continued to peddle his wares throughout Alsace and Lorraine. His stall could be found twice a year at the fairs in Strasbourg, at Colmar, among the fashionable crowds taking the waters at Plombières, and "under the hall of the château in Lunéville."[4]

Matthieu's letters to the STN—sixty-nine of them, in minimal, misspelled French—and those of other booksellers in the province suggest he was a tough customer.[5] He drove hard bargains, shouldered competitors out of business, and rarely took risks. But he always paid his bills, unlike many marginal dealers in Lorraine, who overextended themselves and then went bankrupt. His business seemed to prosper throughout the 1770s. In 1779 he bought out Babin, one of the more solid of Nancy's seventeen booksellers, and issued an impressive catalogue, announcing that he could provide all sorts of books and journals.[6]

The catalogue contained nothing but impeccably legal works, most of them religious. But Matthieu's letters to the STN reveal a healthy appetite for "philosophical" books, which he imported through Strasbourg until the route became too dangerous and he retreated to the safe sectors of the trade. Almost from the beginning, he called for something "by M. de Voltaire or some other item that isn't common. You know what I mean."[7] His meaning became clearer as his orders accumulated. First he sent for Voltaire's *Questions sur l'Encyclopédie* and d'Holbach's *Système de la nature*. Then, as soon as he got word of Mercier's *L'An 2440*, he sent in a rush order for fifty copies, followed by a request for political *libelles* (slanderous tracts about public figures) like *Le Gazetier cuirassé* and a smattering of pornography. The pattern stands out clearly in Table 2.1. It lists all the forbidden books from Matthieu's orders—like most

TABLE 2.1. The Trade of Matthieu in Nancy

	15 nov. 1770	juin 1771	19 juillet 1771	27 sept. 1771	24 fév. 1771	7 avril 1772	6 sept. 1772	25 sept. 1772	28 oct. 1772	31 déc. 1773	7 août 1774	29 mai 1775	18 nov. 1775	6 déc. 1775	4 mars 1777	juin 1777	20 fév. 1778	Total*
Questions sur l'Encyclopédie, Voltaire	7						6											13 (2)
Système de la nature, d'Holbach		12	24		6					2	3	3	4	4		2		60 (9)
L'An 2440, Mercier				50		6				2	4				2	2		66 (6)
Confidence Philosophique, Vernes					4													4 (1)
Le Gazetier cuirassé, Morande					6													6 (1)
Œuvres, Rousseau								1	2									3 (3)
Épîtres, satires, contes, Voltaire								4										4 (1)
Contes, La Fontaine										1								1 (1)
Système social, d'Holbach										6			4	4				14 (3)
Œuvres, Diderot										3								3 (1)
Le Bon Sens, d'Holbach													4					4 (1)
Œufs rouges, Mairobert?													2	2				4 (2)

Mémoires de Louis XV, anon.	4	4 (I)
Œuvres, La Mettrie	I	I (I)
Dictionnaire philosophique, Voltaire	2	2 (I)
La Fille de joie, Cleland	2	2 (I)
L'Adoption, ou la maçonnerie des femmes, Saint-Victor?	2	2 (I)
Les Plus Secrets Mystères des hauts grades de la maçonnerie dévoilés Koeppen	2	2 (I)
Les Devoirs, Statuts ou Règlements généraux des F.M., Anon.	2	2 (I)
Le Christianisme dévoilé, d'Holbach	I	I (I)
L'Académie des dames, Nicolas	2	2 (I)
Les Loisirs du chevalier d'Eon, d'Eon	I	I (I)

*The first figure in the right-hand column represents the total number of copies ordered. The figure in parentheses represents the total number of orders. The legal works ordered by Matthieu have been eliminated from this table.

booksellers, he usually requested a mixture of legal and illegal works, but only the strictly illegal ones are given here—and it shows how their incidence evolved from 1770 to 1778.

The figures indicate that two works stood out in Matthieu's trade: *Système de la nature* and *L'An 2440.* In each case, he placed an unusually large first order for them and continued to order them over several years as his customers kept asking for more. The number of orders confirms the importance of the number of copies ordered and demonstrates the continued strength of the demand. Should one therefore conclude that those two books were the best-sellers in Matthieu's business and perhaps throughout Nancy or even all Lorraine?

Not at all, first, because the statistical base is too small to support a strong conclusion; and second, because Matthieu drew only a small proportion of his stock from the STN. His letters indicate that he went to other suppliers whenever he could get a better price. In 1773, for example, he wrote that he would not order any copies of the STN's edition of *Recherches philosophiques sur les Américains,* an undoubtable best-seller, which went through at least fourteen editions between 1768 and 1777, because he had bought a cheaper version from another publisher. And in 1779 he said that he preferred to purchase the collected works of Voltaire from Lausanne, evidently for the same reason. Neither title appears in the pattern of Matthieu's trade with the STN, yet he probably sold a considerable number of each.

Nevertheless, Table 2.1 provides a valid general picture of Matthieu's business. Although it lacks any reference to the complete works of Voltaire, it includes two of Voltaire's most important books, *Questions sur l'Encyclopédie* and *Dictionnaire philosophique,* as well as his *Epîtres, satires, contes.* And its Voltairean tenor is confirmed by remarks in Matthieu's letters, which repeatedly called for "some good new work by Voltaire."[8] The letters also show a strong interest in popular writers like Louis-Sébastien Mercier and in scandalous political tracts like the apocryphal *Mémoires de Louis XV.* The qualitative and quantitative evidence reinforce one another, pointing to the same general pattern, even though the information isn't thorough enough for one to assess the demand for individual titles.

A similar pattern shows up in the orders of Alphonse Petit of Reims, another occasional customer of the STN. Unlike Matthieu, Petit was a man of some learning, who could turn a phrase and did not hesitate to advise the Swiss about which books to reprint: "The Buffon that you are thinking of printing will always be a good commercial item. . . . But it is essential to include the habits and characters of the animals, because if you simplify it too much it will be nothing more than an excerpt, which will no longer satisfy book lovers." Champagne, like Lorraine, was good book country, and Petit occupied a strong position in its capital, especially after 1776, when the police raided the shop of his principal competitor, Martin-Hubert Cazin, and confiscated 6,000 pounds of forbidden works while sending Cazin to the Bastille.[9] This bust had a sobering effect on the trade throughout the province. Petit seems to have been cautious in any case. In his letters he constantly exhorted the STN to avoid risks and always limited his orders to the number of copies that he felt sure of selling—or, more often, had already sold. In a typical order dated February 3, 1781, he selected an assortment of sixteen titles from the STN's current catalogue, added several works that he wanted it to procure for him from other publishers, then drew a line and listed eight "philosophical" books that required special handling—a typical selection, ranging from Rousseau's works to *Anecdotes sur Mme la comtesse du Barry*.

As Table 2.2 shows, Petit's orders (fourteen of them, from 1779 to 1784) differed from Matthieu's (seventeen orders, from 1770 to 1778) in that they contained books that were current in the 1780s. Yet they included a larger number of works about the political crisis during the last year's of Louis XV's reign, 1771–74. And they show the same fascination with atheism, Freemasonry, and voyeuristic pornography. Petit's letters confirm the impressions conveyed by the statistics. His customers were "tormenting" him for the expanded edition of Mercier's *Tableau de Paris,* a work that criticized many aspects of the Old Regime, he wrote in 1783: he had sold all the copies he had ordered long before they arrived. At the same time, the customers were "harassing" him for the new volumes in Rousseau's collected works. Petit spotted a best-seller as soon as he

TABLE 2.2. The Trade of Petit in Reims

	oct. 1779	31 mai 1780	3 fév. 1781	27 août 1781	16 fév. 1782	24 avril 1782	16 déc. 1782	20 jan. 1783	10 mars 1783	10 mai 1783	29 juin 1783	31 août 1783	30 mars 1784	31 août 1784	Total
La Fille naturelle, Restif de la Bretonne	2	3													5 (2)
Histoire philosophique, Raynal	2			13										4	19 (3)
L'An 2440, Mercier		2			2			4		4					12 (4)
Œuvres, Rousseau		12													12 (1)
La Pucelle, Voltaire			2												2 (1)
Le Bon Sens, d'Holbach			1												1 (1)
Système de la nature, d'Holbach			1												1 (1)
Œuvres, La Mettrie			1												1 (1)
Œuvres, Fréret			1												1 (1)
Thérèse philosophe, d'Argens ?			2												2 (1)
Histoire de dom B, Gervaise de Latouche ?			2												2 (2)
Anecdotes sur Mme la comtesse du Barry, Mairobert ?			1											2	3 (2)
Œuvres posthumes de J.-J. Rousseau				13		13	2								28 (3)

Tableau de Paris, Mercier	13	13	13			6	32 (3)
L'Espion anglois, Mairobert ?		6			4	2	12 (3)
Le Gazetier cuirassé, Morande		1					1 (1)
Recherches sur l'origine de l'esclavage religieux, Pommereul			6				6 (1)
Mémoires sur la Bastille, Linguet				25	24	3	52 (3)
Collection complète de tous les ouvrages pour et contre M. Necker					13	6	19 (2)
Théorie des lois criminelles, Brissot					2		2 (1)
Les Devoirs, Statuts ou Règlements généraux des F. M., Anon.						2	2 (1)
Vie privée de Louis XV, Mouffle d'Angerville						4	4 (1)
Errotika biblion, Mirabeau						2	2 (1)

heard of S.-N.-H. Linguet's *Mémoires sur la Bastille,* and rushed off an unusually large order for twenty-five copies, followed two months later by another for two dozen more. An anthology of polemical tracts about Necker's ministry also drew a large order. In fact, in reordering it, Petit placed a blanket request for two copies of all new "critical works," meaning political *libelles.* Politics clearly sold well in Reims.[10]

Does it follow that political literature dominated the illegal book trade in Champagne? Certainly not. Like Matthieu and the other occasional customers of the STN, Petit drew most of his stock from other sources. He mentioned shipments from Maastricht, Rouen, and Lyon; and he probably dealt with several suppliers in the Low Countries and the Rhineland. If their books differed greatly from those of the STN, his business with Neuchâtel would prove very little. That, however, seems unlikely, because Petit complained that the overproduction of reprints had made the same works available everywhere and that his competitors often undersold him. In fact, the bartering and swapping among publishers and wholesalers had gone to such lengths that he could procure some of the STN's own editions cheaper from Lyon than from the STN itself.[11] For those and other reasons—especially his reluctance to take risks, owing to the severity of the local book inspector[12]—Petit's trade with Neuchâtel never amounted to a great deal. The pattern of his orders looks like a blurred snapshot: enough to convey a general impression, but not a definitive, detailed picture.

The Profile of a Business

In order to see more deeply into a book business, one must examine the STN's relations with its steady customers, those who sent in orders at regular intervals and drew a large proportion of their stock from Neuchâtel. Consider the case of Jean-Félix Charmet, the most important bookseller in Besançon. Located in a provincial capital with a population of 32,000 in the 1780s, he served a clientele composed primarily of royal officials, army officers, country gentlemen, and men of the law. Besançon lacked manufacturing, but it was well endowed with the institutions that brought customers into bookshops: a parlement, an intendancy, an army base, a baroque profusion of fiscal and judicial offices, a university, an academy, a theatre, and three Masonic lodges—not to mention a cathedral and a dozen monasteries and convents.[13] The *Almanach de la librairie* (a yearbook that claimed to include all booksellers and printers in the Kingdom) listed twelve booksellers and four printer-booksellers in 1781. But Charmet told the STN that only four of them did much business; and he was the most active of the four, although he worried about Dominique Lépagnez, an energetic young man who creamed off most of the market for the *Encyclopédie*.[14]

Charmet's orders, and those of his wife, who took over the business after his death in 1782,[15] arrived in Neuchâtel every three or four months from December 1771 to March 1785. There were fifty-five in all, and they included ninety-seven titles of forbidden books, as well as a wide variety of legal literature. The statistics compiled from the orders are so extensive that they cannot be compressed into a single table, as in the case of Matthieu and Petit. Therefore, I have incorporated all of them in a general statistical sampling of orders by the STN's customers, which will be discussed below, and I have listed Charmet's nineteen best-sellers in Table 2.3.

This table reveals demand in two ways: for each forbidden book, it shows the total number of copies and the total number of orders that Charmet placed. The latter figure, which appears in parentheses on the far-right column, serves as a supplement or corrective to the former, because it indicates continuity in demand—that is, instances when Charmet's initial order proved to be inadequate and he sent in additional orders for the same book as his own customers continued to request it.

The best-seller list stands on a statistical base that is solid enough to support a general interpretation, but it cannot be read literally; it does not reveal the exact demand for every title. For example, the top book on the list, *Lettre philosophique de V****—an anonymous collection of impious and scabrous tales that should not be confused with Voltaire's *Lettres philosophiques*—could represent a gamble on some unusually large orders, even though Charmet renewed his stock of it twice.

TABLE 2.3. The Trade of Charmet in Besançon*

1. *Lettre philosophique* de V***, Anon.	150	(3)
2. *L'Arrétin*, du Laurens	137	(4)
3. *Anecdotes sur Mme la comtesse du Barry*, Pidansat de Mairobert?	107	(5)
4. *La Lyre gaillarde*, Anon.	105	(3)
5. *Vie privée de Louis XV*, Moufle d'Angerville? or Laffrey?	104	(4)
6. *Essai philosophique sur le monachisme*, Linguet	93	(5)
7. *Pucelle d'Orléans*, Voltaire	75	(3)
8. *L'Espion dévalisé*, Baudouin de Guémadeuc	60	(1)
9. *Histoire philosophique*, Raynal	59	(7)
10. *L'An 2440*, Mercier	57	(6)
11. *Les Confessions*, Rousseau	54	(2)
12. *Contes de Boccace*, trans. from Boccaccio	49	(3)
13. *Pièces heureusement échappées de la France*, Anon.	45	(2)
14. *Des Lettres de cachet*, comte de Mirabeau	44	(3)
15. *Tableau de Paris*, Mercier	42	(3)
16. *Ma Conversion*, comte de Mirabeau	32	(2)
17. *La Putain errante*, Aretino or Franco Niccolò	31	(2)
18. *Journal historique . . . par M. de Maupeou*, Pidansat de Mairobert and Moufle d'Angerville	31	(2)
19. *Mémoires de Louis XV . . .*, Anon.	28	(1)

*Charmet made 55 orders, from December 1771 to March 1785. They included 97 illegal works, of which the following 19 were most in demand. (The first number in the right-hand column represents the total number of copies ordered; the number in parentheses the total number of orders.)

And the book at the bottom of the list, the *Mémoires de Louis XV,* could have been more popular than it appears, because Charmet might have procured additional copies from other suppliers. Moreover, the titles do not represent strictly comparable units. The *Lettre philosophique de V*** was a hack compilation, printed "without typographical luxury," as the publishers put it; and its price varied from 17 sous to 1 livre, 5 sous. It did not cut much of a figure next to the magnificent *Histoire philosophique* of the abbé Raynal, which appeared in editions of six to ten volumes, usually stately octavos embellished with illustrations and elaborate, fold-out tables. The price of the *Histoire* *philosophique,* not counting an atlas available in an additional volume, ranged from 10 livres, 10 sous to 20 livres. Because of its expense, Charmet did not dare to order it in large quantities; but he renewed his orders for it more often than for any other book on the list. So the demand for the *Histoire philosophique* was probably stronger than is indicated by its position, ninth from the top, on the best-seller list.

These and other considerations serve as a warning:[16] best-seller lists must be handled with care. They provide only an approximate picture of literary demand, and they cannot be used to calculate the precise importance of every book that appears on them. But if studied in the light of other sources, they can reveal significant patterns of trade. Charmet's trade is especially important because he drew so much of his stock from the STN and discussed his affairs so frankly in his letters. His correspondence, a magnificent dossier of 179 items, provides a running commentary on demand as he saw it from his shop. Because the shop was located only 50 miles across the Jura Mountains from Neuchâtel, Charmet occasionally visited the home office of the STN. He became something of a friend, as well as a customer, of the STN's directors, and therefore mixed personal and professional observations with unusual openness when he wrote to them.

The tone of Charmet's letters became particularly cordial after a visit in October 1774, when he and the STN made arrangements for smuggling. He cleared a path through the border by bribing the customs officials and cultivating the intendant, Bourgeois de Boynes, an enlightened administrator with a taste for good literature. The intendant provided Charmet's shipments with special passes, and in return Charmet offered him "palpable civilities"—not money but "philosophical" books.[17] When some bumbling at the border station of Frambourg led to the confiscation of three of the STN's crates in 1775, Charmet presented the intendant's library with two magnificent copies of Raynal's *Histoire philosophique,* bound in Moroccan leather embossed with gold. "There will be a bonfire in the courtyard of the intendancy in order to pacify some blockheads," Charmet wrote. But he would see to it that they burned unsellable works, like Charles Christin's *Dissertation sur*

Saint-Claude, in place of the best-sellers like *Thérèse philosophe,* which had been impounded with the crates.[18]

For its part, the STN did not merely provide hospitality in Neuchâtel. When it marketed new editions, it favored Charmet against Lépagnez, his main rival in Besançon, who in turn ordered from the STN's competitors, including Samuel Fauche in Neuchâtel. As the years went by, the ties of mutual interest developed into reciprocal esteem, and esteem into something close to friendship. After passing through Neuchâtel in March 1777, Charmet wrote to the STN's directors, who were on a business trip in Paris, that their wives and children were in good health. "I was touched by their expressions of affection, politeness and goodwill."[19] When their trade went into a decline in 1779, Charmet assured the Neuchâtelois, "Your house . . . is the one I esteem; I am more attached to it than to any other in my business."[20] At this time he became syndic of the new booksellers' guild in Besançon, a position that made him responsible for inspecting all shipments for illegal works—and that also made him ideally suited to speed the STN's crates on their way through the underground railroad for illegal literature.[21] He helped his Swiss suppliers in a hundred ways, but a vigilant royal inspector of the book trade looked over his shoulder during the inspections. So Charmet had to be extremely careful. Like many of the established provincial booksellers, he never took great risks, and the STN never found the northwest passage for its shipments to Paris that it hoped would open up through Besançon.

While his business grew, Charmet's health declined. The first symptom that surfaced in his correspondence was a letter written by his wife in September 1781, because, she explained, he was too ill to leave his bed. A symptom of what? Cancer; tuberculosis? Mme Charmet lacked the vocabulary as well as the knowledge to convey what overtook her husband, and the historian can only watch helplessly as death invades the dossier. Charmet fell ill again during a trip in the summer of 1782. His wife, who had minded the shop in his absence, reported in September that "He had wanted to defeat the evil, and it defeated him. His lack of care for himself and ineffective remedies have made the disease tenacious and resistant. But I hope he'll pull through."[22] A month later, her optimism had increased. But in early November she wrote that he could not get out of bed, and by November 15 he could not even sign his name. The directors of the STN did not merely send their sympathy. They instructed a local agent to delay collecting one of Charmet's bills of exchange; and that unusual gesture "made him weep tears of gratitude toward everything that is yours," according to his wife.[23] Six weeks later he was dead.

Mme Charmet continued the business. Her letters were not only literate—unlike many widow booksellers who could not manage grammatical French, she did not shrink from using the past subjunctive; they also showed plenty of savvy about the trade. She complained that the STN could not supply Mirabeau's *Lettres de cachet* as rapidly as its competitors in Lausanne, and she warned that she expected quicker service for her order of his pornographic tract, *Le Libertin de qualité.*[24] As soon as she heard of Linguet's *Mémoires sur la Bastille,* she caught the scent of a best-seller: "There is a lot of talk here about a history of the Bastille said to be written by Linguet. I am informed from Geneva that this book can be had at Lausanne. Could you procure some copies of it for me fast? It is sure to sell well, and I would appreciate being supplied in time."[25] And she speculated on an edition of Turgot's *Oeuvres posthumes,* because after studying the text she felt convinced it would appeal to her clients: "This book is written with power and energy."[26]

In ordering books, Mme Charmet adhered to the strategy of her husband: "My husband had as a principle to take a great many items and a small number of each."[27] He, too, tried to read books before stocking them in quantity. Above all, he sought to arrange advance sales with his customers and to restrict his orders to a minimum number of copies per title. He preferred to renew his orders for the same work several times, if his customers kept requesting it, rather than run the risk of having unsold copies on his hands. Far from taking chances, he remained as close as possible to demand: "I am weak and therefore tremble. Sales serve as my compass, and I cannot deviate from them without exposing myself to danger. That's why I don't want to take any risks."[28]

Charmet's letters also make it clear that he drew a large proportion of his stock from the STN. They mention other suppliers, especially in Lausanne and Geneva. But they indicate that whenever possible, Charmet and his wife gave their preference to the STN: "We would prefer to do all our business with your house, to which we are attached by ties of gratitude and esteem."[29] For example, in 1781 they turned down opportunities to buy *Vie privée de Louis XV,* a four-volume work that usually sold for 10 livres wholesale, from other Swiss houses and placed an unusually large order, twenty-six copies, with the STN. But the demand was so great that it strained the exchange system among the Swiss publishers. The STN had expected to stock up on two hundred copies by means of an exchange with the book's publisher in Geneva, Jean-Abram Nouffer. Nouffer, however, was struggling under a heavy burden of debt. Seizing an opportunity to pacify his creditors, he held back the STN's allotment and sold off most of his edition to other wholesalers for cash. They supplied retailers in France long before the STN could get its own copies to market. Charmet therefore complained that his customers had seen the book in the shops of his competitors for nearly two months before he received his shipment. Even so, he renewed his order three times and sold a total of 104 copies, a remarkable success for "a small retailer," as he described himself.[30] The *Vie privée de Louis XV* ranks fifth on his best-seller list, and the inside story of its marketing suggests that the demand for it was even greater than one would judge from the list alone.[31]

In fact, a close reading of Charmet's correspondence makes the dominant tendency of the list, its emphasis on scandalous political literature, seem understated rather than the reverse. To be sure, the best-sellers included a smattering of all the illegal genres—pornographic and irreligious works alongside tomes by famous *philosophes.* But Charmet wrote that the public had lost interest in abstract treatises by 1781.[32] Instead, his customers wanted polemical tracts, like Mirabeau's *Des Lettres de cachet et des prisons d'Etat;*[33] *libelles,* like *Vie privée de Louis XV;* and *chroniques scandaleuses* (gossipy accounts of contemporary events) like *Journal historique de la révolution opérée dans la constitution de la monarchie française par M. de Maupeou, chancelier de France.* As soon as he heard of the *Journal historique,* Charmet said he would take 25 copies sight unseen and 100 if, upon inspection, he considered it "well done."[34] He also expected to sell one hundred copies of the *Mémoires de Louis XV* but, as in the case of any large order, wanted to read it first: "If the work is good and well suited for sales, I will take a hundred. But if it's in the same style as the *Précis de Mme du Barry,* I will be satisfied with a dozen."[35]

Indeed, Charmet's letters suggest that the market was flooded with this sort of literature. When the STN asked his advice about a project to reprint an anthology of polemical works on Necker's ministry in 1781, he said the local market could not absorb any more. But, he added,

> A new reprint of the *Espion anglais* in four volumes is still likely to sell. It's a good work, although it, too, is beginning to wear thin. Twenty-five copies would do for me, since a hundred have already been sold here. *L'Observateur anglais,* the *Mémoires secrets,* the *Espion français,* and this other one {*L'Espion anglais}*—that makes a great many books about the same subject, and the public is already abundantly supplied.[36]

That did not stop him, ten months later, from jumping at the chance to order fifty *Espion dévalisé,* as soon as he heard that yet another *chronique scandaleuse* had come off the presses.[37]

Charmet's letters reveal the human element behind the statistics. His proximity to Neuchâtel, his friendship with the directors of the STN, his cautious way of assessing demand and placing orders—everything about his dossier makes it an ideal source for correcting any misimpressions that might arise from reading the best-seller list alone. In fact, it suggests that the market for political works was even stronger than is indicated by the list, where five of the nineteen titles can be classified as *libelles* or *chroniques scandaleuses.* Taken together, the two kinds of evidence point to the existence of a public hungry for bawdy, slanderous, and seditious literature.

The Trade Throughout a Town

But the public in Besançon, a parlementary city in the highly literate northeastern quarter of the kingdom, might have been very different from that in other parts of France.[38] As a final case study, consider the STN's trade in Montpellier, a city far to the deep south, well beyond the range of friendly visits and personal solidarity with the Neuchâtelois.

Montpellier had a population of about 31,000 and a rich array of cultural institutions, which a proud citizen catalogued in a marvelously detailed and opinionated *Etat et description de la ville de Montpellier* in 1768: a cathedral and four collegial churches, sixteen monastic communities, two large primary schools run by the Frères des Ecoles Chrétiennes, several smaller schools directed by masters who also did tutoring, a royal *collège* or secondary school, a university (the famous faculty of medicine alone had seven professors, who enjoyed stipends of 2,000 livres and the right to wear a "gown of red damask with an ermine-lined bonnet"), a prestigious Royal Academy of Science, an Academy of Music, a municipal theatre, and twelve Masonic lodges. Although it lacked a parlement, Montpellier was a legal and administrative center— the seat of the provincial estates of Languedoc, an intendancy, two important fiscal courts (a *Chambre des Comptes* and *Cour des Aides*), a lower or *présidial* court, and a profusion of lesser administrative and judicial bodies. The town had an important textile industry (blankets, calicoes, stockings, handkerchiefs, bonnets) and a splendid variety of shopkeepers and artisans— not merely joiners and cobblers, but craftsmen whose trades have disappeared from dictionaries, like *plumassiers* and *pangustiers,* and who sent too many of their children to school in the opinion of their social superiors: "These schools, as I have said, are full of children from the dregs of the common people, who should be learning how to till the earth and do other hard labor instead of how to read and write."[39]

A large Protestant population and a garrison of soldiers served as reminders of the religious troubles from the time of Louis XIV, but sectarian passions had died out, according to the *Etat et description:* "No one quarrels any more over Calvinism, Molinism, and Jansenism. All that has been replaced by the reading of philosophical books, which has now become so prevalent, especially among the young, that there are more deists than anyone has ever seen." An old-fashioned bourgeoisie dominated the town and probably provided the bookstores with most of their customers, for Montpellier was good book-selling territory: "The book trade is quite extensive for a city like this," the *Etat et description* explained. "Booksellers have carried good assortments ever since the taste for having a library spread among the inhabitants."[40]

According to the *Manuel de l'auteur et du libraire,* a yearbook that claimed to list all French booksellers and printers, Montpellier had nine booksellers in 1777:[41]

Printers and Booksellers	Aug.-Franc. Rochard
	Jean Martel
Booksellers:	Isaac-Pierre Rigaud
	J. B. Faure
	Albert Pons
	Tournel
	Bascon
	Cézary
	Fontanel

Upon closer inspection, however, the field looked less dense. A traveling salesman of the STN sent the following report to the home office from Montpellier in 1778:

> I called on M. Rigaud, Pons & Co., which is the best house in this city. They keep asking for the works of Mme Riccoboni; herewith their order. I also saw Cézary, who isn't as rich as the former but is considered to be an upstanding gentleman; his order is enclosed. Jean Martel and Picot are two printers who don't sell books. J. B. Faure is actually the widow Gonthier, who is quite good, but she doesn't want to do business. Bascon and Tournel aren't worth anything; I didn't see them. Ab. Fontanel doesn't amount to much. When I first saw him, he said he needed several things from our stock.[42]

In short, the merged firm of Rigaud, Pons dominated the local trade. Two lesser firms, Cézary and Faure, occupied intermediary positions in the commercial hierarchy, and three others did a rather marginal business. Aside from these legal booksellers, various peddlers descended on Montpellier from the mountains of the Dauphiné every year after the autumn harvest. They sold all sorts of illegal literature under their cloaks, as did some of the local lowlife: "There are several unauthorized persons in Montpellier who do a considerable trade in all kinds of books, much to the detriment of the established booksellers," the legal dealers complained. ". . . They are said to include Father Marcellin, an agent of the Capuchins; a man called Tournel [a binder]; and the widow Arnaud, known as 'the students' mother.' "[43] The students actually had two "mothers," for the demoiselle Bringand, alias "the students' mother," also kept them supplied with forbidden books, which she hid "in a room on the right-hand side of the first floor . . . under the bed," according to the report of a police raid instigated by a legal dealer.[44]

This pattern existed nearly everywhere. In most provincial cities the book trade resembled a set of concentric circles: at the center, one or two prominent merchants drew most of the business into their well stocked stores; on the periphery, a few small shopkeepers struggled to resist the gravitational pull of the large firms; and beyond the fringe of the authorized booksellers, a motley collection of binders, peddlers, schoolmasters, down-and-out priests, and intellectual adventurers hawked their wares outside the reach of the law. The further from the center, the greater the tendency toward speculation in forbidden books; for profits increased in proportion to risks, and risks seemed less daunting to men who had little to lose or who were teetering on the edge of bankruptcy. But illegal literature penetrated all the circles of the system, including the inner core: that is the main lesson to be learned by studying a cross section of the trade in Montpellier, beginning with the dossier of the man at its center, Isaac-Pierre Rigaud.

Rigaud embodied the supreme virtue of a bookseller, "solidity"—that is, wealth combined with absolute dependability in the payment of his bills. He published books himself, mainly medical treatises and theses for the university, and he did a large retail business. Even before his merger with Pons in 1770, he carried an inventory worth at least 45,000 livres, which was far more than that of any other bookseller in the city.[45] A catalogue of his holdings in 1777 shows that he kept all kinds of books in stock, although he specialized in medical works and, to a lesser extent, in devotional books for the Huguenots of the region.[46] He drew his supplies from Paris, Rouen, Lyon, Avignon, and the most important publishers in Switzerland. When possible, he would buy a half dozen copies of a book from each of several different wholesalers so that he could play them off against one another and make sure they sent his shipments first. He protested vehemently if he failed to get the lowest price, if a competitor's shipment arrived before his own, if the printer used cheap paper, or if the shipper failed to find the cheapest route.

For example, when the government levied a heavy duty on book imports in 1771, Rigaud decided to cancel all foreign orders rather than risk his capital in smuggling. The confiscation of one crate would wipe out the profit from thirty, he explained: "One must know when to bend to circumstances and hard times."[47] Then, when the government lowered the tariff, he insisted that the STN pay two thirds of it. And finally, when the tariff was repealed, he demanded that the STN pay all transport costs as far as Lyon and cut their wholesale prices by 10 percent: "Without those terms, we will be unable to order merchandise from you, unless we want to beat a path to the poorhouse, which is what we're trying to avoid."[48] Rigaud bargained everyone to the wall and then complained if he failed to get the quickest, cheapest, safest service.[49] But the STN never flinched at his scoldings and *gasconnades* (he bargained with a verbosity that made its northern customers seem to be made of stone), because unlike most booksellers he never cheated and never failed to pay a bill of exchange when it became due. He was tough, but as solid as they came.

It was his toughness that stood out in the eyes of Montpellier's other booksellers. To Cézary, the "upstanding gentleman" who represented the middle rank of the city's trade according to the STN's traveling salesman, Rigaud was the incarnation of aggressive entrepreneurship: "I have learned with great pain that a certain gentleman of this city, consumed with cupidity and determined to destroy me in order to diminish the number of booksellers in Montpellier and to get my books for nothing, has written to some of my creditors in an attempt to dissuade them from making this arrangement."[50]

Cézary was referring to an episode that illustrates the dog-eat-dog kind of capitalism practiced by bookdealers everywhere in France and particularly in the south. By 1781, he had built up a fairly large business. His stock was worth 30,000 or 40,000 livres, and he owned two houses valued together at 30,000 livres. But he had 64,410 livres in debts, and he could not scrape up enough cash to avoid a suspension of payments at the beginning of the year.[51] In an attempt to save himself from bankruptcy, he sent letters to all of his creditors, begging them to let him continue his business, while paying them back gradually from earnings and the sale of assets—a common strategy among merchants with an unfavorable balance sheet. The STN felt inclined to be lenient (Cézary owed it only 285 livres for one shipment of legal books, mostly on medicine). But Rigaud persuaded the principal creditors, who were pirate publishers in Avignon, to insist on the payment of their bills. After Cézary failed to honor a bill of exchange, one of the Avignonese, Jean-Joseph Niel, had bailiffs break into his stockroom and impound 3,000 livres' worth of the most sellable books. Fearing debtor's prison, Cézary then fled town, while his mother had the shop closed and sealed by court officers in order to prevent further depletion of the stock. Cézary negotiated frantically from his hiding place, hoping to arrange a provisional settlement with his creditors and a safe conduct with the municipal authorities. But when he felt safe enough to return to Montpellier, he was locked up in prison.

After the creditors scheduled a meeting to decide whether to auction off his assets or to let him work off his debts, Cézary was released. Rigaud then tried to collect enough proxies from distant creditors to control the meeting, vote Cézary out of business, and buy the books on the cheap at the auction. Cézary countered with a desperate letterwriting campaign. After denouncing the "reprehensible maneuvers of the principal booksellers of Montpellier,"[52] he pleaded for mercy and attempted a maneuver of his own. A speculator named Luc Biron had offered to bail him out, Cézary claimed, so he could pay his creditors half of what he owed them if they would write off the other half. The STN asked a local merchant to investigate the affair. He reported that Biron was probably a strawman, whom Cézary would use to liquidate half his debts, but that the STN stood to lose even more from the auction and that Rigaud really did mean to squeeze Cézary out of business. The STN and a majority of the creditors chose the lesser swindle. "Biron" paid out 142 livres, but he did not save Cézary, who struggled to stay afloat for three more years and finally went under in 1784.

Meanwhile, Rigaud was doing everything possible to destroy another dealer, Abraham Fontanel, who operated on the outer fringes of the trade. Having been trained as an artist and engraver, Fontanel had developed a small print and book business in Mende. In 1772 he tried to break into the ranks of the official booksellers in Montpellier by purchasing a dealer's certificate *(brevet de libraire)*. But when his first shipments arrived, he found it impossible to get the books bound, because the binders either worked exclusively for Rigaud or did some under-the-cloak bookselling on their own and wanted to keep the trade to themselves. Eventually Fontanel arranged for his books to come assembled and stitched instead of in sheets. But once he had stocked his shop, he still had trouble enticing customers into it. So he sought an outlet for his wares at the fairs of Beaucaire and Bordeaux and probably did a little peddling en route, while his wife, like many booksellers' wives, stayed behind to mind the store. Then, in a final effort to prop up the business in Montpellier, he reinforced it with a *cabinet littéraire,* or commercial library.

Marginal dealers often established such societies by making their stock double as the holdings of a library, ordering an assortment of journals, and setting up a reading room behind their shop. The members paid a subscription fee, sometimes only 3 livres a month (a day's wages for a skilled artisan); and in return they could read all they wanted. If the bookseller recruited enough members, the income from the subscriptions could make the difference between survival and bankruptcy; and the stream of readers coming through the shop often stimulated sales.[53]

The kind of literature that Fontanel offered his subscribers can be surmised from one of his orders to the STN, which he said was to serve as the core of the *cabinet*'s collection. He wanted sentimental novels, poems, and essays by fashionable contemporaries like Dorat, Mercier, Gessner, and Young. Among Enlightenment authors, he favored the Voltaire of the *contes* (philosophic novels) and the Montesquieu of the *Lettres persanes*. His non-fiction also tended to be light and amusing—mainly travel adventures and popular histories—although he made room for Bayle's *Dictionnaire* (abridged) and Rollin's *Histoire romaine*. Six months after his arrival, Fontanel diagnosed Montpellier as "a town where new works and especially [philosophical] ones sell quite well." He asked for the writings of Helvétius and "two or three copies of everything in that genre, like *L'Homme par alphabet, Dieu et les hommes,* etc."[54] To guide himself in building up his stock of "philosophical" books—"those that sell the best," as he explained—he requested a copy of the STN's clandestine catalogue.[55] But after comparing prices, he decided to buy them from François Grasset in Lausanne. On the whole, Fontanel's orders resembled Rigaud's. The difference between them did not consist so much in the books they sold as in the positions from which they operated. Both were driven by the same motive: "I work to make money, not to lose it," Fontanel said.[56]

He made enough to pay his bills on time throughout the 1770s. Apparently he gained a foothold at the edge of Montpellier's intelligentsia, for his letters, written in elegant French, mention contacts with professors and lovers of the arts. But he did not feel well enough established to witness the collapse of Cézary's business without fearing that he might be next on Rigaud's list, especially when Rigaud tried to prevent him from recovering some books that had been sent to him by the STN in one of Cézary's impounded crates. That maneuver failed (Rigaud also removed the STN's catalogue from the crate in order to sabotage Fontanel's next order), but it confirmed Fontanel's suspicion that Rigaud was consumed by "excessive jealousy" and would do anything to ruin him.[57] He shored up his finances by winning a small pension as compensation for establishing an "academy of painting and sculpture."[58] Meanwhile, however, booksellers continued to drop out of the middle ranks of the trade. Tournel retreated back to binding. Faure died, leaving a business that was not prosperous enough for his son-in-law to continue. And Rigaud gobbled up the rest. "My book business is going to grow," Fontanel reported in 1781, "since I am now alone here with M. Rigaud, the others having given up, as it appears. But that has further inflamed the jealousy of M. Rigaud, who wants to have the field to himself and expresses his hatred of me every day."[59]

The polarization of the trade did not bring prosperity to Fontanel. For the first time, in January 1781, he failed to redeem one of the STN's notes on him. "Times are hard," he complained in March;[60] and soon afterward he confessed that he could not pay for six subscriptions to the quarto edition of the *Encyclopédie* (Rigaud paid for 143 subscriptions without difficulty). A severe illness, which overcame him at the fair in Bordeaux, prevented him from balancing his books at the end of the year. In August 1782, he failed to pay a bill of exchange for 300 livres. Although he acquitted a note for 666 livres in December, he continued to fall behind in his payments to the STN and to his other suppliers for the next two years. After his debt passed 1,000 livres and he failed to respond to several dunning letters, the STN threatened to take him to court. Finally, "by means of all sorts of threats and sollicitations," its local bill collector wrung 574 livres out of him in November 1784.[61] More threats produced another 300 livres in May 1785 and 150 livres in September 1786. But Fontanel still owed the STN 218 livres in 1787, when it lost contact with him. Whether he enrolled in the army, shipped out to the colonies, or merely took to the open road like so many other broken booksellers is impossible to say. But local businessmen had long since written him off, having concluded that "he takes on far more than he can handle."[62]

Thus hard work and entrepreneurship did not necessarily make for success. They did in Rigaud's case; but he occupied a strong, central position in the local economy and used that strategic advantage to pick off his competitors. Although he sold the same sort of books as Fontanel, he never took risks or overextended his credit. Unlike the marginal dealers, he could retreat to the legal sector of the trade whenever he smelled danger. So his best-seller list, shown in Table 2.4, reveals the clandestine trade at its most conservative.

TABLE 2.4. The Trade of Rigaud, Pons in Montpellier*

1. *L'An 2440*, Mercier	346	(16)
2. *Lettre de M. Linguet à M. le comte de Vergennes*, Linguet	200	(2)
3. *Correspondance secrète et familière de M. de Maupeou*, Pidansat de Mairobert	100	(1)
4. *Questions sur l'Encyclopédie*, Voltaire	70	(4)
5. *Lettre d'un théologien*, Condorcet	70	(3)
6. *Anecdotes sur Mme la comtesse du Barry*, Pidansat de Mairobert?	68	(2)
7. *Dieu. Réponse au Système de la nature*, Voltaire	50	(1)
8. *Requête au conseil du roi*, Linguet	48	(3)
9. *Système de la nature*, d'Holbach	43	(3)
10. *Histoire philosophique*, Raynal	35	(4)
11. *Journal historique . . . par M. de Maupeou*, Pidansat de Mairobert and Moufle d'Angerville	25	(1)
12. *Recueil de pièces fugitives*, Voltaire	24	(2)
13. *Œuvres*, Rousseau	23	(5)
14. *Tableau de Paris*, Mercier	22	(3)
15. *Lettre philosophique*, Anon.	20	(1)
16. *Pièces échappées du portefeuille de M. de Voltaire*, Anon.	20	(1)
17. *De la Philosophie de la nature*, Delisle de Sales	17	(3)
18. *Les Plus Secrets Mystères . . . de la maçonnerie*, Bérage, trans. by Koeppen	16	(4)

*Rigaud, Pons made 64 orders, from April 1771 to July 1784. They included 53 illegal works, of which the following 18 were most in demand.

This list represents the eighteen best-sellers out of the fifty-three illegal works that Rigaud ordered from the STN on sixty-four occasions, from 1771 to 1784. It does not correspond exactly to Charmet's list. One would hardly expect to find an isomorphic fit, title by title, between the two trade patterns. But they are quite similar. Several of the same works—Mercier's *L'An 2440, Anecdotes sur Mme la comtesse du Barry*, Raynal's *Histoire philosophique*— appear toward the top of each list. The same authors—Mercier, Linguet, Voltaire, Pidansat de Mairobert—dominate both of them. And both have a heavy proportion of political tracts, especially of the "Maupeouana" variety—*Correspondance secrète et familière de M. de Maupeou* and *Journal historique . . . par M. de Maupeou.* They differ in that Rigaud favored standard works of the Enlightenment—*Questions sur l'Encyclopédie, Système de la nature*—whereas Charmet ordered more pornography—*La Lyre gaillarde, La Putain errante.*

Like Charmet, Rigaud offered a running commentary on what sold best in his shop, and he did not hesitate to advise the STN on what to pirate. In March 1774, he warned that the market was satiated with so many editions of Raynal's *Histoire philosophique* "that one can consider its sales potential as destroyed."[63] But sales picked up again in 1781 after the public hangman burned it in front of the Parlement of Paris, and Rigaud renewed his orders for it three times. Certain classics—the works of Molière rather than those of the ancients—would always find buyers, he proclaimed.[64] But he did not favor one genre over another. He ordered the Bible and the atheistic *Système de la nature* at the same time; and although he indicated a preference for the latter, he praised its selling power, not its contents. He would have ordered one hundred copies of the *Système* instead of a dozen, he wrote in one of his scolding letters, but the STN had failed to reprint the book while the demand was hottest: "You missed a chance to make a coup."[65] The same calculation made him encourage the STN to reprint Delisle de Sales's atheistic *Philosophie de la nature:* "We have reason to believe that a new edition of *Philosophie de la nature,* 6 volumes in octavo, would sell. We would take 25 or 30 copies."[66]

When rumors about the existence of Rousseau's *Confessions* first reached Rigaud, he immediately recognized a best-seller.[67] But he pronounced *Rousseau juge de Jean-Jacques* a flop, and he worried that the boom in Rousseauism following the *philosophe*'s death in 1778 would flood the market: "We are inundated by different editions of the works of that author, which are proposed to us from everywhere."[68] Rigaud kept his eye on the demand for the works of all the *philosophes,* but he gave no indication of sympathy for their cause. He simply liked books that sold. To him, Voltaire was above all a writer who made life difficult for booksellers, owing to his habit of tinkering with the later editions of his works:

It is astonishing that at the end of his career, M. de Voltaire cannot resist fooling booksellers. It wouldn't matter so much if all those little ruses, frauds, and deceptions were attributed to him. But unfortunately they are usually blamed on the printers and still more on the retail booksellers.[69]

Raynal was also a man to be watched, because he was rumored to be writing a book that would make a fortune for the first person to get to the market with it—a projected history of the Revocation of the Edict of Nantes, which in fact Raynal never completed.[70] Mercier, Linguet, and Mme Riccoboni were the other authors who appealed most to Rigaud's customers, and therefore to him, for he seemed to transmit demand directly to the supplier without any distorting admixture of his personal taste. Whatever Rigaud's literary preferences and philosophical views might have been, they did not show through his commercial correspondence. He acted with absolute neutrality as a cultural agent, because he followed a basic principle: maximize profits and minimize risks.

When he ordered political works, Rigaud showed the same spirit of calculation and caution. "If you could ever get Linguet's *Lettre* to me without any danger via Lyon, I would take 100 copies," he wrote to the STN in 1777. "But no risks, please."[71] He especially wanted spicy topical works (*nouveautés piquantes*)[72]—scandalous accounts of current affairs (*L'Espion anglais, Mémoires secrets*), libels against ministers (*La Casette verte de M. de Sartine*), and scurrilous attacks on the court and the king (*Anecdotes sur Mme la comtesse du Barry, La Putain parvenue, Vie privée de Louis XV*). But these books represented only a small fraction of his business, and he ordered them only when the risk seemed slight. Whenever the government intensified its intermittent measures against the clandestine trade, Rigaud withdrew to safe ground. He finally stopped ordering altogether in 1784, after the government's last and most effective attempt to crack down on the importation of prohibited books.[73] Never in the ninety-nine letters that he sent to Neuchâtel between 1770 and 1787 did Rigaud indicate that he had the slightest difficulty with the police or with his finances. His orders for *livres philosophiques* were small side bets, taken without much of a gambling spirit, in a large and legitimate business. It would be wrong to imagine him sidling up to the lawyers and merchants of Montpellier with a wicked expression on his face and a *libelle* under his cloak. Instead, one should picture him in a large, well-appointed store, surrounded by shelves full of medical treatises, travel books, histories, and sentimental novels—with a few denunciations of ministerial despotism hidden under the counter.

Behind every book business there is a story, each different from the others, each intensely human. A dozen more case studies might reveal a great deal about the human comedy in general, but it would not advance us further toward our objective: understanding the demand for forbidden books and the means of transmitting and satisfying it.[74] Despite the variety in the character of the booksellers, the books that got sold were essentially the same. What varied was the propensity to take risks. At the heart of the trade in each town, the established booksellers often marketed illegal works from beneath their counters, just as the peddlers did from under their cloaks and the "students' mothers" from below their beds. But when the police and the customs agents got tough, the "solid" dealers generally retreated to the safe sectors of the trade. Those on the fringes could not afford such a strategy. They peddled their wares wherever they could find customers, whatever the circumstances.[75] On the whole, then, marginality and illegality went together; but the illegal material circulated everywhere. And although dealers in different parts of the system might be mortal enemies, they ordered the same books from the same suppliers and behaved according to the same imperative: to make money. As André of Versailles put it, "I don't neglect the sale of books that I myself would never read, and that is because one must live amongst the common horde and because the best book for a bookseller is a book that sells."[76]

Whether solid or ragged, the dealers in forbidden books transmitted demand as accurately as they could. They remained ideologically neutral in their role as cultural middlemen, not because they had no personal convictions but because they pursued their own interests. Whatever one thinks of their business practices, their struggle to make a living shows how supply met demand. They got books to readers, books that readers wanted. A systematic sampling of their orders will therefore reveal the nature of the illegal literature that was bought and sold in France on the eve of the Revolution—if the sources of the sample represent the book trade as a whole. That, however, is a monumental "if," large enough, certainly, to give one pause and to merit a digression about the problems of understanding the literary marketplace two centuries ago.

The Problem of Representativeness

There is no getting around the fact that all the statistics come from the same source: the archives of the STN. Nothing like it exists elsewhere. I have beaten a path to all the known papers of dealers in French books under the Old Regime, but none of them contains anything that could be used to test the representativeness of the material in Neuchâtel. The general account book (*Grand livre*) of the Cramers in Geneva says nothing about the sales of individual works; the papers of the Société typographique of Bouillon contain only scraps of correspondence; and the sales registers of Struykmann in Amsterdam are far too meager to provide a point of comparison with the records of the STN. Unless a treasure turns up in some other attic or cellar, the 50,000 letters and dozens of account books of the STN that sat for 150 years in an attic in Neuchâtel will remain the only adequate source of statistics about the trade in forbidden French books.[77]

It is a magnificent source, a historian's dream: first-hand accounts of life in the book trade from all of its sectors and all of the cities in France. But can one reconstruct the whole world of forbidden books from the contents of a single attic, however rich it may be? Isn't some distortion bound to falsify the view, if one studies the clandestine commerce of the entire French kingdom from the perspective of one publisher in one Swiss city? Those objections have considerable weight, and I must admit that I have lost some sleep over them. By way of reply, I would stress two aspects of the book trade in the eighteenth century that made it fundamentally different from the book trade today. The first concerns the way publishers marketed books; the second, the way booksellers ordered them.

When the STN began business in 1769, publishing had not yet become distinguished from bookselling and printing as an autonomous activity. The French term for publisher, *éditeur,* had appeared in the 1762 edition of the *Dictionnaire de l'Académie française,* although in a rather blurred manner: "Someone who takes care of another's work and has it printed." And the role of the publisher was beginning to be defined through new marketing strategies developed by Philip Erasmus Reich in Leipzig, Charles-Joseph Pancoucke in Paris, William Strahan in London, and, somewhat later, Robert Cadell in Edinburgh. But the production and sales of new books remained bound up with antiquated trade practices, above all the old system of exchanges.[78] As explained above, a bookseller-printer (or "publisher," if the anachronism be permitted) frequently traded a large proportion of a new edition against an assortment of books that he chose from the stock of allied houses. The exchange was usually calculated in sheets, with special allowances for disparities in format, difficulties in typesetting, and quality of paper. In this way a publisher could market an edition quickly, without incurring damages from pirates, and at the same time vary his own stock, without dispensing capital. Arranging exchanges was an art, which took up a great deal of a publisher's time and energy. A partner in an exchange might swap sheets of blotchy *bâtard* paper printed in widely spaced and badly worn *cicéro* for sheets of fine *carré* printed in densely set and elegant *petit romain;* he might say he was producing another boring novel by Baculard d'Arnaud when in fact his presses were turning out a wicked new satire by Voltaire; he might suppress information about the best-selling books in his stock and trade only his remainders (known as *drogues* or *gardes-magasin* in the publishers' slang); or he might agree to swap desirable works and then delay his shipment so that he could get to the market first with his own share of those works and also with the books that he received in exchange for them.[79]

There were a thousand ruses in this game, and everyone had to play it or risk being frozen out of the business altogether. Publishers sometimes slipped spies into the offices of their allies and / or competitors and bribed workers in printing shops to send them freshly printed sheets. The intrigues became so fierce that in 1778 three of the big Swiss houses—the sociétés typographiques of Neuchâtel, Bern, and Lausanne—formed a confederation to protect themselves and pirate everyone else by means of joint enterprises. After deciding together on what to reprint, they shared the production costs and sold the common stock separately, so that each house could draw on its own network of retailers. Then they divided the profits at an annual settlement of accounts, basing their calculations on the number of sheets they sold and settling the balance in cash.[80]

The sheet was a fundamental unit in bookkeeping as well as in bookselling and printing. Publishers, who needed to be experts in all three areas, kept "exchange accounts" calculated in sheets along with accounts reckoned in the standard currency of *livres tournois*. In studying the bookkeeping of the STN, one gets the impression that the "exchange accounts" *(comptes de changes)* were almost as important as the "money accounts" *(comptes d'argent)*. In fact, the two could not be separated, because swapping books was an integral part of the process of selling them. As already explained, "philosophical books" commanded special exchange rates, usually one sheet for two of a legal book or a pirated edition of a legal one. The high rate resulted from the high risk, for publishers could be imprisoned in Geneva or Lausanne just as well as in Paris.

Large and respectable firms like the STN rarely published hard-core "philosophical" works. In its early years, the STN put out an edition of d'Holbach's atheistic *Système de la nature*. Its production costs and sales registers show that it stood to make a profit of 243 percent. But in the end, after all sorts of difficulties with smuggling and bill collecting, it earned only about 50 percent; and the affair caused such a scandal within Neuchâtel itself that two of the STN's directors were suspended from their positions within the governing bodies of the local elite— Frédéric-Samuel Ostervald from the command of the civil militia and Jean-Elie Bertrand from the Venerable Class of Pastors.[81]

After this episode, the STN procured almost all of its prohibited works by exchanges with specialists in the genre, obscure entrepreneurs who set up shop in between prison terms and bankruptcies and made as much as they could as fast as they could by producing anything that would sell. Jean-Samuel Cailler, Jean-Abram Nouffer, Gabriel Grasset, Pierre Gallay, and Jacques-Benjamin Téron in Geneva; Gabriel Décombaz in Lausanne; Samuel Fauche in Neuchâtel; Louis-François Mettra in Neuwied; Clément Plomteux in Liège; Jean-Louis Boubers in Brussels—their names are forgotten today, but they produced the bulk of France's forbidden literature. Instead of selling it all themselves, they traded it for the less dangerous works printed by the well-established houses. In this manner, they accumulated a legal stock that they could sell without difficulty in their hometowns, while the big firms acquired the illegal books that they needed to satisfy customers throughout their network of retailers in France and throughout Europe.

The widespread reliance on the exchange system affected publishing in two fundamental ways. First, it meant that the important publishing houses had to operate as wholesalers. As they accumulated books procured through exchanges, they became increasingly involved in marketing large and varied inventories. Second, the swapping meant that their inventories became increasingly similar, because they drew their general stock *(livres d'assortiment)* from the same general sources. Of course, the complex set of alliances and enmities among the major publishers prevented them from filling their warehouses with exactly the same books. But the alliances overlapped enough for all of them to be able to procure almost any current book by means of an exchange. A kind of invisible, floating stock came into existence throughout the area bordering France from the Low Countries to Switzerland. It was available to all the major publisher-wholesalers; and in placing orders with one or two of them, a retailer in France could get virtually everything he wanted.

As the publishers outside France scrambled to supply the booksellers within it, allied houses sometimes competed for the same business. But each publisher had its own network of customers, so the contradictions built into the system were less severe than one might expect. In a letter to its main customer in Marseille, the STN explained, "Despite the fact that we compete with several of our neighbors, we nevertheless cooperate with them. Having by now a very extended business, we succeed in selling their books along with our own."[82] The STN's catalogue in 1785 contained 700 titles; an inventory of its stock in 1787 ran to 1,500 titles. Back in 1773 it had boasted, "There is no book of any importance that appears in France that we are not capable of supplying."[83]

Seen from the perspective of the retailer, the system for ordering books differed from modern practices in one, crucial respect: it did not permit returns. Booksellers therefore tended to be cautious. As Mossy of Marseille explained to the STN:

> You mention some new works. I have to look them over before I can commit myself to ordering them. If prudence does not guide our affairs, we will soon be wiped out. When one has a good idea of a book's value and can foresee its success with some assurance, then one may take a chance on it. But don't be surprised if I balk at all sorts of propositions. I prefer to [order only a few copies and then] come back for more.[84]

As a rule, retailers ordered only as many copies as they felt sure of selling to their own customers. In fact, they often arranged sales in advance and adjusted the size of their order accordingly. A typical order would contain only four or five copies per title (although occasionally the bookseller would request a dozen copies in order to get the free thirteenth), but it would include a great many different works. The idea was to procure a general assortment of books rather than a few books in large quantity.

This practice minimized risks while maximizing the variety of the retailer's stock. It also responded to another prosaic consideration, which has escaped the conventional histories of literature: the need to save on transport costs. Costs were cheapest for bulk shipments that went by wagon (*voiture*), but the wagoners would not take anything that weighed less than fifty pounds. The lighter shipments had to travel by coach (*carrosse*) at a rate that could be ruinously expensive. Thus, for example, Matthieu decided not to forward a shipment of Voltaire's *Questions sur l'Encyclopédie* from Nancy to Paris, because "the nineteen copies of the *Questions sur l'Encyclopédie* don't weigh fifty pounds, and so I couldn't give them to the wagoner, which left the Paris coach as the only other possibility."[85] The distinction between wagon and coach became one of the most important elements in the ordering strategy of booksellers. It meant that they could save money by grouping many titles in the same order, even if they could get some of the titles cheaper elsewhere. In general, therefore, the retailers ordered large assortments of books from a small number of suppliers instead of scattering small orders among a large number of suppliers.

Of course, when they caught the scent of an unusual bargain or a possible coup, booksellers would order from anyone who could supply the goods. But they tended to develop stable relations with a few wholesale houses. So a compilation of their orders with one major supplier over several years can reveal the general pattern of their business. Conversely,the business of one big supplier with a wide variety of retailers can serve as a window, albeit an imperfect one, through which to see the configuration of the illegal trade as a whole.

In short, the practices of the book trade—the way publishers evolved into wholesalers, wholesalers built up their inventories, and retailers placed their orders—help one to understand why the papers of the STN can be taken to provide a fairly accurate picture of the play of supply and demand everywhere in France. Moreover, the correspondence of the booksellers provides a rich running commentary on the state of the market. The qualitative evidence confirms the statistics compiled from their orders. And after reading thousands of their letters, one develops a sense of what sold best. Perhaps subjective judgments should be shunned. But having spent nearly every spare summer and sabbatical for the last twenty-five years (half of my life) with my nose in the STN's archives, and in related archives in France, I have come to trust my sense of smell, the *pifomètre,* as the French call it. I have concluded that the STN's papers do indeed represent the general character of the trade in forbidden books.

But I *want* them to be representative. After 25 years and 50,000 letters, the hunger for significant conclusions can be overwhelming, and that is dangerous, because as soon as a historian desires a certain result, he or she is likely to find it. So in order to control for bias built into my work in Neuchâtel, I have undertaken three research projects in other archives. It would be misleading to refer to these as "control" studies, because no attempt to measure literary demand two hundred years ago can be conducted with scientific rigor. All the sources are imperfect; none of the methods for studying them is fool-proof; and there are no publishers' papers comparable to those of the STN. But it is possible to find some points of comparison by culling statistics from three other kinds of documents: registers of books confiscated in the Paris Customs; inventories of bookshops made during police raids; and catalogues of *livres philosophiques* from other Swiss publishers.

A detailed description of all this supplementary research can be found in the companion volume to this book. Suffice it to say here that a systematic sampling of the booksellers' orders in the STN papers yields a list of 457 titles of illegal books, which can be compared with lists compiled from the other three sources.

The first of the three is the richest. Every time the French authorities confiscated a book in the Paris Customs, they noted the reason for the confiscation—whether it was pirated, or relatively inoffensive but "not permitted," or unambiguously illegal—in a register. A magnificent set of registers, now in the Bibliothèque Nationale, covers all the confiscations from 1771 to 1789. By compiling all the entries for the illegal books, I have made a list of 280 titles and calculated which ones were confiscated most often.

The second list comes from police reports on their raids of bookshops. When they caught a bookseller with a substantial stock of illegal works, they confiscated the books and listed them in inventories. The archives of the Bastille contain nine such inventories, from raids in Paris, Strasbourg, Caen, Lyon, and Versailles between 1773 and 1783. They also contain records of all the confiscated books sent to the *pilon* (pulping room) of the Bastille. This material yielded a list of three hundred titles, which also shows which works were confiscated in two or more raids.

The third list comes from six catalogues of *livres philoso-*

phiques drawn up by publishers in Geneva, Lausanne, and Bern between 1772 and 1780. The catalogues were used for marketing illegal works and circulated clandestinely among the booksellers. Although they vary in size, they give a good indication of the stock of forbidden books kept by a half dozen houses like the STN. Altogether, they provide a further harvest of 261 titles, including several that appeared in more than one catalogue.

The information from all the lists of illegal books can be summarized as follows:

STN list: 457 titles.
Customs confiscations: 280 titles, of which 166 (59%) are on the STN list.
Police raids: 300 titles, of which 179 (60%) are on the STN list.
Clandestine catalogues: 261 titles, of which 174 (67%) are on the STN list.

All this compiling and comparing confirms the conclusion that the STN list does in fact represent the illegal trade in general, although of course it does not cover every book that circulated outside the law. The representativeness of the Neuchâtel material can be judged best by examining the titles at the top of all four lists, where the overlap is greatest. In this way, by comparing rates of incidence, it becomes clear that the books ordered in the largest quantity and with the greatest frequency from the STN were also the books most often confiscated by the Paris Customs, most often impounded in the police raids, and most often listed in the clandestine catalogues of other publishers.

Finally, by amalgamating all four sources, one can produce a fairly complete bibliography of the illegal literature that was bought and sold in pre-Revolutionary France, 720 titles in all. And by closer analysis of the orders to the STN, one can measure the relative importance of individual works, authors, and genres.

The General Pattern

In order to take account of discrepancies and to build up the largest possible statistical foundation, the analysis can be extended in different directions. The basic information comes from the compilation of every illegal book in every order from twelve regular customers of the STN, the "major dealers" located on Map 2.1. The statistics from this first round of sampling make it possible to draw a profile of the business of a dozen booksellers like Charmet and Rigaud (for details see the companion volume). I have supplemented these case studies with surveys of the illegal market in three especially active areas—Paris, Lyon, and Lorraine—where I could amalgamate statistics from many different businesses. Then, in a second round of sampling, I compiled the orders from seventeen "minor dealers" in other locations (see Map 2.2) and also from four peddlers *(colporteurs).* As in the case of Matthieu and Petit, they did not place enough orders with the STN for me to draw firm conclusions about their trade as individuals. But taken as a whole, their orders fall into a significant pattern. In fact, it is virtually the same as the pattern that emerges from the orders of the major dealers. So all the statistics can be combined in a survey which, by eighteenth-century standards, is remarkably exhaustive, covering 28,212 books and 3,266 orders. It is as valid, I believe, as most best-seller lists today.

Table 2.5 shows the top thirty-five best-sellers from the illegal trade in France from 1769 to 1789. It should not be read literally, because the place of individual books cannot be determined with absolute accuracy. Also, it overrepresents the importance of books published by the STN, which are therefore marked off by asterisks, and it underrates a few works published at the very end of the period, when the STN had cut back on its business in France.[86] But the table provides enough information for one to allow for irregularities and to look for convergences among different kinds of evidence.

Are there any surprises on this list? One would expect to find notorious works by famous authors at the top of it. So there is no reason to be astonished at the success of Raynal's *Histoire*

MAP 2.1. Major Dealers in Illegal Books

MAJOR DEALERS, including three areas with composite statistics: Lorraine (on Nancy), Lyon, and Paris.

Bergeret, Bordeaux	Augé, Lunéville	*Lyon:*
Blouet, Rennes	Babin, Nancy	Baritel
Buchet, Nîmes	Bergue, Thionville	Barret
Charmet, Besançon	Bernard, Lunéville	Cellier
Letourmy, Orléans	Bertrand, Thionville	Flandin
Malherbe, Loudun	Bonthoux, Nancy	Jacquenod
Mauvelain, Troyes	Carez, Toul	
Manoury, Caen	Chénoux, Lunéville	*Paris:*
Mossy, Marseille	Choppin, Bar-le-Duc	Barré
Pavie, La Rochelle	Dalancourt, Nancy	Barrois
Rigaud, Pons,	Gay, Lunéville	Cugnet
Montpellier	Gerlache, Metz	Desauges
Robert et Gauthier,	Henry, Nancy	Lequay Morin
Bourg-en-Bresse	L'Entretien, Lunéville	Prévost
	Matthieu, Nancy	Védrène
Lorraine:	Orbelin, Thionville	
Audéart, Lunéville	Sandré, Lunéville	

MAP 2.2. Minor Dealers in Illegal Books

MINOR DEALERS:

Boisserand, Roanne
Billault, Tours
Bonnard, Auxerre
Caldesaigues, Marseille
Cazin, Reims
Chevrier, Poitiers
Fontaine, Colmar
Habert, Bar-sur-Aube

Jarfaut, Melun
Lair, Blois
Laisney, Beauvais
Malassis, Nantes
Petit, Reims
Resplandy, Toulouse
Sens, Toulouse
Sombert, Châlons-
   sur-Marne

Waroquier, Soissons

Itinerant hawkers:

Blaisot
Giles
Planquais
'Troisième'

SOURCES: Maps 2.1 and 2.2 from the Papers of the STN.

TABLE 2.5. Best-Sellers: Total Orders (Major and Minor Dealers)

TITLE [AUTHOR]	BOOKS	ORDERS	EDITIONS	SOURCES†
1. *L'An 2400,* Mercier	1,394	(124)	25	ABCD
2. *Anecdotes sur Mme la comtesse du Barry,* Pidansat de Mairobert?	1,071	(52)		ACD
3. **Système de la nature,* d'Holbach	768	(96)	13	ABCD
4. **Tableau de Paris,* Mercier	689	(40)		AD
5. **Histoire philosophique,* Raynal	620	(89)		ABCD
6. *Journal historique . . . par M. de Maupeou . . . ,* Pidansat de Mairobert and Moufle d'Angerville	561	(46)		ACD
7. *L'Arrétin,* Du Laurens	512	(29)	14	ABCD
8. *Lettre philosophique,* Anon	496	(38)	9	ABCD
9. *Mémoires de l'abbé Terray,* Coquereau	477	(24)		AC
10. *La Pucelle d'Orléans,* Voltaire	436	(39)	36	ABCD
11. **Questions sur l'Encyclopédie,* Voltaire	426	(63)	5	ABCD
12. *Mémoires de Louis XV,* Anon	419	(14)		AD
13. **L'Observateur anglais,* Pidansat de Mairobert	404	(41)		ABCD
14. *La Fille de joie,* trans. by Lambert? or Fougeret de Montbrun?	372	(30)	16	ABCD
15. *Thérèse philosophe,* d'Arles de Montigny? or d'Argens?	365	(28)	16	ABCD
16. *Recueil de comédies et . . . chansons gaillardes . . . ,* Anon	347	(27)		ABCD
17. **Essai philosophique sur le monachisme,* Linguet	335	(19)		A
18. *Histoire critique de Jésus Christ,* d'Holbach	327	(36)	3	ABCD
19. *Les Plus Secrets Mystères . . . de la maçonnerie,* trans. by Bérage?, ed. by Koeppen	321	(36)		A
20. **Requête au conseil du roi,* Linguet	318	(17)		AD
21. *La Putain errante,* Aretino or Niccolò Franco?	261	(27)	10	ABCD

TABLE 2.5. *(Continued)*

TITLE [AUTHOR]	BOOKS	ORDERS	EDITIONS	SOURCES†
22. *Le Christianisme dévoilé,* d'Holbach	259	(31)	12	ABCD
23. *Œuvres,* Rousseau	240	(58)	21	ABCD
24. *Le Paysan perverti,* Restif de la Bretonne	239	(19)	10	AD
25. *L'École des filles,* Milot	223	(16)	3	ABCD
26. *Le Bon-Sens,* d'Holbach	220	(16)	11	ABCD
27. *Lettre de M. Linguet à M. le comte de Vergennes,* Linguet	216	(4)		A
28. *De l'homme,* Helvétius	215	(21)		ABCD
29. *Système social,* d'Holbach	212	(32)	4	ABCD
30. *Le Monarque accompli,* Lanjuinais	210	(18)		ACD
31. *Dictionnaire philosophique portatif,* Voltaire	204	(27)	11	ABCD
32. *Vie privée de Louis XV,* Moufle d'Angerville? or Laffrey?	198	(17)		AD
33. *La Lyre gaillarde,* Anon.	197	(14)		ABCD
34. *Les Lauriers ecclésiastiques,* Rochette de la Morlière	191	(22)	13	ABC
35. *Histoire de dom B . . . , portier des Chartreux,* Gervaise de Latouche? or Nourry?	190	(20)	20	ABCD

*An STN edition.
†A = STN; B = Catalogue; C = Police confiscations; D = Customs confiscations.

philosophique and Voltaire's *La Pucelle d'Orléans,* or of pornographic classics like *La Putain errante.* But *L'An 2440, Anecdotes sur Mme la comtesse du Barry, L'Arrétin, Thérèse philosophe, Le Christianisme dévoilé, Vie privée de Louis XV, Histoire de dom B . . . , portier des Chartreux?* Those works also figure at the top of the lists of the books confiscated most often by the customs officials and by the police.[87] All the evidence points to the same conclusion: the literary marketplace of eighteenth-century France overflowed with best-sellers that have been almost completely forgotten today.

Table 2.6 lists the writers whose works sold best. Almost all

TABLE 2.6. Authors by Number of Books Ordered

1. Voltaire, François-Marie Arouet de	3,545
2. Holbach, Paul-Henri-Dietrich Thiry, baron d' (and collaborators)	2,903
3. Pidansat de Mairobert, Matthieu-François (and collaborators)	2,425
4. Mercier, Louis-Sébastien	2,199
5. Théveneau de Morande, Charles	1,360
6. Linguet, Simon-Nicolas-Henri	1,038
7. Du Laurens, Henri-Joseph	866
8. Raynal, Guillaume-Thomas-François[a]	620
9. Rousseau, Jean-Jacques	505
10. Helvétius, Claude-Adrien	486
11. Coquereau, Jean-Baptiste-Louis[b]	477
12. Argens, Jean Baptiste de Boyer, marquis d'[c]	457
13. Fougeret de Monbron, Charles-Louis[d]	409
14. Restif de la Bretonne, Nicolas-Edmé	371
15. Bérage/Koeppen, Karl-Friederich[e]	321
16. Mirabeau, Honoré-Gabriel Riqueti, comte de	312
17. Aretino, Pietro Bacci[f]	261
18. Pauw, Cornelius de	235
19. Milot (or Mililot)[g]	223
20. Goudar, Ange	214
21. Lanjuinais, Joseph[h]	210
22. Moufle d'Angerville, Barthélemy-François-Joseph[i]	198
23. Rochette de la Morlière, Charles-Jacques-Louis-Auguste	197

[a] One title: *Histoire philosophique . . . deux Indes.*

[b] One title: *Mémoires de l'abbé Terrai.*

[c] Includes *Thérèse philosophe* (365 books, 28 orders) which is also attributed to d'Arles de Montigny. D'Argens, however, has six other titles attributed to him, so he is not disproportionately high on the list.

[d] Includes *La Fille de joie,* his translation of *Memoirs of a Woman of Pleasure (Fanny Hill)* by John Cleland. This translation has also been attributed to a certain Lambert.

[e] One title: *Les Plus Secrets Mystères des hauts grades de la maçonnerie dévoilés, ou le vrai Rose-Croix; traduit de l'anglais, suivi du Noachite traduit de l'allemand.* By usage, the translator is cited as "Bérage" (e.g., Barbier and Caillet). Fesch gives Koeppen as the editor, without citing any original English or German works.

[f] One title: *La Putain errante.*

[g] One title: *L'École des filles.*

[h] One title: *Le Monarque accompli.*

[i] One title: *La Vie privée de Louis XV,* attributed to both Moufle d'Angerville and Arnoux Laffrey (198 books, 17 orders).

illegal books appeared anonymously, but most of their authors can be identified. Some authors, like Raynal, conquered the market with a single work, while others, like Voltaire and Mercier, wrote several best-sellers. Indeed, Voltaire's output was amazing: sixty-eight of the books on the STN list, in nearly all the genres of illegal literature. By cultivating his secretaries and the great man himself, the STN gained access to his infernal factory at Ferney. For that reason, one might suspect a Voltairean bias in its sales. But Voltaire's works also stood out among those most confiscated in the Paris Customs and police raids. Everything suggests that they flooded the kingdom.

More surprising is the strong showing of the baron d'Holbach and his collaborators, whose systematic materialism appears rather bloodless today. But eighteenth-century readers seem to have been fascinated by the opportunity of seeing atheism advocated openly in print. Most of the printing took place in Holland, while the Voltairean stream of Enlightenment flowed from presses in Switzerland.[88] But the strong Holbachean element in the STN's sales suggests that there was little geographical bias in the demand registered in Neuchâtel. For the first time in the 1760s and 1770s, a whole repertory of atheistic works became available in relatively cheap editions, and the French public snapped them up.

Rousseau's place, sandwiched between Raynal and Helvétius, puts him among the top ten writers but not within the range of those at the very top, such as Mercier and Linguet, whose popularity also stands out in the correspondence of the booksellers.[89] To be sure, the list does not take account of Rousseau's supreme best-seller, *La Nouvelle Héloïse,* because it was not an illegal book. But the STN sold only six copies of his *Emile,* which was both prohibited and highly popular in the 1760s. Evidently the market had been saturated with it by 1770, when the STN began to trade heavily in livres philosophiques.[90]

Saturation, however, is difficult to detect. Occasionally the booksellers themselves noted that a work had sold so well that the market for it had been exhausted. For example, Jean-Marie Barret, one of the most astute publisher-book dealers in Lyon, said that he had slashed the price of his stock of Bayle's *Dic-*

tionnaire historique et critique because "that work is dead in France; it can only be sold outside the country."[91] Some important writers of the Enlightenment might have occupied a more prominent place on a best-seller list drawn up in the 1750s and 1760s, when the demand for their works was fresh. A relatively poor showing in the 1770s and 1780s need not prove that the French had ceased to read them, for their books may have been available in private libraries rather than bookstores. By 1776, Parisian booksellers had nearly stopped carrying individual works by Diderot, although editions of his collected works continued to be sold.[92] But even if one allows for the possibility of market saturation, the fact remains that some titles from the midcentury continued to sell well right until the Revolution. The demand for the most notorious of them, *De l'Esprit* by Helvétius, which was first published in 1758, held up until the 1780s, eclipsing by far the demand for *Emile.*

Keeping these complications in mind, is it possible at last to solve the problem of the diffusion of Rousseau's *Du Contrat social?* Only once did the STN receive an order for the book— from a peddler named Planquais, who wanted four copies. So the *Contrat social* did not figure among the top four hundred ordered from the STN. It did not appear in any of the clandestine catalogues of the other publishers, although the STN offered it in its own catalogue of *livres philosophiques;* and it did not get seized in any of the police raids, although it was confiscated four times in the Paris Customs. In short, Mornet was probably correct in claiming that Rousseau's treatise did not circulate widely in France before the Revolution. But he overstated his case, because the *Contrat social* was included in many editions of Rousseau's works; and those editions appear near the top of the best-seller list, even though they contained as many as thirty-eight volumes and often cost 24 livres or more. (The common and relatively cheap duodecimo edition published in thirty-one volumes by the Société typographique de Genève sold for 25 livres in 1785.)

The sales of collected works also help to put the demand for the writings of the *philosophes* in perspective, even though the size and price of the sets varied greatly:

Works of Rousseau: 240 sets, 58 orders[93]
Works of Helvétius: 110 sets, 24 orders
Works of La Mettrie: 90 sets, 20 orders
Works of Voltaire: 59 sets, 29 orders
Works of Grécourt: 56 sets, 12 orders
Works of Piron: 50 sets, 10 orders
Works of Crébillon fils: 40 sets, 12 orders
Works of Fréret: 37 sets, 11 orders
Works of Diderot: 33 sets, 9 orders

There is no denying the appeal of a few famous writers, but they did not dominate the market for forbidden books. After a few great names at the head of the list of the best-selling authors comes a string of others that are now unknown, except to a handful of specialists in eighteenth-century literature: Pidansat de Mairobert, Théveneau de Morande, Du Laurens, Coquereau, d'Argens, Fougeret de Monbron, de Pauw, Goudar, Moufle d'Angerville, Rochette de la Morlière. . . . Those were the men who wrote most of the best-sellers of pre-Revolutionary France, yet they have disappeared from literary history.

Their disappearance may seem less surprising if one views literary history itself as an artificial construct, passed on and reworked from generation to generation. "Minor" authors and "major" best-sellers inevitably get lost in the shuffle. We do not expect the best-sellers of our own day to be read two hundred years from now. But do we not think that literary history should take account of the literature that reached most people? Should not literary historians study the ordinary varieties of Mornet's *la littérature vécue,* the sort of thing that we refer to loosely by expressions such as "taste" and "demand" among "the general public"?[94]

Table 2.7 provides some preliminary answers to those questions by showing which genres of illegal literature were most popular. To be sure, its categories, like those in any classification system, are arbitrary. They may be inadequate as a means of sorting out data, and the sorting itself involves a good deal of subjective judgment: is a work primarily irreligious, or seditious, or pornographic, or does it manage to be all three at the same time? Nonetheless, the rubrics in the table work reason-

TABLE 2.7. General Pattern of Demand

CATEGORY AND SUBCATEGORY	TITLES		COPIES ORDERED	
	NO.	%	NO.	%
RELIGION				
A. Treatises	45	9.8	2,810	10.0
B. Satire, Polemics	81	17.7	3,212	11.4
C. Irreligious ribaldry, pornography	18	3.9	2,260	8.0
Subtotals	144	31.5[a]	8,282	29.4
PHILOSOPHY				
A. Treatises	31	6.8	723	2.6
B. Collected works, compilations	28	6.1	1,583	5.6
C. Satire, polemics	9	2.0	242	0.9
D. General social, cultural criticism	33	7.2	4,515	16.0
Subtotals	101	22.1	7,063	25.1[a]
POLITICS, CURRENT EVENTS				
A. Treatises	20	4.4	986	3.5
B. Topical works	50	10.9	2,213	7.8
C. Libels, court satire	45	9.8	4,085	14.5
D. *Chroniques scandaleuses*	17	3.7	1,051	3.7
Subtotals	132	28.9[a]	8,335	29.5
SEX	64	14.0	3,654	12.9
OTHER				
A. Occultism	2	0.4	111	0.4
B. Freemasonry	6	1.3	639	2.3
Subtotals	8	1.7	750	2.7
UNCLASSIFIED	8	1.8	128	0.5
TOTALS	457	100.0	28,212	100.0

[a]Rounding creates the discrepancy in the subtotals of percentages.

ably well; the classifying proved to be a manageable task; and the result, however approximate, provides a general picture of the proportions within the corpus of forbidden literature as a whole.[95]

What was the place of philosophy among the "philosophical" books? Everywhere and nowhere—that is, omnipresent as a critical spirit but barely visible in the form of systematic thought embodied in treatises. A few treatises can be found scattered across the landscape of illegal literature, even in the remote sector of occultism, where the "natural" and cabalistic magic of

Albert le Grand was dressed up in some editions to look like systematic philosophy. But French readers did not demand many closely reasoned tomes.

One countercurrent ran against this tendency to favor light and informal literature. It took the form of a powerful and sustained demand for anti-Christian treatises. Some of them, like d'Holbach's *Histoire critique de Jésus-Christ* and *Le Christianisme dévoilé,* concentrated their fire on the most exposed flanks of Catholic dogma. Others, like Helvétius's *De l'Homme* or Delisle de Sales's *Philosophie de la nature,* developed alternate philosophies. (For the best-selling titles under each category and subcategory, see the companion volume.) Taken together, these works constituted the heavy artillery of the radical Enlightenment, and they may have inflicted considerable damage on the belief system of educated readers.

Although we have only anecdotal evidence about reader response, it seems likely that the Holbachean blockbusters shook orthodox opinions by exploiting the power of the book as a medium of communication: here was heresy laid out systematically as a series of reasonable arguments; here was Christianity exposed on open pages as a jumble of contradictions. And it all took place in print—not sotto voce, like shameful secrets exchanged in furtive meetings, but openly, in bold type and imposing volumes. The physical qualities of the books reinforced their message in a way that may escape the perception of modern readers, who are used to seeing heterodoxy packaged and sold on the market. For the first time, during the last three decades of the Old Regime, ordinary readers had access to atheism in book form. And the books had all the marks of respectability: frontispieces, title pages, prefaces, appendices, and notes. Unlike the unmanageable folio volumes of orthodox theology, still chained in some cases to shelves in draughty reading rooms, the little tomes of atheism could be carried in pockets and consulted in private. While their layout gave them an air of legitimacy (a favorite type was known as *philosophie*), their size made them seem designed to appeal to the realm of reason, where pros and cons could be pondered in the quiet of one's conscience.

The popular compilations and collected works of the *philo-*

sophes shared those characteristics. Some appeared in magnificent editions, like the Kehl Voltaire published by Beaumarchais. But most avoided "typographical luxury." They were sober: cheap reprints on plain paper, bound in boards or sold in sheets for 20 or 30 sous a volume. Here are some typical prices culled from the catalogues of publisher-wholesalers in the 1770s:[96]

J.-E. Dufour of Maastricht:
Works of La Mettrie, 2 vols.	4 livres
Works of Chevrier, 3 vols.	4 livres, 10 sous

Gabriel Décombaz of Lausanne:
Works of La Mettrie, 4 vols.	4 livres, 10 sous
Works of Diderot, 5 vols.	12 livres

J.-L. Chappuis and J.-E. Didier of Geneva:
Works of Du Laurens, 8 vols.	8 livres
Works of Helvétius, 5 vols.	5 livres

STN:
Works of Helvétius, 5 vols.	4 livres, 7 sous
Works of Voltaire, 48 vols.	72 livres

(And separate volumes at 30 sous each.)

Miniature libraries of materialism, atheism, and deism could be had for reasonable prices in a form that seemed to embody reasonableness itself. Freethinking was not free, but by 1770 it had come within the purchasing power of the middle classes and the upper ranks of artisans and shopkeepers.

While the treatises made full-scale, frontal attacks on orthodox doctrines, smaller and less serious works sniped at everything held up for respect by the Church and State. It was as if a division of labor had occurred among the anti-Christian forces: the Holbacheans tried to destroy the theoretical basis of the "infamous thing" (*l'infâme*), and the Voltaireans tried to cover it with ridicule. To be sure, Voltaire in his *Questions sur l'Encyclopédie* had also turned his wit against d'Holbach's *Système de la nature*. Instead of expressing a party line or a common front, the best-sellers sometimes undercut one another, and Voltaire-anism shaded off into what today would be considered pornography.

Voltaire himself could not keep all the laughter in his own corner. Some of it belonged to the belly variety, which had echoed in taverns since the Middle Ages. The same stock figures appeared in nearly all the sectors of illegality: lascivious monks, ruttish nuns, impotent bishops succumbing to venereal disease, and lesbian abbesses surrendering to "uterine fury." Brother Bugger *(Histoire de dom B . . . , portier des Chartreux),* the gatekeeper of the Carthusian monastery, and his sluttish sister *(Histoire de la tourière des Carmelites),* who tended the gate of the Carmelites, are descended from characters in Boccaccio and Rabelais. All of them, even Joan of Arc in *La Pucelle* and the unchaste nuns of *La Chandelle d'Arras,* belonged to a tradition of bawdy anti-clericalism, which could be classified either under irreligion or pornography. Because of their obsessive slandering of the clergy, I have placed most of these hybrid books (8 percent of the total) under the general rubric of attacks on religion. But if they were classified with sex books, the share of pornography would rise from 12.9 percent to 20.9 percent of the whole—an impressive score, but not what one would expect from the century of Restif de la Bretonne and the marquis de Sade.

"Pure pornography" may be an oxymoron as well as an anachronism. But the monks and nuns in many of the books appear to be incidental to the main business of providing sexual titillation. Writing and reading for erotic pleasure had existed since the time of Aretino, not to mention that of Ovid and all his precursors in antiquity. The most popular sex books of pre-Revolutionary France included some classics—*La Putain errante, L'Académie des dames, Vénus dans le cloître*—as well as the inescapable *Fanny Hill (La Fille de joie* in French). French readers had a strong taste for bawdy songs, which sold well in collections like *La Lyre gaillarde.* So an old-fashioned spirit of *gauloiserie* (Gallic sauciness) permeated much of the erotic literature. But if any tendency distinguished this category as a whole, it was voyeurism. Everywhere in the libertine tales, characters observed one another through keyholes, from behind curtains, and between bushes, while the reader looked over their shoulders. Illustrations completed the effect. In fact, they often showed couples copulating before the secret gaze of a narrator, who might be masturbating as if he or she (frequently she) were inviting the reader to do the same. Lascivious putti or shocked prudes frequently looked down on the scene from pictures within the picture. The interplay of illustration and text multiplied the effect of mirrors within mirrors, giving an air of theatricality to the whole business. Sex in the *livres philosophiques* was rococo—and as we shall see in the next chapter, it was often philosophical as well.

Philosophy as a distinct category included both theoretical treatises and general works, which criticized all sorts of abuses without being predominantly religious or political or pornographic in nature. The treatises amounted to only 2.6 percent of the whole, although they seem more important if one also takes into account the collected works of the *philosophes*. A lively market existed for sets of works by Rousseau, Helvétius, La Mettrie, and Voltaire, as we have seen. But the general philosophic books made up the largest subcategory (16 percent) in the entire corpus of *livres philosophiques*. "Philosophy" in this respect did not take aim at a single target, but scattered its shot across a wide spectrum of subjects. Top best-sellers like Mercier's *L'An 2440*, Raynal's *Histoire philosophique*, and Voltaire's *Questions sur l'Encyclopédie* contained something to offend practically everyone in authority under the Old Regime and at the same time appealed to the broadest range of readers. It was through philosophy of this kind that the Enlightenment reached the general reading public.

Instead of dealing in abstractions, these general works of philosophy moved rapidly from topic to topic, unearthing concrete abuses and condemning specific institutions. They held everything up to reason as a standard; but when they contrasted the evils of society with the rational order of nature, they sounded more impassioned than rationalistic. Even Voltaire, whose spicy *petits pâtés* (anti-clerical tracts) filled many of the works in the subcategory of satire and polemics, appealed at least as much to the passions as to reason. The Voltaire who dominated the best-seller list was the late Voltaire, the Voltaire of the Calas Affair,

A voyeuristic scene: *Histoire de dom B . . . , portier des Chartreux.*

Department of Rare Books and Special Collections,
Princeton University Libraries

of the crusade against cruelty, of the cause of humanity—the irreverent, wicked, immortal Voltaire of the *Dictionnaire philosophique.* To this Voltaire add the crusading fervor of Raynal, Rousseau, Mercier, and Linguet, and one can appreciate the explosive power of "philosophy" during the last years of the Old Regime.

A final category—politics—turned out to be the largest of all. Its boundaries and subdivisions were as blurred as those in the other categories, all the more so as politics itself remained ambiguous under the Old Regime: it could refer to political theory, current events, foreign affairs, the king's secret machinations, or the collective concerns of the general public. When seen as a subject of literature, therefore, politics had none of the self-evident quality that defines political writing today. A few treatises—d'Holbach's *Système social* and Mably's *De la législation*—sold well, certainly much better than *Du Contrat social*. Mirabeau's *Essai sur le despotisme* brought theory closer to current events, and Claude Mey's *Maximes du droit public français* showed that there was still life in the Jansenist challenge to Bourbon absolutism. But the vast majority of the political works, 26 percent of the forbidden books as a whole, concerned current events.

They fall into three subcategories, although the dividing lines are so indistinct that all this literature could be treated together as variations on a common set of journalistic themes. The books in the first subcategory were topical works about notorious incidents and personages: hence Voltaire's *Fragments sur l'Inde et sur le général Lalli* on the condemnation of the French commander in India; the *Mémoires d'une reine infortunée* on the tribulations of Queen Caroline Mathilde and the Danish crisis of 1772–73; and the *Mémoires de M. le comte de Saint-Germain* on the career of the former Minister of War.

The most successful of these works came from the pens of the two writers who did more than anyone else to turn public opinion against the government in the 1780s: Simon-Nicolas-Henri Linguet and Honoré-Gabriel Riqueti, comte de Mirabeau. Linguet's *Mémoires sur la Bastille* and Mirabeau's *Des Lettres de cachet et des prisons d'Etat* provided parallel, first-person accounts of an author imprisoned without trial by an all-powerful state. Each writer presented his story as a cosmic conflict between outraged innocence and ministerial despotism. And each turned his personal narrative into a Gothic horror tale by taking the reader inside dread dungeons and revealing all: the repulsive food, the sadistic turnkeys, the vermin-infested mattresses, and the underground cells where innocent victims vented their despair, cut off from all humanity and all recourse to legal procedure. Although it read in places like *The Castle of Otranto,* the rhetoric rang true, for such things really happened. Linguet and Mirabeau could vouch for them. They recounted their supposed sufferings with such an air of authenticity that they guaranteed the frisson and doubled the emotional charge. With their own hands, they ripped off masks, pulled back curtains, tore down facades, and exposed the *secret du roi.* So they, too, dealt in voyeurism, but theirs was political. They revealed the inner workings of a police state; and in so doing, they popularized the myth of a France governed by dungeons, chains, and *lettres de cachet.*[97]

The same themes also appeared in the subcategory of political libels or *libelles* (the French term conveyed the notion of political rather than private defamation). But the *libellistes* operated in another register. Instead of melodramatic accounts of despotism's victims, they told the inside story of life among its high priests and powerbrokers. They dealt in scandal rather than sentiment; and they told their tales according to the still unannounced principle that names make news. So they concentrated their fire on the most eminent personages of the kingdom, beginning with the king himself, and working their way down through ministers and royal mistresses to the common run of courtiers and *filles d'Opéra.*

The stuff of *libelles* was gossip, but the authors dressed it up to look like history. They offered authentic accounts of what had really happened behind the facade of power; and to prove their case, they printed excerpts from the correspondence of ministers, confidential reports by valets, or dialogue that came from their own unerring ability to be at the right place at the right time, behind a curtain, peering through a window, or simply assuming the omniscience of an invisible, third-person narrator. So *libelles,* too, exploited voyeurism. Their version of it took the reader inside the secret recesses of Versailles, between the sheets of the king's bed or even into his mind. In order to sustain that illusion, the *libellistes* wrote sober prefaces, casting themselves as "historians" or "editors" of memoirs whose authenticity could not be doubted. Sometimes, too, they announced that they were publishing the contents of a portfolio of letters, which had been lost or stolen but were absolutely genuine, as they themselves would guarantee. Whatever pose they struck, they promised to obey the strictest rules of evidence, although they also indicated by some well-placed winks that the reader would not be bored.

The result was a kind of journalism disguised as contemporary history and biography. The demand for it seemed to be inexhaustible, as the booksellers indicated in their letters; and it included several of the top best-sellers in the entire corpus: *Anecdotes sur Mme la comtesse du Barry, Journal historique de la révolution opérée dans la constitution de la monarchie française par M. de Maupeou, chancelier de France, Mémoires de l'abbé Terray, Mémoires de Louis XV,* and *Vie privée de Louis XV.* These works did not discuss abstract principles or complex questions of policy. They reduced politics to "private lives," especially that of the king. In doing so, they created an imaginary world of boundless, arbitrary power and peopled it with stock figures: evil ministers, intriguing courtiers, pederastic prelates, depraved mistresses, and bored, ineffectual Bourbons.

In the *libelliste*'s view of history, these types were concentrated most heavily in the court of Louis XV, especially during the ministry of the so-called triumvirate of Maupeou, Terray, and d'Aiguillon. Between 1770 and 1774, these ministers provoked the greatest crisis of the century (the short eighteenth century, which ran from 1715 to 1787) by restructuring the judicial system in such a way as to destroy the political power of the parlements and to give the government a free hand for increasing taxes. Maupeou, the mastermind of the coup, drew so much of the *libellistes'* fire that his name became attached to a genre: "Maupeouana," the variety of mud slinging popularized by the best-selling *libelle* from 1771, *Correspondance secrète et familière de M. de Maupeou.*[98]

The libeling did not end with the fall of the triumvirate and the advent of Louis XVI in 1774. On the contrary, the "private lives," pseudo-memoires, and Maupeouana sold best during the 1780s, when they could be read as a warning of what might come as well as a history of what had really happened, behind closed doors, in the last reign. The historical dimension of these works gave them more weight than one might realize today, when stores abound in books about the recent past. Contemporary history hardly existed as a genre in the eighteenth century: it was too sensitive to be permitted by the censors. So it went underground, taking the form of slanderous biographies and scandalous political narratives. Sophisticated readers would recognize them as *libelles,* but to the innocent eye they offered a thorough and seemingly authoritative version of how the present emerged from the past. The *Vie privée de Louis XV* ran to three volumes and gave a more detailed—and more amusing—account of political history from 1715 to 1774 than one can find in almost any modern work.

While reading about the private life of Louis XV, the French were treated to an extraordinary unveiling of the domestic world of Louis XVI. Until a minor operation relieved him of a genital abnormality (phimosis), the new king had been notoriously unable to produce an heir to the throne. Fat, awkward, and ineffectual, he looked the perfect picture of a cuckold. In 1785, the cardinal de Rohan became implicated in a baroque drama, played out before the Parlement of Paris, involving a fabulous diamond necklace. He supposedly used the necklace to seduce the queen behind some bushes in the park of Versailles. Although the story eventually turned out to be a badly bungled confidence game on the part of some adventurers, it seemed to epitomize the depravity and extravagance of the court. A king cuckolded by a cardinal! Never had *libellistes* been offered such a supply of muck to rake. The defamation poured from the presses in the last years of the Old Regime. But for the most part, it took the form of handwritten, clandestine gazettes *(nouvelles à la main),* and of pamphlets, which could be produced quickly within France. Publishers located outside the kingdom generally restricted themselves to books. But the French government cracked down so effectively on book imports, both legal and illegal, during the last few years of the Old Regime, that many publishers, including the STN, had cut back on their business in France by 1785. So the Diamond Necklace Affair does not appear in the STN statistics. The French learned about it through other media; and while they did so, they continued to read books about scandals under Louis XV.

Far from being irrelevant, however, the *libelles* against Louis XV took on new meaning under Louis XVI. They provided a way for the reading public to put the Diamond Necklace Affair in perspective, because they showed how the monarchy had been degenerating since the time of Louis XIV. They supplied a master narrative for contemporary history, and they made it available, in vast quantities, just before the last ministries of the Old Regime made a final appeal for public support in order to save the monarchy from bankruptcy. As developed by Charles-Alexandre de Calonne and Loménie de Brienne, the "reform" program of 1787–88 seemed to steal its material from the discredited measures of Maupeou, Terray, and d'Aiguillon. So the pamphleteers of 1787–88 stole theirs from the anti-ministerial propaganda of 1771–74 and even reprinted some of it word for word. A new literature of "Calonniana" hammered away at the same themes developed by the "Maupeouana" sixteen years earlier. Thus books, pamphlets, and manuscript news sheets reinforced one another; and France was flooded by waves of political slander, which carried the detritus of earlier crises across the century and sent it crashing into the midst of the supreme crisis, or "pre-Revolution," that destroyed Bourbon absolutism in 1787–88. Louis XV may not have pronounced the prophecy, but it was correct: "Après nous le déluge."[99]

Libelles overlapped with the third subcategory of political literature, *chroniques scandaleuses,* because both responded to the reading public's hunger for news. News, however, was as problematic as politics under the Old Regime. It did not officially exist, at least not as a public concern. The public had no more right to know about the affairs of state than to participate in them, and "news"papers of the modern kind, the sort that already existed in Britain, the Netherlands, and parts of Germany, remained strictly forbidden. A few privileged periodicals like the *Gazette de France* provided official accounts of court ceremonies and diplomatic exchanges. A great many foreign journals like the *Gazette de Leyde* were permitted to circulate in France, provided they said nothing offensive about delicate subjects such as the crown's running battles with the parlements. But if a Frenchman wanted to know who was maneuvering to supplant the ministers in Versailles or who was squiring around the actresses of the Comédie française, he had to find a *nouvelliste* (newsmonger).[100]

These came in two varieties: *nouvellistes de bouche,* who exchanged verbal reports in public places like the Palais-Royal and the Jardin des Tuileries in Paris, and *nouvellistes de main,* who reduced the talk to handwritten bulletins *(nouvelles à la main),* which circulated under the cloak. When foreign publishers collected these news sheets and produced them as a book, the *chronique scandaleuse* was born. News had passed from word of mouth into writing and finally into print. Each stage of its metamorphoses took place outside the law. So it showed no compunctions about defamation; and when it assumed book form, it joined the ranks of the "philosophical" works.

In contrast to the other books in the corpus, however, the *chroniques scandaleuses* had no consistent narrative voice or tone. Like the *libelles,* they concentrated on the private lives of the great. But like journals, they contained a little of everything, theatre reviews and battlefield reports as well as heavy doses of gossip, *bons mots,* and impertinent verse. They might pack all this material into a single volume, as in the work that took its name from the genre, *La Chronique scandaleuse, ou mémoires pour servir à l'histoire des moeurs de la génération présente,* by Guillaume Imbert de Bourdeaux. Or they might string it out indefinitely, as in the *Mémoires secrets pour servir à l'histoire de la République des Lettres en France,* which grew from edition to edition until it finally reached thirty-six volumes and provided a running account of everything that fascinated the Parisian public—and especially the group of *nouvellistes* who frequented the salon of Mme Doublet de Persan—from 1762 through 1787. No matter what their size and form, their contents remained disparate; and their authors made no effort to blend the material into a single story line.

Indeed, the *chroniques scandaleuses* did not really have authors. They appeared as an anonymous amalgam of everything thrown up by public discussions of public affairs. They *were* the public discussing. They expressed the *on dit,* or talk of the town, as conveyed by the neutral, third-person *on,* or "one":

"One says that . . ."; "One has just learned that . . ."; "One can hardly believe that . . ." As employed in French, the impersonal pronoun could include the reader as well as the narrator. In fact, it could stretch far enough to represent the general public, so that the *chroniques* seemed to give voice to public opinion and to register reactions to the news in the act of transmitting it. Often, to provide more piquancy, the news was narrated by a "spy"—a Turk, or an Englishman, or a Frenchman in London, or an undercover agent who had lost his briefcase (*l'espion déval-isé*). As in the *libelles,* the reports could also be dressed up as memoirs or as correspondence, which an anonymous "editor" had somehow intercepted and was publishing with an absolute guarantee of its authenticity. The titles did a great deal to lure the reader and to orient him toward the contents. Thus *L'Obser-vateur anglais, ou correspondance secrète entre Milord All'Eye et Milord All'Ear (The English Observer, or Secret Correspondence between Lord All-Eyes and Lord All-Ears),* which appeared in four volumes in 1777 and grew to ten volumes as *L'Espion anglais (The English Spy)* by 1784.

Many of the spies also spoke as *"on"* and recorded *"on dits"* along with letters they had stolen from the correspondence of a minister and secrets they had heard from a closet or under-neath a bed. The result was an omniscient insider's view of what was really happening behind the scenes—and still more voyeur-ism. So the *chroniques scandaleuses* completed the work of the *libelles,* which also complemented the mythological view of cur-rent events developed by Mirabeau and Linguet. Taken together, all this literature provided a massive indictment of the regime. It was history, biography, journalism, and scandalmon-gering all at once and all aimed at the same target: the Bourbon monarchy and everything supporting it.

The seditious political message of the *livres philosophiques* should not, however, be taken as evidence of an intention, much less a conspiracy, to overthrow the Old Regime. The for-bidden books may have undermined the regime by striking at the roots of its legitimacy, but they did not do so in order to bring it down. Most of them were simply a response to demand in the illegal sector of the literary marketplace—the demand for information as well as titillation, the curiosity about contemporary history as well as private lives, the hunger for news as well as for the forbidden fruit of abstract thought. By putting all these subjects outside the law, the regime ruled out self-restraint in the way they were treated. By forcing philosophy into the same corner as pornography, it invited the uninhibited attacks that it received. So it was attacked on all fronts, from metaphysics to politics.

But it is too easy, looking back across 1789, to conjure up revolutionary sentiment and to imagine the monarchy battered into impotence by the force of the printed word. It seems unlikely that anyone stormed the Bastille because he had read forbidden books. Instead of assuming a continuity between literary experience and revolutionary action, we need to investigate the disparities between them. Now that we have surveyed the domain of "philosophical" literature as a whole, we can begin by taking a closer look at some crucial texts.

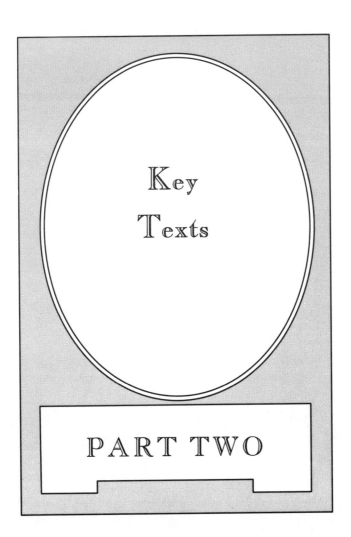

Key
Texts

PART TWO

Chapter 3

Philosophical Pornography

❦

HAVING IDENTIFIED, CLASSIFIED, and counted books at such length, the time has come to read them. But how? Not, alas, by kicking off one's shoes, sinking deep into a chair, and plunging into the texts. The problem does not concern the availability of the forbidden best-sellers; they can be found in most research libraries. Nor is it a matter of accessibility; they are naughtier, funnier, bolder, or bizarrer than most of the books on best-seller lists today. The difficulty lies with reading itself. We hardly know what it is when it takes place under our nose, much less what it was two centuries ago when readers inhabited a different mental universe. Nothing could be more misleading than the assumption that they made sense of typographical signs in the same way that we do. But they left little record of how they performed that feat. Although we have some information about the external circumstances of eighteenth-century reading, we can only guess at its effects on the hearts and minds of the readers. Inner appropriation—the ultimate stage in the communication circuit that linked authors and publishers with booksellers and readers—may remain beyond the range of research.

Still, it should be possible to steer clear of anachronisms while studying the way the texts work. Like all others, the texts of "philosophical books" operate within generic and rhetorical conventions peculiar to their time. They develop implicit strate-

85

gies for evoking responses from readers. So, even if the actual responses elude us, we can learn enough by examining texts and contexts to make some well-informed inferences about what the books meant to readers of the Old Regime.

Instead of working through all the books on the best-seller list, I will concentrate on three which stand at its top and which epitomize different varieties within the corpus as a whole.

The first book, *Thérèse philosophe,* probably written by the marquis d'Argens and published in 1748, seems to come as close as possible to "pure" pornography. But what is pornography, or rather, what was it in eighteenth-century France? The word itself hardly existed, although Restif de la Bretonne coined the term *pornographe* in a work of 1769, which argued, rather non-salaciously, for a state-run system of legal prostitution.[1] Of course, erotic works had existed since antiquity, and in the early sixteenth century Aretino outdid Ovid by celebrating copulation and the language of lust in print. His *Sonetti lussuriosi* and *Ragionamenti* set standards and established themes— the sixteen classical "postures," the provocative use of obscene words, the interplay of text and illustrations, the use of the female narrator and of dialogue, the voyeuristic tours of brothels and convents, the stringing out of orgies to compose a narrative line—that made him famous as the father of pornography. The eighteenth century constructed its own Aretino, *L'Arrétin moderne,* celebrated in the title of one of its best-sellers and in the texts of many others. He combined obscenity with slander, as he had done two centuries earlier, and he also held "modern" views, above all a disbelief in the teachings of the Church.[2]

Meanwhile, erotic literature had taken a great leap forward in the seventeenth century. The early novel celebrated love, both refined, as in *La Princesse de Clèves,* and crude, as in *La France galante.* Works that in retrospect seem central to the history of pornography also belonged to the rise of the novel as a genre: *L'Ecole des filles* (1655), *L'Académie des dames* (published originally in Latin around 1660 and in French by 1680), and *Vénus dans le cloître* (about 1682). So the narrative properties of erotic fiction had been established long before the publication of *Thérèse philosophe,* and the publication took place in the middle of a second wave of "pornographic" writing.

This new cycle began in 1741 with the appearance of three books: *Le Canapé couleur de feu,* by L.-C. Fougeret de Monbrun; *L'Art de foutre,* by François de Baculard d'Arnaud; and especially *Histoire de Dom B . . . , portier des Chartreux,* probably by J.-C. Gervaise de Latouche, an obscene and anti-clerical tour de force, which along with *Thérèse philosophe* dominated the best-seller lists until the end of the Old Regime. Salacious fiction continued to pour off the presses in the midcentury years. It included works of well-known writers—*Les Bijoux indiscrets* (1748) by Diderot, *Le Sopha* (1742), by Crébillon fils, *La Pucelle* by Voltaire (first published in 1755, then touched up and reprinted in more obscene versions by others)—along with grosser and more graphic best-sellers: *Les Lauriers ecclésiastiques* (1748), by C. J. L. A. Rochette de la Morlière; *Margot la ravaudeuse* (1750), by L.-C. Fougeret de Monbron; *La Chandelle d'Arras* (1765), by H.-J. Du Laurens; and *Histoire galante de la tourière des Carmélites* (1743), by A.-G. Meusnier de Querlon. All these books were reprinted throughout the 1760s and 1770s, when the production of original works declined. The genre picked up again in the 1780s with the pornographic works of Mirabeau: *Errotika Biblion* (1782), *Ma Conversion, ou le libertin de qualité* (1783), and *Le Rideau levé ou l'éducation de Laure* (1785). And the century ended with the marquis de Sade. To specialists in the Sade industry, all this writing may look like a prelude to the masterpieces of the divine marquis. But it can be viewed in its own right, as the flowering of a vast literature peculiar to the Old Regime in France and especially to the middle years of the eighteenth century.

Can it be considered pornography? Certainly, if one goes by current dictionary definitions and legal judgments. They usually stress the prurient character of such literature, its explicit descriptions of sexual activity, and its implicit purpose, which is deemed to be the sexual arousal of the reader. But Frenchmen in the eighteenth century did not normally think in such terms, nor did they distinguish a genre of "pure" pornography from erotic fiction, anti-clerical tracts, and other varieties of "philosophical books." The notion of pornography, like the word itself, was developed in the nineteenth century, when librarians sorted out books that they considered dirty and put them under lock and key in taboo sections like the Enfer of the Bibliothèque Nationale and the Private Case of the British Museum. Strictly speaking, pornography belonged to the bowdlerization of the world undertaken in the early Victorian era. It did not exist in the eighteenth century.[3]

But one should not relativize the concept out of existence. The legislation on the book trade under the Old Regime always distinguished three categories of forbidden books: those that offended the Church, the state, and morality. Of course, the last category could include a great deal besides pornography, but in practice the police confiscated only works that they considered unambiguously obscene; and they developed a whole vocabulary to characterize such literature. It was *obscène, lascive,* or *lubrique*—not merely *grivois, libre,* or *galant.*[4] In his *Mémoires sur la librairie* (1759), C.-G. de Lamoignon de Malesherbes, the royal official in charge of the book trade from 1750 to 1763, drew a line between "obscene" books, which the police should always confiscate, and the "merely licentious," which they should pretend not to notice. Without such a guideline, he warned, they might find themselves impounding all of Rabelais, the *Contes* of La Fontaine, and many other works that had become standard reading for educated persons.[5] Such distinctions did not merely exist in the minds of the authorities; they belonged to everyday life, as Diderot indicated in describing a fleeting moment of flirtation between himself as a young man and a salesgirl in a bookshop:

> At that time she worked in a little book shop on the quai des Augustins: a doll-like figure, white and straight as a lily, red as a rose. I entered with that dashing, ardent, crazy manner I had in those days; and I said to her, "Mademoiselle, the *Contes de La Fontaine,* a *Petrone* [i.e., acceptable erotic literature], if you please." "Here they are, sir. Do you need any other books?" "Well, excuse me, Mademoiselle, but . . ." "Yes, do say . . ." "*La Religieuse en chemise* [*Venus in the Cloister* or *The Nun in a Nightgown,* a work considered obscene]. "Fie, Monsieur! Does one sell, does one read such wicked things?" "Oh, oh, they are wicked, are they, Mademoiselle? I had no idea . . ." And then, another day, when I passed by again, she smiled, and I did, too.[6]

The boundary between the erotic and the obscene can even be found in the books themselves. "Wicked" books celebrated reading as a stimulus of sexual pleasure and sometimes recommended works that provided it. *Le Portefeuille de Madame Gourdan* (1783) described the library of the finest, three-star brothel in Paris. It contained all the early classics, from *L'Ecole des filles* to *Histoire de Dom B . . .* in what was later to be defined as canonical pornography. A "gallant library" also appears in the climactic chapter of *Thérèse philosophe,* where reading opens the way to the final stage in Thérèse's education as a voluptuary. And in an earlier chapter one of her role models, a philosophic widow, employs *Histoire de Dom B . . .* as a sex aid. It works so well that she offers herself to her companion, the abbé T., despite her fear of pregnancy: "Reading your awful *Portier des Chartreux* has set me all on fire. Its portraits are so well wrought! They have an air of truth about them which is irresistible. If it were less dirty, it would be an inimitable book of its type."[7]

When Sade looked back on this literature in *Histoire de Juliette* (1797), he described the contents of another "gallant library": *L'Académie des dames, Histoire de Dom B . . . , L'Education de Laure,* everything was there. But nothing measured up to his standards, except one work, *Thérèse philosophe.* "A charming work of the marquis d'Argens; the only one that has shown the goal, without however quite attaining it; the sole book that has agreeably linked luxuriousness with impiety and that, if made available to the public as the author had originally conceived of it, would at last provide the idea of an immoral book."[8] By the end of the century, *Thérèse philosophe* stood out as the supreme work in a body of literature that may not yet have been labeled as pornographic but that took sex far beyond the boundaries of decency that had been generally recognized under the Old Regime.

Thérèse also stood for something else in the eyes of her contemporaries: Enlightenment. She was a *philosophe.* Her title echoed a key work of the early Enlightenment, *Le Philosophe,* an anonymous tract which appeared in 1743, was absorbed in the text of the *Encyclopédie,* and later republished by Voltaire. It defined the ideal type of the worldly, witty freethinker, who held everything up to the critical light of reason and especially scorned the doctrines of the Catholic Church. The publication of *Thérèse philosophe* in 1748 occurred precisely at the moment when the first great barrage of Enlightenment works burst into print:

1748: Montesquieu, *De l'Esprit des lois*
Diderot, *Les Bijoux indiscrets*
La Mettrie, *L'Homme-machine*
Toussaint, *Les Moeurs*

1749: Buffon, *Histoire naturelle,* vols. I–III
Diderot, *Lettre sur les aveugles*

1750: *Encyclopédie,* Prospectus
Rousseau, *Discours sur les sciences et les arts*

1751: *Encyclopédie,* vol. I
Voltaire, *Le Siècle de Louis XIV*
Duclos, *Considérations sur les moeurs*

It was an extraordinary moment. In the space of just a few years in the middle of the eighteenth century, the intellectual topography of France was transformed. *Thérèse philosophe* belonged to that transformation just as much as it belonged to the simultaneous outburst of erotic literature. In fact, the double explosion was fueled by the same source: libertinism, a combination of freethinking and free living, which challenged religious doctrines as well as sexual mores. Free spirits like Diderot fought on both fronts; so the police of the Old Regime knew what they were doing in 1749 when they put Diderot down in their files as a "dangerous boy" and locked him up in Vincennes as the author of the erotic *Bijoux indiscrets* as well as the irreligious *Lettres sur les aveugles.*[9] Some of his contemporaries believed that he also wrote *Thérèse philosophe.*[10] A few modern scholars do, too.[11] There is little evidence for that attribution, but Diderot and Thérèse belonged to the same world—the bawdy, naughty, cheeky world of the early Enlightenment, where everything was held up to question and nothing was sacred.

However well it fits the context of its time, the combination of sex and philosophy in *Thérèse philosophe* is bound to astonish the modern reader. As in many classics of the pornographic tradition, the narrative consists of a series of orgies; but they are strung together by metaphysical dialogues, which take place while the partners catch their breath and restore their forces for the next round of pleasure. Copulation and metaphysics—nothing could be further from the modern mentality or closer to the libertine outlook of the eighteenth century. To understand how the themes complemented one another, it is best to begin at the beginning of the book, which combines a fictitious narrative of Thérèse's girlhood with an account of an actual episode announced in the subtitle: *Memoirs About the Affair Between Father Dirrag and Mademoiselle Eradice.*

The Dirrag Affair belonged to the great chain of *causes célèbres,* or courtroom dramas, which ran through the eighteenth century, crystalizing and radicalizing public opinion right up to the Revolution. Behind the anagrams "Eradice" and "Dirrag," eighteenth-century readers would have recognized the names of Catherine Cadière, a devout young beauty from Toulon, and Jean-Baptiste Girard, her confessor, who was also the Jesuit rector of Toulon's Séminaire royal de la marine. The demoiselle Cadière accused Father Girard of exploiting his role as her spiritual guide *(directeur de conscience)* in order to seduce her. After a great deal of hesitation and a close vote, the Parlement of Aix finally acquitted him in October 1731. But the case touched off several waves of sensational pamphlets. It had everything to appeal to the anti-clerical imagination: sex and fanaticism, foul play in the confessional, and the unmasking of Jesuitry, a favorite motif of the Jesuits' enemies among the Jansenists. In playing on those themes, *Thérèse philosophe* seemed to be telling a true story. It set the narrative in a recognizable place and teased the reader into seeing the action as part of a genuine *chronique scandaleuse* by the use of transparent anagrams: "Volnot" for Toulon and "Vencerop" for Provence, in addition to "Eradice" and "Dirrag." It also identified some of its fictitious characters by initials—"Mme C." and "abbé T."—as if their true identity had to be protected. So the book appeared to be a *roman à clef,* or fact disguised as fiction, although it was actually a *fake roman à clef* and the disguise worked in the opposite manner—dressing up a fantasy in the alluring guise of a scandal taken from current events.

The slippage from fact to fiction took place through the account of the Dirrag Affair given by Thérèse, who describes it as a key event in the development of her own metaphysical-sexual education, which is the subject of the book. She writes in the first person; so the story, as in many erotic novels, takes the form of a first-person narrative in an ostensibly female voice. Thérèse addresses it to her lover, whom she identifies only as "my dear Count." In the Preface, she explains that she is writing at his request and for the good of humanity. Having been a close friend of Mlle Eradice and an equally fanatic disciple of Father Dirrag, she could reveal the inside story of their affair. Indeed, she observed it with her own eyes from a hiding place in Eradice's room.

Dirrag, she reveals, seduced Eradice by playing on her ambition to outdo her peers in holiness. He prescribed spiritual exercises based on the principle of freeing the spirit by mortifying the flesh. Flagellation was his favorite technique. He used it to purge the body of impurities and lift the soul into an ecstatic state, which could even lead to sainthood. Eradice explained it all to Thérèse, while extending an invitation to be a secret witness of her prowess. Soon Thérèse is watching, fascinated, from a closet. Eradice is on her knees, bent over in prayer, with her skirts tucked about her waist. Dirrag whips her buttocks, working her into such a state of excitement that she is ready for his ultimate weapon, a holy relic, which he describes as the hardened segment of the original cord that St. Francis wore around his habit. Thérèse, who has played sex games with some other precocious children, recognizes it for what it really is—or rather for what another priest had told her it was: a serpent, the kind that all men carry between their legs and that Adam used against Eve in the Garden of Eden. Dirrag's serpent stiffens and strains toward Eradice's upper orifice—sodomy was equated with Jesuitism throughout libertine literature—but by a heroic effort of the will, the good father chooses the "canonical path." He humps and heaves in rhythm with his disciple, who believes herself in heaven. Finally, as she nears the high point of her ecstasy, Eradice cries out:

I'm feeling celestial happiness. I sense that my mind is completely detached from matter. Further, Father, further! Root out all that is impure in me. I see . . . the . . . an . . . gels. Push forward . . . push now . . . Ah! . . . Ah! . . . Good . . . St. Francis! Don't abandon me! I feel the cord . . . the cord . . . the cord . . . I give up . . . I'm dying![12]

No reader could miss the blend of sacrilege and sex, but eighteenth-century readers probably saw something else in the description. Graphic as it was—and the full text includes plenty of anatomical detail—it conveyed a metaphysical message. The distinction between mind and matter went beyond the traditional Christian opposition of soul and body and neo-Aristotelian notions of form and substance. It expressed the dichotomy of Descartes, a radical distinction between the world of thought and spirit on the one hand and that of matter in motion on the other. Father Dirrag seduced Eradice by persuading her to take one side of the dichotomy for the other—that is, to experience her orgasm as a spiritual epiphany. He got away with the ultimate stroke of priestcraft, all the more delicious to the trained, anti-clerical eye of the eighteenth-century reader in that it was accompanied by materialist philosophizing dressed up as Christianity. In order to prepare Eradice for sainthood—that is, deflowering—Dirrag gives her a radical Cartesian lecture. First, he announces the dichotomy: "God desires from men only their hearts and their minds. Only by forgetting the body can we find unity with God, approach sainthood, perform miracles." Then he describes the action of matter as if it could lead to the exaltation of the spirit:

The mechanism is infallible, my dear girl: we feel, and we receive our ideas of physical good and evil as well as moral good and evil . . . only through our senses. When we touch or hear or see an object, little particles of thought flow into the hollows of our nerves, and continue on to alert the soul. If, by the force of your meditations on your love of God, you have enough energy to gather together all the little particles of thought which are within you and apply them all to this end, not one will be left to warn your soul of the blows which your flesh is about to receive. You won't feel them at all.[13]

Father Dirrag applying the cord of St. Francis to Mlle Eradice:
Thérèse philosophe.

The informed reader would recognize that Dirrag's philosophy could not be distinguished from that of La Mettrie. The Jesuit was a closet materialist. He possessed the secret that would be progressively unveiled throughout the entire book: the spiritual half of the famous dichotomy did not exist; everything was matter in motion. So Dirrag manipulated the bodies of his disciples according to the most up-to-date principles of philosophy. He even developed his own technology, a materialist version of spiritual exercises, which included a chemical solution to produce false stigmata, a dildo disguised as a holy relic, flagellation to make sexual excitement appear as mortification of the flesh, and copulation itself, which he passed off as religious ecstasy, the kind that had been experienced as spiritual by St. Theresa of Avila and that would be understood as material by Thérèse the *philosophe.* In short, the Dirrag Affair demonstrated that seduction was an inverted form of Christianity, and it prepared the reader to consider the proposition in reverse: Christianity was a form of seduction.

Sex and metaphysics therefore belonged together. Thérèse made that clear in the Preface to the book, addressed to her anonymous lover, the Count: "You would like an account in which the scenes that I have described to you, or those in which we have taken part, should be rendered in all their lasciviousness, and the metaphysical arguments should be preserved with all their force." The intertwined themes run through the entire novel, which is Thérèse's story of her life, divided into four parts: (1) her youth and the Dirrag Affair; (2) her first exposure to philosophy in the company of Mme C. and abbé T.; (3) her education in polymorphous perversion through conversations with Mme Bois-Laurier, a retired Parisian prostitute; and (4) the full flowering of both her sexuality and her philosophy as the mistress of the Count.

In part one, Thérèse discovers sex and cryptomaterialism by exposure to Father Dirrag. But her notions remain confused; and her body wastes away, because her mother puts her in a convent, where her "divine liquid"[14] clogs up and atrophies as a result of sexual repression. Her body comes back to life in part two, thanks to the counsel of two family friends, the good Mme C. and the wise abbé T., who take her under their wing after her release from the convent. They explain that this liquid is "the principle of pleasure."[15] It must be allowed to run its course, or her whole "machine" (i.e., body) will be thrown out of order. But, the abbé warns, Thérèse must not release it by putting her finger up her vagina, because if she damages her virginity she will lose her chance to get a husband. Social conventions may be arbitrary, but they must be respected, out of self-interest as well as a concern for others. For the same reason, she must not allow any man to penetrate her. Penetration could lead to pregnancy, which should never take place outside "the sacrament of marriage."[16] So there is but one solution: masturbation.

Part two turns into an apology for masturbation. Thérèse perfects her own technique and learns about that of others by spying on Mme C. and abbé T. from behind bushes, curtains, and keyholes. She also listens carefully to their conversations, for they philosophize and masturbate deliciously together, page after page, throughout the most substantial quarter of the book. They agree that pleasure is the highest good. Why then do they not indulge in sexual intercourse? "Women have only three things to worry about," the abbé explains: "fear of the devil, their reputations, and pregnancy."[17] The danger of pregnancy especially obsesses Mme C., because she nearly lost her life in childbirth. The child later died, and so did her husband, leaving her free to pursue pleasure and avoid pain according to the principles she shares with the abbé. She disagrees with the abbé on only one point. Having learned through experience to appreciate the full danger of childbirth, she will not accept his proposal of *coitus interruptus,* despite his eloquent and rational argument in favor of it.

Meanwhile, the abbé develops another set of arguments in his conversations with Thérèse. Replacing Father Dirrag as her confessor, he takes up Dirrag's line of reasoning but turns it in a positive direction—toward the promotion of happiness rather than the exploitation of credulity. In doing so, he seems to defend conventional values and ideas—not merely virginity and matrimony, but a reasonable view of religion that could almost pass for Christianity: "as we are assured that natural law is divinely inspired, how could we fear that we offend God in relieving our needs by the means He has afforded us, the objects of His creation, especially when these means in no way disturb the social order?"[18] Such sentiments corresponded to the moderate strain in Enlightenment thought. They allowed for a Supreme Being and a normative order of natural law, without challenging the hierarchical structure of society. But the abbé completely undercut them when he withdrew to masturbate with his philosophic mistress. Then he developed ideas that could not be exposed to tender ears. Thérèse heard them, nonetheless, when spying on the lovers: Nature was nothing but a concept invented by the founders of religions to separate God from the source of suffering. No, God did not hide behind nature. He was everywhere—but if everywhere, nowhere; for everything could be reduced to matter in motion, leaving "God" as an empty word and morality as a utilitarian calculus based on pleasure and pain.

Thérèse cannot fully absorb these truths, because it is only at this point, as she later realizes, that "Perhaps for the first time in my life, I began to think."[19] Meanwhile, her sexual education proceeds apace in part three, where she falls under the influence of Mme Bois-Laurier. Actually, this part does not harmonize well with the rest of the book, because it is merely a catalogue of the curious sexual practices that Bois-Laurier has encountered in her career as a prostitute. Instead of erotic philosophizing, it reverts to a form of female sexual dialogue that had become developed in such standard works as *L'Académie des dames,* *L'Ecole des filles,* and Aretino's *Ragionamenti.* Thérèse finds herself in Paris, alone and with only a small inheritance to live on after the death of her mother. She falls in with a woman in her boardinghouse, who turns out to be a stock figure of obscene literature: the warmhearted whore. Bois-Laurier's narrative-within-the-narrative takes the reader on a tour of Parisian brothels but adds little to the development of the novel until it introduces a new character, the Count, who provides a transition to part four.

While accompanying Mme Bois-Laurier to the Opéra, Thérèse meets a man for whom she feels a visceral sympathy. The Count reciprocates her feeling, although both know that there can be no question of matrimony between them. Not only does the disparity of their estates argue against it—Thérèse is the impecunious daughter of a *bon bourgeois*,[20] and the Count is a nobleman with a château and a handsome income of 12,000 livres a year—but the Count has a personal aversion to marriage. He therefore proposes to retire with Thérèse to his country estate. She will become his mistress, with an annuity of 2,000 livres; but she needn't give in to his desire for sexual intercourse, for he understands her horror of pregnancy, her mother, like Mme C., having nearly died in childbirth. Yet just as Thérèse adopts the position of Mme C., the Count takes up that of abbé T.: he has enough self-mastery to be confident that he can withdraw in time to ejaculate outside of her. He does not insist, however, because he holds to the code of the *honnête homme*,[21] an aristocratic version of the hedonistic calculus preached by abbé T. He can find happiness in making Thérèse happy. So he will settle for mutual masturbation.

Thérèse accepts the contract. The couple lives happily for many months, masturbating and philosophizing exactly as Mme C. and abbé T. had done. Eventually, however, the Count gives in to his desire for a higher form of happiness. He proposes a wager: Thérèse is to spend two weeks reading through his "library of gallant books"[22] and studying his erotic paintings. If she can make it to the end without masturbating, the collection is hers. Otherwise, she will be his, although she can trust him to pluck her flower without planting his seed in her womb.

Soon Thérèse is plunged into sexual reverie while poring over the classic texts of the erotic tradition, including several that still figured among the STN's best-sellers in the pre-Revolutionary years: *Histoire de Dom B . . .* , *Histoire de la tourière des Carmélites*, *Les Lauriers ecclésiastiques*, and *L'Académie des dames*. Five days of reading under two lascivious paintings, *The Feast of Priapus (Fêtes de Priape)*, and *The Love Affair of Venus and Mars (Amours de Mars et de Vénus)*, do the trick. Thérèse slips her finger between her thighs and calls out for her Count. He, of course, has been secretly observing her all along. Like Mars in the painting, he strides into the room, sweeps her into his arms, and at the critical moment, by a supreme effort of the will, withdraws and spills his semen safely outside her. *Coitus interruptus* triumphs over masturbation. The couple lives happily ever after, copulating continuously, "without a problem, without a worry, without children."[23]

When Thérèse tells her story, ten years after its climax, she has become a full-fledged philosopher. Her apprenticeship

The happy ending of *Thérèse philosophe*.

ended with her final lesson from the Count, who perfected the teaching of abbé T., who in turn had corrected the half truths preached by the hideous Dirrag. As the narrator of her own story, she speaks in her own voice and announces truths that she has made her own. The last chapter summarizes them in the form of a hedonistic-materialistic credo, and the caption to the frontispiece fixes them epigrammatically:

> Voluptuousness and philosophy produce the happiness of the sensible man.
> He embraces voluptuousness by taste. He loves philosophy by reason.

Thérèse's sex story turns out to be a *Bildungsroman,* the tale of an education; and as it is an education in pleasure, the philosophizing and the pleasure seeking run together through the narrative until they converge in the end as philosophical hedonism. Studied closely, this philosophy would reveal an admixture of elements derived from many sources—Descartes, Malebranche, Spinoza, Hobbes, and the whole gamut of libertine literature that circulated in manuscript throughout the first half of the eighteenth century.[24] The strongest influence probably went all the way back to Lucretius, for Thérèse and her teachers constantly reduce reality to tiny particles of matter, which determine the will by acting on the senses. Ultimately, then, they describe man as a machine driven by a pleasure principle that he cannot control:

> Reason serves only to make a man aware of the strength of the desire he has to do or not to do something or other, relative to the pleasure or displeasure he will derive from it. . . .
> The arrangement of our organs, the disposition of our fibers, a certain movement of our fluids, all determine the type of passions which work upon us, directing our reason and our will in the smallest as well as the greatest actions we perform.[25]

But it would serve little purpose to sort out all the sources and put them back together again in a consistent system,

The message of *Thérèse philosophe*, encapsulated in its frontispiece.

because *Thérèse philosophe* does not pretend to be a work of systematic philosophy. It is a novel. Rather than developing an elaborate argument through a series of logical steps, it asserts propositions as if they were self-evident truths and gets on with the story. What are the "little particles of thought" that course through the body?[26] How does the "divine liquid" determine sexuality?[27] Thérèse does not explain. She does not bother about technical difficulties or logical connections. Instead, she relies on rhetoric and narrative to make her argument stick. But those techniques assume the existence of a certain public with shared conventions, expectations, and linguistic usages.

For a sex book, the language of *Thérèse philosophe* is extraordinarily proper. Never does it use vulgar expressions for sexual organs and activities, except in the narrative by Mme Bois-Laurier, a street urchin and a whore. Thérèse, who comes from a solidly bourgeois background, keeps to terms like "member" and "orifice." Not that she fails to be explicit. Thus two sentences from her description of Father Dirrag's copulation with Eradice:

> I saw also that with each backward movement of the father's rump, as the cord withdrew and its head appeared, the lips of Eradice spread open, revealing a crimson hue wondrous to behold. I noted that, in the next moment, as the father thrust forward, these same lips, of which one could now see only the short black hairs covering them, grasped the member so tightly that it seemed all but swallowed up.[28]

The reader is induced to see the scene through the eyes of an innocent eighteen-year-old. Verbs like "I saw" and "I noted" recur throughout the entire paragraph, reinforcing the voyeurism that runs through the whole book. While the studied naïveté of the language provides piquancy, the concreteness of the details makes a further point: as in all the sex scenes, the bodies appear as machines. Fluids, fibers, pumps, hydraulic pressure—such is the stuff of sex. So in her next breath, Thérèse comments: "What mechanics!" And in describing the effects of sexual repression in the cloister, she noted that her fluids had backed up into the wrong conduits, producing "disorder throughout my machine."[29] Inherited from the mechanistic philosophies of the seventeenth century, the metaphor of the machine provided later libertines with a congenial way to make sense of the world.[30] Thérèse talked the same language as Diderot, d'Holbach, and La Mettrie. Her story appeared in the same year as La Mettrie's *L'Homme-machine,* and it made the same point: in copulation as in gravitation, everything could be reduced to the identical principle, matter in motion.

Of course, the technique of persuasion in *Thérèse philosophe* differs completely from the cold, flat prose of *L'Homme-machine.* It seduces the reader in the same way as the Count seduces Thérèse—by the evocative power of reading itself. Only after she reads through a whole library of erotic fiction is Thérèse ready for sexual intercourse. Mme C. got so excited from a reading of *Histoire de Dom B . . .* that she offered herself to abbé T. despite her fear of pregnancy. Eighteenth-century readers understood that such books were meant to be read, as Rousseau put it, "with one hand"—that is, for masturbation.[31] Mirabeau expressed the general attitude at its crudest in the preface to *Ma Conversion, ou le libertin de qualité:* "May the reading [of this book] make the whole universe beat off!"[32] The apology for masturbation preached by abbé T. to Mme C. is aimed less at his mistress, who is already converted, than at the reader, who might still have compunctions. In the eighteenth century, masturbation, "self-abuse," was widely believed to cause everything from emaciation to blindness.[33] *Thérèse philosophe* could be seen as a mortal threat, to the body as well as the soul. Its rhetoric therefore proceeds from the assumption that the reader (he or she, but more probably he) must be reassured. His defenses must be broken down in the same way as Thérèse's. He must be made complicit.

The basic strategy of this approach is the first-person narrative; the basic tactic, voyeurism. By addressing her story to the Count—an awkward device, as he is living with her and doesn't need an autobiography to be kept informed—Thérèse orients the reader. He need not feel implicated in the story, because he can read it as an outsider looking in. He can peer into the most intimate activities of the characters without their knowing it. And after looking hard enough, he learns to see with the eyes of Thérèse. She is always spying on copulating or masturbating couples from hiding places. So the reader looks over her shoulder:

> I was placed in such a way as not to miss the smallest detail of this scene. The windows of the room I was observing were directly opposite the door of the closet where I was hiding. Eradice was kneeling on the floor, her arms crossed on the step of the prayer stool and her head resting on her arms. Her shift had been carefully raised to her waist, and I had a view, in half profile, of her admirable loins and buttocks.[34]

Perspectives of this sort appear throughout the text, and they often reflect one another, like mirrors in mirrors, producing tales within tales. For example, Mme Bois-Laurier recounts her own autobiography to Thérèse, and in so doing she produces a string of stories, which often include dialogue that puts other characters into play. The reader therefore has the illusion of witnessing a scene-within-a-scene-within-a-scene. Behind it all, an invisible, anonymous author has arranged the parts to max-imize the refraction, so that wherever the reader turns, he seems to see throbbing sexuality. Illustrations double and triple this multiplier effect. They vary from elaborate to primitive and edition to edition, but they often show someone watching someone else under the watchful gaze of pictures on a wall or statues in a garden.[35] The voyeur frequently masturbates, implicitly inviting the reader to do the same; for the chain of voyeurs finally comes to rest with the reader himself, the only unseen seer. Because he alone cannot be seen, he need not avert his eyes. Nor need he worry about pollution, as the entire spectacle is filtered through the eyes of Thérèse, who for all her sexual appetite remains purity itself, as pure as her lan-guage.

The avoidance of dirt and vulgarity belongs to the strategy of the text, because the book is aimed at an audience of *honnêtes gens,* the French equivalent of "gentle readers" in England. There is a class element in this appeal, for *honnêteté* (gentility) did not extend to the unwashed masses. Yet it no longer had an exclusively aristocratic ring, as it did in the seventeenth century.

The viewpoint of the narrator in *Thérèse philosophe*.

Varieties of voyeurism, as illustrated in *Thérèse philosophe.*
Department of Rare Books and Special Collections,
Princeton University Libraries

Although he is a true-blooded nobleman, the Count embodies general qualities: "Everything about him proclaims him to be a man who thinks, a gentleman *{honnête homme}*, who is such by virtue of reason, taste, and lack of prejudice."[36] He represents the ideal of "man master of himself," of "the sensible man, the *philosophe*"—in short, of the Enlightenment.[37] So, too, does Thérèse, a *philosophe* who is a woman from the bourgeoisie. What sort of Enlightenment was this? How far into society did it cast its appeal?

In expounding her version of deterministic materialism, Thérèse gives a revealing example of the kind of experience she assumes will be shared by her public. "Am I not free to drink with my dinner either Burgundy or Champagne?" she asks rhetorically. Her answer suggests the kind of readers who would take her truths to be self-evident: If I order oysters, Burgundy is impossible; "the dish demands Champagne."[38] A remarkable argument against the freedom of the will!

Thérèse philosophe is addressed to a Champagne-and-oyster readership—as were most of the works of the early Enlightenment. Montesquieu cut up *De l'Esprit des lois* into tiny chapters laced with epigrams so they would suit salon society. Voltaire made his *petits pâtés* (anti-clerical tracts) comestible in the same way. A great deal of what passed for philosophy before 1748 took the form of short pamphlets rather than formal treatises. They remained confined, for the most part, to salons and princely courts, and they often circulated in manuscript. The most important of them, *Le Philosophe* (1743), insisted that philosophy belonged in *le monde,* the world of high society as opposed to that of scholars and literary drudges. It should be witty, well written, free of prejudice, and in good taste.[39] *Thérèse philosophe* fit the formula perfectly. Like the *Lettres persanes, Candide,* and *La Religieuse,* it presented its philosophy as a story, sliced into bite-sized chapters and served with a sauce that would sit easily on the delicate stomachs of *le monde.*

The point needs emphasizing, because it bears on the social implications of the philosophy in *Thérèse philosophe.* Truth, as abbé T. makes clear, is not the sort of thing to be aired openly. It should be brought up only at certain dinner tables, with great discretion, and after the servants have been dismissed.

Let's be careful not to reveal to fools truths that they could not appreciate or that they might misuse. . . . Out of a hundred thousand persons, there are scarcely twenty who are accustomed to thinking, and out of these twenty, you could hardly find four who think, in effect, for themselves.[40]

What then is to be served up to the unthinking 99.996 percent of the population? Religion. From the beginning of history, religion has served to keep the masses in their place, and only religion will make them respect the social order today.[41]

In the meatiest chapter of the book, "An Examination of Religions by Natural Light," abbé T. delivers a secular sermon to Mme C. in the privacy of her boudoir, while Thérèse secretly listens. After clearing his pupil's mind by means of masturbation, he reveals all. Religion is nothing but priestcraft. As a priest himself, he knows all its tricks and can appreciate the particular absurdities of Catholic doctrine. He goes over them, one after another, in a series of short paragraphs, which read like an anthology of the irreligious arguments that had been circulating for half a century in the manuscript libertine tracts. In fact, many of them come directly out of one of the most important tracts, *Examen de la religion dont on cherche l'éclaircissement de bonne foi,* which was first published in 1745. But in attacking Christianity, the *Examen* stopped short of materialism. It defended a deistic notion of God like the one favored by Voltaire and freethinkers in England (it pretended to be "translated from the English of Gilbert Burnet"). The author of *Thérèse philosophe* would have nothing to do with such moderation. So, in cribbing his text from the *Examen,* he trimmed passages that left too much room for a non-Christian Supreme Being. For example:

Examen de la religion:
In a word, God is everywhere, I know; and Scripture, in order to accommodate my weakness [in conceiving of God], tells me that God looked for Adam in paradise; that He called him, "Adam, Adam, *ubi es?* [where art thou?]; that God walked about there; that God talked with the devil about Job. My reason tells me that God is a pure spirit.

Thérèse philosophe:
God is everywhere. Yet the Holy Scripture says that God looked for Adam in paradise: "Adam, *ubi es?;* that God walked about there; that He talked with the devil about Job.[42]

But passages that mentioned the social function of religion remained untouched or were even strengthened:

Examen de la religion:
Man was not made to be idle; he must occupy himself with something and always have society as his end. God did not only propose the happiness of a few individuals but the general good and happiness of all men. So men must naturally render services to one another, whatever differences may exist among them.

Thérèse philosophe:
Man was not made to be idle; he must occupy himself with something whose end is his particular advantage reconciled with the general good. God did not only want the happiness of a few individuals but the happiness of all. We should therefore mutually render all possible services to ourselves, provided that those services do not destroy any branches of the established society.[43]

In short, *Thérèse philosophe* drew on a common stock of libertine arguments to attack Christianity as a philosophy and to defend it as a social policy. Like Voltaire, abbé T. insists that the anti-Christian truth must be confined to a small elite; for if the vulgar herd got wind of it, they would stampede. No one's property or person would be safe in the general rush to satisfy desire. Thus all religions are false, and all are necessary.[44]

These propositions come wrapped in a paradox, however. Abbé T. confides them to Mme C. under the seal of secrecy, yet they reach the reader in a book that could be bought by anyone. How is the reader supposed to respond? If he accepts the abbé's argument, he may flatter himself that he belongs to the tiny elite who dare to think for themselves. He may enjoy the frisson of seeing secrets unveiled, so that his ego swells along with his libido. Exposing priestcraft belongs to the same general strategy as exposing sex: it panders to intellectual voyeurism. But the exposure takes place in a book, not a boudoir. And books have a way of falling into the wrong hands.

The author of *Thérèse philosophe* may well have aimed it at a narrow public of salon sophisticates. Certainly he could not have known that it would be a best-seller twenty-five years after its publication and that it would carry Thérèse's philosophy far outside the orbit of the early Enlightenment. But the potential for spinning out of control had been inherent in its rhetoric in the first place. If literary criticism has demonstrated anything in the recent past, it is the tendency of texts to undermine themselves and to burst through self-imposed constraints. *Thérèse philosophe* does precisely that. It trumpets its respect for all established institutions, but it protests too much. Abbé T. lectures Thérèse about the need to protect "the tranquility of families," "the sacred bonds of marriage," and "the natural law that teaches us to love our neighbors as ourselves."[45] He harangues Mme C. on the necessity of limiting themselves to "pleasures that cannot trouble the inner order of the established society."[46] The Count echoes the same theme.[47] And Thérèse proclaims it in the very last sentence of the book: "Finally, kings, princes, magistrates, and all high officials, according to their rank, who serve the needs of the state, should be loved and respected, because each one of them contributes by his actions to the good of the whole."[48] The message could hardly be clearer, but it has an undertow that carries the argument into dangerous waters.

Put simply, the hedonistic calculus might operate quite differently for someone weighing pleasure against pain at the bottom of society. Why should a peasant, a worker, even an artisan or a shopkeeper respect the established order, if its only justification is the maximization of happiness and he or she is miserable? *Thérèse philosophe* dispatches with this difficulty by directing its hedonism to gentle readers, leaving religion for the rest. But the ranks of the rest had swollen by 1770. Many of them could read.[49] And those with ears to hear could pick up a refrain sent round the world in 1776 by the American Declaration of Independence: "The pursuit of happiness." Thérèse and

Thomas Jefferson—odd bedfellows, but fellow revolutionaries, each in their own way.

The way of Thérèse led through the bedroom. It had more to do with the war between the sexes than with other kinds of conflict, and its gender dimension may have been the most unsettling aspect of its message for the reader of the Old Regime. "The reader, he," I have been saying all along, not simply for stylistic convenience but also because it seems likely that sex books were written by males for males everywhere in early modern Europe.[50] Whether or not *Thérèse philosophe* was actually written by the marquis d'Argens, it probably was aimed at the male animal. By casting Thérèse as the narrator and presenting sexuality from a supposedly feminine perspective, it merely added to the erotic charge—a device as old as Aretino. Should Thérèse's account of sex therefore be dismissed as just another literary version of men exploiting women, as many feminist critics would have it?[51] I think not.

Of course, it would be anachronistic to read feminism into a novel written before feminism existed; and it must be admitted that if *Thérèse philosophe* is an argument for the rights of women, the men do most of the arguing. Thérèse finds her own voice by the end of the book, but through most of it she is reduced to the role of a listener. She sits back passively and receives lessons from abbé T. and the Count, both of whom, to the modern ear, are bores: they drone on and on about liquids and fibers, like tedious schoolmasters who have everything figured out. But eighteenth-century ears may have picked up different messages.

Consider the question of love. The word almost never appears in *Thérèse philosophe,* except as part of a double-barreled noun that means something very different, *amour-propre,* or egotism. The only passion that propels the characters through the plot is self-interest, even when—especially when—they lock in an embrace. Men and women couple like machines. Love for them is a tingling in the epidermis, a surge of liquids, a rush of particles through the fibers, and nothing more. Even when she gazes into the eyes of the Count, Thérèse feels only an affinity of "organs."[52] The relentlessly mechanical descriptions of male-female relations reduce them to matter in motion.

And in such a world, all bodies are ultimately equal, whether noble or plebeian, male or female.

Romantic love was unthinkable in that world. It had not yet been invented by Rousseau. Of course men and women felt strong affections for one another before the publication of *La Nouvelle Héloïse* (1762). The main problem in their affective lives had to do with demography, not literature. A quarter of all babies died before their first birthday; and so many women died while giving birth that marriages lasted on average only fifteen years, despite the impossibility of divorce.[53] Pregnancy represented a mortal danger for women in the eighteenth century. Both Mme C. and Thérèse have such a horror of it that they renounce sexual intercourse. They decide it is simply not worth the risk—a reasonable calculation, given the demographic odds. Mme Bois-Laurier survives a long career as a prostitute, but only because a membraneous growth in her vagina prevents her from conceiving (and has the additional advantage of permitting her to be repeatedly sold as a virgin). The danger of conception underlies the book's emphasis on masturbation and the trajectory of its plot, which leads from masturbation to *coitus interruptus.* When the Count successfully withdraws from Thérèse at the climax of the narrative, he behaves in accordance with the how-to sermon on *coitus interruptus* that abbé T. preached to Mme C. *Thérèse philosophe* is not just a sex book and not only a philosophical tract; it is also a treatise on contraception. It may even have had some influence on the peculiar pattern of French demography.[54]

To be sure, *coitus interruptus* subjects the woman to the goodwill and self-mastery of the man; and when the Count executes it successfully in *Thérèse philosophe,* he is described as a conquering hero. However willingly, Thérèse lets herself be manipulated and seduced. She might be considered as the ultimate target of the book's pervasive voyeurism—that is, as a sex object. But she emerges in the end as the true hero of her story. Unlike Mlle Eradice, who accepts Father Dirrag's injunction to be passive—"Forget yourself and let yourself go"[55]—she takes charge of her life and lives it on her own terms, making her own decisions.

Admittedly, the terms are dictated by the Count. At the crucial turning point of the plot, he proposes to let Thérèse live with him in his château—but as his mistress and at a fee. Nonetheless, the way he makes the proposal does not suggest that he is buying her, but rather that he is explicating the pros and cons of a hedonistic calculus, which illustrates the book's main argument. Never in the history of literature did a lover unbosom himself less passionately. No roses, no poems, no throwing himself at the lady's feet. The Count does not even venture a kiss. Instead, "rather laconically," he lays out the conditions of the contract and turns on his heel. But not before delivering himself of a utilitarian homily:

> In order to achieve happiness, one should seize the pleasure which is peculiar to oneself, that suits the passions with which one is endowed. In doing so, one must calculate the good and the bad which result from the enjoyment of this pleasure, taking care that this good and evil be considered not only in relation to oneself but also in relation to the public interest.[56]

This Romeo is no altruist. He explains that by making Thérèse happy he will achieve happiness for himself, and he draws the line at 2,000 livres, without matrimony. When Thérèse calculates things on her side, she, too, exhibits a hardheaded sense of social realities:

> I felt an inexpressible pleasure in imagining that I could contribute to the pleasures of a man who thought as you did. . . . But how powerful are our prejudices and how difficult to destroy! The social position of a kept woman, to which I had always seen a certain shame attached, filled me with fear. I was afraid also of having a child: my mother and Mme C. had almost died in childbirth.[57]

She takes the château and the 2,000 livres, adding a codicil of her own: Mutual masturbation, yes; sexual intercourse, no. Although she changes her mind after the refresher course on sex in the Count's library, the decision remains hers. She retains her independence to the end. Even if she is the creation of a male fantasy, Thérèse speaks for the right of women to pursue their own pleasures and to dispose of their own bodies.

Whatever its authorship, therefore, *Thérèse philosophe* could be read as a challenge to the accepted values of the Old Regime—a more radical challenge, in some ways, than most French feminism in the nineteenth century, which failed to win the vote for women (they did not get it until 1944) or to free them from their husband's authority over their property and persons.[58] To be sure, there is something unreal about Thérèse's solution to the woman question. Few if any unprotected girls faced the option of a château. But there is also something unsettling about her choice, because she resolutely rejects the roles of wife and mother. So do the other women who are portrayed positively in the book, Mme C. and Mme Bois-Laurier. They make up a formidable trio: three free and freethinking voluptuaries. The independent, libidinous female represented a powerful threat to the social order of eighteenth-century France. Such women actually existed. They were salon lionesses like Mme Tencin and Mlle de Lespinasse, who charged the atmosphere around them with erotic energy and inspired audacious thought experiments like Diderot's *Rêve de d'Alembert*. *Thérèse philosophe* was a thought experiment, too. It weighed the institutions of marriage and motherhood in an imaginary scale, subjected them to the hedonistic calculus, and found them wanting.

When historians calculate the weight of institutions in the past, they rarely allow for fantasy. Yet eighteenth-century Frenchmen often played with conundrums. Could a society of atheists survive? they asked. And a society of libertine women? *Thérèse philosophe* gave them an opportunity to imagine both dangers combined in a single fantasy: a free-loving, freethinking, female *philosophe*. It was an extraordinary feat of the literary imagination. It took the reader outside the law into a fluid zone, where he could play with notions of a different social order. Montesquieu and Rousseau did the same thing in *Lettres persanes* and *Du Contrat social*. Indeed, all the "philosophical" books inhabited this unrestricted space of luddic experimentation, notably *L'An 2440*, to which we now must turn. But none made so free with its subject as *Thérèse philosophe*, the most uninhibited fantasy in the freethinking of the Old Regime.

Chapter 4

Utopian Fantasy

MENTAL EXPERIMENTATION is the main characteristic of *L'An 2440 (The Year 2440)* by Louis-Sébastien Mercier, yet no book could be more different from *Thérèse philosophe*. Where *Thérèse* is impertinent and audacious, *L'An 2440* is heavy and bombastic. The former shocks; the latter moralizes. Instead of teasing the reader's fantasy, Mercier overwhelms it with great waves of rhetoric, always straining for sentimental effect, never betraying the slightest sense of humor. Nothing could be further from modern taste. But the readers of pre-Revolutionary France loved it. *L'An 2440* stands out as the supreme best-seller on the STN list; it went through at least twenty-five editions. It is a crucial work for anyone who wants to understand what appealed to a readership so different from our own.

The first edition of *L'An 2440* came out in 1771, twenty-three years after the first publication of *Thérèse philosophe*. A great deal took place during those years, including a major international conflict, the Seven Years' War, which ended ingloriously for France in 1763, and a major political crisis, the collapse of the Choiseul ministry, which led to the destruction of the parlements in 1771. It was during this period that the most important works of the Enlightenment appeared and that Rousseau carried the Enlightenment beyond the sophisticated circles to which it had been confined in the first half of the century.

Louis-Sébastien Mercier, from the frontispiece to the
1799 edition of *L'An 2440*.

The Henry E. Huntington Library and Art Gallery

Mercier wrote for a public that was bathed in Rousseauism. Of course, other currents continued to run through French literature after 1771. Many surfaced in Mercier's own works, which refer frequently to Diderot's dramaturgy and Voltaire's campaigns against judicial injustice. But Rousseau supplied the main point of reference. It is not simply that he released a tidal wave of sentiment that might be labeled "pre-Romanticism," but rather that he created a new relationship between writer and reader and a new orientation of readers to texts. He rejected the devices that works like *Thérèse philosophe* had used to appeal to readers: sly allusions, hidden meanings, parodies, puns, the whole bag of tricks perfected by Voltaire. In place of wit and word games, Rousseau spoke with his own voice and addressed the reader directly, as if the printed word could carry unmediated effusions from heart to heart. Although other writers had appealed from the head to the heart before Rousseau, none succeeded so spectacularly in creating the sense of contact and in sustaining the illusion of exposure to an overflowing soul. Rousseau seemed to abolish literature and create life. Many of his readers took the characters of *La Nouvelle Héloïse* to be living persons and lived their own lives, or tried to, in accordance with its precepts. Of course, Rousseau had actually substituted one kind of rhetoric for another, drawing on a religious idiom at a time when readers were ripe for a religious revival. But in doing so, he made literature into a democratic force and opened a way toward a democratic political culture.[1]

It is important to insist on Rousseau's originality rather than his sentimentality, because so much of the sentiment rings false today. Sweet tears and soulfulness became such stock features of the novel in the late eighteenth and nineteenth centuries that modern readers often cannot stomach them. But they were still fresh in 1771, when Mercier took up the rhetorical position staked out by Rousseau. Mercier belonged to the growing population of "Rousseaus du ruisseau," sentimental hack writers or "gutter Rousseaus." To be sure, he did not live in penury like his friend Nicolas-Edmé Restif de la Bretonne, for whom the term was coined. Although he came from a rather humble family—his father was a skilled artisan who polished swords and metal arms—Mercier received a decent education and made a decent living by churning out plays, books, and pamphlets. He published prodigiously by recycling passages from one book to another and stretching essays into multi-volume tracts. His major works—*L'An 2440, Tableau de Paris,* and *Mon Bonnet de nuit*—therefore have a formless character. They are composed of short chapters on a wide variety of subjects, which Mercier cobbled together without worrying about narrative coherence. When a book caught on, he expanded it, cutting and pasting and fighting off pirates as he advanced from one edition to the next. The result was never elegant, but it often had a gripping quality, because Mercier knew how to observe the world around him and to make it come alive in anecdotes and essays. There is no better writer to consult if one wants to get some idea of how Paris looked, sounded, smelled, and felt on the eve of the Revolution.[2]

Ostensibly, *L'An 2440* describes a completely different world—a fantasy that Mercier locates far off in the future. The plot is simplicity itself. After a heated discussion with a philosophic friend, who rails against the injustices of the Paris of 1771, the narrator (unnamed, but clearly a version of Mercier himself) falls asleep and wakes up in the Paris of the future. A long beard and a weakened body tell him he has aged. When he stumbles into the street and discovers a poster with the date on it—2440—he realizes just how old he is: seven hundred. A curious but friendly crowd gathers around him, marveling at the strangeness of his appearance. Then a philosophic antiquarian steps forward, straightens out the situation, and offers to guide the stranger through the city. The rest of the book is the narrator's account of their tour. It proceeds from site to site, without following any particular itinerary, so Mercier could insert new passages and extend the text indefinitely in later editions. When the tour is over, the narrator wakes up again, this time in the present; and the book comes abruptly to an end.[3]

Today's reader, accustomed to futuristic fantasies and Rip Van Winkle effects, may find the whole business rather heavyhanded. But eighteenth-century readers found it irresistible. They had never encountered science fiction. Nor had they dreamed of a Utopia set in the future. Plato, Thomas More, Francis Bacon, and all the other architects of Utopias had imag-

The narrator of *L'An 2440* discovers that he is seven hundred
years old.

Department of Rare Books and Special Collections,
Princeton University Libraries

ined societies located far away in space and cut off from the
real world by impossible journeys or extravagant shipwrecks.[4]
Those worlds looked unobtainable; but Mercier made his seem
inevitable, because he presented it as the outcome of a historical process already at work and he placed it in Paris. Thus,
despite its self-proclaimed character of fantasy—A Dream If
Ever There Was One, according to its subtitle—L'An 2440
demanded to be read as a serious guidebook to the future. It
offered an astonishing new perspective: the future as a fait
accompli and the present as a distant past. Who could resist the
temptation to participate in such a thought experiment? And
once engaged in it, who could fail to see that it exposed the
rottenness of the society before his eyes, the Paris of the eighteenth century?

Mercier magnifies this effect by means of three basic techniques: concrete description, which makes his vision of the
future read like reportage; elaborate footnotes, which create a
dialogue between two voices, the narrator in the main text, who
speaks in the future, and the commentator in the notes, who
declaims in the present; and a Rousseauistic rhetoric, which
assigns roles to writer and reader, producing a common align-
ment against the institutions of the Old Regime.

The first technique is the most effective, because it gives full
rein to Mercier's journalistic talent. He records everything that
strikes the eye of the seven-hundred-year-old narrator and
accompanies it with a running commentary by the philosophic
guide. First, they stop by a haberdasher in order to outfit the
narrator in the style of 2440, which will make him look less
conspicuous and feel more comfortable. The Parisians of the
future wear functional, loose-fitting clothes, which do not con-
strict the movements of the body: leggings, covered by a light
undervest, and a togalike robe gathered at the waist with a sash.
Sensible shoes make walking a pleasure, and a skullcap with a
fold-out brim protects them from both sun and rain. Of course,
they do not wear swords, emblems of "the old prejudice of
Gothic chivalry,"[5] and their hair is gathered into a simple braid
behind the head, instead of being piled up and plastered in the
unnatural manner of the men-about-town in the eighteenth century. In his day, the narrator confesses, clothing oppressed the

body: neckbands stifled breath, vests "imprisoned" chests, and garters cut off circulation in the legs.

The description continues in this vein, using homely details about everyday life to build up a general indictment of life under the Old Regime. The narrator can barely recognize Paris, it is so clean and well ordered. Wagons drive slowly along the right-hand side of the road and stop deferentially before pedestrians, who always have the right of way. And nearly everyone goes on foot, even the king. Although a few carriages can be seen, they bear no resemblance to the gilded coaches that mowed down the common people in the eighteenth century. They are reserved for aged citizens who have performed some extraordinary service for humanity. These heroes, and a few outstanding craftsmen who have been nominated by their peers and recognized by the king, make up the only true nobility of the country. The king presents them with a brocaded hat, which gives them free entry everywhere and immediate access to the royal council. The brocaded hats are the only mark of distinction, for everyone wears the same kind of smocks and lives in the same kind of houses—modest structures, all the same height, all filled with simple furniture, and all topped with roof gardens. The gardens contain so much greenery that, seen from above, Paris looks like a forest. By perfecting urban life, the Parisians have returned to nature.

Above all, they have reorganized public space. They celebrate civic festivals in a gigantic square formed by an imposing set of monuments: the Tuileries and the Louvre joined by a new palace, which is reserved for artists; a new Temple of Justice, which has replaced the old parlement; and a transformed Hôtel de Ville. Further down the Seine, a Temple of Clemency stands on the site of the Bastille, and the pestilential Hôtel-Dieu has been replaced by a Hôtel of Inoculation. Thanks to preventive medicine, fewer people fall sick. If they do, they are given private beds and excellent care in twenty public hospitals staffed by dedicated doctors. Extreme poverty has also been eliminated; so the Hôpital Général (poorhouse) no longer exists. All the prisons have disappeared as well, for crime has ceased to be a serious problem. When by some aberration one citizen takes the life of another, he is made to recognize his guilt and to confess before his countrymen, who weep for the injury done to the social contract while he is shot by a firing squad under the direction of the president of the Senate.

The Sorbonne still stands in the Latin Quarter, but it has been converted into a dissecting theatre for research in preventive medicine. Applied sciences and civics have replaced metaphysics and theology throughout the education system. Trained at an early age according to the principles in Rousseau's *Emile,* children learn so quickly that they use the *Encyclopédie* as a primer in grade school. They also assimilate a Rousseauistic cult of the Supreme Being. Churches and monasteries no longer clutter the urban landscape, because Catholicism has collapsed. So Paris now is pious. The narrator visits one of its new temples and marvels at the general simplicity. Nothing adorns the walls but the word "God" inscribed in many languages, and a glass-covered dome reminds the congregation of the Creator in the great Beyond. The pope, reduced to a civic bishopric in Rome, has recently published a "Catechism of Human Reason." Priests have been replaced by philosophic pastors and secular "saints," who inspire love for the fatherland by heroic feats of civic virtue, such as cleaning out cesspools and rescuing people from burning buildings. The theatre has also become a "school of morality." When the narrator spends an evening in one of the four playhouses erected by the government in main squares of the city, he encounters a pastor leading a gaggle of children. They have come in order to have their civic consciousness raised by a double bill: a tragedy about the Calas Affair (the judicial murder of a Protestant that horrified Voltaire) and a comedy glorifying Henri IV (after defeating the Catholic League, the populist king enjoys a feast and clears the table himself).[6]

The modern reader is likely to be surprised at much of this description. When we imagine the future, we fill it with technological marvels. Mercier's had none—no ray guns, no space machines, no time-warp television, no intergalactic gimmickry of any kind. The dimensions of his Utopia were moral. His rhetoric was designed to provoke moral indignation. Yet he did not use most of the devices favored by novelists who wanted to arouse strong emotions in their readers. Because it simply takes the reader through the Paris of the future, *L'An 2440* has no plot that can engage his affections and no characters with whom he can identify. It therefore adopts a strategy that would be unthinkable today. Having captured the reader's attention by means of exotic descriptions, it moralizes through the use of footnotes.

The notes to *L'An 2440* are so extensive that they often overwhelm the main body of the text, which is reduced on some pages to only a line or two. The reader is meant to tack back and forth between the text at the top of the page and the notes at the bottom. In doing so, he switches time frames, because the text is set in the year 2440 and the notes in the eighteenth century. The same narrative voice prevails in each—an unidentified "I" who clearly stands for the anonymous author. (The book was considered so dangerous that Mercier did not publicly acknowledge his authorship until he put his name to the Preface in the edition of 1791.) But the voice changes register as it changes venue. In the main text, the narrator remains stupefied and humbled by the marvels of the future. He listens raptly while the guide lectures him on the superiority of French society in 2440. In the notes, "I" hurls jeremiads directly at the reader, denouncing the abuses in the reader's own world and defying all the authorities of the Old Regime.

In Chapter VIII, for example, the guide informs the narrator that Paris no longer has any prisons or poorhouses, and he offers a restrospective, Rousseauistic explanation for their abuse in the eighteenth century: "Luxury, like a burning acid, had spread gangrene throughout the healthiest parts of your state, and your political body was covered with ulcers." Then, in a footnote to this passage, the author of the subtext harangues the reader in a declamation that covers the better part of two pages. At one point, he flings his invective directly at the judges sitting in the French courts: "Oh cruel magistrates! Men of iron, men unworthy of the name of man, you outrage humanity more than they [the imprisoned criminals] have outraged it themselves! Never has the ferocity of brigands equaled yours."[7]

The footnotes bring out the main tendency of Mercier's fantasied future: it was negative. He describes a society without monks, priests, prostitutes, beggars, dancing masters, pastry cooks, a standing army (all nations have accepted an arrangement for perpetual peace), slavery, arbitrary arrest, taxes, credit (everyone always pays in cash), guilds, foreign trade (every country is essentially agricultural and self-sufficient), coffee, tea, or tobacco (according to the narrator, snuff destroys one's memory). The accumulation of negatives adds up to a massive indictment of the Old Regime. But it hardly constitutes a blueprint for a new kind of society. In fact, Mercier merely imagined the France of his day purged of its abuses. *L'An 2440* does not differ fundamentally from *Le Tableau de Paris,* Mercier's other best-seller, first published in 1781. The former was a walk through the Paris of the future, the latter a promenade around the Paris of the present. The two works complemented one another, providing a positive and a negative picture of the same subject. But the negatives prevailed to such an extent that both books really represent the same side of the same coin.

For example, the chapter on "The Princely Innkeeper" in *L'An 2440* seems, at first glance, to offer a picture of an entirely new and egalitarian society. Instead of living in outrageous luxury, the prince holds an open house for travelers and the poor. Yet he still inhabits a palace with his coat of arms carved above the entrance way—and the poor still exist. Although Mercier abolishes the extremes of wealth and misery, he cannot imagine a society without the needy at its bottom and the aristocracy at its top.

Nor can he conceive of economic and demographic development. In seven hundred years, the population of France has increased by only 50 percent; and the increase merely represents an adjustment of the proportions between Paris and the provinces: the capital remained the same, while the countryside grew. Mercier's vision of rural prosperity corresponds to the common contemporary view of agriculture as the source of all wealth, but it has no theoretical component to it. Instead of embracing the free-trade agronomy of the Physiocrats, he warns that in economics the heart is to be trusted rather than the head: "It is an unfortunate century that submits happiness to reason."[8] He allows for state granaries to protect the poor from disastrous harvests, but he will have no unregulated commerce, no extensive manufacturing, not even any banks or credit mechanisms.

And insofar as he redesigns social relations, his most important innovation is the one that would seem least progressive today. Like Rousseau, he takes women out of the workplace and consigns them to their homes, restricting them severely to their roles as mothers and housekeepers. They cannot participate in politics or any form of public life. They cannot even sit with the men in services to the Supreme Being.

For all its Rousseauism, Mercier's Utopia remains rooted in the society of the Old Regime. So his dream keeps running into contradictions. On one page he abolishes poverty and the nobility; on another he describes wealthy nobles caring for the poor. The court has disappeared in one passage, and courtiers cluster about the throne in another. At the beginning of the book the king exercises only symbolic power; by the end he seems to lay down the law for the entire society. Instead of worrying about inconsistencies, Mercier follows his fantasy wherever it leads him. That is what makes his Utopia so interesting: its contradictions show how far fantasy could be stretched before 1789. Of course, more serious thinkers—Morelly, Mably, and d'Holbach as well as Rousseau—entertained plenty of bold speculations. The Utopian strain in their thought sometimes shaded off into socialism—but only in the abstract. Mercier's reads like a dream come true. He takes the reader by the hand and walks him through the society of the future. Once set in motion, in an everyday world composed of clothing and housing and traffic in the street, the narrative keeps bumping up against the outer boundaries of the thinkable; and by doing so it reveals the limits of the social imagination under the Old Regime.

Yet Mercier later claimed to have prophesied the coming of the French Revolution: "Never, I dare say, did a prediction come closer to an event, nor did one give a more detailed account of an astonishing series of transformations. I am therefore the true prophet of the French Revolution."[9] In one dramatic passage of *L'An 2440*, Mercier does indeed seem to play with the idea of a revolutionary upheaval. Looking back on the political history of the eighteenth century, the guide explains to the narrator that monarchies inevitably degenerate into despotisms; but

Just one loud voice was needed to awaken the multitude from their slumber. If oppression thundered over your heads, you had only your own weakness to blame. Liberty and happiness belong to those who know how to seize them. All is revolution in this world: the greatest one of all grew to maturity, and we are harvesting the fruits of it.

In a footnote to this passage, Mercier makes it clear that he is talking about a violent upheaval:

. . . For some states there is a stage which is unavoidable—a bloody and terrible stage, though it announces freedom to come. I speak of civil war. . . . This is a horrible remedy! But after the long slumber of the state and its inhabitants, it becomes necessary.[10]

Two pages later, however, the blood and thunder have disappeared, and the narrator explains that the revolution actually consisted of sweetness and light: "Would you believe it? The revolution came about quite easily, by the heroism of a great man."[11] A "philosopher-king" voluntarily surrendered his power to the ancient estates of the realm and agreed to rule henceforth as a figurehead. He also destroyed the Bastille and abolished all arbitrary arrest by means of *lettres de cachet*.[12] As for the Catholic Church, "Its power derived from public opinion; opinion changed and the whole thing evaporated in a puff of smoke."[13] The entire power structure of the Old Regime collapsed of its own weight, helped by a little push from the throne and the pressure of public opinion, both of which were set in motion by the ultimate driving force in history: men of letters working by means of the printing press.

Despite its radical rhetoric, Mercier's text actually throbs with monarchist sentiment—not the Louis Quatorzean variety, of course, but a populist, egalitarian monarchism inspired in large part by the myth of Henri IV. Henri IV is celebrated everywhere in the Paris of 2440, both as a man of the people and as a father of the people. The Pont-Neuf has been renamed Pont-Henri IV; Henri IV is applauded on the stage; and the current king is adored as "a second Henri IV":

He has the same greatness of soul, the same grit *{entrailles}*, the same magnificent simplicity, but he is more fortunate. The footprints he leaves on the public pathways are sacred and revered by all. No one would dare to quarrel there; one would blush to commit the smallest disorderly act. "If the King were to pass," they say. This warning alone would, I think, stop a civil war.[14]

Against this positive image, Mercier plays off its opposite: the monarch as despot, or Louis XIV. Surrounded by flatterers, sunken in luxury, Louis XIV epitomizes the worst abuses of the monarchy and the lowest point in the history of France. He lost contact with his people and lived off their ruin.[15] Seen from the perspective of the year 2440, Versailles stands out as the supreme symbol of the process by which the monarchy degenerated into a despotism. In the last chapter, the narrator makes an excursion from Paris to Versailles. But instead of finding a historical monument, he discovers a desolate landscape strewn with ruins. Overgrown with weeds, infested by snakes, the remains of the palace have been forgotten by everyone except an old man, who weeps over them from a perch on a fallen pillar. He turns out to be a reincarnation of Louis XIV, condemned to expiate his guilt on the site of his sins. But before the narrator can learn how it all came crashing down, a snake bites him and he awakes from his dream.

Although it reads like a pastiche of Arthur Young's *Night Thoughts*,[16] this scene provides Mercier with a way to end the book on a dramatic note and to take a final swipe at what he most detests about the politics of the Old Regime. But he never contests the legitimacy of the monarchy as such. On the contrary, he follows Montesquieu in praising a limited monarchy as the best form of government in contrast to democracies, which decline into anarchy, and despotisms, which generate slavery.[17] Monarchies, however, degenerate into despotisms, "just as rivers flow into the sea";[18] and despotisms, as Montesquieu also showed, were systems of power built up over the ages, not passing phases of tyrannical rule. The ultimate target of Mercier's rhetoric is therefore the system itself, rather than Louis XIV or any other individual.

In 2440, according to the main text, citizens pay voluntary contributions instead of taxes, and the small cadre of royal officials live like patriotic monks, without salaries or property of any kind. In contrast, as the footnotes make clear, the ministers of eighteenth-century France bled the people dry in order to give full vent to their depraved taste for luxury.[19] Thus the real disease that threatens to destroy the monarchy in 1771 is "ministerial despotism," as the French then called it—that is, the abuse of power by top officials who exploit the people in the name of the king. In one of his fiercest footnotes, Mercier fulminates against this form of despotism and then imagines a cure for it. A fearless *philosophe* strides into the midst of the king's council and apostrophizes the monarch thus:

> Do not believe these misguided counselors; you are surrounded by enemies of your family. Your security and greatness are founded less on your absolute power than on the love of your people. If they are miserable, they will ardently long for a revolution, and they will overturn your throne or that of your children. The people are immortal, but you will pass. The majesty of the throne resides more in paternal love than in unlimited power.[20]

Mercier did not name names, but the Walter Mitty quality of the fantasy suggests that he imagined himself in the role of saviour of the fatherland and that the government he railed against was the one he had before his eyes—the Maupeou ministry, which in the view of its enemies was then transforming the monarchy into a despotism by destroying the independence of the judiciary. To be sure, Mercier had some harsh things to say about the parlements[21] (the highest courts in the various judicial districts of the kingdom); and it would be wrong to dismiss his Utopian dreaming as anti-ministerial propaganda. He wrote most of it between 1768 and 1770, before Maupeou struck down the parlements. But Mercier might well have added the angriest footnotes in late 1770 or early 1771, when the Maupeou "revolution" was already under way. He later wrote that he produced the first edition "under the reign of chancellor Maupeou."[22] That reign ended with the death of Louis XV on

May 10, 1774. By 1775, when it had risen to the top of the best-seller list, *L'An 2440* provided readers with a retrospective view of the France of Louis XV, not a preview of the French Revolution, to say nothing of the twenty-fifth century.

Should one therefore conclude that Mercier's text had nothing revolutionary about it, despite his subsequent claims? It is easy, two centuries after 1789, to believe that the French should have seen the Revolution coming two decades before it arrived. But in fact no one imagined anything comparable to the explosion of 1789. No one could, because the modern concept of a revolution did not exist until people had experienced one. So Mercier's imagination never broke through the confines of an Old Regime mentality, one that could accommodate notions of parlementary rebellion and civil war but not of a transformation of the regime itself. Nonetheless, Mercier challenged some fundamental principles of the sociopolitical order, especially in two sensitive areas: religion and government.

He did not merely attack the most visible institutions of the Catholic Church—its monasteries, tithes, prelates, and papacy. He also contested its spiritual legitimacy. The deistic pastors of 2440 appeal to religious sentiments that go beyond deism itself, or at least the frigid deism of Voltaire. When they invoke the Supreme Being from their glass-covered temples, they stir an ecstatic sense of the divine in the manner of Rousseau's Savoyard Vicar. Instead of winding up the universe and letting it run according to Newton's laws, their God sees into the blackest souls and intervenes to maintain the moral order. The narrator's guide assures him that evil persons "will be pursued by that absolute eye that penetrates everywhere"[23] and that they will be reincarnated as snakes and toads, while the souls of the good will migrate among the planets and suns until they merge with their creator.

This perspective is unveiled to adolescent boys (apparently girls are not considered susceptible to deep religious emotion) at an initiation rite known as "the communion of the two infinities." When a youth has been seen to sigh and roll his eyes toward the heavens, his parents pack him off to an observatory, where a glimpse through a telescope reveals the grandeur of

God. A session with a microscope then reveals the other infinity, and an ecstatic sermon completes the job. The youth bursts into tears, resolving to adore the Creator and to love his fellow creatures for the rest of his life. No one can resist this demonstration of elementary metaphysics. If, by some aberration, an atheist were to appear among them, the Parisians would bring him around with "an assiduous course of experimental physics."[24] And if that should fail, they would banish him.

For Mercier, as for Rousseau, politics and religion are inseparable, so civic festivals reinforce the citizen's devotion to both God and country. By remaining close to the hearth, breastfeeding their newborn, and applying a Rousseauistic pedagogy, mothers make sure their sons blossom like Emile. Schools and temples perfect the young men's education. And therefore, by the time they reach adulthood, their individual desires harmonize with the General Will. Mercier follows Rousseau's reasoning exactly: law is "the expression of the General Will,"[25] and sovereignty remains in the hands of the people. But because the General Will is essentially a moral consensus about the welfare of society as a whole, the actual form of government remains relatively unimportant. The guide explains that the government is "neither monarchical nor democratic nor aristocratic: it is reasonable and adapted to mankind."[26] As if that were not obscure enough, he goes on to describe a political system that sounds like an impossible amalgam of institutions from the Old Regime. "Estates" (something that seems to resemble the Estates General) assemble once every two years to pass legislation. A "Senate" (evidently an improved version of the Parlement of Paris) administers the laws. And a king (but one who only "conserves the name of king") oversees their execution.[27]

Mercier does not pause to untangle these ideas, because he is more interested in the sentiment that sustains them—a general spirit of equality and civic virtue. He therefore devotes most of the chapters on government to an account of the republican atmosphere surrounding the throne and the Spartan upbringing of the prince. Dressed like a peasant and raised by foster parents among the common people, the Dauphin does not learn about his royal blood until he is deemed ready to

L'ETERNITÉ

The throne room: *L'An 2440.*

Department of Rare Books and Special Collections,
Princeton University Libraries

ascend the throne. As a final lesson in equality, he wrestles with a worker and is pinned to the ground. Then, for three days every year throughout his reign, he must fast and sleep in rags in order to keep the lot of the poor foremost in his mind. The prince-and-pauper fantasy typifies Mercier's way of dealing with ideas. Instead of combining them into a logical argument, he works them into anecdotes and depends on a strong storyline to get his point across.

But what drove the point home? Although it is impossible to find any first-hand testimony by the readers, one can study the way Mercier's rhetoric anticipated and directed their responses. In fact, he prescribed roles for both writer and reader, and then went on to make writing and reading the crucial ingredients that held his vision of utopia together.

Mercier oriented the reader from the outset by an extraordinary dedication and preface. Instead of paying homage to a patron in the conventional manner, he dedicated the book "to the year 2440":

> August and respectable Year . . . thou shalt judge both the dead monarchs and the writers who lived in submission to their power. The names of the friends and defenders of humanity will be honored; their glory will shine pure and radiant. But that vile rabble of kings who tormented the human race will be buried in oblivion. . . .

On the one hand, despots; on the other, writers. Such were the contestants in the cosmic drama of history. This opposition cast Mercier himself in a heroic role, although he spoke only as the anonymous "I" within the text. No matter, his voice would be heard seven centuries from now, while the glory of the great would be forgotten:

> While the thunderbolts of despotism strike and die out, the pen of a writer reaches across time, absolving and punishing the masters of the universe. I have used the power that I received at my birth. I have called before the tribunal of my reason the laws, customs, and abuses of the country where I lived unknown and obscure.[28]

When the reader reached the Preface, he learned that "I" was a prophet, crying in the wilderness like the heroes of the Old Testament, while the police tried to drive him into the Bastille.[29] But the modern Jeremiah was a *"philosophe,"*[30] and he addressed a modern public:

> As for me, I dream like Plato. My dear fellow citizens! You whom I have seen suffering so long from a multitude of abuses, when will we see our great plans, our dreams come true? Let us dream then; it is our only consolation.[31]

The distribution of roles cast the readers with the writer in a community of citizens bound together by a common dream and united against a common enemy. To read the book was to share the dream, to imagine how a coalition of writers and readers would overcome despotism and shape society in the future.

Readers and writers against despots—it was a simple script for the future, but it had a gripping quality, because it made the reading of the book seem to be part of the historical process whose outcome it revealed. The print on the page declared the printed word to be the supreme force in history. Mercier did not merely announce this truth, which was a commonplace of contemporary theories of progress;[32] he also showed how it would be realized, or rather, he asserted its existence as a fait accompli in the year 2440, so that in imagining the future, the reader could also see what the present would look like when it had become the past.

This narrative strategy shows up most clearly in a chapter on the royal library. Expecting to be overwhelmed by a mountain of books, the narrator is astonished to find only four cupboards, one for each of the major literatures in the world. What happened to the vast quantity of printed matter that already cluttered up the royal library in the eighteenth century? he asks. We burned it, the librarian replies: 800,000 volumes of law, 50,000 dictionaries, 100,000 works of poetry, 1,600,000 travel books, and 1,000,000,000 novels all went up in a gigantic bonfire of vanities. Is the regime of 2440 therefore hostile to the printed word? Not at all: printing has proven to be the most important force in history, and the French protect their free-

dom by keeping their press entirely free. They did not burn
the books because they despised them but rather because they
feared their power. Most literature from the past spread poison
through the body politic by flattering the great and catering to
corrupt tastes. A commission of virtuous scholars therefore filtered all the healthy ingredients from everything printed in previous centuries and distilled it down to its essence, which fit
nicely into a small, duodecimo volume. They permitted some
volumes of theology to survive, but only as secret weapons,
stored under lock and key, to be used against the enemy as a
kind of germ warfare in case France should ever be invaded.

The French keep history books out of the hands of their children for a similar reason, because history provides little more
than bad examples of how the rich and powerful exploited the
poor. Of course, by 2440 Enlightenment has triumphed: hence
the four small collections of literary and philosophical works,
which testify to the progressive march of reason. The smallest
of the four contains what the French thought worthy of preserving from their own literature. The narrator searches through it
for the canon of classics familiar to him from the eighteenth
century, but he finds a world turned upside down: nothing
before the sixteenth century, a little Descartes and Montaigne,
no Pascal or Bossuet, and a good selection of works by the *philosophes,* above all Rousseau. Half of Voltaire has gone up in
flames, but every word of Rousseau is still revered, and the
librarian scolds the narrator for the inability of his contemporaries to understand the greatest genius of their age.

Mercier's vision of the future therefore operates as a theory
of progress that runs backward, vindicating the writers who
contributed most to humanity and suffered most from the
agents of despotism. Statues of them stand in public squares
with the heads of their persecutors carved beneath their feet.
Corneille treads Richelieu under his heel, and Voltaire and
Rousseau march on the heads of prelates and ministers whom
the narrator declines to name.[33] Indeed, statues, images, and
inscriptions are to be found everywhere in the Paris of 2440.
The Pont-Neuf, now Pont-Henri IV, is lined with statues of
statesmen who served the people. It has become a "book of
morals,"[34] which instructs the pedestrians who cross it. In fact,

the entire city functions as a book, and citizens read their way through it, imbibing civic lessons at every step.

Mercier puts so much stress on the civic function of reading and writing that he argues himself into a corner. If writers have so much power, how can they be prevented from abusing it? The press is free. Indeed, any threat to its freedom is treated as "a crime of *lèse*-humanity."[35] So instead of censorship, the Parisians force anyone who publishes an immoral or uncivic book to wear a mask and to submit to an interrogation twice a day by two virtuous citizens. When their superior reasoning forces him to see his errors, he is permitted to remove the mask and rejoin the citizenry. The life of the republic depends on moral policing of this sort, because literature is a form of politics and every writer is a "public man" who molds the civic spirit.[36] The greatest writers actually determine the course of history, "like suns who set in motion and direct the circulation of ideas. They are the prime movers; and because the love of humanity burns in their generous hearts, all other hearts respond to them and to their sublime victories over despotism and super-stition."[37]

Every citizen is also an author in his own way. When each man (women remain excluded from all public functions) reaches a certain age, he distills what he has learned into a book. It is read aloud at his funeral. In fact, it is his "soul,"[38] and it is studied along with the books of all his ancestors by his descendants. The French have therefore become a "people of authors" *(tout un peuple auteur)* as well as a nation of readers.[39] Reading and writing sustain all civic life, which is organized around notions of the book—the soul as a book, the city as a book, the book of nature read by means of telescopes and microscopes. Mercier imagines natural law "engraved in indelible characters in every heart,"[40] and describes the stars as "sacred letters," which spell out the divinity.[41] Just as man reads God in the Gutenberg galaxy, God reads the heart of man; for He is the "absolute eye that penetrates everything," "the eye . . . that effortlessly reads the most hidden corners of our hearts."[42]

Writers partake of this divine attribute. It serves as their main weapon in the struggle against despotism. Hence a court scene from the eighteenth century as Mercier imagines it:

A villainous courtier and minister of justice says to his valet while speaking of *philosophe* writers: "My friend, those people are pernicious. You can't get away with the slightest injustice without their noticing it. An artful mask will not shield our true face from the most penetrating looks. When they pass by, those men seem to say to you: 'I know thee.' *Messieurs les philosophes,* I'll teach you that it is dangerous to know a man like me: I do not want to be known."[43]

Thanks to the invention of printing, the insight of the *philosophes* spread throughout the whole society; "nothing could be hidden," and despotism was doomed.[44] By the twenty-fifth century, despotism had become impossible, because everything had been driven out of hiding. "Our eye does not stop at the surface of things," the guide explains to the narrator.[45] Seeing, unmasking, penetrating surfaces has become the primary duty of the citizens. They constantly read one another, while God, the Supreme Reader, looks over their shoulders and into their souls. In case they falter, secret "spies" penetrate everywhere, and moral "censors" maintain the general vigilance.[46] Utopia, in short, is a state of perfect transparency.

To the modern reader, it sounds suspiciously like totalitarianism. But Mercier could not foresee the horrors of the twentieth century when he imagined the twenty-fifth century, nor could he know that Utopian speculations would lead from 2440 to 1984. To the readers of his time, his Utopia promised liberation. It offered them a vision of a world where writers and readers made Rousseau's dream come true and where life was at last an open book.

Chapter 5

Political Slander

ANECDOTES SUR MME LA COMTESSE DU BARRY (1775), the second work on the best-seller list after *L'An 2440,* plunged the reader into an entirely different world—the secret world of brothels and boudoirs, where he could watch the most famous figures of the realm make sport with one another's lives and the destiny of France. It was, in a word, a *libelle,* a classic of the genre. But as the genre is now extinct, the book has been forgotten. One cannot even penetrate the anonymity of its author, although there is no reason to doubt the attribution in standard bibliographies, which ascribe it to an obscure Parisian pamphleteer, Mathieu-François Pidansat de Mairobert. Certainly the text resembles other works attributed to Mairobert and the members of his circle, the *nouvellistes* (newsmongers) who gathered in the salon of Mme Doublet de Persan and Louis Petit de Bachaumont.[1]

This group combed Paris so assiduously for news that it can be considered as a remote ancestor of the modern tabloid's city room. It produced an underground manuscript gazette, which was later printed in thirty-six volumes as *Mémoires secrets pour servir à l'histoire de la république des lettres en France* and which contains some of the same passages, word for word, that appear in *Anecdotes sur Mme la comtesse du Barry.* But the passages also show up in other *libelles* and *chroniques scandaleuses.* The *libellistes* lifted material from one another with such abandon that it is impossible to know where it originated or who wrote what. The modern notion of plagiarism will not do as a way to characterize the practices of men who carried scraps of hand-written *nouvelles* in their sleeves, exchanged them in cafés, copied them into journals, and reworked them into books. To speak of a fixed text or even an author would be equally anachronistic, for libel was a collective enterprise, and *libelles* belonged to the mass of printed matter floating amidst the rumors, gossip, jokes, songs, cartoons, and broadsides that swirled through the streets of early modern Paris. Only a small proportion of those words and images found their way into books, and only a few of the books made it into our libraries. But they include many of the works that circulated most widely in the underground book trade. Of the top one hundred works on the STN best-seller list, fifteen were *libelles* or *chroniques scandaleuses:*

Anecdotes sur Mme la comtesse du Barry (2nd on the list)

Journal historique de la révolution opérée dans la constitution de la monarchie française par M. de Maupeou (6th)

Mémoires de l'abbé Terray (9th)

Mémoires de Louis XV (12th)

L'Observateur anglais, ou correspondance secrète entre Milord All'Eye et Milord All'Ear (13th)

Vie privée de Louis XV (32nd)

Correspondance secrète et familière de M. de Maupeou (37th)

Les Fastes de Louis XV (39th)

Mémoires secrets pour servir à l'histoire de la république des lettres en France (49th)

Le Gazetier cuirassé (53rd)

L'Espion dévalisé (68th)

Mémoires authentiques de Mme la comtesse du Barry (70th)

La Gazette de Cythère . . . {et} Le Précis historique de la vie de Mme la comtesse du Barry (77th)

Mémoires de Mme la marquise de Pompadour (98th)

La Chronique scandaleuse (100th)[2]

ling through Champagne, when he agreed, on a whim, to
it some *noblesse oblige.* The wife of a *rat de cave* (a tax
ctor roundly hated by the peasants) had just given birth in
illage of Vaucouleurs, and the child needed a godfather.
onceau agreed to hold her at the baptismal font and to pay
village-style feast, complete with nuts and candies. Then
ntinued on his way, forgetting his charge until she turns
er at a critical juncture of the story, as the reader soon
arn. The reader will also learn that the child's mother had
been seen in the company of a certain friar Ange, whom
ssed off as her brother-in-law. Moreover, soon after the
birth, her husband died and she found employment as a
But no matter: the future mistress of the king went down
parish register as the daughter of a *rat de cave,* and a public
ted with questions of genealogy could be assured that
s ostensibly legitimate.

way of launching his lady in life establishes the narrator's
It is authoritative, moderate, and objective. Also, it
an elevated tone—a trifle high, perhaps, for the baseness
subject, but that only adds piquancy. And more
nt, it demonstrates the author's determination to do jus-
is theme. He will have nothing to do with legends and
True, he reports them in exquisite detail, but only to
hem. If the refutations sometimes seem a little weak,
ld never be taken to impugn his commitment to set
rd straight. He has read through all the evidence and
ved all the witnesses. Sometimes in order to rebut the
calumnies, he has to produce information that makes
es look true. But isn't the lesser evil better? And does
illingness to let his heroine occasionally look bad con-
general dedication to her defense, and, above all, to
? No, the reader can pursue the story with complete
e in its narrator, and can settle back for a learned dis-
f questions such as: who first had the heroine's maid-

rrator refuses to pronounce. He finds too much ambi-
much conflicting evidence to make a responsible
. His interview with du Barry's godfather suggests that
play may have occurred in the convent school where

Anecdotes sur Mme la comtesse du Ba
this literature as one of the supreme l
Revolutionary era. What made it so aj
public?

First, it was and is a very good read
entertaining and informative, and it ha
which carries the heroine from humbl
the king. It reads like an off-color Ci
success story, because du Barry sleep
to the throne. But the sex only added
of the plot, which gave uninformed
the inside story of life in Versailles. F
saw: the formula was still new, and i
new genres of literature that were
biography and contemporary history

The Preface sets the tone for th
the pleasures that are in store for "al
frivolous to the philosophic: on the
the other, matter for serious ref
never come close to Versailles wil
inner workings of the court. But
thing but the strictest truth, becau
anonymous but clearly knows a
great—has not produced a *libelle*.
He will cite his sources, weed o
substantiated, and defend his her
sip. True, the reader can expect s
will all be true. As a "historian,"
treat: an accurate account of life
read like a novel.

He begins the story with a
Barry's origins. They are, he cc
nantly rejects the legend that
spring of a wandering friar anc
godfather, Billard Dumonceat
Ministry, he has discovered tha
bottom of society. In an excl
coup for our historian, as the
off all such sources—Dumor

trav
exhi
insp
the
Dum
for a
he cc
up la
will l
often
she pa
baby's
cook.
in the
fascina
she wa
This
voice.
strikes
of the
importa
tice to
rumors
refute
they co
the rec
intervie
grossest
lesser or
not his
firm his
the truth
confiden
cussion c
enhead?
The na
guity, to
judgment
some fou

clerk in the Naval Ministry. He, however, deserted her for a decrepit countess, so she moved in with a coiffeur. There she enjoyed a few months of bliss: continuous hairdressing and an ever-expanding wardrobe. But she drove the poor man into bankruptcy. He escaped to England and she to her mother, who had become a cleaning woman by day and a streetwalker by night. Mlle Lançon, who now reverted to the family name of Vaubergnier, also turned tricks with her mama in the Tuileries Gardens. Unfortunately, an undercover agent caught the mother-daughter duo *en flagrant délit.* He was about to pack them off to prison when the mother's old lover, Father Gomart alias Ange, providentially appeared and rescued them with a bribe. He then placed the girl in the household of a wealthy tax farmer's widow, who employed him to say Mass and share her bed.

The widow soon preferred to bed with young Vaubergnier, who meanwhile dallied with her two sons and probably with some of her lackeys, although the narrator pretends to reject that calumny. In any case, Vaubergnier's conduct aroused the jealousy of the servant girls. Their protest made the lover's triangle (mother-son-brother) fall apart. Mlle Vaubergnier returned to her own mother, now the wife of a clerk in the Paris Customs, and then found employment in a gambling den. There she met the comte du Barry, who was not a count at all but a pimp. He specialized in call girls for the high and mighty; and he succeeded prodigiously in this profession, thanks to an extraordinary talent for intrigue and for dominating women. Although not particularly handsome, he seduced them, satiated himself with them, abused them, and rented them out. Mlle Vaubergnier, arrayed in new finery and a new name, Mlle L'Ange, did not love him. In fact, she feared him. But she could not escape from his spell. He completed her education in the art of love. And when she had reached full ripeness—astonishing beauty, fabulous clothes, and enough polish to consort with the great, despite her fundamental vulgarity—he introduced her to the sieur Le Bel.

Le Bel was the first valet of Louis XV. His main function: to flush out "game" from the female population of France and to serve up "royal morsels" to his master in the Parc-aux-Cerfs,

Louis's pleasure house in Versailles.[6] Le Bel had them "cleaned up" *(décrassées)*, dressed up, and married off after one-night stands with dowries of 200,000 livres apiece. At an average of one a week, the cost came to 10 million livres a year. It was enough, our author calculates, to bankrupt the treasury, except that Louis began to run out of libido by 1768. That was when "comte" du Barry saw a chance to take the greatest gamble of his life. He would stake everything on Mlle L'Ange. If he could make her the mistress of the king, she would make him the master of the kingdom.

Thus, when Le Bel came by in search of "a real morsel for a king,"[7] du Barry proposed Mlle Ange, but with a crucial proviso: Versailles, not the Parc-aux-Cerfs. She would be presented to the king as "comtesse du Barry," the wife of du Barry's brother, and they could count on her temperament and training to do the rest. She soon succeeded in reviving Louis's senile sensuality beyond their wildest expectations. His previous women had been either ladies of quality, who knew little about lascivious technique, or commoners, who were too awestruck to employ it. Mme du Barry opened up a new world of pleasure to the aging voluptuary, and from that moment on he could never do without her.

At this point, located somewhere in mid-1768, Mme du Barry's story merges with the history of France, and the *Anecdotes* turn into a behind-the-scenes account of politics in Versailles. The generic shift from biography to contemporary history, or from *libelle* to *chronique scandaleuse,* occurs almost imperceptibly, thanks to the focus on du Barry. The author uses her as a foil to expose the nature of the political system around

Frontispiece to *Anecdotes sur Mme la comtesse du Barry.*
The epigraph reads:
Without wit, without talent, from the bosom of infamy
She was carried to the throne.
Never did she plot
Against an enemy cabal.
Oblivious to the threats of ambition,
A puppet of intriguers, she reigned by her charms alone.

MADAME LA COMTESSE DU BARRY.

her. So in order to understand the *Anecdotes* as a version of political history, it seems best to begin with its portrayal of du Barry herself.

Instead of blackening du Barry's character in the manner of most *libelles,* the narrator works in various shades of gray. He even expresses sympathy for her, despite the obvious bad faith of his arguments in her defense. She has no morals, it is true. But neither does she have any ambition, jealousy, or ill will, even toward her enemies. She simply improvises her way through life, following her "temperament," and picking up as many clothes as possible along the way. No matter how often she lets herself be sold, she remains essentially innocent, more sinned against than sinning. But she retains another trait that made her version of the standard story—the innocent provincial in the wicked city—particularly piquant: vulgarity. No matter how well covered with powder and perfume, she is always dropping a gross remark or slipping back into the behavior of a shopgirl. The author stresses her commonness more than her sexual misconduct, and it may have had more shock value for his readers. For other kings had had mistresses. But they were ladies, and they had added luster to the court. Du Barry provided nothing but lust, and she was bought, not conquered by means of royal gallantry.

Vulgar sensuality could look vital, however, in contrast to the general feebleness in high society. Once du Barry rose above the level of clerks and coiffeurs, she discovered a remarkable inverse correlation amongst her lovers: the higher their status, the lower their sexual capacity. Between the sheets (our omniscient author takes us everywhere) the wealthy and well-born prove to be incompetent or perverted. Dukes cannot have erections; prelates require flagellation; countesses favor lesbianism. When she wanted satisfaction for herself, du Barry descended to the servants' quarters.

This subtheme, the lackey as stud, had become a commonplace of erotic literature, but in the *Anecdotes* it acquired an almost democratic tone, as if to suggest the native superiority of the common people. It expressed du Barry's own philosophy, insofar as she had one. At the beginning of her career, she developed a fancy for a clerk who was trying to seduce his way upward in the world along a path that ran parallel to hers. He had caught the eye of an aged countess, but du Barry (then Mlle Lançon) warned him that he would get more pleasure from women like her. He could have her for 100 livres a month plus room and board, she explained in a note which our author quotes at length after correcting its primitive French (his heroine, he confesses, never really learned to write). She was far better value than "that old boat" of a countess or any woman over forty, even a princess of the royal blood. Social standing had no importance in matters of love. Did he not know that many great ladies preferred their lackeys to their husbands? Why else was his countess interested in the likes of him? He should consider that women came in two classes, the beautiful and the ugly. If he should choose the wrong one, too bad for him! She would move in with her hairdresser, who had a prettier face than he did anyhow.[8]

This primitive variety of sexual egalitarianism hardly amounts to an apology for the rights of man, much less woman. Mme du Barry never philosophizes like Thérèse. But by her indomitable naïveté, her disarming vulgarity, and her simpleminded passion for finery and sex, she serves as a perfect foil for everything around her. Her way of playing Cinderella exposes the hypocrisy and decadence of all the other players in the court. She acts out a story, and at the same time she supplies a moral to it— that is, her tale works in the manner of folklore, providing unsophisticated readers with a way to make sense of the baroque politics of Versailles. Before attempting to unravel that tale, however, we should take a quick look at the last years of Louis XV's reign as they have been understood by historians; for it is impossible to appreciate the import of *Anecdotes sur Mme la comtesse du Barry* without measuring the disparity between its account of events and the versions that have since gone down as history.

When historians look back over the political history of eighteenth-century France, they usually see the period 1769–74 as the greatest political crisis before the onset of the Revolution in 1787. Although they advance different interpretations of the crisis, they agree on its components. The government, dominated at first by the duc de Choiseul, labored under a triple burden. In foreign affairs, the humiliation of France in the Seven Years' War (1756–63) had badly damaged its position in the balance-of-power system. While Britain extended its empire overseas, France remained bound by ineffective alliances with Austria and Spain. The Family Compact, Choiseul's supposed masterstroke in diplomacy, committed France to defend Spain's claim to the Falkland Islands against Britain, but France could not afford another war on a global scale. Nor could it do anything to defend Poland, its ally in the East, against the other East European powers, who soon would carve it up in the first of the partitions (1772).

France's weakness in foreign affairs derived from its inability to put its finances in order at home, the second major problem of the government. An inadequate tax base—rooted in all sorts of exemptions and inequalities—and an archaic fiscal system made it impossible for the state to shake off a crippling deficit. It could not increase its revenues, because the parlements (law courts, not elected bodies like the British Parliament) fought new taxes tooth and nail by refusing to register royal decrees. Parlementary agitation constituted a third source of instability. In Brittany, the parlement became involved in a judicial battle with the duc d'Aiguillon, who as royal governor embodied the prestige of the crown. What had begun as a court case turned into a spectacular "affair," which was taken up by the Parlement of Paris and turned into a campaign to protect provincial liberties against the centralizing power of the state. In Versailles, d'Aiguillon was supported by the chancellor, R.-N.-C.-A. de Maupeou, and the so-called devout party, which opposed the "Choiseulistes" in the power alignments of the court. Choiseul and his partisans generally favored the parlements, having thrown their weight behind the parlementary crusade for the expulsion of the Jesuits (1764). In the end, Maupeou and his supporters persuaded Louis XV to crush the proceedings against d'Aiguillon, to override the parlements' opposition to new taxation, and to give in to Britain on the Falklands question. The realignment of policy meant the repudiation of Choiseul and nearly everything the government had stood for during the last twelve years.

The overthrow and exile of Choiseul on December 24, 1770,

reverberated throughout Europe as the most dramatic coup in French politics since the 1720s. But it seemed mild in comparison with the "revolution" produced by Maupeou in 1770–71. ("Revolution," as the French used the term in describing Maupeou's policies, implied a sudden, drastic change of policy, not the modern notion of the violent overthrow of a regime.) The chancellor dismantled and reconstructed the entire judicial system in a way that destroyed the parlements' ability to resist royal decrees. Magistrates from the Parlement of Paris went into exile; lawyers went on strike; but the new government held firm until the death of Louis XV on May 10, 1774. It was a government of vigorous reforms, which set out to restructure the kingdom's taxation system as well as its judiciary, while retreating from its exposed position in foreign affairs. Maupeou was joined by the parlements' nemesis, the duc d'Aiguillon, in the Foreign Ministry, and by the abbé Terray, a hard-liner on deficit reform, in the Finance Ministry. Despite some internal rivalries, they ruled together as a triumvirate; and they ruled firmly, promoting the centralized power of the state at the expense of traditional liberties and vested interests. Some historians have therefore interpreted the Maupeou government as a French version of enlightened despotism, although to many Frenchmen at the time it looked more like despotism pure and simple.[9]

Of course, we do not really know how the French perceived the great crisis of 1769–74: that is the fascination in reading *Anecdotes sur Mme la comtesse du Barry* today, because it provides a contemporary account of the events with a running commentary on them. Just as the narrator has ferreted out every scrap of evidence about du Barry's early life "according to the duty of a truthful, impartial, and perspicacious historian,"[10] so, he assures us, he has combed through every possible source about her life at court. He has captured letters, overheard conversations, and amassed a huge collection of all the political gossip that flowed between Versailles and Paris. By sifting through this material and piecing together "anecdotes," he has constructed a general history of the last years of Louis XV's reign.

The story goes as follows. When du Barry first appeared in Versailles, she cultivated the Choiseul party, following instructions sent from Paris by "comte Jean" du Barry, her former pimp and present brother-in-law, who directed her every move. (Immediately after her *mariage de convenance* to "comte Guillaume" du Barry, her husband was hustled off to the provinces, where he drank himself into oblivion.) But Choiseul's sister, the depraved duchesse de Grammont, rejected those advances, because she herself wanted to succeed to the position of *maîtresse en titre* left vacant by the death of Mme de Pompadour. She slipped into the king's bed and managed virtually to rape him. But she was too old and ugly to defend that territory once Mme du Barry appeared on the scene. So an epic battle began. On one side, Choiseul and his sister blackened du Barry's name by spreading information about her past which was supplied to them by the lieutenant general of police. On the other, du Barry tightened her grip on the king in the intimacy of the *petits apartements,* always taking her cues from comte Jean.

The courtiers studied every move in the daily life of the court for signs of shifts in the power system. Thus the appointment of his brother to the governorship of Strasbourg suggested that Choiseul still had the upper hand at the beginning of 1769, but he left earlier than usual for an Easter vacation in his country estate; and at a dinner before his departure, the king did not sit near him. Worse, after the dinner, the maréchal de Richelieu, a weathervane of royal favor, played twenty-one with Mme du Barry instead of whist with Choiseul.

By April 1769 it looked as though nothing could stop Mme du Barry's presentation to the court, which would amount to recognition as *maîtresse en titre* and would give her a powerful role to play in negotiations with ambassadors and ministers. True, no one of such low extraction had ever been elevated to such a position in Versailles, and the Choiseulistes still maneuvered desperately to save the situation. They enlisted Mesdames, the king's bigoted daughters and leaders of the "devout" party, in a campaign to create a united front against the bogus countess among the greatest ladies of the court. But comte Jean parried the blow by producing some documents from England, which supposedly proved that the du Barrys descended from the noble house of Barrymore. He also persuaded a down-at-the-heels lady-in-waiting, the comtesse de Béarn, to break ranks and act as du Barry's "godmother" in the presentation ceremony. Still, the king hesitated, undecided as always and susceptible to pressure from the "devout" party, which did not care for former prostitutes. But finally, after some rehearsing with comte Jean, du Barry threw herself at Louis's feet in a tearful scene, which brought him around. The great event took place on April 22, 1769. The news flew around the kingdom. Swarms of carriages descended on Versailles. Ambassadors dashed off dispatches to all the courts of Europe. And then everyone settled down to watch for the next world-historical event, the fall of Choiseul.

It seemed inevitable, given the passions of the women and their managers at court. The duchesse de Grammont withdrew in disgrace to her country estate, and du Barry was observed tossing two oranges in the air and chanting, "Jump Choiseul, jump Praslin!" meaning that she would catapult both the duke and his cousin, the duc de Praslin, a secretary of state who directed the Royal Council of Finance, out of office. But the king prevaricated; and the ladies of the court hesitated to rally to his mistress, fearing that a false step would make her fall from grace. Du Barry remained vulnerable because of her vulgarity. Thus, after losing a small fortune in after-dinner gambling one evening, she cried out, "I've been fried." While pocketing her money, a sharp-tongued courtier replied, "You should know what you are talking about, Madame"—a verbal slap, which everyone recognized as an allusion to her origins as the daughter of a cook.[11] But the king found her forthright manner refreshing. When du Barry moved into the rooms formerly occupied by Mme de Pompadour, her position began to look unassailable. Driven to desperation, Choiseul attempted a frontal attack. He planted a ravishing Creole marquise directly in the king's path. But Louis hardly looked at her; and from that point on, the courtiers drifted into du Barry's camp, while Choiseul's enemies secretly began to allot ministries and sinecures among themselves.

It took nearly two years to consummate the shift in power, so difficult was it for the monarch to get his mind around affairs of state. The du Barrys worked with Maupeou, who in turn forged an alliance with the duc d'Aiguillon based on their common hatred of the parlements. Not that the chancellor and the duke opposed the courts in principle. On the contrary, questions of principle did not interest anyone in any of the camps, including that of the parlements themselves. But d'Aiguillon's case before the Parlement of Paris provided Maupeou with an opportunity to cut the last shreds of favor that bound Choiseul to the king. The chancellor informed Louis that Choiseul was secretly plotting with the parlements to destroy d'Aiguillon, even at the cost of undermining the authority of the throne. The only solution was to quash the procedure against d'Aiguillon, dismiss Choiseul, and crush the parlements.

Such a spectacular change of policy far exceeded the capacity of the royal will: that was where du Barry came in. When she disappeared with the king into the *petits apartements,* she filled him with drink, dragged him to bed, and got him to sign anything she wanted. Comte Jean prepared the scenario and Maupeou the texts. Again and again between the sheets the king put his name to a fatal *lettre de cachet* exiling Choiseul. But he reversed himself when he came to his senses on the mornings after. In the end, however, his resistance collapsed, and on December 24, 1770, he banished Choiseul from court.

With Choiseul out of the way, his enemies took over the government and began to distribute plums. D'Aiguillon did not assume control of the Foreign Ministry at once. The scandalous suppression of his trial made him wait in the wings until he felt confident enough of du Barry's support to defy the disapproval of the public. The gift of a fabulous gold carriage—according to the narrator's calculations, it cost the equivalent of feeding all the poor of an entire province for several months—did the trick. Du Barry had him named Foreign Minister, while Terray fleeced taxpayers from the Finance Ministry and Maupeou completed the destruction of the parlements from the chancery.

All these machinations required a great deal of prowess in the royal bed. Du Barry succeeded remarkably in restoring the king's appetite, but his doctors warned that she was killing him. Comte Jean therefore did everything possible to milk the treasury before their time ran out. He wrote chits on the abbé Terray as if the Finance Minister were his private banker: 168,000 livres to cover losses from one session at a gaming table;

300,000 livres for one night with a whore; and so on. By mid-1773, he had run the treasury 5 million livres into the red, and Terray tried to stop the hemorrhaging by appealing to d'Aiguillon for support. For a moment, their combined opposition seemed likely to bring comte Jean to heel. But he threatened to run them out of office just as brutally as he had rammed them in. He never lost his grip on power, ruling the kingdom from gambling dens and brothels by means of runners whom he dispatched to Versailles, where du Barry awaited his orders, always subservient to his perverted will.

The scramble for booty opened up fissures within the triumvirate. Sensing that d'Aiguillon had supplanted him in du Barry's favor, Maupeou secretly cultivated d'Aiguillon's enemies in the "devout" party, which regrouped around the Dauphin (the future Louis XVI), who detested the royal mistress, owing to her mockery of his impotence and his wife's complexion. D'Aiguillon fought back by conspiring with Maupeou's enemy, the duc d'Orléans, in a plot to restore the parlements. More important, he gained access to the ultimate source of power by seducing du Barry himself and thus, in effect, cuckolding the king. Meanwhile, Terray felt threatened by both his colleagues; so he took over the Administration of the Royal Buildings and wooed the du Barrys by sprinkling châteaux throughout their clan. For her part, Mme du Barry settled for the modest château de Lucienne; but she took in so much jewelry (notably a pair of earrings worth 80,000 livres and a diamond hairpiece valued at 300,000 livres) that she passed as the most expensive mistress in the history of France. By the end of 1773, she had drained the treasury of 18 million livres, and the kingdom was as exhausted as the king.

While all these plots came to a climax and the treasury teetered on the verge of bankruptcy, Louis saved the situation by dying. What did him in? The narrator revealed the awful secret. Having become increasingly incapable of arousing the king in his last days, Mme du Barry turned procuress and held on to his favor by slipping fresh young girls into his bed. One girl, the daughter of a carpenter and a particularly reluctant victim, had an undetected case of smallpox. She gave it to the king, he died, and all France breathed a sigh of relief.

The moral of the story was clear: A pack of rogues had taken over the state, bled the country dry, and turned the monarchy into a despotism. Nothing could be further from the political history constructed subsequently by historians, however much they disagree among themselves. The *Anecdotes* hardly mentions foreign affairs. It says nothing about the deficit, except to deplore the millions drained from the treasury for gold carriages and gambling. It refers often to the destruction of the parlements, but it provides no details on Maupeou's reforms or on the ideological debates that surrounded them. Policy does not exist in its account of politics, nor do questions of principle. Politics is simply a scramble for power and a contest of personalities, one more evil than the other. The Choiseulistes are no better than the triumvirate. Even the parlements do not get an endorsement: they merely act as the only available obstacle to ministerial despotism, and there is nothing heroic about their demise. On one occasion the text refers favorably to an unnamed "patriot" writer, who defends the cause of the people,[12] but it provides no information about a patriot party or an opposition movement. Although the people themselves appear in a positive light, they remain far off in the background, suffering from an inadequate supply of bread and an excessive burden of taxation. So the story has no hero. It presents Cinderella as a slut, Prince Charming as a dirty old man. But it has a message: The French monarchy has degenerated into the vilest variety of ministerial despotism.

To be sure, it gets the story wrong. We know today that the state's bankruptcy came from an inadequate tax base and an inefficient administration rather than from the bad debts of comte Jean.[13] But we know next to nothing about how contemporaries saw the state. I believe their view of politics, however askew, was as crucial an ingredient of political reality as the collection of the *vingtième* (twentieth tax): hence the importance of understanding politics as folklore.

Of course, the text of *Anecdotes sur Mme la comtesse du Barry* is just a text, not a photograph of contemporary opinion. We do not even know how it was read. But we do know how it addressed its readers and how its rhetoric works. Speaking as a "historian," the author announced in the Preface that he was writing for "the simple citizen who, deprived by his obscure birth of access to the court and its glories, might sigh after such things." The standard moral pose—exposing the wickedness and vanity of life at the top—should not prevent us from seeing a less familiar function: that of the journalist. Now that nearly every moment in the life of the great is beamed into the living room of nearly every citizen, we can barely imagine a world where the great played out their lives in a world of their own, inaccessible to ordinary persons, even by means of newspapers. Neither court gazettes nor unofficial journals carried much information about the inner workings of Versailles in the eighteenth century.[14] But Versailles—the private life of the king, the power plays in the court—fascinated readers, and by 1770 the readers constituted a public. Although we know little about how that reading public developed, we know enough to assert that it was a phenomenon of a different order from the public that existed a century earlier, when the court withdrew from Paris to Versailles. In the last years of Louis XV's reign, the demand for the printed word had spread to the remotest corners of the kingdom; and readers everywhere demanded news.

Our author wrote to satisfy this function. He often used terms like "public" and "news," but he did not define them. In referring to the public, he implicitly distinguished between two types of audiences: a general reading public of "simple citizens" scattered about the kingdom, and a more sophisticated public of Parisians. He addressed his book primarily to the former, who knew little about life in *le monde* (Parisian high society); so he acted as their interpreter, decoding and explaining the puns, jokes, and allusions that seasoned the talk of the town.[15] When he spoke of the public in Paris, he evoked those who did the talking, usually in groups that gathered in parks and cafés to discuss the news of the day. These people belonged to *la ville* (the city) in contrast to *la cour* (the court). *La cour* and *la ville* had developed separate circuits of information.[16] But their systems intersected, and together they produced virtually all the news that circulated in the kingdom.

A typical news story concerned the king's habit of amusing himself in the *petits apartements* by brewing his own coffee. One day, when he was not looking, the coffee began to boil over, and du Barry called out: "Hey, France! Look out! Your coffee has flown the coop." ("Eh! La France, prends donc garde, ton café fout le camp.") The story illustrated du Barry's vulgarity and her familiar way of treating the king in private. It began as gossip spread by courtiers in Versailles; then a Parisian *nouvelliste* reported it in his manuscript gazette; and finally our author took it up as "an anecdote . . . from which one can infer what at that time was the general opinion of the public concerning her [du Barry's] domination of the king."[17] The text will not yield anything more in the way of social description or conceptual elaboration; but like other texts of its kind, it proceeds from the assumption that a public really existed and that its opinions had an important influence on politics, even though politics took place in the court of a supposedly absolute monarchy.

News came in many forms. But our author favored it at its juiciest, in the form of the *chronique scandaleuse,* anecdotes strung end to end to create a running account of misdeeds and malfeasance. The anecdotes operated on the principle, still familiar in popular journalism, that names make news, so they concentrated on the most famous figures in the kingdom. Their authors—known as *nouvellistes, gazetiers,* and *gens à anecdotes*—behaved like ancestors of today's inquiring reporters. They sniffed out scandal in high places. But one should not push the parallels with modern journalism too far, because the early modern newsmen did not belong to a profession. Many of them collected anecdotes for the fun of it. They scribbled them on scraps of paper, exchanged them among themselves, and accumulated them in portfolios, which they drew on in order to regale friends in cafés and salons. By assembling his anecdotes into a bulletin, a *nouvelliste* created a manuscript gazette *(gazette à la main);* and by printing them, a publisher produced a *chronique scandaleuse.*

As its title indicates, *Anecdotes sur Mme la comtesse du Barry* owes a great deal to these underground gazettes. It cites them constantly. In fact, after its first seventy pages, which cover du Barry's biography up to her installation at Versailles, it can hardly be distinguished from them. Unlike *Thérèse philosophe* and *L'An 2440,* whose narratives are cut up into short chapters, it has no chapters at all. It consists entirely of anecdotes, which flow past the reader in a continuous stream of 346 pages.[18] In this respect, the *Anecdotes* reads like the most famous of the printed *gazettes à la main,* the *Mémoires secrets pour servir à l'histoire de la république des lettres en France,* which has also been attributed to Pidansat de Mairobert. Mairobert or his collaborators may well have extracted tidbits about du Barry from their larger gazette or collections of anecdotes, attached them together with passages of fresh prose, and published them as a book, part biography, part *chronique scandaleuse.* Whatever the procedure, the result looks at times like a scrapbook. It contains so much disparate material that one sometimes loses the main thread of the story. But its collage quality makes it especially interesting, because it shows how a picture of events was built up out of all the scraps of news that circulated at the time. In fact, the *Anecdotes* describes this process: it provides not merely information but also information about the information, taking the reader into the heart of the communication system that it activated.

Consider, first, the nature of the anecdotes themselves. In the *Anecdotes sur Mme la comtesse du Barry* as in the *Mémoires secrets,* they appear as short bulletins, or "flashes" of news. The king brews his own coffee, and du Barry makes a vulgar remark when it boils over. The papal nuncio and the cardinal de la Roche-Aymon come to do business in the royal bedroom and hold du Barry's slippers for her as she slides, naked and giggling, out of the king's bed. In order to amuse du Barry, Maupeou presents her black servant boy, Zamore, with a pie. When Zamore cuts into it, a swarm of maybugs flies out. They settle in the chancellor's wig; and in pursuing them, Zamore plucks the wig off, exposing the bald pate of "the supreme chief of the King's justice" to a guffawing chorus of ladies-in-waiting.[19] Each incident takes the form of a tiny story, and each story conveys the same message: everything elevated—the Church, the judiciary, the throne—has been debased through the general depravation of the court.

The stories themselves make the point better than any abstract commentary. But comments also appear, in the form of *bons mots,* jokes, and songs; and they, too, constitute news. Thus the Dauphin is reported to have refused an invitation to dinner with du Barry by replying, "Madame, the Dauphine was not made to eat with a whore."[20] And the marquis de Chabrillant greets the news of du Barry's presentation at court with a cry of jubilation about his venereal disease: "Oh my happy *chaude pisse* [VD]. . . . She's the one who gave it to me, and she will certainly compensate me for it."[21] Most of the songs work variations on the same theme:

Tous nos laquais l'avaient eue,	All our lackeys had her,
Lorsque traînant dans la rue,	In the days when she walked the streets,
Vingt sols offerts à sa vue	And twenty sols offered up front
La déterminaient d'abord.	Made her accept at once.[22]

All the reportage, incidents and comments alike, illustrates a leitmotif embodied by du Barry herself: the degradation of the monarchy.

Thus the anecdotal news bulletins perform the same function on a small scale as the narrative of the book as a whole. They reduce the complex politics of the Old Regime to a storyline that can be grasped by any reader at any distance from the center of the action. And while telling the story, the narrator reflects on the process of storytelling itself. He shows how information flowed through the various media of the capital and how a journalist-historian must sift through it in order to perform two tasks: to understand what was happening, and to understand the contemporary understanding of what was happening. A second story therefore transpires through the first, one that delineates the formation of public opinion. It is directed to the sophisticated reader, just as the first is directed to the simpleminded. Both sophisticated and simple, self-reflective and reductionistic, the *Anecdotes sur Mme la comtesse du Barry* provides an extraordinarily rich view of news and the communication process two centuries ago.

Its richness can be appreciated by an examination of the author's coverage of the Choiseuliste offensive against du Barry during her first few months as Louis XV's mistress. He begins by quoting a *vaudeville,* or popular song, "La Bourbonnaise." The lyrics, composed to be sung to a well-known tune, contain one of the first allusions made in public to du Barry's arrival at court:

De paysanne	From a peasant
Elle est dame à présent	She is a lady now
. . .	. . .
On dit qu'elle a, ma foi,	They say she has, my goodness,
Plu même au Roi!	Even attracted the King![23]

How is one to interpret this piece of news? Our author is less concerned with what it says than with how it is transmitted and received. Its crude versification does not get high marks from Parisian connoisseurs, but it goes down well in the provinces. Such, at least, is the view expressed in one of the manuscript gazettes that he has collected and that he quotes as follows: "Although the words are very insipid, and the tune couldn't be sillier, it has reached the very farthest corners of France and is being sung even in villages. One can hardly move anywhere without hearing it."

The gazette also provides information about the way the song circulates in Paris: "The anecdote collectors {gens à anecdotes} have not been slow to take it up and to fatten their portfolios with it, and with all the commentaries necessary to make sense of it and to render it precious for posterity." Why all the excitement over such a mediocre composition? The insiders know that it announces a major event: the arrival of a new royal mistress. But our author knows still more.

He proceeds from the assumption that popular songs are weapons in power struggles, because power involves reputations and songs are "the surest, the most damaging, and the most indelible means of defamation."[24] Then he notes that "La Bourbonnaise" first appeared with the approbation of the lieutenant general of police, Antoine-Gabriel de Sartine, in a broadside dated June 16, 1768. He quotes it, apparently from this source, observing that the eighth stanza, which applies most explicitly to du Barry, does not exist in any printed version. Clearly he has paid close attention to every mode in which the text appeared—as it was sung in the streets, printed in broadsides, discussed in cafés, and reported in underground gazettes.

In doing so, he takes account of the fact that part of the underground runs through police headquarters. Instead of attempting the impossible task of eradicating all *gazettes à la main,* the police tried to control them by allowing vetted copies to circulate. Therefore, the report on "La Bourbonnaise" in the manuscript gazette was as revealing as the text of the song itself: "One imagines that it would have been difficult to circulate such a bulletin throughout Paris, if the gazeteer had not been secretly put up to it by a powerful protector." Conclusion: both the song and the anecdotes about it belong to a smear campaign being engineered by du Barry's most obvious enemy at court, the duc de Choiseul.

A Choiseuliste spin on news does not make it false; it makes it more interesting. So our author carefully observes the reporting in "the manuscript journal that often guides us in assembling the facts of our history."[25] Although he cites many sources, he refers most consistently to "the manuscript journal," "our manuscript," and "the precious manuscript," as if he drew on one main *gazette à la main* in piecing together his narrative.[26] Some, but not all, of those references coincide with entries in the *Mémoires secrets.*[27] So the *Anecdotes* and the *Mémoires secrets* tapped the same source in the journalistic underground. But our author uses this source to determine the slant of the facts rather than the facts themselves.

Thus, after quoting reports in the *gazette à la main* from October and November 1768 on the campaign to slander du Barry by song, he reproduces three articles from its December issues, which concern rumors about her presentation at court. The first he interprets as a frontal attack, "clever and full of malice," inspired by the Choiseulistes.[28] The second reveals a change in strategy and tone. It praises du Barry, but in a manner that is really meant as an alarm signal for the Choiseul camp: the beauty of the new mistress is so great and her hold on the king so powerful that all of Choiseul's protégés will soon be purged if they do not rally to the defense of their leader. And the third article is genuinely favorable to her, evidently because the gazeteer and the police are now bending to what has become an irreversible though still invisible shift of power.[29]

Meanwhile, acting as a gazeteer in his own right, the narrator continues to report all sorts of café gossip that blackens du Barry's reputation as soon as she begins to emerge as a public figure. He produces his own transcription of another "Bourbonnaise," far nastier than the first. It turns the same tune into a mock eulogy of du Barry's sexual prowess. Having mastered the classic sixteen positions of Aretino and everything else to be learned in the best brothels of Paris, she has succeeded in reviving "the old lecher" on the throne.[30] A similar song also derides the dwindling sexual energy of the king. In a pro-Choiseuliste account of a meeting of the king's council, it has Louis say to Maupeou:

Choiseul fait briller ma couronne	Choiseul makes my crown gleam
De la Baltique à l'Archipel;	From the Baltic to the Archipelago;
C'est là l'emploi que je lui donne:	This is the job I give to him:
Vous, prenez soin de mon B . . . . . {Bordel}	You, take care of my B . . . . [Bordello]

And Maupeou replies:

Que ne puis-je en votre ruelle,	If only at the side of your bed
Raffermir aussi votre V . . ! {Vit}	I could firm up your p . . . . [prick]![31]

The flood of "murmuring, indignation, and protest" vented in "epigrams, songs, and pasquinades"[32] also included prints. Our author cannot reproduce them, but he describes their character. One refers to a declaration by the magistrates in the Parlement of Paris that they oppose the monarch only for the good of the monarchy and that they would sacrifice their wealth, their liberty, and even their heads for that noble cause. The print shows the first president of the parlement presenting a sacrificial offering to the king and his ministers: purses for Terray, heads for Maupeou, and penises for du Barry.[33] The disaffection especially takes the form of jokes, which our author, like most scandalous chroniclers, reports as *on dits* ("one says"), attributing them to the omnipresent *on* who spoke for the general public. Thus one of the many off-color puns based on du Barry's name: "It is said *{on dit}* that the king can now fill a barrel [*baril,* pronounced as "Barry"]."[34] Given the descriptions, it is easy to imagine *on* joking with drinkers in a tavern:

QUESTION: Why was the comtesse du Barry the best street-walker in Paris?

ANSWER: Because she had to make only one leap to get from the Pont-Neuf to the Throne.[35]

Here *"on"* is a Parisian. To get the joke, a reader in the provinces required an explanation. So our author provides it: "The Pont-Neuf is a part of Paris where there are lots of prostitutes, and the Throne is a gate some distance away, at the entrance to the Faubourg Saint-Antoine."[36]

In short, the narrator produces news and commentary at the same time; then he comments on the commentary, building up a text that tells as much about the way news circulated as what the news was. It passed through all the media of the time, visual (prints, posters, graffiti), oral (jokes, rumors, songs), and written (manuscript gazettes and printed pamphlets). And when it appeared in the *Anecdotes,* it can be read not merely as an attempt to influence public opinion but also as an account of how public opinion came into being.

It is, of course, a tendentious account. By writing the *Anecdotes,* the author participated in the process he described, so his descriptions cannot be taken as objective and accurate. In fact, he made his own views clear at several points, when he stepped out from behind his usual rhetoric and addressed the reader in a tone of moral outrage. "It was time for all this depravity to come to an end," he exclaimed, as he began to recount the death of the king.[37] He heaped scorn on all the parties in the court and everyone in public life, including ministers, mistresses, and the king. The basic problem, as he presented it, went beyond the influence of individuals. It was systemic, a matter of corruption at the core of the monarchy, of the monarchy itself.

To be sure, the denunciation of corruption can be dismissed

as another form of rhetoric. Moralists had hurled jeremiads against monarchs since the time of the Old Testament prophets, and Parisians had bad-mouthed ministers for centuries before they exchanged pasquinades about the government of Louis XV. Did all the loose talk and moralizing in the *Anecdotes sur Mme la comtesse du Barry* really provide an indictment of the regime? That question raises a host of problems, which will be discussed in the next chapter. I would like to end this one by venturing out on a limb: the *Anecdotes,* I believe, were not just anecdotal; they were revolutionary.

By "revolutionary," however, I do not mean that they anticipated or promoted anything like the French Revolution. I mean they attacked the legitimacy of the Bourbon monarchy at its very foundation. Telling stories about the sex life of kings was not seditious in itself. The mistresses of François I, Henri IV, and Louis XIV (except for Mme de Maintenon) could be celebrated as conquests, like victories in war. They demonstrated royal virility, and they provided noble sport, for they were noble themselves, great ladies of the kind celebrated since the time of the troubadours. Du Barry was a whore. As the *libelles* insisted, anyone could have had her for a few pennies before she was let loose in Versailles. Many did, including the lowliest of lackeys. Instead of demonstrating the prowess of the king, she stood out in the *libelles* as a symbol of his feebleness and, worse, of the degradation of the throne. For she was merely a tool, used to revive the dying energy of a dirty old man in the sordid politics of a depraved court.

The symbolic dimension of the story shows up clearly, not only in the details selected by the narrator for his own "history" but also in the obscenities of the street talk he reports. "La Bourbonnaise," for example, emphasizes the symbols of the monarchy in recounting du Barry's use of whorehouse techniques to gain control of the king:

. . .

Elle a pris des leçons	She took some lessons
En maison bonne,	In a good house,
Chez Gourdan, chez Brisson;	At Gourdan's, at Brisson's;

Elle en sait long.	She knows all about it.
. . .	. . .
Le Roi s'écrie:	The King cries:
L'Ange, le beau talent!	The Angel, what a talent!
. . .	. . .
Viens sur mon trône,	Come on my throne,
Je veux te couronner,	I want to crown you,
Je veux te couronner,	I want to crown you,
Viens sur mon trône:	Come on my throne:
Comme sceptre prends mon V . . . {vit}	As a scepter take my p . . . . [prick]
Il vit, il vit!	It's alive, it's alive![38]

The feebleness of the royal penis provided street singers with a favorite motif:

Vous verrez sur les fleurs de lys	You will see on the fleurs de lys
Un vieil enfant débonnaire;	A debonair old infant;
Une élève de la Pâris	A student of Pâris [another Parisian madame]
Tient son v . . pour lisière	Holds his p. . . . as guiding strings.
Vous verrez le doyen des rois	You will see the dean of kings
Aux genoux d'une comtesse	On his knees before a countess
Dont jadis un écu tournois	Whom you could have had as your mistress
Eût fait votre maîtresse	For one *écu* some time ago.
Faire auprès d'elle cent efforts	He tries a hundred things with her
Dans la route lubrique,	In their lubricious commerce,
Pour faire mouvoir les ressorts	To set the works in motion
De sa machine antique.	Of his ancient machine.
Mais c'est en vain qu'il a recours	But it is in vain that he has recourse
A la grande prêtresse;	To the high priestess;
Au beau milieu de son discours	Right in the middle of the action
Il retombe en faiblesse.	He falls back into feebleness.

De cette lacune, dit-on,	From this insufficiency, it's said,
En son âme elle enrage;	She rages secretly inside;
Mais un petit coup d'Aiguillon	But a little help from d'Aiguillon
Bientôt la dédommage.	Soon compensates her for it.
Au premier bobo qu'il aura,	At the first infection [i.e., venereal disease] that he gets
Notre bon Sire, en prière,	Our good Sire will, through his prayers,
Pieusement la logera	Send her to dwell
A la Salpêtrière.	In the Salpêtrière [a house of detention used for whores].

As an exegesis, the narrator adds: "It was widely believed in Versailles that the favorite slept with the duc d'Aiguillon: it was Louis XV's lot to be cuckolded by his ministers."[39]

Throne, crown, fleurs de lys all appear as so much ludicrous paraphernalia. The scepter looks as weak as the king's penis, and the king has been reduced to a stock figure in a dirty joke. He is an impotent old lecher and a cuckold. By fouling his body, du Barry has drained him of his charisma and emptied the power from the symbolic apparatus of the monarchy.

This interpretation may seem extravagant, if one forgets that the body of the king was still sacred to many Frenchmen in the eighteenth century. By touching it, many of them believed they could be cured of scrofula. So when the Parisians sang about Louis XV's impotence in the streets, they struck at the religious roots of his legitimacy. Instead of a divine monarch, they spread the idea of a "feeble tyrant":

Tu n'es plus qu'un tyran débile,	You are nothing more but a feeble tyrant,
Qu'un vil automate imbécile,	A vile, imbecilic automaton,
Esclave de la du Barry;	The slave of du Barry.
Du Gange jusqu' à la Tamise	From the Ganges to the Thames
On te honnit, on te méprise.	You are shamed and scorned.[40]

The desascralization of the king was expressed most strongly in a parody of the *Pater Noster:*

Our Father, who art in Versailles. Abhorred be Thy name. Thy kingdom is shaken. Thy will is no longer done on earth or in heaven. Give us back this day our daily bread, which Thou hast taken from us. Forgive Thy parlements who have upheld Thy interests, as Thou forgiveth those ministers who have sold them. Be not led into temptation by du Barry. But deliver us from that devil of a chancellor. Amen![41]

The French could no more see their king as a father than as a god. He had lost the last shreds of his legitimacy. Such, at least, was the message conveyed by the public noises of Paris as picked up by one of the most widely diffused books of the pre-Revolutionary era. Did listeners and readers merely laugh and shrug it off? We do not know. We have only the testimony of another book, *Remarques sur les Anecdotes de Madame la comtesse du Barry* (1777), which circulated in the wake of the first. It, too, quoted the *Pater Noster,* and then by way of commentary it described the *Anecdotes* as

a defamatory libel against the state, which does not stop half-way in its satire, but climbs onto the throne and directly attacks the King. . . . In England, where the King is only the first citizen of the republic, such anti-monarchical satire does not strike home. But in an absolute monarchy, where the prince's authority is the supreme law, it overthrows every-thing, because it strikes at the constitution itself.[42]

Can these *Remarques* be taken literally? Certainly not. They provide only an interpretation of an interpretation, and they occur in yet another *libelle.* So now we must consider the larger dimensions of the problem and leave the story of du Barry where we found it, caught in the midst of a thicket of texts.

Do Books
Cause
Revolutions?

PART THREE

Chapter 6

Diffusion vs. Discourse

AFTER EMERGING FROM THIS THICKET of texts, statistics, and contemporary testimony, the reader may feel an urge to step back, catch a breath, and ask what is at stake in such detailed study. Mornet's question, with which we began, bears on some of the truly big questions of modern history: How did ideas penetrate into society two centuries ago? What was the connection between the Enlightenment and the French Revolution? What were the Revolution's ideological origins? To be sure, those issues are so complex and they have been worked over so often that they may never yield definitive answers. We certainly cannot answer them simply by pointing to the existence of a corpus of forbidden books and by adding up the figures on our best-seller list. On the contrary, I think we should repress the desire for bottom-line solutions. The significant problems in history involve too vast a range of human experience to be reduced to common denominators. In struggling with them, the historian works like a diagnostician who searches for patterns in symptoms rather than a physicist who turns hard data into firm conclusions.

But some diagnoses are more accurate than others. Even if we cannot recreate the literary world of pre-Revolutionary France in all its complexity, we can identify the books that actually circulated outside the law. And a full investigation of the forbidden literature should bring us closer to understanding the collapse of the Old Regime. It might even make it possible to sort out some of the confusion that has fallen upon intellectual history in general. I would like to attempt some preliminary sorting out and then to suggest ways in which the study of forbidden books can be connected with the classic questions about the origins of the French Revolution.

In retrospect, it seems clear that a parting of the ways took place in intellectual history in the late 1960s. On one side, scholars attracted by social history set off in pursuit of subjects such as the spread of ideology, popular culture, and collective *mentalités.* On the other, scholars inclined toward philosophy concentrated on the analysis of texts, intertextuality, and the linguistic systems that constituted schools of thought. The bifurcating and branching produced a profusion of specialized fields, but two main tendencies stood out, one on each side of the main divide. The first can be characterized as "diffusion studies." It especially involved research on books and the printed word as a force in history, and it had its intellectual home in Paris, where Henri-Jean Martin, Roger Chartier, Daniel Roche, Frédéric Barbier, and others built *histoire du livre* ("book history") into a distinctive discipline. The second tendency came to be known as "discourse analysis." It concerned the history of political thought, and it flourished in Cambridge, England, where John Pocock (a New Zealander who later migrated to the United States), Quentin Skinner, John Dunn, and Richard Tuck transformed the understanding of political culture in the English-speaking world.

Each of these tendencies had peculiar strengths and weaknesses. The diffusionists challenged the prevailing great-book, great-man view of literary history. Where earlier scholars had concentrated on a canon of classics, they tried to reconstruct literary culture in its entirety. They traced changes in book production as a whole, studied popular genres like chapbooks and almanacs, examined the role of publishers and booksellers as well as that of authors, and made a start in the investigation of reception and reading. In their ways of conceiving of their subject, they drew on the work of sociologists, notably Pierre

Bourdieu, Norbert Elias, and Jürgen Habermas. In their ways of working, they favored quantitative analysis and the methods of social history developed in the *Annales* school. Their goal, like that of their fellow travelers among the *Annalistes,* was to develop a "total history" of the book, one that would be social, economic, intellectual, and political at the same time. In many ways they actually achieved that goal. If their success can be measured by the influence of their research, they must be credited with setting standards that have been emulated throughout the West—from the publication of the first volume of *Livre et société,* edited by François Furet, in 1965, to the appearance of the last volume of *Histoire de l'édition française,* edited by Henri-Jean Martin and Roger Chartier, in 1986. But the Parisian book historians also ran into problems, some of which they inherited from the diffusion studies developed at the beginning of the century by Daniel Mornet. The Mornet model operated like a French filter coffee machine: it assumed that ideas trickled down from an intellectual elite to the general public, and that once they became absorbed in the body politic, they stimulated a revolutionary spirit—that is, they functioned as a necessary if not a sufficient cause of the French Revolution.

In Mornet's hands, the trickle-down view of intellectual history led to a wonderfully rich tableau of cultural life under the Old Regime. His *Origines intellectuelles de la Révolution française* (1933) served as a blueprint for much of the research produced by the *Annales* historians after World War II—on provincial academies, education, Freemasonry, intellectuals, journalism, libraries, de-Christianization, and public opinion, as well as publishing and the book trade. But Mornet squeezed all this material within a narrow frame. Everything fell into the same pattern, demonstrating a unilinear movement from the Enlightenment to the Revolution. In the end, therefore, Mornet's argument turned tautological. It assumed the cause from the effect, reasoning backwards from 1789 to a starting point in the heads of Voltaire and the other freethinkers of the early century. Despite its emphasis on cultural intermediaries and social institutions, Mornet's version of intellectual history could ultimately be reduced to the formula that it was meant to attack. In the last analysis, the Enlightenment was driven by great men's great books, and the Revolution was inspired by the Enlightenment: it remained "la faute à Voltaire, la faute à Rousseau."

In order to shake off the constraints built into Mornet's model, the historians currently associated with the *Annales* have shifted from intellectual to sociocultural history. Daniel Roche, Roger Chartier, Jacques Revel, Arlette Farge, Dominique Julia, and Michel Vovelle (a fellow traveler, if not exactly a member of the *Annales* school) have studied cultural activities as social phenomena without reducing them to the influence of Enlightened ideas. Their work is excellent enough to stand on its own, but it does not meet the challenge of Mornet's original question, which refuses to go away: If the intellectual origins of the Revolution cannot be identified with the Enlightenment, what were they?

In a recent attempt to take up this challenge, Roger Chartier has argued that the origins were not intellectual at all, but rather cultural. He cites first and foremost an expansion of the realm of private life, and then a series of other changes: secularization of religion, an increase of litigation among the lower classes, a decrease of participation in public rituals by the king, and especially the influence of literature on the development of what Jürgen Habermas calls the "bourgeois public sphere." But although he weaves those arguments in and out of a wonderfully rich synthesis of research on the Old Regime, Chartier never connects them with the outbreak of the Revolution.[1]

The "bourgeois public sphere" won't do as a connection. When translated from German *(bürgerliche Öffentlichkeit)* into French, it came out as "public space" *(espace public),* that is, it became reified, as if it were an actual phenomenon producing effects in history. Habermas had not meant it that way at all. He had used *Öffentlichkeit* ("public," "publicity," or "publicness" in English) metaphorically, to depict the interplay of public opinion and modes of communication in modern society. By "bourgeois," he referred to something much more solid: the conquering class of Marxist social history. But since 1962, when Habermas originally published his thesis, historians have generally abandoned the notion of a rising bourgeoisie as an explanation of the French Revolution. Why should they adopt the rise of the "bourgeois public sphere" in its place?[2]

Other elements of sociocultural history have more substance, but they, too, seem unconnected with the events of 1787–89. Shifts could have occurred in attitudes toward the family, private life, the afterlife, literature, masters of guilds, and even royal ceremonies without disposing the French to overthrow the Old Regime. Such shifts took place everywhere in Western Europe, notably in countries like England and Germany that did not erupt in revolution. They probably belonged to a general transformation of world view—something akin to Max Weber's "disenchantment of the world"—that took place over a long time span everywhere in the West. Why identify them with the Revolution in France? Why substitute them for the Enlightenment, Jansenism, and parlementary constitutionalism in an account of the Revolution's origins? After all, the revolutionaries traced their principles back to Montesquieu, Voltaire, and Rousseau. They did not associate the fall of the Old Regime with anything as nebulous as the expansion of the sphere of private life; and once they seized power, they did everything possible to subordinate the private realm to the all-pervasive demands of the state.

Of course, "origins" are always construed retrospectively, and many of them may escape the consciousness of contemporaries. Perhaps, as Chartier claims, the revolutionaries invoked the Enlightenment in order to legitimate their rule by providing it with a respectable intellectual pedigree.[3] But even if that were so, it does not prove that the ideas of the *philosophes* had no part in the origins of the Revolution. The Enlightenment had established itself firmly in contemporary consciousness by the end of the 1750s. It cannot simply be dismissed by invoking the superior explanatory power of cultural history. If cultural history is really to explain the Revolution's origins, it must establish connections between attitudes and behavior patterns on the one hand and revolutionary action on the other. Otherwise, it will simply displace onto another level—the level of culture, broadly understood—the very difficulty that it found so objectionable in Mornet's account of the diffusion of ideas.

Like diffusion studies, discourse analysis began from a sense of dissatisfaction with the conventional history of ideas. It challenged the very notion of an idea as a unit of thought or an autonomous container of meaning. This notion lay at the heart of the history developed by the *Journal of the History of Ideas* and its founder, Arthur Lovejoy, who was probably the most influential intellectual historian of twentieth-century America. Lovejoy isolated "idea units" as the object of study, and followed them as they were passed on from philosopher to philosopher across the centuries. To his critics, this procedure sailed past the main point in the understanding of meaning. As linguistic philosophers from Wittgenstein onward had demonstrated, meaning did not inhere in ideas. It was transmitted by utterances and construed by interlocutors; it activated conventional patterns of speech; and it operated contextually, so that the same words could convey different messages in different times and texts.

In fact, Lovejoy had shown great sensitivity to philosophical contexts in his masterpiece, *The Great Chain of Being* (1936), which traced notions of ontological hierarchy across two thousand years. But his book seemed fundamentally misconceived to his critics, just as the *Origines intellectuelles de la Révolution française* had appeared inadequate to the successors of Mornet. Instead of isolating key ideas, the new generation of intellectual historians tried to reconstruct discourse—that is, they treated the great works of political theory as part of an ongoing argument about politics, a general debate couched in a particular idiom or a system of meaning peculiar to a certain society at a certain time. Therefore, when they held the conventional history of political thought up to inspection, they found it shot through with anachronism. To them, Hobbes, Harrington, and Locke did not point in a straight line to modern political faiths but looked backward—to the politics of Renaissance courts and a tradition of civic humanism derived from the ancients. The great thinkers of the seventeenth century spoke to seventeenth-century issues in seventeenth-century language. Language itself was the key to understanding them, language as it spilled over treatises and coursed through contemporary debates about the patriarchal character of royal authority, the legitimacy of standing armies, the exclusion of Catholics from the throne, and other questions that have now disappeared from politics.[4]

Because linguistic philosophy remained inscrutably "Anglo-

Saxon" when viewed from across the Channel, the English manner of reworking the history of political thought did not take hold in France. The French combined history and philosophy in their own way, one that began in the history of science with Georges Canguilhem and that broadened out in the work of Michel Foucault to include a wide range of discursive practices. "Discourse," however, meant one thing in Cambridge, another in Paris. To Foucault and his followers, it connoted power—social constraints rooted in cognition and embodied in institutions.[5] So, in effect, there developed two discourses on discourse, each of which went its own way from the early 1960s. Recently, however, they seem to have come together at a strategic site, the Centre Raymond-Aron in Paris. Here, in the protective shadow of the *Annales* school, a remarkable mixing of genres and traditions has occurred. Philosophers and historians, French and Anglo-Americans, have joined forces in an assault on the sector of the eighteenth century that has resisted scholarly understanding since the time of Mornet: the point at which the French Revolution intersected with the Enlightenment; or, to put it differently, the point of convergence between politics and philosophy.

The attack on this problem has been led by François Furet, who began as a social historian attempting to modernize Mornet, and later converted to political history in a philosophical vein. Furet does not hesitate to ascribe the intellectual origins of the Revolution to the Enlightenment,[6] yet he does not revert to the old history of ideas. He and his followers, notably Marcel Gauchet and Keith Baker, understand the Revolution in the last analysis as the working out in politics of Rousseau's theories in philosophy. But they do not assume a straightforward process by which the revolutionaries applied the precepts of the *Social Contract*. Instead, they see a Rousseauistic discourse sweeping everything before it in the course of events from 1789 through the Terror and the Directory.

The strongest version of this argument and the one most influenced by the Cambridge philosopher-historians appears in *Inventing the French Revolution* (1990) by Keith Baker. Baker reduces the political thought of the Old Regime to three discursive "languages": a discourse of will, which he identifies with Rousseau; a discourse of reason, expounded by Turgot; and a discourse of justice, articulated most effectively by the apologist of the parlements, Louis-Adrien Le Paige. As he understands it, the first few months of the Revolution constituted an epic struggle for supremacy among these discourses; and the decisive moment came, not on July 14 or August 4 or October 5, but rather on September 11, when the National Assembly voted for a suspensive rather than an absolute royal veto. At that point, Baker argues, the Assembly committed itself to a Rousseauistic notion of popular sovereignty—that is, the discourse of will gained the upper hand, and from then on nothing could stop the Revolution from sliding into the Terror.[7]

Marcel Gauchet advances a similar argument. He sees a "Rousseauistic category" overwhelming everything else in the debates on the Declaration of the Rights of Man and of the Citizen. In conformity with Rousseau's concept of the General Will, it was "a way of conceiving liberty that prevented the realization of liberty." Once installed at the heart of the revolutionary process, it defined an "intellectual space" that stretched from 1789 to 1795 and made the Terror inherent in the Revolution from the beginning.[8] François Furet also traces the Terror back to discursive moves made in 1789, and he, too, adopts a linguistic concept of power, which he conveys by spatial metaphors. He argues that by claiming in Rousseauistic fashion to express the will of the people, the revolutionaries installed a discourse of sovereignty in the "empty space" vacated by the absolute monarchy. Having displaced absolutism, the word itself, *la parole,* became absolute. To speak for the General Will was to exercise it. Thus the representation of power became power; politics turned into language; and the "semiotic circuit" ruled supreme. Although Furet's notion of semiotics remains obscure, the implications of his argument are clear: from the first months of the Revolution, discourse dictated the course of events, and the philosophizing of the revolutionaries led directly to the Terror.[9]

Furet and his followers produced a bolt of intellectual energy which galvanized the study of the Revolution at a time when it seemed to be stalled after decades of bickering between Marxists and revisionists. Their work provided an intelligent rereading of many treatises and debates, and it had the advantage of confronting the problem of how ideas intermixed with events. But it also suffered from some weaknesses of discourse analysis. I would like to discuss three.

First, by imposing a discursive model on the flow of events, it left no room for contingency, accident, and the revolutionary process itself. Political histories, from the time of Aulard if not Guizot and Thiers, had shown how the Revolution became increasingly radical in response to events that occurred after 1789: religious schism, war, counter-revolutionary uprisings, pressure from the Parisian Sections, and economic disaster. Although he resurrects a great deal of nineteenth-century historiography, Furet disparages this traditional kind of narrative by linking it to Aulard's famous "thesis of circumstances"—that is, the notion that the Terror was not inherent in the Revolution from the beginning but rather was improvised piece by piece under the pressure of contingencies. In his own narrative history, Furet had actually come close to adopting Aulard's thesis. He had treated the Terror as an accidental episode, when the Revolution skidded off course—a course that it had set for itself in 1789 and to which it returned after 1794.[10]

I think there is a great deal to be said for the "thesis of circumstances," unfashionable as it is. Of course, it does not explain everything, and one must allow for an ideological, quasi-religious element in the convictions of many revolutionaries, especially during the tragic "Great Terror" in the summer of 1794. The guillotining continued unabated, even though the French victory at Fleurus on June 26, 1794, removed the threat of military invasion a full month before the overthrow of Robespierre. But the momentum of the Terror and the power of the Robespierrists could not be stopped overnight. The deputies themselves were terrorized, and whatever their philosophical principles, they were eager to dismantle the Terror once they could do so without risking their own heads. Even the men who sat on the Committee of Public Safety were rather ordinary mortals trying to cope with extraordinary events. To see how they did so, imperfectly and from day to day, one need only read through the twenty-eight volumes of Aulard's *Recueil des Actes du Comité de salut public,* or, if the appetite for documentation wanes, take a shortcut through Robert Palmer's *Twelve*

Who Ruled.[11] The old-fashioned narrative history of Aulard and Palmer provides a far more convincing explanation of the Terror than any exegesis of philosophizing in 1789, even the linguistic variety embellished with spatial metaphors. For my part, I confess that I cannot understand what "intellectual space" might be.

Second, the philosophical explanations of the Revolution do not go far enough toward a history of meaning. They restrict themselves to a few treatises and the record of parliamentary debates. But the revolutionaries' understanding of their situation was shaped by all sorts of phenomena, most of which took place outside the debating halls. When they declared feudalism abolished on the night of August 4, 1789, they had a vivid sense of châteaux burning and heads on the end of pikes. Even when they took up positions on parliamentary questions, they did not simply consult political theory; they oriented themselves in a concrete manner by watching the play of factions. For example, there was nothing inherently radical or conservative in the notion of a parliamentary government in which ministers were chosen from and responsible to the National Assembly. But when Mirabeau championed that idea in November 1789, he signaled to the deputies that it belonged to the program of the Right; and when Robespierre opposed it, he indicated its repugnance to the Left—even though he would champion a powerful parliamentary executive in 1793.

In short, meaning did not come prepackaged in pre-revolutionary discourses: it inhered in the revolutionary process itself. It had to do with personalities, factions, perceptions of political strategies, the shifting categories of Left and Right, and all sorts of pressures exerted on the deputies from the surrounding society. Discourse analysis should take account of those factors, and of others still further removed from formal thought: emotion, imagination, prejudice, implicit assumptions, collective representations, cognitive categories, the whole spectrum of thinking and feeling that once belonged to the research agenda of the history of *mentalités*. By turning their back on that kind of history, the discourse analysts have taken up positions that can hardly be distinguished from those of the old-fashioned history of ideas. Their difficulty does not come from embracing a semiotic view of political conflict but from failing to take semiotics far enough—into barnyards and streets, where ordinary people refashioned their view of the world.[12]

Third, discourse analysis acknowledges the need to study the passage from ideas to action but does not come to grips with the difficulties of doing so. That problem remained in the background in Cambridge, where the philosopher-historians limited their inquiry to political theory. But it took stage center in Paris, where they set out to explain events, and above all the supreme event of early modern history, the French Revolution. Like Mornet, they assumed the Revolution had some genetic connection with the Enlightenment. But after raising the "old and immense question" of the Revolution's relation to the Enlightenment, François Furet dismisses it and, like Marcel Gauchet, asserts the existence of an "intellectual space" in a temporal frame that extended from 1789 to 1800 and that derived in some unexplained manner from the philosophizing of the Old Regime.[13]

Keith Baker provides a more satisfactory formulation of the problem, because he relates the revolutionary debates to philosophical positions staked out long before 1789. But his identification of discourses appears arbitrary. Why separate the complex corpus of political writing from the Old Regime into three distinct and autonomous "languages"? Why discourses of will, reason, and justice rather than other ways of talking about and acting out royal authority, such as the paternal, the religious, the ceremonial, and the theatrical? Some attention to diffusion studies might be helpful in this respect, because if one could identify the most widespread political tracts, one could look for intertextuality from the perspective of what appealed to eighteenth-century Frenchmen rather than twentieth-century professors.[14]

Even then, however, problems would remain, above all the problems of understanding how the diffusion of books affects public opinion and how public opinion inflects political action. Both Keith Baker and Mona Ozouf have written excellent articles on the idea of public opinion as it was expressed in the works of the *philosophes,* but they seem to assume that it is adequate to study the idea of the thing rather than the thing itself.[15]

To be sure, historians have no more access than philosophers to things-in-themselves. Events come wrapped in meanings, so we cannot separate action from interpretation or strip history down to pure events. But it does not follow that events are construed exclusively through philosophic discourse or that ordinary people depend on philosophers to find meaning in their lives. The making of meaning occurs at street level as well as in books. The shaping of public opinion takes place in markets and taverns as well as in *sociétés de pensée*. To understand how publics made sense of events, one must extend the inquiry beyond the works of philosophers and into the communication networks of everyday life.

But the subject of public opinion takes us into considerations that belong to a later part of the argument. For the moment, it seems better to pause over the possibility of combining the two strains of intellectual history in a way that would maximize their strong points and minimize their weaknesses.

Chapter 7

Communication
Networks

ზ⚘ლ

"DO BOOKS MAKE REVOLUTIONS?"[1] To put the issue so bluntly is to step into that insidious French trap, the *question mal posée*—that is, to distort the problem by oversimplifying it. An affirmative answer seems to assume a linear notion of causality, as if one can argue from the sale of a book to its reading, the convictions of the readers, the mobilization of public opinion, and the engagement of the public in revolutionary action. Clearly that will not do. The straightforward, cause-and-effect model of diffusion fails to take account of independent factors, not simply non-literary sources of public opinion but reading itself as an active appropriation rather than a passive reception of texts. Is the study of book diffusion therefore irrelevant to the understanding of the Revolution's origins? Instead of rushing to that conclusion, I would like to propose a more complex model.

The advantage of book history as a kind of diffusion study is that one knows precisely what is being diffused: not discourse, not public opinion, but books. Of course, books are many things—objects of manufacture, works of art, articles of commercial exchange, and vehicles of ideas. So the study of them spills over into many fields, such as the history of labor, art, and business. It is particularly valuable in intellectual history, because it provides a way of minimizing anachronism. Instead of beginning with the question, "How widespread was the Enlightenment?", the historian can determine which books actually circulated most widely during the eighteenth century. Then he (or she) can set to work with categories of his own devising in an attempt to measure specific sectors of the literary market. With enough information and a valid set of criteria, he might even be able to calculate the demand for Enlightenment—that is, to determine the place of the works of the *philosophes* within the general pattern of literary culture; to locate the Enlightenment, so to speak, without beginning by looking for it.

This procedure will not yield foolproof results, and it does not bear directly on the problem of relating the Enlightenment to the Revolution. But it will help the diffusionist cope with the criticism of the discourse analysts. The latter rightly object to the notion of ideas as "units" that can be traced through the body politic like radioactive particles being monitored in the bloodstream. But that objection does not apply to books. Books are physical objects that circulate through channels of trade. Their production, distribution, and (to a certain extent) consumption can be studied systematically. One can think of the system as a communications circuit, which runs from author to reader—and ultimately back to the author again, because authors respond to readers, reviewers, and other sources of information and inspiration in the surrounding society. The circuit can be represented schematically as in Figure 7.1:[2]

In comparison with a unilinear conception of diffusion, this model has two advantages. First, it rejects the notion of downward percolation in favor of an organic view, one that posits the penetration of society by a communication network composed of arteries, veins, and capillaries, and that takes account of every stage in the process of production and distribution. It could be designed somewhat differently when applied to other periods of history, other cultures, and other print media such as newspapers, pamphlets, and broadsheets. But the principle remains the same: to represent the communication process in a way that does justice to its systemic nature and the interconnection of its parts.

Second, instead of assuming a self-sufficient, machinelike

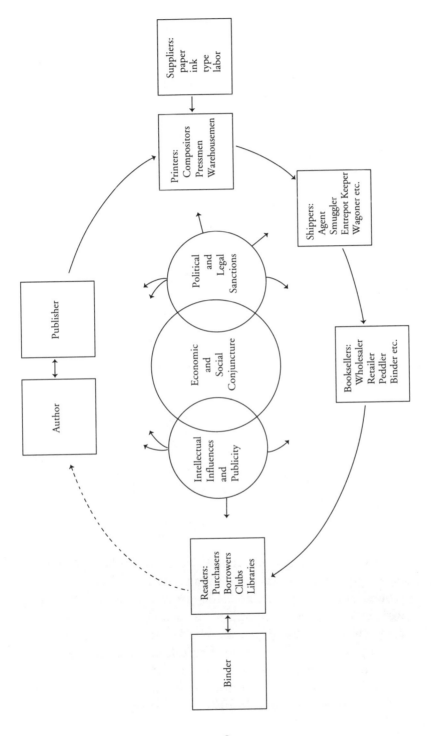

mode of functioning, the model allows for outside influences at every stage. Authors, publishers, printers, booksellers, librarians, and readers constantly modified their behavior in response to pressure from the state, the Church, the economy, and various social groups. Until recently, most research has concentrated on authors. Their texts often bore the mark of patronage, censorship, enmities, rivalries, and the need for income. But when they appeared in print, the texts were shaped by the artisans who set the type, composed the formes, and pulled the bars of the presses. Publishers also molded the meaning of texts when they put together speculations, deciding on market strategies, formats, illustrations, type, and book design. And the importance of booksellers as cultural middlemen can hardly be overestimated. It was in the bookseller's shop—or stall, or wagon, or the pack on his back—that supply met demand and books came into the hands of readers.

Reading remains the most difficult stage in the cycle to understand. We still have only a vague sense of how readers construed texts, whether alone or in groups, aloud or silently, in libraries or under spreading chestnut trees. But the lack of information about reception does not mean that we should abandon the notion of capturing the contemporary experience of literature. For literature was not limited to authors and readers or readers and texts. It took shape throughout the entire communication system; and because the system was permeable at every point to outside influences, we can study all the ingredients that went into the formulation of literature. Our knowledge of production and distribution can compensate, to a certain extent, for the limitations of our knowledge of reception.

Reception remains crucial nonetheless to a fuller understanding of literary experience. How can we devise a strategy to get around our inadequate knowledge of reader response? Playing with models won't accomplish much unless it helps to orient research. In the case of research on French forbidden books, it actually turns out to be quite helpful, because the qualitative evidence complements the quantitative. As indicated in chapter 1, the way publishers and booksellers discussed and handled *livres philosophiques* reveals a great deal about the taste for the taboo among readers, and the statistics of book sales provide a clear picture of literary demand.[3] But to advance the argument beyond that stage, we need to shift from questions of diffusion to questions of meaning—that is, to move into the area of discourse analysis.

One could begin by taking the best-seller list as an adequate index to the preferences of eighteenth-century readers and then read one's way through it. That strategy may sound suspiciously straightforward, but there is much to be said for it. It opens up the possibility of finding intertextual patterns without relying on anachronistic notions of literary culture. If we can identify the entire corpus of literature that circulated outside the law, we should be able to make reasonable inferences about what contemporaries saw as threatening to the regime. But we still must face an uncomfortable question: How can we be sure that our readings of that literature approximate those of Frenchmen who lived two hundred years ago? At this point, we need to take a closer look at the notion of reading as appropriation.

Roger Chartier uses that notion to undercut the argument that the forbidden books produced a consistent pattern of reader response and thus affected public opinion. If readers appropriated texts in their own manner, willfully projecting all sorts of personal ideas onto books instead of passively receiving messages printed in them, their experience could have been endlessly varied. They could have made whatever they wanted out of literature. So it is not very revealing to discover what they read, because one cannot know how they read it.[4]

Chartier draws on the work of Michel de Certeau and Richard Hoggart for a theoretical account of appropriation; and for historical examples, he cites the research of Carlo Ginzburg and myself. De Certeau certainly stressed the "indefinite plurality of meanings" inherent in the act of reading.[5] A generous free spirit himself, he protested against the idea that ordinary people were simpletons who could be molded like wax by the media. But he did not develop that protest into a sustained and substantiated theory of how people actually did read, and his insights are not entirely confirmed by Hoggart's.[6] Although Hoggart also emphasized the positive, independent nature of working-class culture, he did not go on to argue that ordinary readers made whatever they wanted out of books. On the contrary, he emphasized the cultural determinants of their experience. Their culture operated like the snug, protective, overheated, all-enveloping atmosphere of their parlors: it absorbed alien elements into a pattern of its own. Far from promoting individualism or idiosyncrasy, it stamped its own character on everything that came within its range.[7]

Carlo Ginzburg's study of a lower-class reader, the sixteenth-century miller named Menocchio, carries the same argument even further. Ginzburg does not merely demonstrate that Menocchio read aggressively, transforming Renaissance texts into his own terms, but claims that Menocchio derived those terms from a materialist cosmology, which had remained hidden in popular culture since antiquity. In my own research on a reader from eighteenth-century La Rochelle, I tried to show how an individual responded passionately to the works of Rousseau but in so doing conformed to Rousseauism itself as a cultural framework for finding meaning in life. Other research on reader response has confirmed this tendency. It does not demonstrate the prevalence of passivity on the one hand or of indeterminacy on the other. Instead, it suggests that readers found meaning in texts by fitting them within a pre-existing cultural frame.[8]

How is it that we normally make sense of things? Not, I believe, by drawing insights from deep within our souls and projecting them onto our surroundings, but rather by fitting perceptions into frames. The frames we take from our culture, for reality as we experience it is a social construction. Our world comes organized—divided into categories, shaped by conventions, and colored by shared emotions. When we find something meaningful, we fit it within the cognitive order that we inherit from our culture; and we often put it into words. So meanings, like language, are social, whatever the individual inflection we may give to them. In making meaning, we engage in a profoundly social activity, especially when we read. In order to make sense of a book, we must find our way through a dense symbolic field; for everything about a book bears the mark of cultural conventions—not just the language in which it is written, but its typography, layout, format, binding, and even the advertising used to sell it. Each of these elements orients the reader, directing his or her response. The reader also brings a great deal to the text—expectations, attitudes, values, and opinions—and these, too, have cultural determinants. So reading is doubly determined, by the nature of the book as a medium of communication, and by the general codes which the reader has internalized and in which the communication must take place.[9]

To avoid misunderstanding, I should add two caveats. First, in asserting the importance of cultural frames, I am not subscribing to a holistic notion of culture. I think that all sorts of fissures and faultlines run through cultural systems, so that the making of meaning involves conflict just as much as coherence. But conflict mobilizes competing frames—or, to borrow a term from the Cambridge school, rival discursive practices. Readers make sense of political tracts by fitting them to the conventions of a preferred political idiom. So nothing could be more appropriate for the history of reading than discourse analysis.

Second, in emphasizing the cultural constraints on reading, I do not mean to imply that readers must find identical messages in the same book. Almost any cultural system is broad enough to accommodate original and contradictory responses to texts. I am not advancing an argument for overdeterminacy but trying to argue against an underdetermined notion of reading, one that would put it outside the range of cultural history. Appropriation strikes me as a valuable concept, but not if it rules the history of reading out of another scholarly tradition to which it is most suited—the study of attitudes, values, and world views known in France as the history of *mentalités*.

That said, no amount of conceptual clarification will compensate for a lack of empirical research, and research in the history of reading usually runs aground for lack of adequate evidence. Although we know a certain amount about how the French responded to books in the eighteenth century, there is no getting around the fact that we do not know enough to draw general conclusions about reader response. Or is there? I would like to propose a strategy for tackling that problem, and then to put aside questions of method in order to take up some specific issues raised by the study of France's forbidden books.

In order to skirt around the difficulties on the reception side of the communication circuit, we could make a direct attack on the problem of public opinion. It is a major problem, still badly understood. We have only a vague idea of who composed the general public and how their opinions took shape in eighteenth-century France. In principle, politics was the king's business. Affairs of state were restricted to Versailles; and within that small world, the narrow halls of power narrowed into even smaller spaces—the inner circles of cabinet intrigue, with the "king's secret" at their heart. After the consolidation of absolutism under Louis XIV, the general public remained in a prepolitical state, far beyond the boundaries of participation in the political process. In practice, however, many power conflicts took place outside the confines of the court, and the public, as participant observers, became increasingly politicized. Politics of this sort took the form of contestation—petitions, protests, graffiti, songs, prints, and talk, much of it witty *(bons mots)*, disaffected *(mauvais propos)* and seditious *(bruits publics*—"public noises" or rumors) leading to collective violence *(émotions populaires*—"popular emotions" or riots).[10]

Most of this talk evaporated into the air. But some of it was recorded by police spies, because the authorities took it seriously and worked hard to keep track of it. The police reports fill hundreds of dossiers, some so rich that one can almost listen in to conversations held in taverns, cafés, and public gardens. Of course, the spy reports cannot be taken literally, because the spies may have misconstrued what they heard or misrepresented it to conform to agendas set for them by the police. But their reports can be compared with similar material in clandestine news sheets, diaries, and letters. Further documentation can be found in the vast Parisian collections of pamphlets, songs, and prints. Having spent years in these sources, I have come to think of eighteenth-century Paris as a gigantic communications network, wired through every neighborhood and buzzing at every moment with "public noises," as the Parisians called them then, or political discourse, as they would be known today.

The process can be envisaged schematically according to a second model, as in Figure 7.2:

Fig. 7.2. *The Communication Circuit*—News

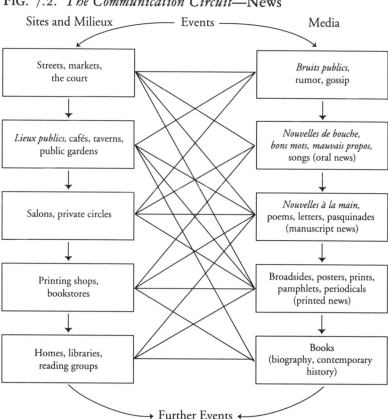

Whether or not this model corresponds exactly to the flow of information in pre-Revolutionary Paris, I think it illustrates the way messages were transmitted through different media and milieux. By imagining some such system of communication, it should be possible to sketch a rough history of public opinion. Despite its difficulties—the unevenness of the archives, the uncertainties about the composition of the public, and the ambiguities inherent in the very notion of public opinion—the task is feasible. We can already see far enough into the sources to posit a connection between the circulation of illegal literature on the one hand and the radicalization of public opinion on the other. But what was the nature of that connection? Not simply one of cause and effect. As the first diffusion model indicates, the production and diffusion of forbidden books was permeated at every point with influences from outside the circuit of the printed word. Political talk drifted up to writers scribbling in garrets, seeped into the calculations of publishers planning editions, and stimulated booksellers ordering supplies. The books themselves, especially certain genres like the *chroniques scandaleuses,* bore the mark of *"mauvais propos."* And they also helped to spread the word. They prevented it from disappearing in the air and carried it, fixed in print, to the farthest corners of the kingdom. Instead of cause and effect, therefore, one should imagine mutual reinforcement, feedback, and amplification.

As illustrated by the second model, this feedback process spilled over into other media, which intersected in a general information system. The same motifs often appeared in discussions waged in cafés, poems improvised in salons, ballads sung in streets, prints pasted on walls, manuscript gazettes circulated under the cloak, pamphlets sold under the counter, and books, where they wove in and out with other motifs to form complex narratives. There is little use in asking whether a particular theme appeared first in gossip or in print, because themes originated from different points and traveled in different directions, passing through several media and milieux. The crucial question does not concern the origin of a message but its amplification and assimilation—the way it reverberated through society and became meaningful to the public. How did forbidden books contribute to this process?

Bons mots and ballads tended to vanish and be forgotten. But books fixed themes in print, preserving them, diffusing them, and multiplying their effect. Even more important, books incorporated them in stories with broad persuasive power. An anecdote or an irreverent aside was one thing in a café, another in a printed book. The transformation into print actually altered its meaning, because books blended seemingly trivial elements into large-scale narratives, which often opened up perspectives into philosophy and history. Of course, some narratives worked more effectively than others. *Le Gazetier cuirassé* is little more than an anthology of scurrilous gossip. But *Anecdotes sur Mme la comtesse du Barry* combines the same material into a biography with a strong story line, and *La Vie privée de Louis XV* reads like a thorough history of contemporary France. As we have seen, the rhetoric of these works reinforced their persuasiveness as *histoires,* even while winking at the reader and nudging him in the ribs. No doubt many readers lifted material from their books and spread it through their table talk at dinners and cafés. They probably also employed the perspectives of their reading to interpret new items picked up from the talk of others. By reading forbidden books they took part in radicalizing public opinion.

Here, admittedly, we venture into speculation, because we do not have precise information about how people selected messages from books and how books incorporated material from other sources. It seems valid, however, to assume that the process worked both ways and that the print media played a key part in it, by preserving and by multiplying the discourse in the streets. In fact, they did much more. By fixing themes in print, books fitted them into narratives and gave them wide significance. The printed version of things organized information—anecdotes, "public noises," "news" *(nouvelles)*—into convincing pictures and strung them out along storylines, defining situations and plotting their direction. In their own way, as a peculiar kind of literature, the clandestine best-sellers reinforced the general way of fashioning meaning: they provided frames for sorting out reality.

How those frames functioned is an empirical question. It cannot be answered directly, owing to lack of documentation about the inner experience of reading. But it may yield an indirect and approximate answer, because if the information about public opinion coincides with the evidence about illegal literature, we may be able to detect a significant cultural pattern. It is not that the themes of the books determined the motifs of "public noises," or vice versa, but rather that the two forms of communication worked together, defining, transmitting, and amplifying messages that undercut the legitimacy of the regime.

To understand how delegitimation actually occurred, it will be necessary to work through a vast amount of material from the 1780s. But for the moment, it seems adequate to insist on a general proposition. Forbidden books molded public opinion in two ways: by fixing disaffection in print (preserving and spreading the word), and by fitting it into narratives (transforming loose talk into coherent discourse).

Objections

The attempt given above to outline two diffusion models should forestall some objections from those who assume "diffusion" implies the imprinting of ideas on a passive public, or linear movement from cause to effect, or trickle-down influences from high to low levels of culture, or an excessively literary process that had little to do with politics and public opinion. But plenty of objections remain. The most important can be formulated as three arguments against my principal thesis, namely, that the diffusion of *livres philosophiques* undermined the legitimacy of the Old Regime. First, it could be objected that the illegal literature may have appealed most to those who had most to lose by the collapse of the Old Regime; so why associate it with radicalization or the revolutionary cause? Second, scurrilous political literature may have existed for centuries: why attribute so much importance to it under Louis XVI? Third, even if the *libelles* were especially outspoken in the 1770s and 1780s, why assume they had much effect on readers? They might have been shrugged off as gossip or trivia, and the radicalization of public opinion might have come from a completely different source.

The first objection certainly has force. Rousseau's most enthusiastic readers included a large portion of aristocrats before 1789 and of aristocratic émigrés afterwards. True, they responded more to the sentiment in *La Nouvelle Héloïse* than to the politics of *Du Contrat social,* but the privileged orders in general provided a large share of the market for the works of the Enlightenment. It even seems likely that Louis XVI read some Voltaire in prison while waiting for his trial after the overthrow of the monarchy. Not that he can be considered a Voltairean. He probably read the plays rather than the irreligious tracts in Voltaire's collected works. Louis had a *Missel de Paris* smuggled in to him, and the royal family generally favored devotional works during their imprisonment. But the emphasis on religion in their literary diet contrasted strongly with the reading habits of other prominent figures in the Revolution. The inventories of twenty-six libraries confiscated during the

Terror from leaders of different factions look remarkably similar. Whether the libraries belonged to counter-revolutionaries like the baron de Breteuil, constitutional monarchists like Lafayette, Girondists like Roland, moderate Jacobins like Danton, or radical Jacobins like Robespierre, they contained relatively few books on religion, a great many on history and current events, and a large number by *philosophes,* especially Voltaire, Rousseau, Mably, and Raynal.[11]

It would not be surprising if *libelles* and *chroniques scandaleuses* occupied favorite places in some aristocratic libraries, because courtiers thrived on scurrilous gossip about the court. They produced and consumed it avidly, even when they were its targets. J.-F. Phélypeaux, comte de Maurepas, the much-maligned minister of Louis XV and Louis XVI, enjoyed the *bons mots* made at his expense and amassed the largest collection of satirical songs and poems in the kingdom.[12] In assessing reader response, it is important to allow for the sophisticated reading of the "political class," which knew how to laugh at itself or at least at the favorite victims within its own ranks.[13] No doubt other insiders, including some of the *libellistes,* also amused themselves in this fashion while maintaining a critical distance between what they read and what they believed.

But having made allowances for disabused reading among the aristocracy, one should take account of a more important phenomenon: many aristocrats read Voltaire, Rousseau, and Pidansat de Mairobert as true believers. Indeed, they may have responded to the forbidden books more passionately than did readers located far below them in the social hierarchy. Although it is difficult to document, their experience of literature does not prove that *livres philosophiques* posed no threat to the regime. Quite the contrary: a political system may be most endangered when its most favored elite ceases to believe in its legitimacy.

The alienation of the aristocracy cannot be measured precisely, but the protests against government abuses stand out just as strongly in the *cahiers de doléances* (petitions of grievances drawn up before the meeting of the Estates General) of the nobility as in those of the Third Estate, and the Enlightenment motifs are even stronger. Noblemen took the lead in opposing the government in 1787 and 1788, and aristocratic liberals figured prominently in events from 1789 to 1792. It is not that the Revolution or even the pre-Revolution deserves to be labeled "aristocratic" rather than "bourgeois," but rather that a mixed elite took charge of both. This elite hardened into a dominant class in the nineteenth century, when old noble families, wealthy landowners, and professional bourgeois fused to form the "Notables." Its origins date back to the Old Regime and especially to cultural life under Louis XV. As Daniel Roche has demonstrated, noblemen and professional men, royal administrators and bourgeois rentiers, came together in provincial academies, Masonic lodges, and literary societies. They subscribed to the same journals, wrote papers for the same essay contests, and read the same books—notably the *Encyclopédie,* whose authors and readers belonged to the same mixed milieux. A great deal went into the fusion of old elites into a new notability, and the process took time, but its key ingredient was the elaboration of a common culture in the eighteenth century.[14]

Tocqueville put his finger on this phenomenon:

> The bourgeois was as cultivated as the nobleman and his enlightenment came from the same source. Both had been educated on literary and philosophic lines, for Paris, now almost the sole fountainhead of knowledge for the whole of France, had cast the minds of all in the same mold and given them the same equipment. . . . Basically all who ranked above the common herd were of a muchness; they had the same ideas, the same habits, the same tastes, the same kinds of amusements; read the same books and spoke in the same way.[15]

As so often, Tocqueville seems to have said it all; except that he did not ask himself what those books were.

They were not, as he assumed, simply the works of the *philosophes;* nor were they solely abstract treatises that showed no knowledge of political realities. As we have seen, the most widely diffused illegal literature included muckraking journalism, social commentary, political polemics, bawdy anti-clericalism, Utopian fantasies, theoretical speculations, and raw pornography—all of it cohabiting promiscuously under the same label, *livres philosophiques.* Its themes ran together and overlapped in such a way as to challenge the orthodoxies of the Old Regime on every front. The challenge lacked all self-restraint, because it all took place outside the law. And it appealed to the emotions as well as the reason, using every rhetorical device at its command to play on a wide range of responses—indignation, anger, scorn, derision, and disgust.

As readers, the aristocrats were exposed to the full gamut of themes in the forbidden books, and it seems likely that their responses also covered a broad spectrum. The cumulative effect probably extended well beyond sympathy for the Enlightenment. For many it doubtless went as far as a general disenchantment with the regime, including a loss of faith in the legitimacy of their own privileges. Of course, these are surmises, which must be hedged with words like "probably" and "doubtless." But it is more reasonable to posit a gradual erosion of belief among the privileged orders than a sudden conversion on the night of August 4, 1789, when they renounced their privileges.[16] They lost their faith in the regime before it fell, and afterwards they found they had a great deal more to lose. But instead of rallying around the old order, they generally joined in its destruction. Some, to be sure, enlisted in the Counter-Revolution, but most of those with right-wing sympathies merely retreated into private life or withdrew across the Rhine. The most striking aspect of the aristocrats' behavior in 1789 is their enthusiasm for the Revolution on the one hand and the ineffectuality of their opposition to it on the other. In either case, their attachment to the Old Regime had been broken, and at least some of the damage can be attributed to the *livres philosophiques.*

It would be extravagant to reduce complex phenomena like loss of faith and failure of nerve to the effect of reading. But it is easy to underestimate the power of print, especially today when the book has lost the place that it once occupied at the center of society's communication systems. To appreciate the force of forbidden books in the eighteenth century—the whole corpus of illegal literature, not just single sectors—one should look at them from an eighteenth-century point of view, or, better still, from the perspective of the absolutism developed a century earlier. This consideration applies to all the arguments against the importance of *livres philosophiques,* so I will take it up at this point, before attempting to answer the other objections.

It was under Louis XIV that the values of the Old Regime hardened into a powerful cultural system. Militantly Counter-Reformation in its religion, relentlessly hierarchical in its social structure, and uncompromisingly absolutist in its government, Louis Quatorzean France stood for everything that was most abominated in the forbidden books published a century later. The most eminent writers of the seventeenth century, patronized, disciplined, and manipulated by the state, worked at the center of the new court culture. They turned literature into an instrument of absolutism. Authors in the eighteenth century also scrambled for patronage, but they often operated outside the state and turned literature against it. Some of them became culture heroes for doing so. "King Voltaire" epitomized the heretic-as-hero, despite his sympathies for Louis XIV and his role as royal historiographer. Voltaire embodied a whole new belief system, one that went far beyond the priest-baiting and libertinism of his youth. In the Calas Affair and the other affairs that succeeded it, he made his cause—the Enlightenment—into the cause of humanity, infusing it with passion and moral indignation.

Other writers in other quarters also mobilized sentiment against the state; for the Enlightenment was not the only cause in eighteenth-century France, and it was not the only ideology represented in the corpus of forbidden books. The *livres philosophiques* covered a vast range of subjects. They included something to offend everyone in power and to challenge everything in the value system inherited from Louis XIV. By 1770, Louis Quatorzean culture appeared antiquated and oppressive. Literature stood for its antithesis—a certain variety of literature, the kind that was produced outside the law and that flooded the market during the last two decades of the Old Regime. As Tocqueville observed, literature spilled over social distinctions, mobilizing public opinion among all the literate classes. Everyone read the same books, including the same *livres philoso-*

phiques. The authors of those books had pried literature loose from its attachment to the state. They had separated culture from power, or rather, they had directed a new cultural power against the orthodoxies of the old. So a contradiction opened up, separating an orthodox value system grounded in the absolutist state from a contestatory ethos rooted in literature. This contradiction defined the situation of the reader, whatever his or her social status. It demonstrated to everyone that times were out of joint, that cultural life no longer synchronized with political power. The Louis Quatorzean synthesis had come apart; and literature, which had done so much to legitimize absolutism in the seventeenth century, now became the principal agent of its delegitimation.

Chapter 8

The History
of Political Libel

THE ISSUE OF DELEGITIMATION raises a second objection, which concerns the subgenre of forbidden books called *libelles*—slanderous attacks on public figures known collectively as "les grands." Why attribute so much importance to these works? one may ask. Scandalous literature had collected around kings and courtiers ever since the Renaissance, when Aretino made smut-peddling into a profession; but no one considered it a threat to the state. Perhaps the *libelles* of the 1770s and 1780s belong to an ancient variety of mud slinging, which should be left where it belongs—in the gutter.

This objection confronts us with a problem: scandalmongering has been regarded as so distasteful and so trivial that no one has ever inquired extensively into its past. We need a history of political libel. Until that history is written, we cannot arrive at anything more than tentative conclusions, and I can offer only some preliminary arguments for taking the smut seriously. They can be summarized as follows: First, although one can dig up plenty of scurrilous remarks about "les grands" during the sixteenth and seventeenth centuries, one cannot find anything comparable to the best-selling, book-length *libelles* of the eighteenth century. Second, even if *libelles* circulated widely in France two centuries before the Revolution, their appeal under Henri III and Louis XIII does not prove that they lacked appeal under Louis XV and Louis XVI: on the contrary, they may have gained in power through their cumulative effect on an ever-growing reading public. Third, a comparison of the early and the late *libelles* does not reveal a pattern of endless repetition but rather a shift from the defamation of individuals to the desecration of an entire regime.

The term used to identify this literature covered a wide front. In the late Middle Ages, *libelle* (from the Latin *libellus,* a diminutive of *liber,* for "book") meant a small book. Although it continued to apply to all sorts of pamphlets, it became associated primarily with short, slanderous attacks on prominent individuals. By 1762, the standard dictionary published by the Académie française defined a *libelle* simply as an *écrit injurieux* or "offensive work." The offense might concern a private person, as in the modern concept of libel; but more often it was an affair of state, for *libelles* could be seditious. That had become clear two centuries earlier, when a royal ordinance of 1560 proclaimed that "all producers of posters and defamatory *libelles . . .* that tend to arouse the people and provoke it to sedition" would be condemned as "enemies of the public peace and criminals guilty of *lèse-majesté.*"[1]

This peculiar combination of slander and sedition seems to have characterized the history of political *libelles* from the sixteenth through the eighteenth century. Whenever crises hit the state, *libelles* compounded the damage. In 1589, at the height of the Catholic League's insurrection in Paris, Pierre de l'Estoile marveled at the proliferation of scandalous pamphlets: "Every day the slightest printer manages to make his press turn out some stupid new defamatory *libelle* against His Majesty."[2] During the revolt of the princes against Marie de Médicis in 1615, a polemical tract, *Avertissement à la France touchant les libelles* warned that "defamatory *libelles*" were the main weapon used by those trying to foment public unrest.[3] In 1649, when the Fronde had reduced the kingdom to something close to anarchy, Parisians were appalled by "this frightening quantity of *libelles.*"[4] By then, the danger of *libelles* was deplored on all sides, even by the *libellistes,* who libeled their opponents by accusing them of libel. "Nothing is more pernicious to a state than *libelles,*" proclaimed one pamphlet, while another made the suppression of scandal the central concern of a program announced in its title, *Censure générale de tous les libelles diffamatoires*.[5]

Whether such pronouncements represented genuine alarm or rhetorical posturing is difficult to say, but the authorities certainly took slander seriously. On May 28, 1649, the Parlement of Paris tried to restore order in the capital by threatening to hang anyone who produced *libelles*. In June, it nearly hanged a lawyer, Bernard de Bautru, for disturbing the peace by a slanderous pamphlet. And in July, it condemned a printer, Claude Morlot, who was caught running off sheets of *La custode du lit de la reine,* which began with a statement about Mazarin and the queen mother, Anne of Austria, that was as crude as anything put out in the 1770s: "Townsmen, don't doubt it any more; it's true that he fucks her." Morlot was saved by a riot of journeymen printers, who snatched him from the hangman; but the point had been made: *libelles* led to sedition, and the first phase of the Fronde ended with a crackdown on the press.[6] In the later stages of the Fronde, the competing factions fought with *libelles* as much as with swords. So when Louis XIV began to reconstruct the monarchy in 1661, he took severe measures to control the press and to subject every aspect of cultural life to his authority. The reorganization of the book trade, of censorship, and of the police all contributed to a new variety of absolutism, which drove the *libellistes* underground or out of the country. Many of them fled to Holland, where they joined ranks with Protestant refugees following the Revocation of the Edict of Nantes in 1685. Religious conflict and foreign war added intensity to the political slander produced by exiles in the 1690s. But the older variety continued to appear from time to time within the kingdom. In November 1694, while Louis reigned over the cult of kingship in Versailles, a printer and bookseller were hanged in Paris for producing an irreverent account of the royal sex life.[7] Thus, by the beginning of the eighteenth century, a genre was established; it had been branded as seditious by the state; and the way was cleared for the clandestine best-sellers of the pre-Revolutionary era.

But does this history, insofar as one can reconstruct it from a few, scattered monographs, demonstrate an essential sameness in the vast literature of libel stretching from the Reformation to the Revolution? There was plenty of variety within the genre itself. *Libelles* could be posters, broadsides, songs, prints, pamphlets, or books. Pierre de l'Estoile included a little of everything in the collection he put together in 1589: more than three hundred items bound in four folio volumes.[8] But for all their differences in form, they had one thing in common: they were intensely personal. In this respect, they owed a great deal to the Renaissance style of politics. Politics in the Renaissance court was a matter of personalities, of patronage and clienteles, ins and outs, intrigues and *combinazione* (plots). To play the game, one had to know how to defend one's prestige; for reputation was a form of power, especially at the level of princes, as Machiavelli had explained:

> The prince must, as already stated, avoid those things which will make him hated or despised; and whenever he succeeds in this, he will have done his part, and will find no danger in other vices. . . . He is rendered despicable by being thought changeable, frivolous, effeminate, timid, and irresolute; which a prince must guard against as a rock of danger, and so contrive that his actions show grandeur, spirit, gravity and fortitude. . . . The prince who creates such an opinion of himself gets a great reputation, and it is very difficult to conspire against one who has a great reputation, and he will not easily be attacked, so long as it is known that he is capable and revered by his subjects.[9]

The defense of reputation became a basic strategy of Renaissance statecraft, not merely in Machiavelli's Tuscany but also in Louis XIII's France. Richelieu placed it at the heart of his notion of power: "The prince ought to be powerful through his reputation. . . . Reputation is so necessary that a prince who benefits from a good opinion can do more with his name alone than those who have armies but no esteem."[10]

In early modern Europe, power did not generally come out of the barrel of a gun. Armies usually amounted to little more than a few companies of mercenaries and guards, police forces to a handful of constabularies. In order to impress their authority on the people, sovereigns acted it out—through coronations, funerals, royal entries, processions, festivals, fireworks, public executions, and touching the diseased (that is, curing scrofula or the "king's evil"). But the dramaturgical form of power was vulnerable to insult. A well-aimed affront could puncture a reputation and destroy an entire performance. To survive in the Renaissance court, one had to know how to parry and thrust with verbal offenses. Although this variety of politics was restricted to princes and patricians, it was played out before the people. So when the play fell apart, the actors could appeal to the audience; the plebes could intervene; and the man with the greatest reputation in the streets might well come out on top.[11]

In Paris as in Florence, politics often degenerated into street fighting; but much of the violence was verbal. "Days of the Barricades," on May 12, 1588, and August 26–28, 1648, released floods of *libelles*—so many, in fact, that they could not have been aimed exclusively at coteries of courtiers. They appealed to the mixed public that gathered at the Pont-Neuf, the Palais de Justice, the Palais-Royal, the Quai des Augustins, and other nerve centers in the systems of communication by print and word of mouth. The plebeian target of the *libelles* was implicit in their style. They were vulgar, obscene, brutal, and simplistic. They drew on popular genres like the burlesque dialogue, the bawdy joke, the broadside ballad, the vituperative harangue, and the stylized narratives of dreams and ghosts and ghoulish *faits divers*. Some *libelles* captured the tone of seditious street talk (*bruits publics, mauvais propos*). Some used the rhetoric of ritual insult and popular pasquinades (slanderous poems displayed in public places like the statue of Pasquino in Rome). Many were stitched in blue wrapping paper like the almanacs and chapbooks of the *bibiliothèque bleue* (popular literature). Many read like broadsides—the *occasionnels, canards,* and *feuilles volantes* that provided news for all sorts of readers for a century before 1631, when *La Gazette de France,* France's first newspaper, began publication, and that continued to inform or misinform the humblest sort for two centuries afterwards. These extraordinary explosions of printed matter demonstrate that politics took place not just at court but in the street, amidst the plebes.[12]

It does not follow, however, that one can distinguish clearly between patrician and plebeian cultures. Some such distinction existed, but it was continually blurred. The most vulgar pamphlets sometimes lapsed into Latin, and much of the fishmongering was a kind of literary slumming, intended to amuse the sophisticates. The more that scholars have studied "popular" genres like the *bibliothèque bleue,* the less confident they feel about the very notion of "popular culture." Who better represents the fusion of the popular and the elite than Rabelais, the supreme genius of sixteenth-century literature? Bawdy and recondite, vulgar and *recherché,* Rabelais plucked his main character, Gargantua, from a chapbook and introduced him in the language of a huckster in a street fair. The literature of libel pulsated with Rabelaisian energy, but it cannot be assigned to a particular public. It belonged to a world where the struggle for power had burst through the confines of the court and spilled into the streets, sweeping up everyone in its path.[13]

The violence of the explosions derived from a final ingredient that hardly existed in the calculations of Machiavelli: religion. For a century, from the death of Henri II in 1559 to the defeat of the Fronde and the beginning of the personal rule of Louis XIV in 1661, France went through a period of intermittent civil war fueled primarily by the struggle between Protestants and Catholics. Although the Protestants did not take part in the Fronde, Louis drove them out of the kingdom in the 1680s. So the most violent *libelles* against him at the end of his reign came from Holland, where the refugees mixed with opponents to absolutism in England—that is, with men like John Locke. The quarrel between Jansenists and Jesuits added another dimension to the ideological conflicts. And every conflict was compounded on an international scale by the rivalries of dynasties and states—Valois, Bourbons, Habsburgs, Tudors, Stuarts, Orangists, Hohenzollerns, and Hanoverians commanding armies that could inflict enormous damage, even before they abandoned cross-bows and armor.

What was the place of verbal violence in this long period of multi-dimensional conflict? We cannot measure the incidence of *mauvais propos* and public noises, but we can identify the greatest explosions of *libelles* from the late sixteenth to the early eighteenth centuries. Four periods stand out: 1588–94, 1614–17, 1648–52, and 1688–97.[14]

The first explosion took place during the chaotic period of religious warfare, when events came so thick and fast that the presses could hardly keep up with them. *Occasionnels* poured out at a rate of one a day in Paris throughout 1589—an extraordinary output in contrast to the annual production of a dozen or so per year in 1585 and 1594. The crisis supplied plenty of good copy: assassinations, coups, heroes, and villains. And the Parisian authorities gave the pamphleteers full rein, provided they concentrated their fire on the enemy: Henri of Valois (Henri III) and his sometime ally, Henri of Navarre (the future Henri IV).

The king certainly made a good target. His reputation was everything it should not be, according to Machiavelli's formula: "changeable, frivolous, effeminate, timid, and irresolute." The *libellistes* hit him with all the insults in their arsenal, calling him a coward, a hypocrite, a prevaricator, a tyrant, and worst of all a Protestant. They did not make much of the behavior that has fascinated many of his biographers, the supposed orgies with his male "minions," because their main concern was religious.[15] Religion provided the basic idiom for politics in the 1580s; so in slandering Henri III, the *libellistes* made him out to be a crypto-Huguenot, a sorcerer, a companion of the devil. From the other side of the barricades, the Protestants replied in kind, accusing the Holy League of betraying France to the satanic forces of the Counter-Reformation, Spain, and the pope. Both sides embellished their arguments with sensational details about signs in the sky and miracles on earth. They reported events in the same spirit of sensationalism, just as *canards* had done for nearly a hundred years. In fact, the *libelles* often resembled *canards*. They were usually crude broadsides or pamphlets of half a sheet or a sheet (eight or sixteen pages in octavo, the most common format). In form, style, and content, they had more in common with old-fashioned *occasionnels* than with the best-sellers of the eighteenth century.

The next great wave of *libelles*, which flooded the kingdom during the revolt of the princes in 1614–17, was similar. Once again a power struggle among "les grands," great noblemen and royal protégés, could not be contained within the court, and the contestants appealed to the public for support, both by taking up arms and by slandering one another in print. This time, however, the religious themes remained relatively muted, and no one challenged the authority of the king—in part because he had so little. Louis XIII was only twelve when the crisis broke. Instead of attacking him, the warring factions tried to seize power by controlling the king's councils and ruling in his name. The queen mother, Marie de Médicis, dominated the councils as regent and through favorites such as Concino Concini, the maréchal d'Ancre. Her main opponent, the prince de Condé, tried to supplant her, first by manipulating the Estates General of 1614, then by backstairs intrigue, and finally by open rebellion. The crisis reached a climax and the pamphleteering a peak of productivity (about 450 new titles, nearly 100 more than the output in 1589) in 1617, when Concini was murdered and Marie de Médicis driven into exile. Sporadic rebellion and baroque intrigue continued for two more decades, but by 1630 Richelieu had restored order. Under his firm hand and that of his successor, Cardinal Mazarin, power was consolidated in a way that laid the foundation for the absolutism of Louis XIV. But when he acceded to the throne in 1643, Louis was a four-year-old boy. So France went through another regency and another rebellion, the Fronde, before absolutism finally emerged as a form of government designed to contain the forces that had been tearing the kingdom apart for a hundred years.

Because the crisis of 1614–17 was primarily a struggle of "ins" against "outs," the pamphlets that it generated were intended to mobilize support among "the politically important public"[16] of noblemen, royal officials, and leading members of municipal governments and guilds. They seem less violent than the pamphlets of the 1580s. Probably they had less resonance among the common people. But they, too, were keyed to events and helped shape events by providing a rhetoric of action. They informed, interpreted, exhorted, and denounced in strategic thrusts and parries, which cut into the flow of action, rallying supporters and exposing enemies at all the crucial points. Although they occasionally referred to religious and constitutional issues, they remained remarkably respectful to the principle of absolute royal sovereignty. And they concentrated their fire on individuals. Condé was a traitor, a hothead, a reckless conspirator; Concini a profligate, a demon, a dissolute usurper; Marie de Médicis a tyrant, a meddler, a protector of corrupt and alien adventurers. The libeling, as always, took the form of ad hominem attacks, but it did not go far beyond *règlements de compte* (settlements of grudges).

During the Fronde, the great bulk of the 5,000 pamphlets published from 1648 to 1653 repeated the same sort of personal vituperation. The situation, too, was similar: a boy king; a queen mother, Anne of Austria, trying to govern through a favorite, Mazarin; and great nobles, led by another Condé (Louis II, the son of Henri II de Bourbon, the opponent of Marie de Médicis), vying for a share in the power. But this time the crisis went deeper. After driving Mazarin, the queen mother, and young Louis XIV from Paris in January 1649, the rebels took over the city. They held out against a blockade until the end of March, while permitting virtual freedom of the press—freedom, that is, to slander Mazarin and everyone associated with him. The pamphlets poured out at a rate of ten a day for the first three months of 1649. Like the broadsides of the Holy League, they struck a popular chord and stayed close to events, commenting and caricaturing without inhibition.

The tone of the pamphleteering began to change after the king's return to Paris in August signaled the end of the first or parlementary Fronde. Conspiracies and coups provided plenty of material for polemics until 1653. But the pamphlets became longer and more reflective. They expressed programs devised in the councils of "les grands" rather than reactions in the street. Nonetheless, many of them continued to slander individuals with such verve and violence that the whole body of *frondeur* pamphleteering came to be known by the *libelle* that epitomized the genre, Paul Scarron's *La Mazarinade* of 1651.

The common name disguised a great variety of themes and forms. Like the polemical literature of the 1580s and 1590s, the *mazarinades* included everything from songs and posters to long-winded political tracts. Some were merely intended for amusement without offering any political message at all. A few even supported Mazarin in company with the Fronde. The main novelty that distinguished them from earlier *occasionnels* was the subgenre of burlesque verse made popular by Scarron. It drew on the tradition of ritual insult and the pasquinade, and it certainly hit below the belt. Thus Mazarin, according to *La Mazarinade,* is defined as:

Bougre bougrant, bougre bougré,	Buggering bugger, buggered bugger,
Et bougre au suprême degré,	Bugger to the supreme degree,
Bougre au poil, et bougre à la plume,	Hairy bugger and feathered bugger,
Bougre en grand et petit volume,	Bugger in large and small volume,
Bougre sodomisant l'Etat,	Bugger sodomizing the State,
Et bougre du plus haut carat . . .[17]	And bugger of the purest mixture . . .

All the players in the Fronde received their share of libel, but the vast majority of it, an unprecedented avalanche of vituperation, fell on Mazarin. The *libellistes* mocked the cardinal for his supposed low birth. (In fact, he came from the minor Italian nobility and grew up in the orbit of the Colonna dynasty in Rome, but some made him out to be the illegitimate offspring of a priest and a servant girl, the same parentage that would be attributed to Madame du Barry 120 years later.) They denounced him for funneling French wealth into Italian pockets or the coffers of Spain and the Ultramontane Church. They derided his love of luxury, good food, opera, and his nieces, whose private lives also got raked over. They dwelt on his sex life, especially his relations with Anne of Austria. And they concluded that he should be run out of office, hunted like an animal, shot down, torn to pieces, or broken on the wheel. These attacks went further than the insults sprayed through earlier texts: they made libel into a genre of mini-biography, although they seem underdeveloped (*La Mazarinade* was only a fourteen-page pamphlet) in comparison with the attacks on Louis

XIV and the elaborate *vies privées* that proliferated under Louis XV.

Did slander on such a scale constitute a revolutionary threat to the Old Regime? The experts disagree. Hubert Carrier, the author of the most recent and most extensive study of the *mazarinades,* finds all sorts of radical messages in the texts—not merely protests against taxation and tyranny, but some attacks on the monarchy itself. In a few of the later pamphlets he detects "authentically revolutionary" demands for a change of regime, even a "popular democracy," by means of a general uprising.[18] But according to Christian Jouhaud, another authority, the violent rhetoric cannot be taken literally. To the men who wrote the *mazarinades* and the public that read them, their meaning was inherent in the complex jockeying for position during the final phase of the civil war. The pamphlets did not try to stir up a popular insurrection against the king. They merely raised that specter in order to demonstrate the preferability of an alternative strategy: a caretaker government under Gaston d'Orléans. By constituting a "third party," the Orléanists hoped to wedge themselves between the princes and the court and to win support from the partisans of the "old," parlementary Fronde. The legalistic rhetoric of the pamphlets—their learned Latin citations, their invocation of natural law, and their emphasis on constitutional history—was designed to promote that appeal. Far from trying to overthrow the monarchy, they sought to capture it. Their most radical-sounding tract, *Le guide au chemin de la liberté,* concluded lamely: "We love royalty and detest tyranny"—a proposition that could offend no one, least of all the magistrates and lawyers in the Palais de Justice.[19]

It is at points such as this, where competing interpretations converge on the same texts, that discourse analysis has most to offer. Despite the rigor of his research, Carrier lets an anachronistic element creep into his reading of the *mazarinades* from 1652. For him, the language is self-evident: an attack on the king smacks of revolution and even of democracy. Jouhaud treats the texts as moves in a strategic contest. They belong to the constant rhetorical crossfire that accompanied all the attacks and counterattacks in the chesslike "Fronde of the princes." By 1652, the spontaneity had gone out of the rebellion. The professionals had taken over—"les grands" like Orléans, Condé, the cardinal de Retz, and Mazarin himself. They shared the same assumptions and competed within the same system, struggling to dominate it, not to destroy it. At critical points, they appealed for support from the "public" and even contemplated popular intervention, as in the Days of the Barricades. But those were tactical moves of an insider's game—truly Machiavellian moments, not of classical republicanism but of *combinazione*.[20]

By the time of the next outbreak of pamphleteering, in 1685, the game looked very different. Louis XIV had domesticated the nobility, cowed the parlements, and gained control of the press. The press itself had begun to assume the modern form of newspapers. True, nothing that made the regime look bad could get past the censors, and nothing comparable to political news as we know it today appeared in the most important periodicals, *La Gazette de France,* the *Mercure,* and the *Journal des savants.* But a lively French-language press had grown up in the Low Countries and the Rhineland, and *nouvellistes* purveyed gossip in Paris through word of mouth and manuscript gazettes. Clandestine presses turned out pamphlet literature, despite the severity of the reorganized Parisian police under the firm hand of G.-N. de La Reynie, while old-fashioned *occasionnels* and *canards* continued to divert all sorts of readers. The reading public itself had expanded, especially in cities. Although the court had withdrawn to Versailles, Paris was full of ordinary persons, artisans and shopkeepers as well as solid bourgeois, who wanted to be informed about politics, even if they knew it was the king's business. The king did indeed keep his business to himself, but he understood the need to satisfy the public and to manipulate it. Royal entries, festivals, theatre, art, architecture, and even science pursued in royal academies kept the cult of the king before the public eye. Richelieu had merely made a start on the state control of culture; Louis made it into a mainstay of the ultimate version of absolutism.[21]

This was hardly a climate in which *libelles* could flourish. The total output of pamphlets during Louis's personal reign, from 1661 to 1715, was about 1,500 titles—fewer than the number of *mazarinades* that appeared in 1649 alone. It is difficult to measure their incidence; but judging from collections in the Netherlands and Switzerland, they came out at a rate of twenty to forty a year, and they especially proliferated during the critical last years of the century, from 1688 to 1697.[22] The proportion of *libelles* within the pamphlet literature cannot be estimated: too much uncertainty surrounds the statistics and too much fuzziness obscures the notions both of a pamphlet and of a *libelle*. But the slandering of Louis XIV and his ministers seems to have been trivial in comparison with the mud slung at Mazarin, Anne of Austria, Marie de Médicis, Concini, and Henri III. Of all the illegal books seized in the Paris Customs from 1678 to 1701, only 2 percent concerned the private life of the king.[23]

The relative paucity of the *libelles* against Louis XIV derived in part from the state's control of the printed word in France. The earlier outbursts of slander took place in the midst of civil wars during periods of virtual freedom of the press. In the late seventeenth century most of it came from outside the kingdom, above all from the Netherlands, which had been locked in a life-and-death struggle against France since 1672 and had begun sheltering Huguenot refugees even before the Revocation of the Edict of Nantes in 1685. The *libelles* naturally stressed foreign affairs and religious themes. They also contained an admixture of theoretical arguments derived partly from the political literature produced during the upheavals in England and partly from the older Calvinist literature such as François Hotman's *Franco-Gallia* (1573) and *Vindiciae contra tyrannos* (1579). But for the most part they relied on old-fashioned insult delivered in the form of scandalous news sheets *(lardons)* and short pamphlets, including pasquinades in dialogue with stock characters like Pasquin and Morforio.

The new ingredient that set this literature apart from the *mazarinades* and earlier pamphlets came from an unexpected source: Versailles itself and the sharp wit of one of its libertine courtiers, Roger de Rabutin, comte de Bussy. Bussy-Rabutin transformed court gossip into novellas, which circulated in manuscript and recounted the sexual adventures of the greatest ladies in the kingdom—but always in the purest French, without any obscenity, political comment, or indeed any reference to the world outside the court. Unfortunately for Bussy-Rabutin, the the success of his non-fictional romances inspired imitators, who took their material from the sex life of the king. Bussy-Rabutin's enemies attributed the sequels to him. Then sequels to the sequels, published in the Netherlands, turned the sexual yarns into an indictment of the political as well as the moral character of Louis Quatorzean absolutism. From gossip to manuscript, manuscript to print, and sex to politics, the scandal-mongeuring developed into a whole new branch of literature.

In the end, Bussy-Rabutin went to the Bastille, then into exile; and his slim, little *Histoire amoureuse des Gaules* expanded into a five-volume politico-sexual epic, *La France galante, ou histoires amoureuses de la cour de Louis XIV*. Its nastiest novella, *Les Amours de Mme de Maintenon,* presented the biography of the king's mistress as a picaresque adventure story. In sleeping her way to the throne, Mme de Maintenon passed through the hands of loutish provincial nobles, the hunchbacked *libelliste* Scarron, and finally the king's confessor, Father de La Chaise, who disguised himself as a valet in order to gain access to her bed, and then made her the agent of a Jesuit plot to take over the kingdom. But contrary to what the modern reader might expect, the narrative shows far less interest in politics than in voyeuristic revelations of sex life at the court. Few of the attacks on Louis XIV went as far as the most radical *mazarinades* in their protest against the abuse of power. Their significance lies less in their comments on current events than in the creation of a new genre. They took the *libelle* beyond the sniping of the old-fashioned pamphlets and broadsides, and into the range of a more destructive weapon, the full-scale political biography. By the beginning of the eighteenth century, the way had been cleared for the best-sellers that did so much to damage the legitimacy of Louis XV and of the monarchy itself.[24]

This survey hardly does justice to the history of an ignoble, unfamiliar, and enormously influential strain of literature; but it should provide enough information to help answer a fundamental question: What distinguished the *libelles* of the 1770s and 1780s from the earlier varieties?

The first characteristic that comes to mind is their scale.

Unlike their predecessors, the eighteenth-century *libelles* were long, complex narratives, which ran from one volume (*Anecdotes sur Mme la comtesse du Barry*) to four (*Vie privée de Louis XV*), or ten (*L'Espion anglais*), or even thirty-six (*Mémoires secrets pour servir à l'histoire de la république des lettres en France*), if one includes *chroniques scandaleuses* in the genre. Almost all the earlier literature had circulated in pamphlet form, even the novellas about Louis XIV, which were not collected in multi-volume editions until the 1730s. The pamphlets probably had a powerful effect on public opinion, at least during some crises such as the Fronde. But they tended to be ephemeral. *Libelles* in book form incorporated the pamphlet material into a literary genre that remained accessible for many years and that provided an elaborate account of the recent past.

Second, the book *libelles* had a wider distribution than the previous pamphlet literature. Although some *mazarinades* reached bookshops in remote cities like Grenoble, most of the early literature seems to have circulated locally in small editions turned out overnight or in a few days by clandestine presses.[25] The later *libelles* belonged to a vast industry, which supplied the entire kingdom through an extensive distribution network. They were best-sellers, produced simultaneously in editions of a thousand or more copies by several publishers, who competed to satisfy a greatly expanded market.

Third, the attacks on Louis XV went far beyond those on Louis XIV by setting the royal sex life within a general narrative of contemporary history. *La France galante* reduces the reign of Louis XIV to a series of amorous intrigues. The *Vie privée de Louis XV* covers sixty years of politics. Even the *Anecdotes sur Mme la comtesse du Barry* refers constantly to power struggles in the government, the opposition of the parlements, and the hard lot of the common people. In this respect, it continued the hard-hitting political commentaries of the *mazarinades;* but it incorporated them in an expanded version of the novelesque narrative developed under Louis XIV.

Fourth, even as sex yarns the later *libelles* differed greatly from those of the previous reign. In *La France galante,* the king is gallant. He combines gallantry with power, cutting a wide swath through the ladies of his court in the manner of François

I and Henri IV. Except in a few pamphlets, mostly from the last years of the reign, he is an imposing figure, the virile master of a powerful kingdom, usually referred to respectfully as "le Grand Alcandre." Thus, despite its occasional irreverence, the scandal often puts Louis XIV in a favorable light; in some cases it may actually have reinforced the cult of the Sun King. The *libelles* against Louis XV present a very different picture of a monarch. By 1770, he has lost two world wars and all interest in the affairs of state. He cares only for women. But he is barely capable of an erection, so he falls under the spell of a common whore, who dominates him and the entire kingdom by applying the tricks that she learned in the brothel. The commonness of du Barry, her base origins and vulgarity, make her a very different heroine from the noble mistresses of Louis XIV. In dragging the king down to her level, she strips him of his charisma and drains the monarchy of its symbolic power. As several *libellistes* insist, the scepter in her hands appears as feeble as the royal penis.

Fifth, the early *libelles* often protested against tyranny, a notion that goes back to antiquity and that underwent a revival during the Renaissance. But the late *libelles* accused the monarchy of degenerating into a despotism, a concept that began to acquire a powerful new range of meaning at the end of the seventeenth century.[26] Both terms conveyed the idea of the abuse of power, but tyranny connected it with the arbitrary rule of an individual, someone whose removal would eliminate the problem, whereas despotism indicated that it pervaded an entire system of government. The shift from an individual to a systemic view of power abuse began during the last years of Louis XIV's reign, the period of disasters in domestic and foreign affairs from 1685 to 1715 that Paul Hazard characterizes as "the crisis of the European conscience."[27] Louis XIV did not simply pursue disastrous wars abroad while eliminating all opposition at home and bleeding his subjects dry with taxes; he also imposed an oppressive bureaucracy on the kingdom, continuing the work of administrative centralization where Richelieu and Mazarin had left off. To the aristocratic intellectuals who witnessed the catastrophes, the problem lay with the apparatus of the state as much as with the king himself. And to Montesquieu, who pursued their train of thought into the early reign of Louis XV, the problem pointed to a peculiar kind of state: a despotism, as distinct from a monarchy or a republic.

Earlier classifications had generally followed Aristotle's method of distinguishing states according to the locus of their power: government by one (monarchy), many (aristocracy), or all (democracy). But Montesquieu concentrated on the historical development of political systems, and Louis Quatorzean France, as it appeared in the *Lettres persanes* and *De l'Esprit des lois,* looked like a monarchy in the process of degeneration into a despotism. The Jansenist quarrels and the battles between the parlements and the crown reinforced this view. So, when the kingdom was shaken by the great crisis of 1771–74—the attempt under Chancellor Maupeou to destroy the parlements as a check on the power of the king—the *libellistes* could draw on a theoretical and historical explanation of events. Of course, they did not write political theory, nor did they simply produce propaganda for the parlements. But they had a larger view of affairs than was available to their predecessors in the seventeenth century. The experience of Louis Quatorzean absolutism and the political thought of the Enlightenment gave them what they needed to make sense of the Maupeou crisis: they saw it as the final stage in the development of despotism. From 1771 to 1789, despotism would be the main theme of *libelle* literature, one perfectly suited to the standard, scabrous details about royal orgies and *lettres de cachet.*

Was this sort of literature revolutionary? The short answer is no: none of the *libelles* urged the French to rise against the monarchy or to overthrow the social order. Many of them repeated motifs that went back to the sixteenth century and that would continue into the nineteenth—in Victor Hugo's *Le Roi s'amuse,*

A *libelliste,* pictured as "the armor-plated gazeteer," sending off cannon blasts in all directions against the abuses of the Old Regime: from the frontispiece to *Le Gazetier cuirassé, ou anecdotes scandaleuses de la cour de France,* by Charles Théveneau de Morande, a typical *libelle* of 1771, "printed a hundred leagues from the Bastille, at the sign of liberty."

for example, and Rigoletto's aria, "Cortigiani, vil razza dannata" (Vile, damned race of courtiers). Such themes composed a political folklore, which had a very long life and probably a long-term effect on general attitudes: like the drip, drip of water on a stone, the denunciations of dissolute kings and wicked ministers wore away the layer of sacredness that made the monarchy legitimate in the eyes of its subjects. Although individual episodes disappeared from the collective memory, general patterns remained. They formed a narrative frame, which could be imposed on situations as circumstances evolved. While the meaning of individual texts was keyed to current events, it also derived from a metatext elaborated over three centuries. Thus the *libelles* against Louis XV belonged to the sparring between Maupeou and the parlements, and at the same time they expressed a defiant stance toward royal authority that went back to the Catholic League and the Fronde. They called up images of Henri III and Mazarin, and in doing so they made Louis XV look like Louis Capet.

The long-term continuity in the history of *libelles* does not mean that it should be understood as endless repetition of the same thing. The *libelles* acquired new motifs and new forms as they evolved. From the artful slander of the Renaissance to *frondeur* pamphleteering, erotic political biography, and muck-raking protest against despotism, the literature of libel gathered force and transformed itself into a full-scale indictment of the regime, even if it did not call for a revolution. In fact, no one foresaw the Revolution or urged it on the French before 1787. The ideological origins of the Revolution should be understood as a process of delegitimating the Old Regime rather than as a prophecy of the new one. And nothing sapped legitimacy more effectively than the literature of libel.

Such, at least, is the conclusion to be drawn from a preliminary survey of the literature. It must be put tentatively, however, not only because the subject requires further study but also because it opens onto another range of problems: How did readers respond to illegal literature, and how did the forbidden books contribute to the formation of public opinion?

Chapter 9

Reader Response

DESPITE SOME PRELIMINARY FORAYS into the history of reading, we know very little about the ways readers responded to books under the Old Regime.[1] We have learned only enough to distrust our own intuition, for whatever the responses might have been, they took place in a mental world so different from our own that we cannot project our experience onto that of French readers confronted with texts two hundred years ago.

I think it valid nonetheless to make a minimal assertion: readers' reactions, though varied, tended to be strong. In an era when television and radio did not challenge the supremacy of the printed word, books aroused emotions and stirred thoughts with a power we can barely imagine today. Richardson, Rousseau, and Goethe did not merely wring tears from their readers; they changed lives. *Pamela* and *La Nouvelle Héloïse* inspired lovers, spouses, and parents to reconsider their most intimate relations and, in some well-documented cases, to modify their behavior. *The Sorrows of Young Werther* drove a few of Goethe's readers to take their own lives, even if the "Werther fever" did not produce a wave of suicides, as some Germans believed.

Those early romantic novels may seem unbearably sentimental today, but to readers in the eighteenth century they had an irresistible ring of authenticity. They established a new rapport between author and reader and between reader and text. Of course, there were many other genres and many different kinds of readers under the Old Regime. Compared with the sparse diet of earlier eras, the reading matter consumed in the eighteenth century seems so enormous that some have associated it with a "reading revolution." According to this thesis, the experience of reading was basically "intensive" until the mid-eighteenth century and "extensive" thereafter. "Intensity" derived from the practice of reading a few works, particularly the Bible, over and over again, usually aloud and in groups. When readers took up "extensive" reading, they raced through a wide variety of printed matter, especially periodicals and light fiction, without considering the same text more than once.

This formula was developed by some German scholars to explain the peculiar course of German history: while France had a political revolution and Britain an industrial revolution, Germany's route to modernity led through a "reading revolution," which opened up a domain of culture peculiar to a nation of *Dichter und Denker* (poets and philosophers). The thesis had a beguiling simplicity, but it rested on little evidence, except in the case of the densely Protestant and commercial regions around cities like Leipzig, Hamburg, and Bremen. Insofar as it could be applied to other parts of Germany and of Europe, it made a useful distinction between an older pattern of culture in which people owned only one or two books and read them repetitively, and a more prosperous and more literate phase in which people read one text after another. But this distinction did not correlate with the more important opposition between "intensive" and "extensive" reading. It ignored evidence that the old-fashioned, repetitive reading was often mechanical or ritualistic rather than intensive, while the new vogue for novels produced a more not a less intensive experience. Many Germans read *The Sorrows of Young Werther* over and over again (Napoleon read it seven times), and some even memorized it.[2]

True, readers turned increasingly to periodicals and other kinds of literature that had been relatively scarce in the seventeenth century. Reading habits no longer conformed to the picture of the paterfamilias declaiming Scripture to his household. But that picture never corresponded closely to practices in France, despite the sentimental evocation of it by Restif de la

Bretonne in 1779.[3] In fact, Parisians may have read more ephemera in 1649, when the presses of the Fronde turned out a half dozen pamphlets a day, than they did a century later. The first evidence of new reading habits can be detected around 1750, when catalogues of private libraries and registers of book privileges show a decline in religious works as opposed to fiction, history, scientific and travel literature.[4] But truly "extensive" reading on a mass scale did not predominate until late in the nineteenth century, when cheap paper, steam-powered presses, and greatly increased literacy brought new varieties of popular literature within the range of the general public. Nothing comparable happened in the eighteenth century. The technology of printing, the organization of the book trade, and the education of children did not differ fundamentally from what had existed a hundred years earlier. Although tastes changed and the reading public expanded, the experience of reading was not transformed. It became more secular and more varied, but not less intense. It did not undergo a revolution.[5]

Historians have discovered and dismissed so many hidden revolutions of the past that the "reading revolution" might be safely ignored, except that it has been invoked to explain the possible reaction of readers to the forbidden literature of the Old Regime in France. If reading had been revolutionized and readers had adopted a radically new attitude of casualness and skepticism toward texts, then perhaps they shrugged off the *livres philosophiques* as a trivial form of amusement.[6] This argument employs a hypothetical cause to account for a hypothetical effect, but it deserves to be taken seriously, because it is the only argument that has been advanced to dispute the influence of forbidden books. We cannot submit it to much of a test, however, because we have so little documentation of readers' responses, especially in the clandestine sector of the book trade. Pending further investigation, I can offer only a few scraps of evidence culled from the correspondence of authors, publishers, booksellers, and the book police.

Book reviews, unfortunately, provide little help. Forbidden books could not be discussed in periodicals that circulated in France, and in any case reviewing usually involved little more than publishing extracts or plugging works of allies and attacking those of enemies. But the Parisian literati often reported on scandalous works in newsletters that they wrote for foreign princes. Although these private gazettes could be even more biased than the official press—the gazeteers frequently reviewed their own books and those of their friends—they were uninhibited enough to contain some clues to the reception of illegal literature in the literary circles of Paris.

The most influential of the newsletters, Grimm's *Correspondance littéraire* (established in 1753 by F. M. Grimm with help from Diderot, Raynal, and others, and continued by J. H. Meister during the 1770s and 1780s), discussed many *livres philosophiques*. Its favorable reviews of atheistic tracts like *Le Christianisme dévoilé* do not prove much, because they were written by the Holbacheans within its own ranks.[7] But its reviews of the *libelles* against Louis XV indicate that sophisticated readers took political slander seriously, even if they disapproved of its vulgarity. Although he could not identify the authors of *Vie privée de Louis XV* and *Anecdotes sur Mme la comtesse du Barry*, Meister showed no sympathy for them: the first wrote like a lackey, he said, and the second like a valet. Nonetheless, the substance of their writing deserved serious attention. By endeavoring to separate fact from fiction, the *Vie privée* provided a fairly balanced account of Louis XV's reign.[8] And the *Anecdotes* deserved high marks for impartiality and verisimilitude if not for style: "His [the anonymous author's] history is neither absolutely false nor absolutely true: although it falls short of the truth, it comes close to it most of the time."[9] Meister had an even higher opinion of *Lettres originales de Mme la comtesse du Barry,* a collection of obviously apocryphal letters that were "all the more true for having been invented." They captured the spirit of Louis XV's reign:

> The very anonymous author of these letters not only seems to be quite well informed about all the minor intrigues that filled the last years of the reign of Louis XV, but he also seems to have an excellent knowledge of the character and turn of mind of most of the personages that he represents. . . . But the first reflection one is tempted to make after reading this extraordinary work is that in all the dazzling social whirl sur-

rounding Mme du Barry during the time of her favor there was no one, truly no one, any more worthy of respect than she was. One sees the greatest dignitaries, the most powerful figures of the kingdom debase themselves at her feet, beg for her credit, exhibit incomparably more greed than she does. They promote general disorder in the hope of profiting from it, alternately seek and betray her trust, undergo the most well deserved humiliations, and merit all the contempt that hatred and envy sought to heap on her.[10]

In short, the folkloric view of du Barry and politics in the court of Louis XV seemed convincing to a sophisticated contemporary in the Parisian intelligentsia.

The letters that have survived in the correspondence of publishers demonstrate the public's fascination with a half dozen authors of illegal books: Voltaire, Rousseau, Raynal, Linguet, and Mercier. But they almost never discuss the readers' responses. A rare exception in the papers of the STN is a letter from a merchant in Nantes named Barre, who sold a few books on the side. Barre had nothing good to say about the book trade in his town: "Merchants hardly think of literature at all."[11] But Raynal's *Histoire philosophique* was an exception:

The public has received this work with enthusiasm. The author has genius, true knowledge, and an honest heart. He paints things in vivid colors, and in reading him you feel your heart has been set on fire. He has torn away a great deal of the fatal blindfold that covers the eyes of the human race and prevents it from seeing the truth.[12]

The STN received a similar report from Pierre Godeffroy, a merchant in Rouen, who also dabbled in the book trade. He, too, was an enthusiast, but for the more rationalist side of the Enlightenment. He asked the STN to send him a half dozen copies of the *Système de la nature* so that he could supply friends who had developed an appetite for forbidden fruit. Everyone in his circle "venerated" Voltaire, he wrote; and he himself especially admired the rustic liberty of the Swiss, which he contrasted with the slavish spirit in France. While reading a travel book about a journey into the Swiss mountains, he said that he was moved by "the advantages that liberty produces. We need to show as many examples of that as we can to people here, who don't even have an idea of what liberty is."[13]

The professional booksellers did not write personal commentaries of this sort, but as explained in chapter 1, their letters provide plenty of testimony about the demand for *livres philosophiques*—"the philosophical genre, which seems to be this century's favorite," according to Pierre-Joseph Duplain of Lyon.[14] In the course of their shop talk, they offered observations about their customers' interest in particular authors and genres. For example, a peddlar named Le Lièvre who operated out of Belfort noted the peculiar "curiosity" concerning bawdy and irreligious works among the officers of the local garrison.[15] In Loudun, Malherbe picked up a strong interest in anti-clericalism: "The new works of M. Voltaire will certainly be in great demand. . . . As to sermons, their sales don't amount to much. Devotional works are common and religious ardor has cooled."[16] Everywhere booksellers sensed a powerful desire for political *libelles*—"critical works," as Petit of Reims called them, or "piquant articles" (Waroquier of Soissons), or "works on current affairs" (Carez of Toul).[17] They always mentioned the same texts, above all, *Anecdotes sur Mme la comtesse du Barry, Mémoires authentiques de Mme la comtesse du Barry, Journal historique . . . par M. de Maupeou, Correspondance secrète et familière de M. de Maupeou, Vie privée de Louis XV, Mémoires de Louis XV, Fastes de Louis XV, Mémoires de l'abbé Terray, Mémoires secrets, L'Espion anglais.* Their letters leave no doubt about the interest in such books; but, alas, they say nothing about how their customers read them.[18]

Of course, the texts themselves contain many clues about the responses anticipated by their authors and publishers. It was assumed, for example, that pornographic books were read for erotic stimulation. Hence Rousseau's famous remark about "books that one reads with one hand,"[19] and the climax of *Thérèse philosophe,* entitled "The Effects of Painting and Reading," where the Count provokes Thérèse to masturbate by plying her with *Histoire de dom B . . . , portier des Chartreux, Histoire de la tourière des Carmélites, L'Académie des dames,* and other pornographic best-sellers. But how can one test such assumptions against the actual experience of readers?

Some indications, especially about the effect of political works, are scattered through the memoranda and letters exchanged within the Book Trade Department (Direction de la librairie) of the royal administration. In June 1771, the subdelegate of the intendant of Caen warned the authorities that Normandy was flooded with forbidden books and that the readers took them seriously: "Reading these bad books produces a disturbed spirit among the citizens and provokes them constantly to shake the yoke of submission, of obedience, and of respect."[20] Labadie, a retired bookseller from Valenciennes, advised the police to take strong measures, although they could not expect to turn the tide of public opinion: "Today, everyone wants to think philosophically and to discuss governmental affairs. Everyone discourses on such matters and rushes to get even the most dangerous works that appear on them."[21] Not that the police informants connected this danger with an impending revolution. They perceived voguishness as well as discontent in the rage for "bad" books. Hence an anonymous memoire of 1766, which warned the police that the spread of *livres philosophiques* seemed to be unstoppable:

> Never has one seen so many forbidden works as today. . . . No one is ashamed to be occupied with a bad book. Instead, people take pride in it; it's enough for a book to be known as such for people to desire it all the more. And someone who can hardly spare an hour a day for healthy reading will talk about staying up whole nights with something bad.[22]

The professionals on both sides of the law realized that forbidden books attracted different kinds of readers who read in different ways. In a memo written from the Bastille, the sieur Guy, who peddled *livres philosophiques* while working for the Veuve Duchesne in Paris, described the varieties of readers and reading as follows:

> People are bent on getting them [forbidden books], no matter what the price. And who are these people? Precisely those

who by their birth, their position, their knowledge, and their attachment to religion should be the first to condemn them. But on the contrary, if they merely hear something mentioned in a hushed tone about a new work of this kind, they run after it—the courtier for his amusement, the magistrate in order to be kept informed, the clergyman to refute it, and members of the Third Estate in order to say that they have something rare and difficult to get. In short, it's a way of cutting a figure and being fashionable; and a man who doesn't have a six-livre *écu* to pay his cobbler will spend four louis [96 livres] in order to swim with the tide.[23]

To be in fashion, to be informed, to be aroused or moved—readers turned to illegal literature for many reasons and reacted in many ways. No one in the book business expected the reactions to be the same. But everyone treated the forbidden literature as a serious matter, important enough to demand attention from the highest officials in the kingdom and to occupy a whole department of the police.

Of course, police archives have a bias of their own. Inspectors of the book trade could curry favor with the lieutenant general by discovering threats to Church and State, and the lieutenant general could ingratiate himself with his superiors in Versailles by detecting and suppressing slander of "les grands." The papers of Jean-Charles-Pierre Lenoir, the most important lieutenant general of the Parisian police during the pre-Revolutionary years, must be read with particular caution, because Lenoir composed them at different times between 1790 and 1807, when he had fled from the French Revolution. He wanted to defend his administration against the revolutionaries, who had accused him of abusing his power and had run him out of the country. But Lenoir also wanted to understand what had brought about the collapse of the Old Regime. And he knew so much about its inner workings that his observations, scribbled in drafts for memoirs that he never completed, provide valuable information about the attitudes and policies toward forbidden books at the highest levels of the French government.[24]

According to Lenoir, *libelles* did not cause much concern in Versailles during the first years of Louis XVI's reign. The comte de Maurepas, the dominant minister in the government and a veteran of court intrigue, collected slanderous songs and epigrams: "In private gatherings, M. de Maurepas gaily declamed the verse written against him. He said that such things always were and always would be an amusement, something that occupied Parisians who had little to do and who wanted to impress people in high society."[25] But policy changed under the ministries of Necker, Calonne, and Brienne. By 1780, the ministers secretly subsidized writers to undercut one another. *Libelles* that had circulated in manuscript during the stormy last years of Louis XV now appeared in print, attacking the monarch himself. Then the slander turned on Louis XVI, deriding his supposed impotence, and on Marie-Antoinette, deploring her supposed sexual orgies. Defamation of this kind could not be laughed off, not even by Maurepas, who reversed his policy and organized secret missions to cut off the production of *libelles* in foreign countries. The Foreign Minister, the comte de Vergennes, dispatched undercover agents to kidnap *libellistes* in London. The police sent agents to Vienna and Brussels and kept raiding bookstores in Paris. But the slander appeared faster than they could repress it, so "the law was particularly ineffective against anti-government *libelles* during the years before the Revolution."[26]

In retrospect, it seemed to Lenoir that the mud slinging had "caused great harm to domestic tranquility, to the public spirit, and to [the spirit of] submissiveness."[27] The public believed the wildest stories, despite the government's attempts to counter them with accurate reports in propaganda of its own: "Parisians put more faith in wicked rumors and *libelles* that circulated clandestinely than in the facts, which were printed and published by order of the government or with its permission."[28] By 1785, Lenoir had to bribe the crowds to shout "Vive la reine!" when Marie-Antoinette appeared in Paris. But despite great efforts, he managed to produce "only some scattered applause, which everyone knew to be bought."[29] Years of slander had damaged something fundamental in the people's attachment to the monarchy.

Lenoir's remarks can be confirmed by documents in the Ministry of Foreign Affairs and the archives of the Bastille. In 1783, the Foreign Minister spent almost as much time trying to stamp out the London *libellistes* as he did negotiating the Treaty of Paris, which put an end to the American war. Slander was despicable, he wrote to the French chargé d'affaires in London, but when it struck at crowned heads it could not be ignored: "You know how evil our century is and how easily the most absurd fables are accepted."[30] After a great deal of hugger-mugger, the police bribed off some of the *libellistes* and lured others to France, where they were clapped up in the Bastille.[31] But soon afterwards, the Diamond Necklace Affair—the scandal involving the queen and the cardinal de Rohan—produced an even more disastrous wave of pamphleteering, and many Frenchmen went into the Revolution convinced that the king had been cuckolded by a cardinal.

Nowhere in all this material can one find any suggestion that books were simply "machines made to produce effects" and that readers were simply recipients with minds like "soft wax" ready to accept any message stamped on them.[32] Eighteenth-century Frenchmen understood enough about communication to expect readers and readings to be diverse. But they believed that *livres philosophiques* could produce powerful responses and that *libelles* could upset the stability of the state. We have no access to the minds of men and women as they manipulated texts two centuries ago. We can only study them indirectly, through the testimony of authors, publishers, booksellers, government officials, and the occasional reader who left some record of his reaction. But all the evidence points to the same conclusion: readers took forbidden literature seriously. All of it, that is, except one final document.

In his *Tableau de Paris,* Louis-Sébastien Mercier seems to minimize the effects of the *libelles:*

The more a *libelle* is forbidden, the more it is coveted. But when you have read it and seen that it provides no reward for your audacity, you are ashamed to have run after it. You hardly dare say, "I have read it." It's the froth produced by the lowlife of literature.... What *libelle* after two weeks has not been condemned by public opinion and left to its own infamy? ... An excessive *libelle* is revolting, disgusting, and undercuts itself by its own violence. But if it is more moderate, it sometimes counterbalances an excessive concentration of power; it goes beyond the limits of decency in the same way as the authorities abuse their power. It was often provoked by insolent little despots, and the public perceives the truth between two extremes.[33]

This passage does indeed suggest that the public did not believe everything purveyed by the *libellistes,* but it does not prove that readers refused to take *libelles* seriously. On the contrary, it makes a distinction between exaggerated slander, which could produce a counterreaction, and more moderate attacks on abuses of power, which could turn the public against the despots in the government. In this case, Mercier's description of "the public" seems to apply primarily to people like himself—that is, well-informed people, the insiders in the world of publishing and public affairs. In a similar discussion of satirical posters and pamphlets, he noted, "People in high society are amused by them but take them with a grain of salt."[34] Thus, like the booksellers and police agents, Mercier distinguished between sophisticated and ordinary readers. He never defined the latter, although he wrote a suggestive essay on "Monsieur le public" as an "indefinable composite" made up of ill-assorted and incompatible social traits.[35] Nonetheless, he insisted that a public did exist, in the form of a tribunal above the ebb and flow of fashion, which sifted through conflicting opinions and ultimately pronounced the truth.[36] The conviction that the truth would out also shaped Mercier's view of libeling, because he maintained that "a few good truths" in a lowly *libelle* could make a minister quake, and he even argued that the infamous Maupeou ministry was brought down by one of the most popular *libelles* on the best-seller list, *Correspondance secrète et familière de M. de Maupeou.*[37]

But suggestive as it is, Mercier's *Tableau de Paris* cannot be taken literally, as if it were a window into the minds of eighteenth-century Parisians. Like all texts, it has a rhetorical undertow, which carries it in contradictory directions. The contradictions stand out strongest in Mercier's references to reading, because on the one hand he celebrates the printed

word as the supreme power in history and on the other he dep-
recates journalism, hack writers, and *libelles*. Why this aversion
to the humbler forms of literary activity? Basically, I believe,
because Mercier did not want to be identified with them. He
had acquired a reputation as a "Rousseau of the gutter" *(Rousseau du ruisseau)* very much like Restif de la Bretonne, for
whom that phrase had been coined. In the literary newsletter
of Jean-François de La Harpe, Mercier appears as a failed play-
wright, vulgar compiler, and bosom companion of Restif.[38] In
the *Mémoires secrets* of Bachaumont, he appears as a hack, who
threw all sorts of garbage into the *Tableau de Paris* in order to
increase the number of volumes and squeeze the maximum
return from the market.[39] And in the files of the police, he is

> [a] lawyer, a fierce, bizarre man; he neither pleads in court
> nor consults. He hasn't been admitted to the bar, but he takes
> the title of lawyer. He has written the *Tableau de Paris,* in four
> volumes, and other works. Fearing the Bastille, he left the
> country, then returned and wants to be attached to the
> police.[40]

All the reviews concurred on the audacity of Mercier's criticism of the government and the social order. Like *L'An 2440,*
the *Tableau de Paris* became a best-selling *livre philosophique.*
But was it also a *libelle?* A review of the first, two-volume edition in the *Courier de l'Europe* said categorically, "This is not a
libelle; it is the work of a courageous and sensitive citizen." That
may sound like praise, but it cut Mercier to the quick. In volume IV of the next edition, Mercier devoted a long, vehement
chapter to the *Courier's* remarks, the only review he ever mentioned: "The criticism hardly amounts to an absolution! You
who have read me, tell me, can this work conceivably conjure
up any notion linked with that odious word *libelle?* Why use it?
It oppresses me."[41] Mercier's horror of *libelles* gave vent to his
anxiety that his own work could be classified as one, just as his
deprecation of hack writing expressed his fear that he might be
considered a hack.[42]

Indeed, everything that Mercier published about writers and
readers is revealing, not so much about actual practices as about

dominant themes in the contemporary discourse on literature. In nearly all his works, he returned obsessively to the same topic: Enlightenment is spreading everywhere; writers are the unacknowledged legislators of the world; the printing press is the most powerful engine of progress; and public opinion is the force that will sweep despotism away. One example should be enough to illustrate his tone:

> A great and momentous revolution in our ideas has taken place within the last thirty years. Public opinion has now become a preponderant power in Europe, one that cannot be resisted. In view of the progress that has occurred and will occur, one may hope that enlightened ideas will bring about the greatest good on earth and that tyrants of all kinds will tremble before the universal cry that echoes everywhere, awakening Europe from its slumbers. . . . The influence of writers is such that they may now openly proclaim their power and no longer disguise the legitimate authority they exercise over people's minds.[43]

Reading occupied a central position in this bundle of leitmotifs. Mercier drew on the stock images of early Romanticism to describe its operation: a moral force, as irresistible and invisible as gravity or electricity, was generated by a genius, released from his pen, transmitted through type, and imprinted in the soul of the reader.[44] Hence the chapter on printing in *De la Littérature et des littéraires,* which Mercier reprinted in *Mon Bonnet de nuit:*

> It [printing] is the most beautiful gift of heaven. . . . It soon will change the countenance of the universe. From the compositor's narrow cases in the printing shop great and generous ideas emerge, which man cannot resist. He will adopt them, despite himself; their effect is already visible. Printing was born only a short while ago, and already everything is heading toward perfection. . . . A despot, surrounded by guards, by fortresses, defended by two thousand naked swords, may be deaf to the call of conscience; but he cannot resist a stroke of the pen: this stroke will fell him in the heart of his grandeur.

. . . Tremble, therefore, tyrants of the world! Tremble before
the virtuous writer![45]

Mercier did not allow anything ignoble to spoil this picture.
In the Utopian fantasies of *L'An 2440,* he eliminated all unworthy books, filled public spaces with statues of writers, and made
reading and writing into solemn spiritual exercises. In his
essays, he often protested against overly sophisticated or trivial
literature, which undercut the moral purpose of reading.[46] And
in his plays and novels, he inserted reading scenes to redirect
the plot at crucial turning points. For example, *Jezennemours,* a
sentimental tale about the triumph of love over religious big-
otry, recounts a Jesuit plot to seize control of the hero's soul
and to turn him into a priest by force-feeding him with theological and devotional works in a boarding school in Strasbourg.
One day, a peddler accosts him in the street and offers him
some *livres philosophiques* under the cloak. His curiosity piqued,
the hero buys four Voltairean tracts. A preliminary skim
through the texts is enough to whet his appetite. He stays up
all night, devouring them in his cell. Then the scales fall from
his eyes. He abandons the priesthood and escapes to his true
love, Suzanne, the "belle luthérienne."

In telling the story, Mercier uses all sorts of concrete details
to evoke the sensation of consuming forbidden literature: the
ample folds of the peddler's cloak in which the books were hidden; the cheap paper and crude printing of the underground
editions; the fascination evoked by the diabolical name of Voltaire; the peddler's assurance that such things sold like hot
cakes; the sensation of cutting the first pages with a pocket
knife; the excitement of carrying the small volumes under a
shirt and in a pocket; and the final immersion in the texts late
at night, as the wick of the lantern sputtered and burned down
to a stub. The description, narrated in the first person, goes on
for two chapters, providing one of the richest accounts of reading as an author of forbidden books liked to imagine it:

> Anyone who had seen me reading would have compared me
> to a man dying of thirst who was gulping down some fresh,
> pure water. . . . Lighting my lamp with extraordinary caution,

I threw myself hungrily into the reading. An easy eloquence, effortless and animated, carried me from one page to the next without my noticing it. A clock struck off the hours in the silence of the shadows, and I heard nothing. My lamp began to run out of oil and produced only a pale light, but still I read on. I could not even take out time to raise the wick for fear of interrupting my pleasure. How those new ideas rushed into my brain! How my intelligence adopted them![47]

Overblown as it is, this description actually corresponds to the experience of many eighteenth-century readers.[48] Of course, it represents an ideal type rather than a common practice. But that is the point: far from providing unambiguous evidence about the diminished power of the printed word and the casualness of readers, Mercier articulated a widespread conviction that reading could move mountains—and remove despots, especially if the books were "philosophical."

How could *livres philosophiques* produce such extraordinary effects? Even Mercier did not invoke simple notions of causality. Like many of his contemporaries, he envisioned an indirect process by which books determined the course of public opinion and public opinion shaped events. But that notion, too, is an ideal construct, expressed in its noblest form by Condorcet in the *Esquisse d'un tableau historique des progrès de l'esprit humain*. Having examined what people thought happened to them and ought to happen to them when they read forbidden books, we now face a final problem: How did *livres philosophiques* contribute to the radicalization of public opinion?

Chapter 10

Public Opinion

THE QUESTION OF PUBLIC OPINION cannot be dispatched in a few pages any more easily than the problem of reader response. But a brief discussion of it may help clear the way for further study and also for an answer to a final objection: Perhaps forbidden books did not affect public opinion at all; perhaps they merely reflected it. This thesis rests on two kinds of arguments about the autonomous character of attitudes toward the monarchy among the common people in Paris. According to the first, a "desacralized" view of kingship can be detected from spontaneous, small changes in the daily life of Parisians.[1] According to the second, the Parisians began to express open hostility to the king in the 1750s and perhaps even earlier.[2]

The first argument derives from some other observations about everyday life in the *Tableau de Paris*. Mercier noted that second-hand dealers sold old, wrought-iron signs painted with images of kings and queens and that Parisians thought nothing of buying a picture of Louis XVI or Catherine II to hang outside their taverns and tobacco shops. Nor did they hesitate to purchase "cakes à la royale" and "beef à la royale" in food stores.[3] According to Roger Chartier, this casual use of images and words demonstrates a "symbolic and emotional disinvestment" that desacralized the monarchy, robbing it of all "transcendent significance." Indeed, it explains the success of the *livres philosophiques,* because the desacralization of attitudes came before the publication of the books rather than vice versa.[4] In fact, the chronology does not serve this interpretation very well, because the first edition of the *Tableau de Paris* came out in 1781, long after the first *libelles* against Louis XV, and *libellistes* had been slinging mud at monarchs for two centuries before Mercier noticed the familiarity with royal accoutrements in Parisian shops. More important, casual and even irreverent handling of sacred objects does not provide evidence of desacralization. In the Middle Ages, people chatted with, leaned against, and defecated near holy objects with a familiarity that seems sacrilegious to us but that actually expressed the all-pervading power of their faith. And even today, royal signs outside pubs and labels on toiletries in England proclaiming, "By special appointment from Her Majesty the Queen," do not bespeak any disaffection for the monarchy; quite the contrary.[5]

The second argument is more serious; and as it leads directly into the problem of charting public opinion, it must be examined carefully. Like everyone else, the French authorities failed to define "the public," but they knew it had opinions and they took those opinions seriously. The Paris police developed an elaborate network of informers in order to keep track of discussions in cafés, taverns, and other public places. Reports of these *propos*—loose talk about current events—provide a rough index to the state of public opinion in Paris throughout the eighteenth century.

Here, for example, is what was being said in cafés during the late 1720s, according to the police spies. At one point in 1728, the customers in the Café de Foy could hardly believe that N.-P.-B. d'Angervilliers had been appointed Minister of War, because his rival, F.-V.-L. de Breteuil was protected by the queen. Those in the Café Rousseau thought the appointment presaged further changes, probably a new intendant of Paris and perhaps a new lieutenant general of police. Meanwhile, at the Café de l'Enclume, a heated argument broke out between those who condemned d'Angervilliers for his brutal, autocratic manner and those who admired his character. The controller general Philibert Orry won the applause of the regulars at the Café de la Régence, because he had just humiliated the directors of the General Tax Farm (wealthy financiers who contracted with the crown to collect indirect taxes) in a quarrel over a *Te Deum* to be sung by the Jacobins. Talk at the Café Cotton was about maneuvers on the Bourse, at the Café de la Veuve Laurent about the price of bread, at the Café de Poinselet about speculation on grain, at the Café de Basteste about speculation on gold, at the Café du Puits on the pregnancy of the queen, at the Café de Conti on the French sympathies of the king of Spain, at the Café Gradot about the prohibition of a play, at the Café Procope about the poor health of the cardinal de Fleury, at the Café de Moisy about Jansenist agitation, and so on, in stupendous detail, including plenty of remarks about non-political events— a highway robbery, a prison break, a fire in Troyes, and a storm in Champagne that damaged vineyards with hailstones as big as chicken eggs. The reports covered about fifty cafés scattered throughout the city. Other agents informed the police about conversations in working-class taverns, *bons mots* in salons, and general gossip in public gardens. Strategically placed at the center of this vast information system, the lieutenant general of police had a remarkable knowledge of the talk of the town. By means of his weekly reports to the king and the minister of the *maison du roi* (in effect the Ministry of the Interior), the government kept a firm hand on the pulse of the public. It lacked pollsters, but it followed the course of public opinion.[6]

Some of the reports were written in the form of dialogue, so that in reading them, one can imagine eavesdropping on political discussions held 260 years ago. That fantasy should be resisted, however, because the police spies were not stenographers, and their reports, like all historical documents, are just texts, not transparent windows into the past. Nonetheless, the reports reveal enough for one to get a general idea of how Parisians talked about Louis XV early in his reign. Here is an example:

At the Café de Foy someone said that the king had taken a mistress, that she was named Madame Gontaut, and that she was a beautiful woman, the niece of the duc de Noailles and the comtesse de Toulouse. Others said, "If so, then there could be some big changes." And another replied, "True, a rumor is spreading, but I find it hard to believe, since the cardinal de Fleury is in charge. I don't think the king has any inclination in that direction, because he has always been kept away from women." "Nevertheless," someone else said, "it wouldn't be the greatest evil if he had a mistress." "Well, Messieurs," some others added, "it may not be a passing fancy, either, and a first love could raise some danger on the sexual side and could cause more harm than good. It would be far more desirable if he liked hunting better than that kind of thing."[7]

As always, the royal sex life provided plenty of material for gossip, but the talk tended to be friendly. In 1729, when the queen was about to give birth, the cafés rang with jubilation:

Truly, everyone is delighted, because they all hope greatly to have a dauphin. . . . One of them said, *"Parbleu,* Messieurs, if God graces us with a dauphin, you will see Paris and the whole river aflame [with fireworks in celebration]." Everyone is praying for that.[8]

Twenty years later, the tone had changed completely. Here are some typical extracts from the archives of the Bastille for 1749:

Jules-Alexis Bernard, chevalier de Bellerive, esquire, former captain of dragons: In the shop of the wigmaker Gaujoux, this individual read aloud . . . an attack on the king in which it was said that His Majesty let himself be governed by ignorant and incompetent ministers and had made a shameful, dishonorable peace [the Treaty of Aix-la-Chapelle], which gave up all the fortresses that had been captured . . . that the king, by his affair with the three sisters [the daughters of the marquis de Nesle, whose affairs with Louis XV were commonly considered both incest and adultery] scandalized his people and would bring down all sorts of misfortune on himself if he did not change his conduct; that His Majesty scorned the queen and was an adulterer; that he had not confessed for Easter communion and would bring down the curse of God upon the kingdom and that France would be overwhelmed with disasters.[9]

Fleur de Montagne, defrocked Jesuit . . . Among other things, he said that the king didn't give a fuck about his people, as shown by his enormous expenditures; that he [Louis XV] knew the people were destitute and that he would make them still more miserable by burdening them with a new tax [the *vingtième* proposed by Machault d'Arnouville], as if to thank them for all they had done for him. "The French are crazy to stand for this," he added. He whispered the rest into somebody's ear.[10]

Jean-Louis Leclerc, lawyer in the parlement: Made the following remarks in the Café Procope: that there was never anything as rotten as the court, that the ministers and that whore Pompadour were making the king do unworthy things, which completely disgusted the people.[11]

Despite the imperfections of the sources and the fuzziness surrounding the very idea of public opinion, it seems clear that the public's respect for the monarchy plummeted in the mid-eighteenth century. One can find plenty of reasons for this change: the humiliation in foreign affairs after the War of the Austrian Succession, the fiscal crisis and the controversy over the *vingtième* tax, and the Jansenist agitation, which produced a new round of fierce conflict between the crown and the parlements. Much of the discontent became attached to the king's private life, which fed "public noises" at the very time when the king lost touch with the public and abandoned some of the key rituals of kingship. After 1738, when he began to parade his mistresses at court, Louis XV found it impossible, as an open adulterer, to confess himself and take communion on Easter with the traditional pomp. Having failed to maintain the rites of confession and communion, he then discontinued the rite of touching people afflicted with scrofula. His brush with death at Metz in 1744 brought a brief period of penance for his notorious love affairs and a brief resurgence of his popularity. But Louis soon took up again with the de Nesle sisters, then with Madame de Pompadour and Madame du Barry—all of them so hated by the Parisians that he finally stopped coming to Paris. By 1750 there were no more ceremonial *entrées* to the city, no more masses graced with the king's presence, no more touching of the sick in the Great Gallery of the Louvre, and no more reaffirmation of God's protection of "the Eldest Son of the Church" at Easter. The king had lost the royal touch, and with it he had lost contact with the common people of Paris.[12]

Sea-changes in attitudes cannot be dated precisely, nor can they be assigned exact causes. But it seems likely that many French people—not salon sophisticates but shopkeepers and artisans—felt that the king's sins had brought down the wrath of God upon his people. Bad harvests and military defeat could be interpreted as signs of the loss of God's favor. And they occurred just when a wave of chiliastic, popular Jansenism swept through the lower classes of Paris and the main provincial cities. By persecuting the Jansenists, Louis seemed to be doing the work of the devil, or even acting as Anti-Christ, a role in which Louis XIV had been cast by the Huguenot pamphlets. Although the government vacillated in its handling of the Jansenist agitation, it generally supported the archbishop of Paris in his campaign to prevent Jansenists, whom he considered as crypto-Protestants, from receiving the last sacraments on their deathbed. In 1750 most Frenchmen still adhered to a highly ritualized, "baroque" variety of Catholicism. For them, the deathbed ritual remained the most important moment in the quest for salvation. By making a "good death," they could repair a lifetime of sinning. But Louis, a sinner himself, seemed to snatch that possibility away from his most saintly subjects, the Jansenist leaders whom the common people revered. It was as if he stood between them and their sacraments, and so condemned their souls to Purgatory.[13]

In short, by tampering with the sacred, in both royal and personal rituals, Louis XV seems to have ruptured the lines of legitimacy that bound the people to the crown. The monarch himself may have done more to desacralize the monarchy than any *libelliste*. And the damage took place in midcentury, at least twenty years before the publication of the most important books attacking him. Does it follow that the *libelles* had little impact on public opinion, that they should be understood more as an effect than as a cause of the public's disaffection with the monarchy?

At this point, it seems appropriate to issue a warning about the bag of tricks that historians play on the dead. I have spliced some police reports with a narrative about popular Jansenism, ordering the chronology and adding ethnographic comments in a way to make the years around 1750 appear as a crucial breaking point in the history of the French monarchy. I have done so in good faith. But I have offered an argument, nothing more, and I cannot pretend to know what really makes a value system rupture. Certainly it seems extravagant to think that the French could have read some smutty accounts of the kings' private lives and then suddenly, as a consequence of their reading, lost their faith in kingship. The shattering of belief probably occurs at a more fundamental level, one involving sacred rituals on the one hand and patterns of everyday behavior on the other.

Yet it also seems exaggerated to claim that something, at this visceral level of belief, snapped circa 1750, permanently severing the people from their sovereign. The sound, the pain of the wound do not appear in the documents. I can locate a change of tone in the gossip of cafés and pick up echoes in a few contemporary diaries, but is that enough to support a major claim about the collapse of legitimacy in an ancient political system? One can find plenty of angry talk about kings and queens before 1750. According to Arlette Farge, an expert on police archives and the history of the Parisian poor, the bad-mouthing of sovereigns extends far back into the eighteenth century.[14] I would argue that it contributed to all the political explosions in early modern Paris—especially the great crises of 1648–52, 1614–17, and 1588–94, which made the troubles of the mid-eighteenth century look mild in comparison. Instead of positing a scission that severed the people's attachment to the crown in 1750, I think it more reasonable to envisage a series of shocks and a long-term process of erosion. The mid-century crisis was important, but so were the earlier traumas and the supreme crises of 1770–74 and 1787–88. At every critical juncture, *libelles* and *mauvais propos* appeared together, marking off phases in the emergence of public opinion as an ingredient in the political system of the Old Regime.

Cause or effect? Slander by word of mouth or by print? The questions have a misleading, either / or quality. The *libelles* and the *mauvais propos* existed simultaneously, reflecting and reinforcing one another as they evolved over a long span of time. They both shaped and expressed public opinion as it, too, changed form and gathered force across the centuries. To attach priority to one element or the other would be to lose one's way in a chicken-and-egg hunt for an original cause. The point, as I see it, is not to determine what came first or what caused what, but rather to understand how all the media interacted in the process of forming public opinion.

"The media" conjures up notions of television, radio, and daily newspapers. France had none of those (the first French daily, the *Journal de Paris,* began publication in 1777, but it contained little that we would recognize as "news"), yet the French received a great deal of information through the communication systems peculiar to the Old Regime. Word spread through gossip, songs, letters, prints, posters, books, pamphlets, manuscript gazettes, and newspapers of sorts—foreign periodicals and the official, heavily censored French press. How did these modes of communication—oral, visual, written, and printed— insert themselves into contemporary consciousness, articulating and directing that mysterious force called "public opinion"? No one knows. In fact, no one has even raised the question, because public opinion has rarely been taken seriously as an ingredient of Old Regime politics. Insofar as historians have studied it at all, they have generally treated public opinion as an idea debated by philosophers rather than a force shaping events. I cannot dispense with the subject in what remains of this chapter, but I would like to try to dispel some of the confusion surrounding it by discussing the importance of libel literature in the 1780s.[15]

On the face of it, books would seem to have little influence on events. According to diffusion studies like Mornet's *Origines intellectuelles de la Révolution française,* they contribute to the formation of a climate of opinion—a general outlook or set of attitudes—which provides the background of events. They do not determine public opinion, which occupies the foreground and can best be studied by consulting pamphlets, gazettes, and gossip. But the relation between these phenomena remains unclear. How does a climate of opinion turn into public opinion, or background connect with foreground? Not simply by the popularization in journals of ideas developed in books. Journals convey news. So did café gossips and clandestine gazeteers, two varieties of *nouvellistes* who spread the news through oral and written circuits of communication. To follow the flow of public opinion, one must consult the work of these premodern newsmen. But the historian who sifts through such sources looking for signs of the oncoming Revolution is bound to be disappointed. Let us say he reads all the available police reports on *mauvais propos* (regrettably thin for the 1780s), all the issues of the *Journal de Paris* (the heavily censored Parisian daily), all of the *Courrier de l'Europe* (a French periodical produced twice a week in London and Boulogne-sur-Mer and tolerated by the French government), and every entry in the *Mémoires secrets pour servir à l'histoire de la république des lettres* (a highly illegal, printed version of a manuscript gazette): he will get the impression that the French were interested in little more than balloon flights, the miraculous cures of Dr. Mesmer, and American rebels. Public opinion in the late 1770s and the 1780s seems to have been oblivious to domestic politics. True, it heated up during the turbulent ministries of Turgot and Necker. But between Necker's fall (1781) and the so-called pre-Revolution (1787–88), political news virtually disappears from all the sources. The French seem to have lapsed into a curious calm before the storm. And when the storm finally broke, it seemed to come from nowhere—neither from a "climate of opinion" produced by books, nor from a public opinion whipped up by journals and seditious talk.

These paradoxes look less puzzling if one considers the nature of news. It is, I believe, a cultural construct: not what happened, but stories about what happened, stories produced by specialists who share conventions about what a story is and how it should be told. Those conventions vary over time; so the news of one century can look bewildering to readers in another, and it can differ greatly from the restrospective stories constructed by historians. We know little about what made stories compelling to eighteenth-century readers; but whatever it was, we may get it wrong if we assume too great a divergence between the narratives of books and the narratives of news. Perhaps *libelles* were newsworthy after all.

They certainly made news immediately after Louis XV's death in 1774. At that time the reading public was hungry for the inside story about the "king's secrets" during the previous reign. But the secrets made such good stories that they continued to fascinate the French for the next fifteen years, as they were recounted over and over again, sometimes in the form of epistolary exchanges, sometimes as reports of an English spy, or as what-the-butler saw, or as memoirs, biography, *chronique scandaleuse,* or contemporary history. The *libelle* literature kept changing form and growing, until it composed a corpus of enormous proportions and dominated the best-seller list throughout the 1780s. Thus, as Lenoir observed, the slandering of Louis XV did most damage long after his death. In fact, it helped to bring down Louis XVI.

Perhaps the interest in royal sex remains strong enough today for us to appreciate the appeal of this literature, but we need to understand how that appeal operated. It involved three basic rhetorical strategies, each of which had affinities with contemporary journalism. First, as in the notion that "names make news," it gave readers a specious sense of familiarity with "les grands." The *libellistes* used devices perfected by Bussy-Rabutin—precise physical descriptions, dialogue, and excerpts from letters—to build up the illusion of witnessing the inner life of the court from the perspective of an invisible voyeur. Second, the *libellistes* crystalized general themes in anecdotes, which seemed to convey the flavor of life at the summit of society. They borrowed this material from the gossip of cafés and the vignettes of the underground gazettes. In fact, as we have seen, the *Anecdotes sur Mme la comtesse du Barry* interrupted its narrative so often with quotes from the gazettes and tidbits from the *nouvellistes* that it reads in places like a news sheet. But its anecdotes always illustrated a general point: the decadence and despotism of Versailles.

Third, unlike non-print media such as gossip and handwritten news sheets, the *libelles* embedded these stories permanently in books, making them available for multiple readings by a multitude of readers. And unlike other print media such as the short pamphlet and the *chronique scandaleuse,* they did not simply recount brief anecdotes or string them out in endless, formless series. Instead, they worked them into complex narratives, amplifying and diversifying their meanings. In *Anecdotes sur Mme la comtesse du Barry,* the anecdotes fit inside a bawdy Cinderella story, which could also be read as a political biography and a contemporary history of France. Moreover, the story belonged to a whole corpus of similar narratives. Together they constituted a repertory of related tales, using stock characters (evil ministers, conniving courtiers, libidinal royal mistresses) in stock plots (sexual success stories, rags to riches, *jeux de l'amour et du hasard*). Taken altogether as it evolved over the centuries, this literature expressed what I have called a political folklore. But segments of it, particular *libelles* published at a propitious moment, could also be news—revelations of hitherto unsuspected scandal in the secret recesses of Versailles.

News of this kind was hardly new. The skeletons, as they came out of the closet, looked remarkably alike and illustrated the same master theme: Following the excesses of Louis Quatorzean absolutism, decadence had set in, and the monarchy had degenerated into a despotism. But the material was lurid enough to engage the attention of the reading public during the quiet years of Louis XVI's reign, when direct discussions of political issues had relatively little appeal. Political messages in the 1780s often became attached to ostensibly apolitical subjects such as foreign affairs, spectacular court cases, and scandals on the Bourse. The private life of Louis XV served them best of all—until the fiscal catastrophe forced the king to summon the Assembly of Notables in 1787, and the Old Regime entered into the last and greatest of its political crises. At that point, the vast corpus of *libelle* literature acquired a new meaning, one that became embedded in the events themselves.

Without attempting to relate the events, I think it fair to contrast two general views of them: one favored by most historians, and another held by most of the Frenchmen who followed them as they happened. Ever since Albert Mathiez launched the idea in 1922, historians have usually begun their accounts of the Revolution with an "aristocratic revolt" that broke out in 1787. This notion fits a general view of eighteenth-century political history, which pits a reforming monarchy allied with a rising bourgeoisie against a reactionary nobility protected by the parlements. Thus, at the climactic moment in February 1787, when the controller general, Charles Alexandre de Calonne, presented the Assembly of Notables with a progressive tax plan that would solve the crown's financial problems, the aristocratic Notables revolted, forced Calonne out of office, and precipitated the Revolution. This "pre-Revolution," or first stage of the overall Revolution, lasted until August 1788, when the king dismissed Calonne's successor, Loménie de Brienne, and summoned the Estates General. Brienne had adopted the main ingredients of Calonne's reform program, while the resistance to it passed from the Notables to the parlements. In a desperate effort to crush the parlements, Brienne reorganized the entire judicial system, repeating in essence the Maupeou "coup" of 1771. But the public refused to support him, and the fiscal pressure remained so intense that the king finally surrendered to the aristocracy, convoking an archaic body, the Estates General, which the privileged orders expected to dominate.

Although some historians have challenged this view,[16] the great majority have adopted it, whether they belong to the Left, like Mathiez, Georges Lefebvre, Albert Soboul, and Michel Vovelle, or to the moderate Left and Center-Right, like Alfred Cobban, Robert Palmer, Crane Brinton, and François Furet. The "aristocratic revolt" provided them with an interpretation that made sense of the whole course of early modern French history, while explaining the immediate cause and the first stage of the Revolution. It also helped to sort out the roles played by individuals. It made the leaders of the Notables and the parlements look like self-interested reactionaries, and cast Calonne and Brienne as progressive reformers. In one supremely anachronistic version, the reform program even appeared as "Calonne's New Deal."[17]

To contemporary Frenchmen, the world looked completely different. They did not perceive the "aristocratic revolt" that supposedly broke out under their noses. Most of them despised Calonne and applauded the Notables' resistance to him. When Brienne tried to force Calonne's taxes through the parlements, the public took the parlements' side. And when he tried to destroy the parlements, it took to the streets. Ordinary Frenchmen did not necessarily support the parlementary cause, but they did not want to pay more taxes. Instead of seeing the ministers' program as a war against tax privileges, they saw it as ministerial despotism. Calonne and Brienne seemed to repeat the authoritarian measures of Maupeou, and 1787–88 looked like a replay of 1771–74 or even of the Fronde.

Never has the historians' version of events and the contemporary perception of them diverged so greatly. This disparity can be explained in several ways, but ultimately it comes down to a dilemma: Either the historians have badly misinterpreted the causes of the Revolution, or the contemporaries suffered from a colossal case of false consciousness. For my part, I believe the historians are wrong, not simply because they see little more than class interest in the stand taken by the Notables and parlements, but also because they fail to see what the contemporaries saw—that is, they do not take adequate account of public opinion. The contemporary view of events was as important as the events themselves; in fact, it cannot be separated from them. It gave them meaning, and in so doing it determined the way people took sides when a truly revolutionary situation came into existence.

We are back to where we started, with the problems of determining public opinion, analyzing discourse, and developing a history of meaning.

I realize, of course, that I may have created a false dilemma, which can easily be resolved by locating the difficulty elsewhere—not with the historians, but with me. How do I, a fellow historian, dare speak for the consciousness of Frenchmen who died two centuries ago? To make my case, I will have to go over the "pre-Revolution" event by event, showing both what happened and how contemporaries construed those happenings. That is the subject of another book. In this one, I can only confess that the argument remains unproven, although I have read enough of the evidence (every pamphlet published between February 1787 and August 1788 in the Bibliothèque Nationale and the British Library) to be convinced of its correctness. I raise the issue here because it bears on the general problem of assessing the impact of forbidden literature.

By 1787, the reading public was saturated with illegal books of all kinds, which attacked the orthodox values of the Old Regime on every front. But the political *libelles* had particular resonance, because they fitted the events of 1787–88 in a specific way. As the crisis broke, lines were drawn and people took sides—informed people, that is, the "public" that constituted public opinion. In April 1787, everyone in this broad segment of society felt compelled to take a stand for or against Calonne. In July 1788, everyone rallied for or against the parlements. Seen through the historical literature, the situation looks hideously complex; and indeed it was—a bewildering mixture of rising expectations and rising bread prices, destitution among the poor and bankruptcy among the rich, impenetrable procedures by royal bureaucrats and unconscionable vexations by semi-public, semi-private tax collectors, all of it ostensibly directed by a government so eaten away by vested interests and special privileges that one can hardly locate power, much less see who was in charge. The more one learns about the Old Regime, the more inscrutable it appears. But in considering public opinion, which complicates things further by adding another dimension to them, I would push the argument in the opposite direction: from complication to simplification.

Instead of splitting the issues into hundreds of fragments, the pamphlets of 1787–88 simplified them. They presented the situation as a radical choice: for or against the government, for or against the parlements. They provoked the drawing of lines; they helped to polarize public opinion—and they also expressed it, because the formation of public opinion and the agitation of pamphleteers reinforced one another, functioning simultaneously as cause and effect. The complexities of tax reform hardly appear in the pamphlets. The vexed question of privileges was rarely raised, at least not before the convocation of the Estates General transformed the situation by posing the question of who would dominate the new constitutional order. Instead of analyzing the issues, the pamphlets heaped scorn on the government. Of course Calonne and Brienne had their defenders, who produced propaganda on the government's side. But the great majority of the pamphlet literature—and as much of the *propos* and "public noises" as one can trace through manuscript sources—reduced the issues to a single theme: despotism.

Or, more precisely, ministerial despotism. Few of the pamphlets attacked Louis XVI. After the Diamond Necklace Affair, he appeared more as an object of derision than as a threat to life and liberty. Instead, the pamphlets vilified Calonne and Brienne, making them look like monsters, depraved, debauched, and ready to fling any honest citizen into the Bastille. So much abuse was heaped on Calonne that it acquired a generic name: "Calonniana," the counterpart to the "Maupeouana" of the 1770s. The pamphlets, too, were *libelles*—shorter, sharper, and more up-to-date versions of the stories that had circulated in book form for the last fifteen years.

In this way, the libel literature from the end of Louis XV's reign became devastatingly pertinent at the end of the reign of Louis XVI. It fitted the events of 1787–88, providing a general frame for a fresh supply of anecdotes and *propos*. It helped contemporaries make sense of things by furnishing them with a master narrative, which went far back in time, beyond Louis XVI and Louis XV to Louis XIV, Mazarin, Marie de Médicis, and Henri III. A literary genre had grown from obscure verbal jousting in the Renaissance court to a full corpus of best-selling books. As it grew, it provided a running commentary on more than two centuries of political history. It assimilated new material and new rhetorical techniques into a body of tales, a political folklore, organized around a central theme with a single moral: The monarchy had degenerated into despotism. Instead of providing space for serious discussion of state affairs, this literature closed off debate, polarized views, and isolated the government. It operated on the principle of radical simplification, an effective tactic at a time of crisis, when the drawing of lines forced the public to take sides and see issues as absolutes: either / or, black or white, them or us. That the Bastille was nearly empty and that Louis XVI desired nothing more than the welfare of his subjects did not matter in 1787 and 1788. The regime stood condemned. It had lost the final round in the long struggle to control public opinion. It had lost its legitimacy.

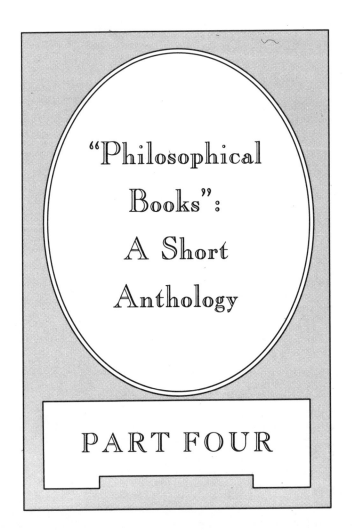

"Philosophical Books": A Short Anthology

PART FOUR

Thérèse philosophe, ou mémoires pour servir à l'histoire du P. Dirrag et de Mlle Eradice

(Thérèse philosophe, Or, Memoirs About the Affair Between Father Dirrag and Mademoiselle Eradice)

[No date or place of publication; probably first published in 1748; probably written by Jean-Baptiste de Boyer, marquis d'Argens]

WHAT, SIR, YOU SERIOUSLY want me to write the story of my life? You wish me to describe for you the mystical scenes between Mademoiselle Eradice and the Reverend Father Dirrag and inform you about the adventures of Mme C. with abbé T.? You are asking for an orderly and detailed description from a girl who has never written a word before? You would like an account in which the scenes that I have described to you, or those in which we have taken part, should be rendered in all their lasciviousness, and the metaphysical arguments should be preserved with all their force. In truth, my dear Count, that's beyond my capabilities. Besides, Eradice was my friend and Father Dirrag my confessor, and I have reason to be grateful to Mme C. and to abbé T. Will I betray the confidence of those to whom I am the most indebted? It is their deeds or, in some cases, their wise counsel which have caused the scales to fall from my eyes concerning my youthful prejudices. But, you say, if their example and their argument have brought me happiness, why wouldn't I try to bring happiness to others by the same means—by example and by argument? Why be afraid to write useful truths for the good of society? Well, my dear benefactor, I will resist no longer: I'll write; my ingenuity will make up for my lack of a polished style—at least for thinking men, and I care little for fools. No, you'll be denied nothing by your dear Thérèse, you'll know all the secret places of her heart from her earliest days. Her soul will be completely revealed through the little adventures which have led her, despite herself, step by step, to the height of sensual delight.

*   *   *

Address to the Theologians on the Liberty of Man

Answer me this, you theologians, either canny or stupid, who tax us with crimes at your whim: Who put in me the two passions which warred within me, the love of God and the love of sensual pleasure? Was it nature or the devil? Choose. But would you dare to assert that either one is more powerful than God Himself? If they are both subordinate to Him, it must be God Himself who ordained that these passions should be in me, who am His creation. But—you reply—God gave you reason to enlighten you. Yes, but not in order to determine my will. Reason certainly helped me perceive the two passions which enveloped me; that's how I concluded finally that, since everything came from God, so also had these two passions in all their force. But this same reason which guided me didn't help me to choose. But—you'll continue—since God had created you mistress of your own will, you were free to opt for good or evil. A pure play on words! This free will and this so-called liberty have no force of their own: they only operate in response to the force of the passions and the appetites which drive us. For example, I would appear to be free to kill myself, to jump out the window. But not at all: while the desire to live is stronger in me than the desire to die, I'll never be able to kill myself. A certain man—you'll say—is perfectly capable of giving to the poor, or to his indulgent confessor, the 100 *louis* which he has in his pocket. Far from it: since the desire which he has to keep his money is greater than that of obtaining a useless absolution from his sins, he will of course hang on to his coins. Anyone, thus, can see for himself that reason serves only to make a man aware of the strength of the desire he has to do or not do something or other, relative to the pleasure or displeasure he will derive from it. From this awareness achieved through reason, we acquire what we call *will* and *determination*. But this will and this determination are just as inferior to the forces of passion and desire which rule us as a two-pound weight trying to tip a scale that has a four-pound weight on the other side.

But—so a debater will insist who sees only externals—am I not free to drink with my dinner either Burgundy or Champagne? May I not choose for my walk either the *grande allée* at the Tuileries or the terrace of the Feuillants?

I agree that whenever the soul is completely indifferent to its fate, that when one's desire to do one thing or another is exactly balanced—in a perfect equilibrium—we cannot perceive this absence of liberty. It exists as a far-off haze in which we can discern no objects. But when we draw a little closer to these objects, we can observe quite distinctly the mechanisms of our actions. And as soon as we understand one, we understand them all, for nature is guided in all things by one and the same principle. Our interlocutor sits himself down at the table and orders oysters: the dish demands Champagne. But, you say, he was free to choose a Burgundy. I object; it is true that another reason, or a competing desire stronger than the first one, might have led him to opt for the Burgundy, but here again, this other whim would just as surely have compromised his supposed freedom of choice.

This same man, entering the Tuileries Gardens, catches sight of an attractive woman of his acquaintance on the terrace of the Feuillants: he decides to join her—unless some other motive propels him down the *grande allée*. But whichever path he chooses, there will always be a reason, a desire, which will lead him invincibly to the decision that reflects it.

To maintain that man is free, one must assume that he is capable of self-determination. But if he is determined instead by the degrees of passion instilled in him by nature and his senses, he is not free, for one degree of desire will tip the balance as surely as a four-pound weight will outweigh a three-pound one. Furthermore, I ask my interlocutor to tell me what prevents him from thinking as I do about the subject here under discussion, or why I cannot bring myself to reckon as he does on this point. He will reply no doubt that his ideas, his notions, his sensations force him to think as he does. But, having said this—and having thus demonstrated to himself that he is as incapable of willing himself to think like me as I am incapable of thinking as he does—he must admit that we are not free to think in one way or another. Moreover, if we have no freedom of thought, how could we have freedom of action, since thought is the cause and action only the effect? Could a *free* effect result from a cause which is *not free?* There is a contradiction here.

In order, finally, to convince ourselves of this truth, let's examine the question in the light of experience. Gregory, Damon, and Philinte are three brothers who have been educated by the same masters to the age of twenty-five. They have never been separated, have received the same upbringing, the same lessons on religion and morals. Gregory, however, loves wine, Damon loves women, and Philinte is very devout. What has caused these three different propensities in these three brothers? It cannot be their learning or their knowledge of moral good and evil, for they have each received the same precepts from the same masters. Each of them must, then, have had within himself different principles and different passions, which determined their dissimilar predilections despite the similarity of their received knowledge. What's more, Gregory, the wine lover, was, when sober, the greatest gentleman, the most sociable, and the dearest friend; but as soon as he had tasted the bewitching brew, he became carping, quarrelsome, and accusatory. He would have delighted in cutting the throat of his best friend. But had Gregory any control over this temperamental change that suddenly took place in him? Certainly not, for when he was sober he detested the actions which he was forced to commit when he was in his cups. Certain fools, however, admired the sexual restraint of Gregory, who had no taste for women, the sobriety of Damon, who hated wine, and the piety of Philinte, who cared not a whit for women or wine but who derived his own and equal pleasure from his devotional urgings.

Thus does most of humankind delude itself as to its virtues and vices.

To sum up, the arrangement of our organs, the disposition of our fibers, a certain movement of our fluids, all determine the type of passions which work upon us, directing our reason and our will in the smallest as well as the greatest actions we perform. Thus are zealots formed, as well as sages and fools. The fool is no freer than the other two, for he acts according to the same principles: nature is uniform. To imagine that man is truly free and capable of self-determination is to place him on a par with God.

Thérèse Leaves her Convent at the age of Twenty-Three Close to Death from the Efforts she has made to struggle against her Temperament

Let's get back to my own story. I have recounted how my mother removed me, at the age of twenty-three and near death's door, from the convent where I had been. My whole machine [i.e., body] was listless, my complexion jaundiced, my lips inflamed. I resembled a living skeleton. The practice of religion had almost dispatched me, when I regained my mother's home. A skilled doctor, whom she had sent to see me at the convent, had immediately spotted the cause of my illness: that divine liquid which affords us the one physical pleasure—the only one which we taste without bitterness—the one, as I say, whose flow is as necessary to certain temperaments as nourishment from food is to others, had flowed out of its customary channels and into unfamiliar ones, all of which had produced disorder throughout my machine.

My mother was advised to find me a husband as the only remedy for this life-threatening situation. She proposed this to me with great tenderness. But, infatuated as I was with my own prejudices, I responded angrily that I would rather die than displease God by accepting such a despicable estate, which He could tolerate only by His great kindness. All her arguments failed to shake my resolve. My weakened state left me no further desire for this earthly world, and I aspired only to the happiness which had been promised to me in the next.

She puts herself under the Direction of Father Dirrag at Volnot and becomes the Friend and Confidante of Mademoiselle Eradice

I continued thus my pious exercises with all imaginable fervor. I had heard much talk of the famous Father Dirrag: I wanted to see him. He became my confessor and Mlle Eradice, his most engaging disciple, was soon my best friend.

You know, my dear Count, the story of these two famous personages. I will make no attempt to repeat here all that the public knows about them and all that has been said on their subject. But one anecdote, in which I was personally involved, might amuse you and help to convince you that, even if Mlle Eradice eventually, with full knowledge of her actions, entered into a romantic relationship with this hypocrite, it is no less clear that she was, for a long time, the unwitting target of his pious lechery.

Mlle Eradice had entered into the most loving friendship with me; she entrusted to me her most secret thoughts. The closeness of our dispositions, our habits, our religious beliefs, perhaps even of our natures, made us inseparable. We were both virtuous, but we were consumed by a passion to gain a reputation for saintliness, together with an outlandish desire to perform miracles. This passion ruled her so completely that she would have endured all imaginable torments with a constancy worthy of the martyrs if she had been persuaded that she could thereby raise a second Lazarus from the dead. Father Dirrag had, first and foremost, the talent for making her believe anything he wanted. Eradice had confided to me on several occasions, with a sort of vanity, that the father would speak freely only with her, and that in these intimate conversations, which they often had in her room, he had assured her that she was only a few short steps away from sainthood, that God had revealed to him in a dream how she was just on the verge of performing the very greatest miracles if she only continued to comport herself with the required degree of virtue and mortification.

Everyone is prey to jealousy and envy, but a pious woman is perhaps the most susceptible of all.

Eradice saw that I was jealous of her happiness, and, more-over, that I seemed skeptical of all that she told me. In fact, I displayed all the more surprise at hearing of these inti-mate conversations with Father Dirrag, because he had always managed to avoid just this kind of encounter with me, in the house of one of his followers, a friend of mine who had received the stigmata, as had Eradice. Probably my sad mien and my sal-low complexion didn't appeal enough to the holy father to excite in him the appetite for his spiritual labors. I was drawn further into the competition. No stigmata! No conversa-tions with me alone! I let my anger show and pretended to believe none of it. Eradice, very moved, proposed that I should, on the following morning, witness her happiness with my own eyes.

"You'll see," she fervently assured me, "the power of my spir-itual exercises and the stages of repentance through which the good father is leading me to sainthood. And you'll no longer be able to doubt the ecstasies and the raptures which these exer-cises produce. My dear Thérèse," she added more calmly, "I do hope that, as my first miracle, my example can awaken in you the force to liberate your spirit from matter, through medita-tion, and to fix it on God alone!"

Mlle Eradice shuts Thérèse in a Closet from which she can View her room, so that Thérèse can Witness her Exercises with Father Dirrag

I arrived at five o'clock the following morning at Eradice's room, as agreed between us. I found her at prayer, a book in her hand.

"The holy man is coming," she told me, "and God with him. Hide in this little closet, from which you can both see and hear just how far divine mercy will extend to save its vile creation through the pious ministrations of our confessor." A moment later there was a soft knock at the door. I hid myself in the closet; Eradice pocketed the key. Through a hole as large as my hand, covered by an old, almost transparent Bergamo embroi-dery, I could easily observe the room in its entirety with no danger of being seen myself.

Father Dirrag Visits the Stigmata placed beneath the Left Breast of Eradice

The good father entered the room.

"Good day, my dear sister in God!" he greeted Eradice. "May the Holy Spirit and St. Francis be with you!"

She attempted to throw herself at his feet, but he raised her and bade her sit near him.

"It is necessary," said the holy man, "that I go over with you the principles by which you must be guided in all the actions of your life. But tell me first about your stigmata. The mark which you have on your breast—is it exactly as it was? Let's have a look."

Eradice made a move to uncover her left breast, just above his gaze.

"Ah, sister!" he cried. "Stop! Stop! Cover your breast with this handkerchief." (He held one out to her.) "Such things are not fit for a member of our society. It will be enough for me to see the wound which St. Francis has imprinted there. Ah! it's still there. Good," he said, "I'm delighted. St. Francis still loves you: the wound is neat and red. I've thought to bring with me the holy remnant of his cord. We'll make use of it later in our devotions."

Physical Demonstration by Father Dirrag in order to Convince Eradice to Suffer Flagellation without Complaint

"I have already told you, sister," the father continued, "that I have singled you out from all my followers, your companions, for I observe that God Himself has chosen you among His sacred lambs, just as the sun is singled out from the moon and the other planets. It is for this reason that I am not afraid to reveal to you His most hidden mysteries. I have advised you, my dear sister: forget yourself and let yourself go. God desires from men only their hearts and their minds. Only by forgetting the body can we find unity with God, approach sainthood, perform miracles. I cannot keep from you, my little angel, the fact that, during our last exercise, I noticed that your mind was still tuned to your flesh. What! Can you not imitate to some extent those blessed martyrs who were flagellated, tortured, roasted without the least suffering, because their imagination was so totally absorbed in God's glory that there wasn't the tiniest bit left over for other thoughts?

The mechanism is infallible, my dear girl: we feel, and we receive our ideas of physical good and evil, as well as moral good and evil, only through our senses. When we touch or hear or see an object, little particles of thought flow into the hollows of our nerves, and continue on to alert the soul. If, by the force of your meditations on your love of God, you have enough energy to gather together all the little particles of thought which are within you and apply them all to this end, not one will be left to warn your soul of the blows which your flesh is about to receive. You won't feel them at all. Consider the hunter: when his imagination is entirely occupied with the pleasure of stalking his prey, he will feel neither the thorns nor the brambles which tear at him as he advances through the forest. You may be weaker than he, but your goal is a thousand times greater. Will you feel the faint blows of the rod if your soul is fully occupied with the happiness which awaits you? This is the touchstone which leads us to perform miracles; this should be the perfect state which unites us with God.

Father Dirrag tells Eradice that he will make her Experience a Host of Pleasures by means of a Remnant of St. Francis's Cord (which he has in his possession)

"We're going to begin, my dear girl," the father continued. "Attend well to your duties and you'll be sure that, with the help of St. Francis's cord and your meditation, this holy exercise will end in a host of inexpressible pleasures. Get down on your knees, my child, and uncover those parts of your body which inspire God's anger. The mortification which they're going to experience will unite your spirit intimately with Him. I remind you once again: forget yourself and let yourself go."

Eradice uncovers her Buttocks to receive the Discipline of Father Dirrag

Mlle Eradice obeyed immediately without reply. She knelt upon a prayer stool with a book before her. Then, raising her skirts and her shift to her waist, she revealed her snow white buttocks, which formed two perfect ovals surmounting two thighs of admirable proportions.

"Raise your shift higher," the father told her. "It isn't quite right . . . Yes, that's it. Now put your hands together and raise your soul to God, filling your mind with the idea of the eternal bliss which is promised you." The father at this point brought over a stool, upon which he himself knelt behind and slightly to the side of Eradice. Under his robe, which he now raised and anchored under his belt, was a thick bunch of long birch rods. He presented them to his charge so that she might kiss them.

Father Dirrag Flagellates her while Reciting Verses

While watching this scene take shape I was filled with a kind of holy terror, and I experienced a sort of trembling which I can scarcely describe. Eradice said nothing. The father meanwhile devoured with his feverish eyes her buttocks, which were within full view of him, and, as he did so, I heard him gloat, under his breath:

"Oh, what a beautiful bosom! What charming tits!" He hunched forward, then backward, rocking rhythmically and muttering a few biblical verses. He gave free rein to his lust. After several minutes, he asked his disciple if her soul were in a state of contemplation.

"Yes, my very holy father," she said. "I feel that my spirit is completely detached from my flesh, and I beg you to begin your holy work."

"That's as it should be," the father replied. "Your spirit will find contentment." He repeated a few more prayers, after which the ceremony commenced with three strokes of the birches applied rather lightly to her behind. These were followed by a recitation of Scripture, succeeded by three more applications of the birches a little harder than the first.

He produces the Supposed Cord of St. Francis

After five or six of these scriptural recitations, interspersed with whippings, to my astonishment I saw Father Dirrag unbutton his pants and pull out an inflamed object identical to the dreaded serpent which had got me into trouble with my former confessor. This monster had the length, the width, and the firmness foretold by the Capucine. I trembled at the sight. Its reddish head seemed to threaten Eradice's buttocks, which had now become quite scarlet. The father's face was aflame.

"You should now be," he said, "in a state of the most perfect contemplation; your soul should be detached from your senses. If my child does not disappoint my holy expectations, she sees nothing, hears nothing, and feels nothing."

As he spoke these words, the torturer delivered a rain of blows over all the exposed parts of Eradice's body. Despite this, she remained motionless and spoke not a word, appearing insensitive to these terrible blows. The only movement I could distinguish in her was the convulsive movement of her two buttocks, which tightened and loosened incessantly.

After a quarter hour of this cruel punishment, "I'm pleased with you," the father said. "The time has come for you to taste the fruit of your holy work. Don't listen to me, my dear child; just let yourself be carried away. Bend forward face down. With the venerable cord of St. Francis I'm going to purge you of all your impurities."

The good father did, in fact, place her in this position—humiliating, truth to tell, but also the most useful for what he had in mind. He had never had such an appealing prospect: her buttocks were spread apart, affording him an unimpeded access to the twin routes of desire.

The hypocrite, after a few moments of contemplation, moistened with saliva what he called "the cord" and, pronouncing some words in the tone of an exorcist chasing the devil from a body possessed, His Grace began to insert it.

I was placed in such a way as not to miss the smallest detail of this scene. The windows of the room I was observing were directly opposite the door of the closet where I was hiding. Eradice was kneeling on the floor, her arms crossed on the step of the prayer stool and her head resting on her arms. Her shift had been carefully raised to her waist, and I had a view, in half profile, of her admirable loins and buttocks.

He is embarrassed by the Choice presented to him by the Two Orifices of Eradice. Prudence rules over his Natural Predilection

This pleasurable perspective commanded the full attention of the very reverend father, who had himself sunk to his knees, the legs of his young disciple between his own, his underpants pulled down, his terrible "cord" in his hand, as he murmured some barely articulate phrases. He remained for several moments in this edifying posture, his excited gaze drinking in the altar, seemingly unable to decide as to the nature of the sacrifice he was going to offer. Two orifices presented themselves to him. He devoured them with his eyes, overcome with the richness of the choice. One was a delicious morsel for a man of the cloth, but he had promised pleasure, ecstasy even, to his disciple. What should he do? He dared to direct the head of his instrument several times to the door he preferred. It knocked lightly against it, but prudence, finally, won out over his natural inclination.

He penetrates her. Exact Description of his Movements, his Positions, etc.

It must be said, in fairness to him, that I distinctly saw His Holiness's ruby red member take the canonical path, after he delicately opened its purple lips with the thumb and index finger of each hand. This work was begun with three forceful thrusts which caused half of it to enter. Then, all of a sudden, the apparent tranquility of the father was transformed into a sort of fury! Oh, God! What a countenance! He was like a satyr, his lips frothing, his mouth ajar, grinding his teeth and snorting like a bull. His nostrils flared, but he kept his hands raised in the air above Eradice's haunches, obviously reluctant to use them as a point of support. His fingers thus contorted and spread apart looked like the feet of a roasted capon. His head was bent and his glistening eyes were fixed on the work of his battering ram, whose thrusts he controlled in such a manner that, as it retracted, it did not leave its sheath completely and, as it shot forward, his stomach did not come into contact with the thighs of his charge, who might thus, upon reflection, have guessed the origin of this supposed cord. What presence of mind! I noted that approximately a thumbnail's width of the holy instrument was always held back, deprived of a role in the festivities. I saw also that with each backward movement of the father's rump, as the cord withdrew and its head appeared, the lips of Eradice spread open, revealing a crimson hue wondrous to behold. I noted that, in the next moment, as the father thrust forward, these same lips, of which one could now see only the short black hairs covering them, grasped the member so tightly that it seemed all but swallowed up. It would have been difficult to say to which of the two actors this tool belonged, as both of them appeared equally attached to it.

What mechanics! What a sight, my dear Count, for a girl of my age who had no knowledge whatsoever of these sorts of mysteries. So many strange ideas passed through my head! I could hardly think straight! I do remember that twenty times I was on the point of throwing myself at the feet of this famous confessor and begging him to treat me just like my friend. Was it a welling up of faith? Or was it a welling up of lust? That's what I still cannot quite sort out in my own mind.

Eradice and Father Dirrag Swoon with Pleasure. The Young Woman believes herself to be enjoying a purely Celestial Happiness

Let's get back to our acolytes. The father's movements were accelerating. He could scarcely now maintain his equilibrium. He had positioned himself so that he formed something resembling an S from his head to his knees, and the belly of this S moved in and out in a horizontal relationship with Eradice's buttocks. Her private part acted as a channel for the work in progress of his battering ram and directed the operations, while two enormous growths which hung down between the thighs of His Reverence seemed to be standing by as witnesses.

"Is your mind at ease, my little saint?" he asked, as a sort of sigh escaped him. "As for me, I see the heavens opening, and sufficient grace is carrying me aloft. I . . ."

"Oh, Father!" cried Eradice. "Such pleasure is penetrating

me! Oh, yes, I'm feeling celestial happiness. I sense that my mind is completely detached from matter. Further, Father, further! Root out all that is impure in me. I see . . . the . . . angels. Push forward . . . push now . . . Ah! . . . Ah! . . . Good . . . St. Francis! Don't abandon me! I feel the cord . . . the cord . . . the cord . . . I give up . . . I'm dying!"

The father, who was feeling the same rush of overwhelming pleasure, stuttered as he pushed, puffing and panting. When at last Eradice's words sounded the signal of retreat, I saw the once-proud serpent, now humble, creep foam-covered from its holder. Everything was promptly put back in its place. The father lowered his robe and, with an unsteady step, approached the prayer stool which Eradice had just left. There, after feigning to be lost in prayer for some moments, he beckoned Eradice to rise and cover herself, and then to come join him in thanking the Lord for the favors she had just received.

What more should I say, my dear Count? Dirrag left the room, and Eradice, having opened the door of my closet, fell upon my neck, crying:

"Ah, my dear Thérèse, do share my happiness! Yes, I have seen Paradise unveiled; I've experienced angelic bliss. So much pleasure, my friend, for only a moment of pain! By virtue of the holy cord my soul was almost freed from matter. You could see just how our good confessor introduced it into me. Well, I promise you that I felt it penetrate practically to my heart. Make no mistake: one degree more of excitement and I would have passed over forever into the realm of heavenly contentment."

Eradice told me a thousand other things, and in such a vivacious tone that I had no doubts at all as to the reality of the supreme happiness which she had experienced. I was so moved myself that I scarcely could find the words to congratulate her. With my heart in a state of the very greatest agitation, I embraced her and went away.

*　　*　　*

{Thérèse then retires to her room, falls asleep, and dreams about the scene she has witnessed. Unable to contain her sexual energy,

she rubs her private parts against a bedpost and wakes up feeling terribly sore. At that point, Mme C., an old family friend, arrives for dinner, accompanied by abbé T. Later, in a private conversation, Thérèse tells Mme C. of her ailment and Father Dirrag's spiritual exercises. Mme C. offers to take Thérèse under her wing, and the narrative continues as follows.}

An Introduction to Mme C. and abbé T.

As it is only fair, my dear Count, that you know who Mme C. and M. l'abbé T. are, I think it's time to give you some idea.

Mme C. was born in a family of good standing. Her parents had forced her, at the age of fifteen, to marry an old naval officer who was sixty. Her husband died five years after their marriage, leaving Mme C. pregnant with a child who, at his birth, almost cost his mother her life. The infant died three months later, and Mme C. found herself, after his death, in possession of a rather considerable fortune. A pretty young widow, self-sufficient at the age of only twenty, she was soon pursued by all the wife-seekers in the neighborhood. But she asserted so firmly her decision never again to run the risk of childbirth, after the miraculous escape from her first experience, that even her most enthusiastic suitors abandoned the field.

Mme C. was very intelligent, and she stood by her opinions, which she adopted only after mature reflection. She read a great deal and enjoyed conversation on the most abstract subjects. Her personal conduct was above reproach. Ever the indispensable friend, she helped out whenever she could. My mother had some useful experience of this when she was twenty-six years old. I will have an opportunity later to paint her portrait for you.

M. l'abbé T. was a particular friend of Mme C. as well as her confessor. He was, moreover, a person of real merit. He was forty-four or forty-five, small but attractive, with an open countenance. He was a witty man and a scrupulous observer of the niceties of his estate. He was much admired and sought out by members of polite society, who delighted in his company. He was intelligent and a man of broad learning as well. These good qualities, which were generally recognized, had earned for him

the post he filled at that time, and about which I must not speak here. He was the confessor and friend of many goodly persons of both sexes, unlike Father Dirrag, who specialized in professional holy women, enthusiasts, quietists [mystics], and fanatics.

Mme C. sends Thérèse to M. l'abbé T. for Confession

I returned the next morning to Mme C.'s at the appointed hour. "Well, my dear Thérèse," she said, as she entered the room, "how are your poor little wounded parts? Did you sleep well?"

"Everything is improving, Madame," I replied. "I did as you advised me. I bathed everything very well. That soothed me, but I hope at least that I haven't offended God." Mme C. smiled, and, after she had given me some coffee, she spoke.

"What you told me yesterday," she said, "is of much greater importance than you imagine. I thought it wise to discuss it with M. T., who is waiting for you at the moment in his confessional. I am asking you to go and find him and repeat to him word for word just what you told me. He's a gentleman and a wise counselor—just what you need. I think he will prescribe a change of conduct for you, something necessary for your health and your salvation. Your mother would die of worry if she knew what I know, for I must tell you that these are horrible things that you have seen at Mlle Eradice's. Now go, Thérèse, and put your complete trust in M. T. You'll have no reason to regret it."

I began to cry, and left all atremble to go in search of M. T., who entered his confessional as soon as he caught sight of me.

Salutary Advice from the Confessor to Thérèse

I hid nothing from M. T., who heard me out attentively, interrupting only to ask for clarification of certain points which he did not understand.

"You have just," he said, "made some astonishing revelations to me. Father Dirrag is a scoundrel, a poor devil who is letting himself be carried away by his passions. He is going to rack and ruin, and he's taking Mlle Eradice with him. However, Made-

moiselle, they are more to be pitied than blamed. We are not masters of our fate and cannot always resist temptation. Our lives are often determined by circumstances. Stay away, then, from these people. Stop seeing Father Dirrag and the young women in his care, without, however, speaking ill of any of them. Charity would have it thus. Spend your time instead with Mme C., who has grown very attached to you. She will give you nothing but good advice and wholesome examples to follow.

"Now let's speak, my child, of these powerful urges which you often feel in that part of your body which has rubbed itself against your bedpost. These are instincts as natural as those of hunger and thirst. You shouldn't search them out or excite them, but, on the other hand, if you feel an active pressure to do so, there's nothing wrong with using your hand, or your finger, to assuage that body part with the rubbing necessary for its relief. However, I expressly forbid you to introduce your finger inside the opening there. It's enough for you to know, for now, that this could arouse doubts in the mind of the man you will marry. Furthermore—I repeat it yet again—just as this need is aroused in us by the immutable laws of nature, it is from the hands of nature itself that we take the measures I've recommended to satisfy this need. Besides, as we are assured that natural law is divinely inspired, how could we fear that we offend God in relieving our needs by the means He has afforded us, the objects of His creation, especially when these means in no way disturb the social order? This is certainly not the case, my dear girl, for what happened between Father Dirrag and Mlle Eradice: the father tricked his disciple. He ran the risk of impregnating her by substituting for the pretended cord of St. Francis his own male member, which is used for procreation. In so doing, he offended against the natural law which teaches us to love our neighbor as ourselves. Is it neighborly love to expose Mlle Eradice, as he did, to the threat of lifelong dishonor and disgrace?

"My dear child, the insertion of the father's member in the private parts of his charge, and its movements which you have seen, are part of the mechanism for the production of the human race and are only sanctioned within the state of matrimony. If engaged in by an unmarried girl, this action could trouble family tranquility and work against the public good, which we must always respect. And so, as long as you are not bound by the sacrament of marriage, you must be careful to avoid such an act with any man, in any posture whatsoever. I have suggested to you a remedy which will moderate the excesses of your yearnings and cool the fire that excites them. This very remedy will improve the state of your health and put some weight on you, too. Your good looks will not fail to attract many suitors who will try to seduce you. Be ever on your guard, and keep in mind the lessons I have taught you. That's enough for today." The wise confessor added, "You can find me here a week from now at the same hour. Please remember that everything which is said here in the confessional is sacred for sinner and confessor alike. It is a heinous sin to reveal the smallest detail to anyone."

Thérèse makes a Happy Discovery while Bathing her Sexual Parts

The precepts of my new confessor had charmed my soul. I perceived in him an air of veracity, a kind of careful reasoning, a charitable philosophy which called into question everything I had heard heretofore.

I spent the rest of the day in reflection, and, when evening came, as I prepared for bed, I thought to bathe my painful private parts. Safe from all interfering hands and eyes, I pulled up my skirts and, sitting on the edge of my bed, I spread my legs as wide as I could and set about to examine in detail that part of my body which makes me a woman. I spread apart the lips of it and searched with my finger for the opening through which Father Dirrag had been able to penetrate Eradice with such a gross instrument. What I discovered left me still in doubt. The smallness of the orifice puzzled me, and I was attempting to introduce my finger into it when I remembered M. T's injunction. I withdrew it promptly. As my finger traveled up the length of the opening, a little protuberance that I encountered there caused me to shiver. I lingered there, rubbed harder, and soon gained the heights of pleasure. What a happy discovery for a girl who had within her an abundant quantity of the liquid which is the principle of pleasure!

For six months thereafter I bathed continually in a river of voluptuousness. During this period nothing else occurred that need concern us here.

My health was completely restored. My conscience was clear, owing to the ministrations of my new confessor, who gave me counsel that was both wise and well suited to human passions. I saw him regularly every Monday in the confessional—and every day at Mme C.'s. I now never left the side of this admirable woman. The cobwebs in my mind were dissipating little by little, and I was growing accustomed to think and combine things in my reason. No more Father Dirrag for me, and no more Eradice.

Precept and example are the greatest teachers in the schooling of the mind and heart! While admitting that they impart nothing, that each of us has within himself the seeds of his future development, it is nevertheless certain that they help to nurture these seeds. They make us aware of the ideas and the emotions to which we are susceptible, and which, in the absence of teaching or example, would remain buried or fettered deep within us.

Meanwhile, my mother continued her wholesale business, which was progressing badly. Many people owed her money, and she feared the looming bankruptcy of a Parisian merchant who might bring about her fall along with his own. After seeking advice on the matter, she decided to travel to this proud city. This loving mother cared too much for me to be out of touch during what might be a prolonged absence: it was decided that I would accompany her. Alas! The poor woman could not foresee that she would end her sad life there, and that I would find there in the arms of my dear Count the source of my own happiness.

We determined to leave in a month's time—a period which I would spend with Mme C. in her country house just a league away from town. The abbé stopped by regularly every day and stayed overnight when his duties permitted. Both of them heaped caresses upon me. They were not at all shy about speaking freely before me. They spoke of moral philosophy, of religion and metaphysical subjects, all in a manner very much at variance with the precepts I had been taught. I felt that Mme C. was quite satisfied with my way of thinking and reasoning, and that she took pleasure in shepherding me through my arguments to the proper conclusions. On occasion, however, I was distressed to note that M. l'abbé T. signaled to her not to forge ahead with certain arguments on certain topics. This discovery humiliated me. I resolved to do all in my power to discover what they were trying to hide from me. I hadn't the slightest suspicion, at that point, of the affection they felt for each other. Soon my curiosity would be satisfied, as you will hear.

You will see, my dear Count, from whence I garnered those moral and metaphysical principles which you have cultivated so well—those same principles which have shown me what we are in this world, and in doing so have assured me of this tranquil life, in which you are the happy centerpiece.

Thérèse Hides in a Thicket, from which she uncovers the Love Affair between Mme C. and l'abbé T.

We were then in a period of fine summer weather. Mme C. rose regularly around five o'clock in the morning and went to stroll in a little wood located at the bottom of her garden. I had noticed that l'abbé T. went there, too, when he spent the night in the country, and that after an hour or so, the two returned together to Mme C.'s apartment, and that neither one of them was seen thereafter until eight or nine o'clock in the morning.

I resolved to arrive in the little wood before them and to hide so that I could overhear them. As I hadn't the slightest suspicion of their love affair, I didn't realize what I might miss by not being able to see them. I went down to look over the terrain and find the most appropriate location for my plan.

That evening, at supper, the conversation turned to the workings of nature and her creations.

"What is this 'nature,' after all?" asked Mme C. "Is it some kind of being? Isn't everything created by God? Could it be some kind of lesser divinity?"

"In truth, you're not very rational when you speak like that," the abbé T. retorted quickly, with a wink in her direction. "I promise on our walk tomorrow morning to explain to you the idea one should have of the mother of all mankind. It's too late now to discuss this subject. Don't you see how boring it would be for Mlle Thérèse, who's nodding off already. If you'll take my advice, both of you should go up to bed. I'll finish my offices and follow your example."

The abbé's advice was heeded: each of us retired to her apartment.

The next morning, at dawn, I stole down to take up watch in my hiding place. I stationed myself in the bushes at the end of a tree-lined alley ornamented with green-painted benches and, here and there, a statue. After an hour's wait, in which I grew increasingly impatient, my heroes arrived and sat themselves on the very bench in front of my hiding place.

"Yes, indeed," the abbé was saying as they approached, "she does grow prettier every day. Her breasts have grown to the point where they could very well fit into the hand of an honest priest. Her eyes have a vivacity that betrays a fiery temperament, for she certainly has a strong one, that saucy little Thérèse! Can you imagine that, since I gave her permission to calm her passions with her finger, she's done it at least once a day! You must admit that I'm a good doctor as well as a kindly confessor. I've cured both her body and her mind."

"But, l'abbé," Mme C. retorted, "haven't we heard enough already about your Thérèse? Did we come here to talk about her beautiful eyes and her temperament? I suspect, my bawdy fellow, that you'd rather like to spare her the trouble she takes to apply your treatment on her own. For that matter, you know that I'm a good sport, and that I'd agree to it willingly if it weren't for the danger to you. Thérèse has lots of spirit, but she's too young and has too little experience of the world to be relied upon. I grant you her curiosity is without equal. In the long run she could develop into a very fine disciple, and, if it weren't for the drawbacks I've just mentioned, I wouldn't hesitate at all to include her in our pleasures. Because let's admit that it's silly to be jealous or envious of one's friends' happiness, especially when their enjoyment takes nothing away from our own."

Why Jealousy is Ridiculous

"You're absolutely right, Madame," said the abbé. "These are two passions which drive to distraction all those who lack an innate ability to reason. We must, however, distinguish between envy and jealousy. Envy is a passion inborn in man; it's part of his essence: babies in the cradle are envious of what their peers receive. Only education can moderate the effects of this passion, which we receive at the hands of nature. Jealousy, in its relationship to the pleasures of love, is something quite different. This passion arises from our sense of self-love and from prejudice. We can point to other nations where men offer their guests the enjoyment of their wives just as we offer ours the finest wines in our cellars. This foreigner gives a pat on the back to the lover in his wife's arms while his companions applaud and congratulate him. A Frenchman, in a similar situation, would pull a long face. He would be mocked and held up to public ridicule. A Persian would no doubt stab both the lover and the mistress, and everyone would applaud this double homicide.

"It is therefore clear that jealousy is not a passion instilled in us by nature. It is our education, our local prejudice, which gives rise to it. From infancy, a young woman in Paris reads and hears it said that it is a humiliation to endure the infidelity of her lover. Young men are assured that an unfaithful mistress or wife wounds their pride and dishonors either her lover or her husband. Out of these teachings, which are imbibed, we might say, with our mothers' milk, jealousy is born—that green-eyed monster who leads men to rack and ruin all because of an imaginary slight. Let's be clear, however, about the difference between inconstancy and infidelity. I love a woman who loves me; her character is at one with my own; the sight of her face, the enjoyment of her person fill me with delight. She leaves me: in these circumstances, my pain is not the result of prejudice, it's reasonable. I'm losing a clear asset, an accustomed pleasure, which I cannot be sure I will be able to replace. But a passing infidelity, which may be only a whim or a libidinal response, perhaps only a demonstration of gratitude or proof of a heart that's tender and sensitive to the pain or pleasure of someone else—what possible harm can come of that? In truth, no matter what people say, you'd have to be pretty silly to get upset over what's called, with reason, 'a swordstroke in the water'—something which has no effect whatsoever."

"Oh, I see where you're heading," said Mme C., interrupting l'abbé T. "You're introducing the idea very gently that you, out of your good heart or just to give pleasure to Thérèse, might be the person to give her a little lesson in sexuality, a little friendly humping which, according to you, would be neither here nor there to me. Well, my dear abbé," she went on, "I'm all for it. I love you both, and you'll both be the better for it, while I'll lose nothing by it. Why would I be opposed to it? If I were upset about it, you'd have to conclude, with reason, that I love only myself and my own selfish pleasure, which I would rather increase at the expense of denying you yours; but that's not at all the case. I know how to find my own gratification independently of anything that can help you to increase yours. And so, my dear friend, without any fear of annoying me, you can frot Thérèse's pussy for all you're worth. It will do the poor girl good. Just watch out, I repeat, and don't be imprudent . . ."

"What folly!" the abbé retorted. "I swear to you that I'm not thinking of Thérèse at all. I simply wanted to explain to you the mechanism whereby nature . . ."

"Well, let's not talk about it any further," replied Mme C. "But, speaking of nature, you're forgetting, it seems to me, that you promised to define this good mother for me. Let's see how you can cope with this assignment, for you claim to be able to explain any and everything."

Abbé T.'s Exercise, which he recommends for the Use of all Reasonable Men

"I'm happy to do so," answered the abbé. "But first, my little mother, you know what I have to do. I'm good for nothing if I haven't done the little job which affects my imagination most. Otherwise I can't sort out my ideas clearly; they all get mixed up in this one preoccupation. I've told you already that, when I lived in Paris and passed my time almost entirely in reading and the study of the most abstract sciences, whenever I felt interrupted by the goading of the flesh, I had a young girl ad hoc, like a chamberpot for peeing, and I also stuck it to her once or twice in the way you'd just as soon do without. Then, with my mind at ease and my ideas clear, I'd go back to work. And I maintain that any man of letters, any studious fellow who has a little temperament should make use of this remedy, which is as salutary for the body as for the mind. I'll go further: I assert that any gentleman conscious of his social obligations should make use of it, just to be sure that he doesn't become so aroused that he forgets his duty and debauches the wife or daughter of one of his friends or neighbors."

Instructions for the Women, the Girls, and the Men who wish to Travel Safely through the Pitfalls of Sexual Pleasure

"Now, Madame, perhaps you'll ask me," the abbé continued, "what women and girls should do. They have the same needs, you'll tell me, as men; they're made of the same stuff. They do not, however, have the same resources at their disposal. Concern for their good name, fear of an indiscreet or clumsy partner, fear of pregnancy—these do not permit them to have recourse to the same remedy as the men. Moreover, you'll say, where could they find these available men like your little ad hoc girl? Well, Madame," T. continued, "they should do just as you and Thérèse. If that game doesn't suit them (for, in fact, it doesn't suit everybody), then they should make use of one of these ingenious instruments called 'dildos.' They're a rather good imitation of the real thing. Add to that the helpful role that imagination can play. When all is said and done, I repeat, men and women must only procure themselves pleasures in such a way as not to trouble the inner order of the established society. Women must consort, then, only with those who are suitable for them, owing to the duties which society imposes upon them. You will cry out against this injustice in vain: what you may regard as injustice for the individual assures the good of the generality, which no one should try to infringe."

"Oh, I've got you now, Monsieur l'abbé," replied Mme C. "You're telling me now that no woman or girl should be permitted to do you-know-what with a man, and that no gentleman should threaten the public order by attempting to seduce her. All this, while you yourself, you dirty old man, have tormented me a hundred times for just this purpose. In fact, you would have made quick work of it, indeed, were it not for the insurmountable fear I have of becoming pregnant. So you weren't at all afraid, when it came to satisfying your particular needs, to act against the common good that you're always preaching about!"

"Good! Here we go again!" replied the abbé. "Are you beginning again with the same old song, my little mother? Haven't I told you already that, if you take certain precautions, you won't run that risk? Didn't we agree that women have only three things to worry about: fear of the devil, their reputations, and pregnancy? Your mind is very much at ease, I think, on the first point. I don't believe that you worry about indiscretion or imprudence on my part, which are the only things that could tarnish your reputation. And finally, women only become mothers through the thoughtlessness of their lovers. Moreover, I've explained to you already more than once, by expounding the mechanism of procreation, that nothing is simpler to avoid. Let's go over it once again, then. The lover, either as a result of reflection or the sight of his mistress, finds himself in the state necessary for the act of procreation: his blood, his spirits, and his erecting nerve have together caused his member to swell and become hard. The two of them, having agreed, assume the appropriate posture, and the arrow of the lover is thrust into the quiver of his mistress; the seed is prepared by the mutual rubbing of their sexual parts. A wave of pleasure engulfs them: already the divine juices are beginning to flow. But now the wise lover, master of his emotions, draws the bird from its nest, and his hand, or his mistress's, achieves, with a few deft strokes, a safe ejaculation. No danger of a child in this case. The thoughtless and brutal lover, on the other hand, pushes deep into the vagina and spreads his seeds there. They penetrate the womb and, from there, into her tubes, where procreation occurs.

"There you have it, Madame," M. T. continued, "since you desired that I go over it once again—the mechanics of sexual pleasure. Knowing me as well as you do, can you imagine that I would be one of the imprudent types? No, my dear friend, I've done it a hundred times the other way. I beg you, let me do it again today with you. Just look at what a triumphant state my funny thing is in . . . Yes, take it; squeeze it in your hand. You see that it's begging a favor from you, and I . . ."

Mme C. affords M. l'abbé T. some Disinterested Pleasure

"No, if you please, my dear abbé," Mme C. quickly replied, "I'll have none of it, not on my life. Nothing you've said can calm my fears, and I would just be giving you a pleasure I couldn't experience myself, which wouldn't be at all fair. Let me do things my way. I'm going to teach this little upstart a lesson. Well!" she went on, "are you satisfied with my breasts and my thighs? Have you had enough of kissing them and squeezing them? Why are you pulling my sleeves up above my elbows? Monsieur is aroused, no doubt, by the sight of bare arms in motion. How am I doing? You can't say a word! Ah, the rascal, what fun he's having!"

There was a moment of silence. Then, suddenly, I heard the abbé cry: "My darling little mother, I can't take it any longer! Go a little faster! Give me your little tongue, now, please! Ah! It's com . . . ing . . . !"

You can imagine, my dear Count, the state I was in as I listened to this edifying conversation. I tried twenty times to raise myself, to try and find some opening through which I would see them. But the noise of the leaves always held me back. I was sitting there, then I lay back as well as I could and, in an effort to put out the fire that was consuming me, I had recourse to my usual little exercises.

M. l'abbé T. proves that the Pleasures of the Little Goose are entirely Lawful

After several moments, during which, no doubt, M. l'abbé T. repaired the disorder in his garments, he spoke:

"In truth, my good friend, after thinking it over, I'm sure you were right in refusing me the enjoyment I asked from you. I felt a pleasure so great, an arousal so powerful, that I suspect that the dam would have broken if you had let me have my way. One must admit that we're very weak animals indeed and very seldom able to master our urges."

"I know all that, my poor abbé," Mme C. replied. "You're not telling me anything I don't know already. But tell me, are we not, by dabbling in these pleasures as we do, sinning against the good of society as a whole? And this wise lover, whose prudence you applaud, who pulls the bird from its nest and spills the stuff of life on the ground, isn't he also committing a crime? Because you must admit that we're all depriving the world of another citizen who might be useful to society."

"Such reasoning," the abbé answered, "would seem at first glance germane, but you're going to see, my lovely lady, how superficial it really is. There is no law, either human or divine, which urges—much less requires—us to work for the multiplication of the species. Young men and women are allowed by law to remain single, giving rise to hordes of underemployed monks and useless nuns. And a married man may lawfully cohabit with his pregnant wife, expending his seed, in these circumstances, fruitlessly. Virginity is even held to be preferable to marriage. However, this being said, isn't it true that the man with his little trick and we, who play the 'little goose' game, are doing nothing more than monks or nuns or anyone else who lives in celibacy? The latter are conserving in their loins, to no avail, the seed which the former are spilling to no purpose. Are they not both then in precisely the same position, with relation to society? None of them are producing citizens. But doesn't sweet reason dictate that we indulge ourselves in pleasure, without harm to our fellow man, by spilling our seed rather than bottling it up in our spermicidal vessels—which is just as useless but also threatens our health and even, in some cases, our lives. And so you see, Miss know-it-all," the abbé added, "that our pleasures do no more harm to society than the celibacy of the monks and the nuns, and so we can go on about our little business."

No doubt that, having said this, the abbé put himself in a position to render a little service to Mme C., for, a moment later, I heard her say:

"Oh, stop that, you rascally abbot! Take your finger away. I'm not up to it today. I'm still suffering a bit from our follies yester-day. Let's put the next one off until tomorrow. In any case, you know I like to be in a comfortable position, spread out on my bed. This bench isn't the least bit right for it. But, wait, just one more thing: the only thing I want from you at present is the definition you promised me of Mother Nature. Here you are at your ease, Monsieur philosopher. Just talk: I'm listening."

Definition of what we should understand by the Word "Nature"

"Mother Nature?" replied the abbé. "My goodness, you'll soon know as much about her as I do. She's a figment of the imagination, a word devoid of sense. The first religious lead-ers—the original political thinkers—were in doubt about the ideas of good and evil they should offer to their public, and so they invented a being who stands between us and God, whom they imagined to be the author of our passions, our sicknesses, and our crimes. In fact, failing this, how could they have recon-ciled their system with the infinite goodness of God? How else could they have explained our desire to rob, to murder, and to bear false witness? Why are there so many ills, so many human frailties? What did man—this poor worm born to crawl along the earth his whole life long—ever do to God to deserve it? A theologian would answer: 'This is a consequence of nature.' But just what is this nature? Is it another god which we don't know or understand? Does she act on her own, independently of the will of God? 'No,' the theologian answers again, dryly. 'As God cannot be the author of evil, evil can only exist by the action of nature.' What nonsense! Is it the stick that hit me I ought to be angry at, or the person who wielded it? Isn't he the real cause of the pain I'm feeling? Why can't we admit, once and for all, that nature is a construct of the mind, a mere empty word; that everything comes from God; that the physical evil which strikes down one contributes to the well-being of another; that, from the point of view of the Divinity, there is no evil in the world, only good; that everything we call 'good' or 'evil' exists only in relation to the interests of society as established by man? In relation to God, we act of necessity according to the first laws laid down by the divine will, the first principles of movement, which He established in all that is. A man steals: he does himself good, he does evil to society, whose laws he breaks, but he does nothing in the eyes of God."

Why Evildoers should be Punished

"I agree, however, that this man should be punished," [the abbé went on] "even though he acted out of necessity, even though I am persuaded that he was not free to commit or not commit his crime. He must be punished, because the punishment of someone who disturbs the public order makes an impression, mechanically, by means of the senses, upon the souls of other potential wrongdoers, who will be reluctant to risk incurring the same, and because the punishment meted out to the poor wretch for his crime will contribute to the general good, which should always be preferred to the good of the individual. I would add that every effort should be made to cover the relatives, friends, and associates of a criminal with opprobrium, to encourage, thereby, the members of society to feel a mutually inspired horror for the crimes or other acts which may disturb domestic tranquility. A tranquility that our natural disposition, our needs, and our individual well-being are always leading us to violate. A disposition that can only be developed in man through education and through the impressions made upon his soul by the teaching or example of his friends and associates—in a word, by external sensations, which, together with internal dispositions, direct all our actions. One must, then, stimulate men and constrain them to arouse among themselves the sensations that promote the general welfare.

"I believe, Madame, that you now understand what one means by the word 'nature.' I plan to address you tomorrow morning on the proper concept of religion. It is a subject which is important to our happiness, but it's too late to take it up today. I have a feeling that I need to take my chocolate."

"I'd be very pleased," said Mme C. as she rose. "The philosopher must need a little physical restoration after all the libidinous losses he has incurred with my help. You've earned it," she continued. "You have done, and you have said, admirable things, none more so than your observations on nature. But allow me to say that I have grave doubts that you'll be as illuminating on the subject of religion, which you have touched on several times already with much less success. How, in effect, can one give proofs in a realm of such abstraction, and one where everything is based on faith?"

"That's what we'll see tomorrow," the abbé answered.

"Oh, don't think you'll get off tomorrow with arguments," replied Mme C. "We'll go home early, if you please, to my room, where I'll have need of you and of my couch."

Several moments later, they started for home. I followed them by a hidden pathway. I stopped for only an instant in my room to change my dress, and took myself immediately to Mme C.'s apartment, where I was afraid the abbé might already have launched into the subject of religion, which I wanted to hear at all costs. His talk on nature had made a powerful impression on me: I saw clearly that God and nature were one and the same thing, or, at least, that nature acted only through the direct will of God. From this I drew my own little conclusions, and I began to think perhaps for the first time in my life.

The abbé affords some Interested Pleasure in his turn to Mme. C.

I trembled as I entered Mme C.'s apartment. It seemed to me that she would be able to perceive by my manner the kind of treachery I had just committed and the many thoughts racing through my mind. Abbé T. watched me closely. I thought all was lost. But then I heard him speak, barely audibly, to Mme C.:

"Don't you see how pretty Thérèse is? Her coloring is so delightful, her eyes so lively, and her expression grows more intelligent with every passing day."

I don't know what Mme C. answered in return. They were both smiling. I behaved as though I'd heard nothing, and I took great pains not to leave their side during the rest of the day.

That evening, when I returned to my room, I formed my plan for the next morning. I was very fearful of not being able to wake myself early enough, with the result that I wasn't able to sleep at all. Toward five o'clock I saw Mme C. head for the little wood, where M. T. was already waiting for her. If all proceeded according to what I had overheard the day before, she would soon be returning to her bedroom and to the couch that she had mentioned. I didn't hesitate to slip into the room and hide, crouching on the floor behind her bed, with my back up against the wall at its head. The hangings of the bed obscured me, but I could draw them aside as needed and have an unobstructed view of the couch, which stood in the opposite corner of the room. Anything said there would be entirely audible to me.

Thus I waited behind the scenes, and my growing impatience was beginning to make me fear that I had missed my chance, when my two actors entered the room.

"Take me, lie with me for real, my dear friend," said Mme C., as she let herself fall back onto the couch. "Reading your awful *Portier des Chartreux* has set me all on fire. Its portraits are so well wrought; they have an air of truth about them which is irresistible. If it were less dirty, it would be an inimitable book of its type. Put it to me today, abbé, I beg you," she added. "I'm dying of desire, and I'll even risk the worst."

"No, not me," the abbé replied, "for two good reasons: first, because I love you and I'm too much of a gentleman to risk your reputation and your justified reproaches by this imprudence; second, because Monsieur the doctor is not, as you see, at his most brilliant today, I'm not a Gascon, and . . ."

"I can see that very well," replied Mme C. "The latter reason is so compelling that you actually needn't have troubled to flatter yourself with the first one. But lie down here, at least, beside me," she added, stretching out lustfully on the bed, "and let's, as you say, 'sing the little service' together."

"Ah! With all my heart, my dear little mother," responded the abbé, who was at that moment standing. He began carefully to uncover the breasts of Madame.

Next he raised her dress and her shift above her navel, then he opened her thighs, elevating her knees slightly, so that her heels, drawn in close to her buttocks, were almost touching and supported by the foot of the bed.

In this position, partly hidden from me by the abbé, who was kissing all the beautiful parts of her body in turn, Mme C.

appeared immobile and deep in contemplation, meditating on the nature of those pleasures of which she felt already the first stirrings. Her eyes were half closed, the point of her tongue was visible between her deep red lips, and all the muscles of her face were drawn up in a frenzy of desire.

"Have done with kissing," she said to abbé T. "Can't you see that I'm waiting for you? I can't stand it much longer . . ."

The obliging confessor didn't wait to be asked twice for his services. He slipped over the foot of the bed between Mme C. and the wall, and passed his left hand under the head of the tender C., pressing her to him. Their mouths met in a kiss, and their tongues made small movements of the greatest voluptuousness. His other hand was occupied with the principal action: it was caressing artfully, massaging that part which makes us women, and which, on Mme C., was abundantly decorated with curly, jet black hair. The finger of the abbé played here the most interesting role.

Never has a picture been placed in a more advantageous light, from my point of view. The couch was positioned so that the fleece of Mme C. was directly before my eyes. Below it I could see, in part, her two buttocks, driven by a slight up-and-down movement which suggested internal ferment. Her thighs—the most round and white and beautiful imaginable—together with her knees, made another small movement, left and right. This doubtless contributed also to the joy of the principal part, which was the center of attention and whose every rise and fall the abbé's finger, buried in the fleece, followed.

Thérèse Crosses the Line and loses her Virginity, forgetting the Interdictions of her Confessor

I couldn't even attempt to tell you, my dear Count, what I thought at that moment: I was so moved that I felt nothing at all. I began mechanically to mimic everything I saw. My own hand did the work of the abbé's hand; I imitated all the movements of my good friend.

"Ah! I'm dying!" she cried all of a sudden. "Stick it in, my dear abbé. Yes, deep in, I beg you. Push hard, push, my little one. Ah! what bliss! I'm melting . . . I'm faint . . . ing!"

Continuing still to imitate exactly all that I saw and without a thought for my confessor's interdiction, I stuck my finger in, in my turn. A slight pain that I felt didn't stop me. I pushed with all my force and reached the heights of sensual delight.

Calm had followed upon these amorous carryings on, and I was dozing off despite my uncomfortable position, when I overheard Mme C. approaching the spot where I was hiding. I thought I was discovered, but I got off with only a fright. She pulled on the bellcord and ordered some chocolate, which they drank while praising those pleasures they had just tasted.

An Examination of Religions by Natural Light

"Why, then, aren't they [sexual pleasures] entirely innocent?" asked Mme C. "Because you may say what you like, they're in no way detrimental to the interests of society, and we're all drawn to them by a need as natural to certain temperaments as hunger and thirst . . . You have demonstrated to me quite thoroughly that we act only in accordance with God's will, that 'nature' is a word devoid of sense and is merely the effect of which God is the cause. But what will you have to say about religion? It denies us sexual pleasures outside the state of matrimony. Do we have here another word devoid of sense?"

"What, Madame," answered the abbé, "don't you remember that we're not free at all, that all our actions are necessarily determined? And if we're not free, how can we sin? But, since you want to, let's get down seriously to the subject of religion. I know well your discretion and your prudence. And I have all the less to fear in setting forth my ideas as I swear before God to the good faith with which I have attempted to sort out truth from illusion. Here is the summary of my works and my thoughts on this important subject.

"God is good, I assert. His goodness assures me that, if I try avidly to find out if there is one true religious practice which He requires of me, He won't mislead me. I will inevitably come to discover this religion; otherwise God would be unjust. He has given me reason so that I can use it, so that I can be guided by it. To what better use could I put it than this?

"If a believing Christian refuses to question his religion, why

would he expect (as he requires) that a convinced Moham-
medan would examine his? They both believe that their religions were revealed to them by God, one through Jesus Christ
and the other through Mohammed.

"Faith develops in us only because men have told us that God
has revealed certain truths. But other men, in other religions,
have said the same thing to their followers. Who should we
believe? In order to know that, we must examine the question
carefully, for everything that comes from men should be subjected to our reason.

"All the authors of the diverse religions of this earth have
asserted with pride that theirs are revelations of God. Which
ones should we believe? We must ascertain which is the true
one. But, as all we know are the prejudices of our youth and
education, in order to judge wisely we must begin by sacrificing
before God all these prejudices, and then examining in the light
of reason a question so important that our happiness or unhappiness hangs by it, in this life and for all eternity.

"I begin by noting that there are four parts in the world, and
that the twentieth part, at most, of one of these four parts is
Catholic, and that all the inhabitants of the other parts say that
we worship a man, and also a piece of bread, that we multiply
the Divinity, and that almost all the Church Fathers have con-
tradicted each other in their writings—which proves that they
were not inspired by God.

"From Adam on, all the changes in religion made by Moses,
by Solomon, by Jesus Christ, and then by the Church Fathers,
all show that all these religions are nothing but the creation of
men. God never changes! He is immutable.

"God is everywhere. However, Holy Scripture says that God
sought out Adam in the earthly paradise (*Adam, ubi es?*); that
God walked there and had a conversation with the devil on the
subject of Job.

"Reason tells me that God is not subject to any passion. However, in Genesis, chapter VI, they have God say that He repents
of having created man, that His anger has not been without
effect. God appears so weak, in the Christian religion, that He
is incapable of making man come to heel. He punishes him by
water, then by fire: man is still the same. He sends the prophets:

men are still the same. He has only one son: He sends him, but men still don't change in the least. What foolishness the Christian religion attributes to God!

"Everyone agrees that God knows what will occur throughout eternity. But, they say, even before He knows what the results of our actions will be, He has foreseen that we will betray His grace and commit these same acts. Thus, with this foreknowledge, God, in creating us, knew in advance that we would be infallibly damned and eternally miserable.

"We read in the good book that God has sent His prophets to warn mankind and to exhort it to change its behavior. But God, who is all-knowing, knew very well that men would not change their behavior. The Holy Scriptures suppose, thus, that God is a cheat and a trickster. Can these ideas be reconciled with the certitude we have of the infinite goodness of God?

"We attribute to God, who is all-powerful, a dangerous rival in the person of the devil, who is forever winning over against Him some three quarters of the small number of the chosen, for whom he sacrificed his Son, with no worry at all for the fate of the rest of mankind. What pitiful absurdities!

"According to the Christian religion, we sin only as a result of temptation. It's the devil, they say, who tempts us. God would only have to destroy the devil and we would all be saved. There must be a lot of injustice or weakness on His part!

"A rather large number of Catholic clergymen assert that God has given us the Commandments but pretend that man cannot fulfill them without grace, which God accords to some as it pleases Him—and then punishes others who do not observe them. What a contradiction! What a monstrous impiety!

"What could be more contemptible than to hear God described as angry, jealous, and vindictive, or to see the Catholics offering up their prayers to the saints, as if these saints were, like God, omnipresent and could look into the hearts of men and hear them? How ridiculous it is to say that we must do everything for the greater glory of God! Can God's glory be increased by the imagination or by the actions of men? Can they increase anything in Him? Does he not suffice unto himself?

"What has made men think that the Divinity would be more

honored, more satisfied, to see them eat a herring rather than a lark, onion soup rather than soup made with bacon, or a sole instead of a partridge—and that this same Divinity would strike them with eternal damnation if, on certain days, they opted for the soup with bacon?

"Lowly mortals! You think you can offend God! Could you offend so much as a king or a prince, if they looked upon you rationally? They would despise your weakness and your ineffectuality. You are told that God is an avenging God, and then that vengeance is a crime. What a contradiction! They assure you that forgiving your trespasses is a virtue, and then they dare to tell you that God will avenge involuntary trespassing with eternal suffering!

"If there is a God, they say, there must be religion. However, you must admit that, before the creation of the world, there was a God and no religious practice. Moreover, since the creation, there are creatures who exist—animals—who do not worship God in any form whatsoever. If there were no men, God would still exist, creatures would still exist, and there would be no religion. Man's obsession is to conceive of God's actions in the light of his own.

"The Christian religion gives a false idea of God. Christians say that earthly justice emanates from divine justice. Yet, by the canons of earthly justice, we could not but censure God's actions toward his Son, toward Adam, and toward pagans and infants who die unbaptized.

"According to the Christian religion, one must strive toward perfection. The state of virginity, for them, is more perfect than that of marriage. It is clear, therefore, that the Christian idea of perfection leads to the destruction of the human race. If the efforts and the preaching of their priests succeeded, in sixty or eighty years the human race would cease to exist. Can such a religion come from God?

"Is there anything more absurd than to ask prayers of God through the intermediary of priests, monks, or others? This is conceiving of God in the image of earthly kings.

"What excessive folly to believe that God has created us to do only what is against nature, what can only bring us unhappiness here below; that He requires that we turn away from sensual satisfaction and our God-given appetites! What more could a tyrant do if he were determined to persecute us from the cradle to the grave?

"To be a perfect Christian, you must be ignorant, have blind faith, renounce all pleasures, all honors, all riches, abandon your parents and your friends, keep your virginity—in a word, do all that runs counter to nature. This nature, however, operates certainly only in accordance with God's will. What contrariness religion attributes to a Being who is infinitely good and just!

"As God is the master of all His creation, it is our task to employ it all to the uses which he intended and to make use of it in accordance with the end for which each thing was created. By means of our reason and the internal feelings He has given us, we can know His design and His goal, and reconcile them with the interests of the particular society in which we live.

"Man is not made to be inactive: he must busy himself with some activity which has as its goal his own personal advantage in concert with the general good. God has not willed the happiness of certain individuals only, but the happiness of all mankind. We should, then, render each other every sort of mutual service, provided that these services destroy no branches of established society. It is this last point which should govern our actions. By adhering to it in everything we do in our estate in life, we fulfill all our duties. Everything else is only prejudice and illusion.

The Origin of Religions

"All religions, without exception, are the work of men," [the abbé continued.] "There's not one without its martyrs and its supposed miracles. What is more convincing about ours than the other religions?

"Religions originated out of fear: thunder, storms, gales, hail—all destroyed the fruits and grains which nourished the first men scattered over the face of the earth. Their powerlessness in the face of these catastrophes led them to have recourse to prayers to a power they recognized as greater than themselves and which they saw as disposed to torment them.

Later, men of genius or ambition—powerful politicians—from different centuries, from different regions, played upon the credulity of their peoples by coming up with gods who were often strange, fantastic, or tyrannical. They established cults, and set out to form societies in which they would be the leaders and the lawgivers. They recognized that, in order to maintain these societies, it was necessary that each citizen sacrifice his pleasures and desires to the good of the others. For this it was necessary to create a system of punishments and rewards which would determine men to make these sacrifices. So these political leaders dreamed up religions. All of them promise rewards and punishments which encourage a large portion of mankind to resist the natural tendencies they have to appropriate another's goods, his wife, or his daughter, to seek vengeance, to malign their fellow man, and to besmirch the reputation of their neighbor so as to improve their own."

The Origin of Honor

"Honor came to be associated, later on, with the religions. This phenomenon was just as illusionary as they were, and just as essential to the happiness of the individual and society. It was designed to confine within the same limits, and by means of the same principles, a certain number of other men."

A Man's Life is compared to a Throw of the Dice

"There is a God, Creator and motive force of everything which exists, make no mistake about it. We are a part of this whole, and we act only as a consequence of the first principles of movement which God has given to it. All is essential and well devised; nothing is left to chance. Three dice cast by a gambler must of necessity give a certain score, according to the arrangement of the dice in their holder or the force or spin given them. This throw of the dice can be taken as a picture of all the actions of a lifetime. One die knocks against another, setting it in motion, and the result of their movements is a certain score. Likewise, in man, his first action—a first movement—determines a second and then a third, etc. To say that man wants something simply because he wants it is meaningless. This would be the same as supposing that something could result from nothingness. Clearly there is a reason or a motive which causes him to desire this thing, and so from reason to reason, all of which are determined one by the other, man's will necessarily determines him to take this or that action throughout the course of his lifetime, whose end is the one set in motion by the throw of the dice.

"Let us love God, not because he requires it of us, but because He is supremely good. Let us fear only men and their laws. We will respect these laws because they are necessary for the good of society, in which each of us plays a part.

"There you have it, Madame," added abbé T., "what my friendship for you has extracted from me on the subject of religions. It's the fruit of twenty years' meditation and study and burning the midnight oil, during which time I have attempted in good faith to sift truth from falsehood.

"Let's conclude from this, my dear friend, that the pleasures which we enjoy, you and I, are innocent and pure, because they harm neither God nor man, owing to the secrecy and the propriety with which we conduct ourselves. Without these two conditions, I agree that we might cause a scandal and that we would be guilty of a crime against society: our example could seduce certain young hearts who were destined, by their families or by their birth, for useful service to society, and who might forget their duties in following the rush of their desires."

Mme C. tries to persuade abbé T. that, for the Good of Society, he should communicate his Inspirations to the Public

"But," replied Mme C., "if our pleasures are innocent, as I now understand them to be, why not, on the contrary, show the whole world how to have the same? Why not communicate the fruit garnered from your metaphysical meditations to your friends and fellow citizens, since nothing could contribute more to their happiness and tranquility? Haven't you told me a hundred times that there is no greater pleasure than that of spreading happiness?"

The Reason which abbé T. advances for Refusing

"I have told you the truth, Madame," replied the abbé. "But let's be careful not to reveal to fools truths that they could not appreciate or that they might misuse. They should only be accessible to those who know how to think, and whose passions are in such a healthy equilibrium that no one of them holds them in its sway. This type of man and woman is most rare: out of a hundred thousand persons, there are scarcely twenty who are accustomed to thinking, and out of these twenty, you could hardly find four who think, in effect, for themselves, or who are not dominated by some passion or other. We must, therefore, be extremely circumspect in regard to the sort of truths we have examined here today. As very few people understand the necessity of assuring their neighbors' happiness as a means to assuring their own, one must be chary of widely communicating these clear proofs of the weakness of religion. Religions still motivate a great many men, and keep them submissive to their duty and to the rules which, after all, are useful to society in their religious guise only because of the fear of damnation and the hope of eternal reward promised to the faithful. It is these hopes and fears which inspire the weak: their number is very large. It is honor, public interest, the laws of society which guide thinking men: their number is, in reality, quite small."

As soon as abbé T. had ceased to speak, Mme C. thanked him in the most glowing terms.

"You are adorable, my dear friend," she said, throwing her arms around his neck. "How fortunate I am to know you, to love a man who thinks as soundly as you! Be assured that I will never abuse your confidence, and that I will unswervingly follow your sound principles."

After still more kisses, given first by one and then the other—which greatly annoyed me because of the uncomfortable situation in which I found myself—my godly confessor and his willing proselyte descended to the drawing room. I promptly regained my room and shut myself in. A moment later, a message was brought from Mme C. calling for me to come to her. I sent word in reply that I had not slept the whole night, and begged to be allowed to rest for several hours more. I used this time to set down in writing all that I had just heard.

*   *   *

{Following this initiation in the mysteries of philosophy, Thé-rèse accompanies her mother to Paris. Her mother dies soon after their arrival, leaving Thérèse with relatively little to live on in the wicked city. While trying to decide what to do with her life, Thérèse moves into a boardinghouse, where she is befriended by Mme Bois-Laurier, a former prostitute who has retired on a small fortune she inherited from the madame of her brothel. Mme Bois-Laurier recounts her sex life to Thérèse in elaborate detail and shows her around the city. Their excursions include an evening at the Opéra, where Thérèse meets the Count to whom she is addressing this narrative. So at this point it shifts to her relations with him.}

The Story of Thérèse, Continued

When Mme Bois-Laurier had finished, I assured her that she could count on my discretion, and I thanked her with all my heart for having overcome, for me, the natural reluctance one feels to speak about one's dissolute past.

The noon hour was sounding. Mme Bois-Laurier and I were exchanging pleasantries when word came that you were asking to see me. My heart leaped with joy. I sprang up and ran to you; we dined and passed the rest of the day together.

Three weeks passed without, so to speak, our leaving each other's sight, and without my having had the wit to notice that you were using this time to decide whether or not I was worthy of you. In fact, my soul, drunk with the pleasure of contemplating you, registered no other emotion whatsoever; and though I had no other desire than that of possessing you all my life, I never dreamed of forming some kind of plan which could assure my happiness.

Meanwhile, the modesty of your language and the modera-tion of your demeanor with me could not but alarm me. If he loved me, I told myself, he would be as lively in my presence as my other suitors who were all assuring me of their undying love. This worried me. I didn't know then that reasonable people love in a reasonable way, and that scatterbrains are scatterbrains in everything they do.

The Count of . . . offers to support Thérèse and to bring her to his Country Estate

Finally, dear Count, after a month's time, you announced one day, rather laconically, that my situation had been weighing on your mind since the first day you met me, and that my expression, my character, my trust in you, all had convinced you to search for some means of freeing me from the labyrinth in which I was about to be engulfed.

"No doubt I appear rather cold to you, Mademoiselle," you added, "for a man who tells you he loves you. Nothing, however, is more certain. But you should know that the strongest passion I feel is the desire to make you happy." I wanted at that moment to interrupt you to express my gratitude.

"Now is not the moment, Mademoiselle," you answered. "Be good enough to hear me out. I have twelve thousand livres of income. I can, with no inconvenience at all, promise you two thousand during your lifetime. I'm single, with the firm intention never to marry, and I'm determined to leave high society, whose vagaries are beginning to weigh on me, and withdraw to a rather beautiful property I have about forty leagues from Paris. I'm leaving in four days' time. Would you like to come along as my companion? Perhaps, in time, you might decide to live with me as my mistress. That will depend on the pleasure you will have in giving me pleasure. But don't forget that this decision should not be taken unless you are certain within yourself that it will contribute to your happiness."

The Definition of Pleasure and Happiness: They both depend on the Conformation of Sensations

"It is folly," you added, "to believe that you can make yourself happy by your way of thinking. It has been shown that you cannot think as you like. In order to achieve happiness, one should seize the pleasure which is peculiar to oneself, which suits the passions with which one is endowed. In doing so, one must calculate the good and the bad which result from the enjoyment of this pleasure, taking care that this good and evil be considered not only in relation to oneself but also in relation to the public interest."

Man, to Live happily, should be careful to Contribute to the Happiness of Others. He should be a Gentleman

"It is axiomatic that man, who, because of the multiplicity of his needs, cannot achieve happiness without the help of an infinity of other persons, should be careful to do nothing to diminish his neighbor's happiness. Anyone who holds himself aloof from this system eludes the happiness he is seeking. Whence one may conclude with certitude that the first principle one should follow to live happily in this world is to be a gentleman and to observe the laws of society, which are like the ties that bind our mutual needs together. It is evident, I say, that those who depart from this principle cannot be happy: they are persecuted by the rigor of the law, and by the hatred and disdain of their fellow citizens. Reflect, then, Mademoiselle," you continued, "upon everything I have just had the honor to tell you. Think about it, see if you can be happy while making me happy. I'm going to leave you. I'll come tomorrow to receive your answer."

Your speech had shaken me. I felt an inexpressible pleasure in imagining that I could contribute to the pleasures of a man who thought as you did. I perceived, at the same time, the labyrinth which loomed before me and from which your generosity could save me. I loved you. But how powerful are our prejudices and how difficult to destroy! The social position of a kept woman, to which I had always seen a certain shame attached, filled me with fear. I was afraid also of having a child: my mother and Mme C. had almost died in childbirth. Moreover, the habit I had of procuring for myself a kind of voluptuousness that I understood to be equal to that which we receive by making love to a man—this habit deadened the fire of my temperament. I wanted for nothing in this regard, because relief followed immediately upon the desire. There was only, then, the prospect of misery to come, or the wish to find my own happiness while making yours, which could influence my choice. The first idea touched me only lightly; the second determined my decision.

Thérèse Surrenders herself to the Count of . . . as a Friend and departs with him for the Country

With what impatience I awaited your return once I had made my decision! The next day you appeared; I threw myself in your arms. "Yes, Monsieur, I am yours!" I cried. "Deal kindly with the heart of a young woman who adores you. Your feelings lead me to believe that you would never restrain mine. You know my fears, my weaknesses, and my habits. Let the passage of time and your teachings do their work. You understand the human heart and the power of the senses over our wills. Use these advantages to inspire in me those sensations you judge to be the most appropriate, so that I may be brought to contribute unreservedly to your pleasure. In the meantime, I shall be your friend, etc."

I remember that you interrupted me in the midst of this tender outpouring of my heart. You promised me that you would never constrain my tastes and my inclinations. Everything was arranged. The next day I announced my good fortune to Mme Bois-Laurier, who burst into tears as we parted. We left, at last, for your estate on the appointed day.

Once arrived in this lovely spot, I accepted quite naturally the change in my status, for my mind was entirely occupied with pleasing you.

The Count is Reduced to Playing the "Little Goose" Game

Two months passed, during which you abstained from pressing upon me those desires which you were trying imperceptibly to arouse in me. I anticipated you in the realization of all your pleasures, with one exception. You extolled the ecstasies it afforded, but I could not believe they could be stronger than those which I normally tasted, and which I offered to have you share with me. On the contrary, I trembled at the sight of the member with which you were threatening to pierce me. How would it be possible, I asked myself, for something of this length and this width, with a head so monstrous, to be inserted into a space where I could barely fit my finger? Moreover, if I became pregnant, I felt, I would surely die of it.

"Ah! my dear friend," I continued, "let's avoid this fateful pitfall. Let me do it my way."

I caressed you. I covered what you like to call your "doctor" with kisses. I aroused a quickening in him which led you to the height of voluptuousness and, as this divine liquid was stolen from you almost unawares, calm returned to your soul.

Discourse on Self-Love, which determines all the Actions in our Lives

I remarked that, once the knife of desire was whetted, under the pretext of catering to my taste for moral and metaphysical issues, you employed the force of argument to help me decide in favor of that which you desired of me.

"It's self-love," you said to me one day, "which determines all the actions of our lives. I mean by 'self-love' that internal satisfaction which we feel in doing one thing or another. I love you, for example, because I take pleasure from loving you. What I have done for you may gratify you, may serve your purposes, but you shouldn't feel any gratitude to me for it: my own self-love caused me to act thus. I have pinned my own happiness on the idea of contributing to yours. By the same token, you cannot make me perfectly happy unless your self-love finds satisfaction in doing so. Men often give alms to the poor; they go out of their way even to comfort them: their actions contribute to the good of society and, to that extent, are praiseworthy; but, from their personal point of view, far from it. They are giving alms because the compassion which they feel for the poor excites in them pain, and they find less discomfort in parting with their money than in continuing to endure the pain excited by their compassion. Or perhaps, yet again, their self-love, flattered by the vanity of passing for charitable men, is the real interior satisfaction which determines their decision. All

our actions are directed by these two principles: to procure ourselves more or less pleasure, to avoid more or less pain."

Discourse on the Soul's Inability to act or think independently in One Manner or Another

At other times, you explicated, and expanded upon, the short
lessons I had received from M. l'abbé T.:

"He taught you," you told me, "that we are no more able to
think independently, to act with a free will, than we are able to
control whether or not we should have a fever. In reality," you
added, "we see, through clear and simple observations, that the
soul controls nothing, that it reacts only in response to the sensations and faculties of the body. The causes which can wreak
chaos in the organs can trouble the soul and alter the mind. A
vessel or a fiber disturbed in the brain can make an imbecile out
of the most intelligent man in the world. We know that nature
acts in the very simplest manner, and has one unvarying principle. Thus, since it is evident that we are not free in some of our
actions, we are free in none of them.

"Furthermore, if souls were purely spiritual, they would all
be the same. Being all the same, if they had the ability to think
and will for themselves, they would all think and all decide in
the same way when similar cases were put to them. However,
such a situation never arises. They must, therefore, be determined by some other thing, and this other thing can only be
matter, because even the weakest thinkers acknowledge only
spirit and matter."

Reflections on the Meaning of the Spirit

"Let's ask these gullible men just what the spirit is. Can it
exist and yet have no location? If it is located somewhere, it
must occupy space, and, if it occupies space, it has extension,
and, if it has extension, it must have parts, and, if it has parts,
it is matter. Thus, either the spirit is imaginary, or it is part
of matter.

"From these arguments," you said, "one can conclude with
certainty the following: first, that we think in one way or

another only because of the organization of our bodies, combined with the ideas we receive daily though feeling, hearing, sight, odor, and taste; second, that our happiness and unhappiness depend upon this modification of matter and upon these ideas, such that thinkers and geniuses must always be at great pains to inspire ideas which are apt to contribute constructively to the public well-being, and, more particularly, to the happiness of their own loved ones. Toward this end, what wouldn't fathers and mothers do for their children, or tutors for their pupils?"

The Count's Wager with Thérèse

Finally, my dear Count, you were beginning to be a little tired of my refusals, when you hit upon the idea of sending to Paris for your library of erotic books and your picture collection of the same sort. The taste which I had developed for books, and even more for painting, suggested to you these two avenues, which met with success.

"So, Mademoiselle Thérèse," you said, in a teasing tone, "you like racy painting and literature? I'm delighted to hear it: you're going to be treated to some of the most outstanding. But give in to this request, if you please: I agree to loan you, and to place in your apartment, my library and my pictures for one year, provided that you promise to refrain for two weeks from touching that part of your body which should, by rights, today be within my domain. You must in good faith accept divorce from 'manualism.' No quarter will be given," you added. "It's only fair that each of us brings a little accommodation to the bargain. I have good reason for asking this of you. Choose: without this arrangement, no books and no paintings."

I only hesitated a moment before I took a vow of abstinence for two weeks.

"That's not all," you told me then. "Let's make the conditions reciprocal. It's not fair that you should make such a sacrifice just for a glance at the paintings or a quick read. Let's make a wager, which you'll no doubt win: I bet my library and my paintings against your virginity that you will not practice abstinence for two weeks, as you have promised."

"In truth, Monsieur," I answered, with a slightly offended air, "you have a very curious idea of my temperament, and you attribute to me very little self-control."

"Oh! Mademoiselle," you replied, "no accusations, please. I can't be happy arguing over legal points with you. I sense, furthermore, that you don't guess the reason for my proposition. Listen to me. Isn't it true that every time I give you a present, your pride is wounded, because you are receiving it from a man whom you are not making as happy as he could be? Well! The library and the paintings, which you will love so much, will not make you blush, because you will have earned them."

"My dear Count," I replied, "you're setting a trap for me, but it's you who'll be caught, I warn you. I accept the wager!" I cried, "and, what's more, I agree to do nothing else every morning but read your books and look at your bewitching pictures."

The Effects of Reading and Painting

Everything was brought, as you ordered, to my room. In the first four days, I devoured with my eyes, or rather, raced through, the story of the *Portier des Chartreux,* followed by *La Tourière des Carmelites, L'Académie des Dames, Les Lauriers ecclésiastiques, Thémidore, Frétillon,* etc., and many others of the same type, which I only put down in order to examine the pictures avidly, where the most lascivious poses were rendered with a coloring and an expressiveness that sent fire coursing through my veins.

The fifth day, after an hour of reading, I fell into a kind of ecstasy. Stretched out on my bed with the curtains opened on all sides, I had two paintings—*The Feast of Priapus* and *The Love Affair of Venus and Mars*—directly before my eyes. As my imagination began to be ignited by the attitudes represented in them, I threw off my sheets and covers and, without pausing to think whether or not the door of my room was well secured, I prepared to imitate all the positions I saw. Each figure inspired in me the feeling which the artist had ascribed to it. Two athletes, in the left-hand part of *The Feast of Priapus,* enchanted me, transporting me by the conformity of the diminutive woman's taste with my own. Without thinking, my right hand

L'An deux mille quatre cent quarante, rêve s'il en fût jamais

*(The Year 2440: A Dream
If Ever There Was One)*

Amsterdam, 1771," by Louis-Sébastien Mercier. Material
dded after the publication of the first edition does not appear in
his translation.]

CHAPTER II

I Am Seven Hundred Years Old

was midnight when my old Englishman departed. I was a
tired. I closed my door and went to bed. As soon as sleep
loped me, I dreamed that I had been asleep for hundreds
ears, and that I was just waking (a). I arose, and found
lf to be of an unaccustomed weight. My hands were
bling, my feet unsteady. When I looked in my mirror, I
scarcely recognize myself. I had gone to bed with blond
a pale complexion, and rosy cheeks. When I got up, my
ead was lined with wrinkles, my hair had grown white, I
unken eyes, a long nose, and a wan and pallid color to my
When I tried to walk, I supported myself mechanically
a stick. But at least I had not inherited that bad humor
is all too often seen in old people.
side my lodgings, I discovered a public square that was
iliar to me. In it, they had just put up a column in the

ne need only have one's imagination powerfully struck by an object
reappear during the night. There are astonishing things in dreams.
e, as you will discover as you read on, is quite powerful.

---

traveled to the spot where the man's hand was placed, and I was
on the point of inserting my finger there when I came to my
senses. I became aware of my illusion, and the memory of the
conditions of our wager obliged me to withdraw my hand.

How little I imagined that you were observing my weaknesses—if this sweet proclivity of nature is, in fact, one—and,
oh God, how stupid I was to resist the inexpressible pleasures
of its actual enjoyment! Such are the effects of prejudice: they
are our tyrants. Other parts of this picture excited, one by one,
my admiration and my pity. Finally I turned my gaze to the
second one. What sensuality in Venus' stance! Like her, I
stretched out lazily. With my thighs slightly apart and my arms
spread open voluptuously, I admired the striking attitude of the
god Mars. The fire with which his eyes, and especially his lance,
seemed to be animated passed directly into my heart. I slipped
under the sheets. My buttocks rocked lustfully as though they
would bear onward the crown destined for the conqueror.

"What!" I cried out. "The divinities even find their satisfaction in this good thing which I must forswear! Ah! dear lover! I
can resist no longer. Come forward, Count, I'm no longer afraid
of your dart. You may pierce your lover. You may even strike
where you will. It's all the same to me. I will suffer your blows
trustingly, without a murmur. And to assure your victory, here!
My finger is in place!"

The Count Wins his Bet and finally Enjoys Thérèse

What a surprise! What a joyful moment! You appeared all of
a sudden, more proud, more brilliant than Mars in the painting.
A light dressing gown that covered you was thrown aside.

"I had too much delicacy," you told me, "to take advantage of
the first opportunity you gave me. I was outside your door, and
saw and heard everything, but I didn't want to owe my happiness to the winning of a clever wager. I only came, my lovely
Thérèse, because you called me. Have you decided?"

"Yes, dear lover!" I cried. "I am all yours. Beat me, I'm no
longer afraid of your blows."

At that very moment you fell into my arms. I seized without
hesitation the arrow which, until then, had appeared so fearful

to me, and I placed it myself at the opening which it was threatening. You drove it in; your redoubled thrusts did not wrest from me the smallest cry. My attention, fixed on the idea of pleasure, did not allow me to register any sense of pain.

Our passion seemed already to have banished any philosophy of self-control, when you articulated these words with difficulty:

"I will not take advantage, Thérèse, of the full right I have earned. You are fearful of becoming a mother: I am going to spare you. The supreme pleasure is coming. Place your hand again on your conqueror as soon as I withdraw it, and help it with some squeezes to . . . it's time, my girl, I . . . from . . . pleasure . . ."

"Ah! I'm also dying!" I cried. "I feel nothing more. I . . . am . . . faint . . . ing . . ."

When I had seized his member, I pressed it lightly in my hand, which enclosed it like a case, and in which he managed to cover the distance which brought him to the threshold of voluptuousness. Afterwards we began again, and have continued to renew our pleasures in the same manner for ten years, without a problem, without a worry, without children.

Here, my dear benefactor, is what I believe you required that I write about the details of my life. How many fools—if ever this manuscript should appear—would cry out against sensuality, against the moral and metaphysical principles it contains! I would answer these fools, these clunking machines, these sorts of automatons accustomed to think with the brain of someone else, who do this or that thing only because they are told to do it—I would answer them, I say, that everything I have written is based on experience and on reason freed of all prejudice.

A Curious Reflection by Thérèse to prove that the Principles contained in her Book should contribute to the Happiness of Men

Yes, you know-nothings! Nature is an illusion, everything is the work of God. It is from Him that we take our needs: eating, drinking, and sensual enjoyment. Why then blush when we fulfill His designs? Why fear to contribute to the happiness of men by preparing for them different dishes which are apt to satisfy

sensually their different appetites? Could I ̶
pleasing God and men when I assert truths wh̶
harm, only enlighten?

She gives a Summary of Everything included̶

I'll tell you once more, you ill-humored ̶
think as we like. The soul has no will, and is ̶
the senses; that is to say, by matter. Reason̶
cannot determine our actions. Self-love (the̶
for or the pain we try to avoid) is the moti̶
our decisions. Happiness depends upon th̶
our organs, our education, and our external̶
laws of man are such that man can be happ̶
them, by living as a gentleman. There is a G̶
Him, for He is a supremely good and perfe̶
nal man—the philosopher—should contrib̶
of society by the regularity of his morals. ̶
for God is sufficient unto Himself. Genufle̶
whatever we mortals have been able to in̶
to increase His glory. Moral good and evi̶
to men, not at all in relation to God. If so̶
someone, it is beneficial to another: doc̶
ciers live from the misfortunes of others;̶
lated. The laws established in each reg̶
society together should be respected. An̶
should be punished, because, just as exan̶
men who are badly organized or wrongl̶
true that the punishment of an infraction̶
eral tranquility. Finally, kings, princes, ̶
officials, according to their rank, who̶
state, should be loved and respected, be̶
contributes by his actions to the good ̶

shape of a pyramid, which was drawing the attention of the curious. I advanced and read very distinctly: "The year 2440." These numbers were engraved upon the marble in gold.

At first I imagined that my eyes were deceiving me, or rather that the artist had made an error. I was preparing to make a remark to this effect, when my glance fell on two or three royal edicts posted on the walls, and my surprise became even greater. I saw the same date, 2440, faithfully printed on all the public documents. "What!" I said to myself, "I must have become very old without noticing! What! I have slept 672 years (b)!"

Everything was changed. All those neighborhoods which had been so well known to me now appeared to my eyes in a new shape, as if recently refurbished. I lost my way in broad and beautiful streets, now perfectly aligned. I entered spacious intersections where such perfect order reigned that I could find not even the slightest eyesore. I heard none of those bizarre and confusing street cries which had long ago smitten my ears (c). I encountered no carriages ready to run me over. A gout-sufferer would have been able to stroll about comfortably. The city had an air of animation, but without turmoil or confusion.

I was so full of wonder that I didn't see the passers-by stop in their tracks and look me over from head to foot with the greatest astonishment. They shrugged their shoulders and smiled, as we ourselves would smile if we saw a mask. In fact, my dress was so different from their own that it could not help but appear singular and grotesque.

A citizen (whom I learned later to be a scholar) approached me and addressed me politely, but with a decided gravity: "My good old man, what is the purpose of your disguise? Do you mean to reenact for us the ridiculous customs of a bizarre age? We have no desire to imitate them. Leave off this silly game playing."

"What?" I answered him. "I'm not at all in disguise. I'm wear-

(b) This work was begun in 1768.
(c) The street cries of Paris form a language unto themselves, which one must know the grammar to understand.

ing the same clothes I was wearing yesterday. It's your columns and your public notices that are lying. You seem to recognize a sovereign other than Louis XV. I don't know what your idea could be, but I warn you: I'm sure it's dangerous. One shouldn't put on such a masquerade. No one can be quite as mad as you seem. In any case, you are all imposters to no earthly purpose, for you can't deny that nothing can prevail against the evidence of one's own existence."

Perhaps the man was persuaded that I was exaggerating; perhaps he thought that the great age that I seemed to have attained made me ramble on foolishly; perhaps he had some other suspicion, but he asked me in which year I was born. "In 1740," I answered. "Well, by my count, you are exactly seven hundred years old. You shouldn't be amazed," he said to the multitude that had surrounded us. "Enoch and Elie are living still; Methuselah and a few others lived nine hundred years; Nicholas Flamel is running about the world like the wandering Jew; and Monsieur has, perhaps, found the fountain of youth or the philosopher's stone."

As he pronounced these words, he smiled, and everyone crowded around me with a pleasantness and a respect that were very marked. They were all avid to put questions to me, but discretion bade them hold their tongues. They contented themselves with murmuring low to each other: "A man from the age of Louis XV! How very strange!"

CHAPTER III

I Outfit Myself from the Second-Hand Store

I was very embarrassed about my appearance. My scholar said to me: "Astonishing old man, I'll offer myself willingly to serve as your guide. But to begin with, I beg you, let's stop in the first second-hand clothing dealer we find, because," he added with candor, "I couldn't accompany you if you weren't decently dressed.

"You'll admit, for example, that, in a well-administered city, where the government outlaws all combat and assures the life of each and every individual, it is useless, not to say indecent, to encumber one's legs with a lethal weapon, and to wear a sword at one's side to go and talk to God, to women, and to one's friends. That's more fitting for a soldier in a town under siege. In your time, they still held on to the old prejudices of Gothic chivalry; it was a badge of honor always to carry an offensive weapon. And I have read in one of the works of your time that even feeble old men paraded about with useless arms.

"How constricting and unhealthy your manner of dressing is! Your shoulders and arms are imprisoned, your body is compressed, your chest is squeezed. You can't breathe at all. And why, if you please, expose your thighs and legs to bad weather?

"Every age brings with it new styles of dress, but either I'm wrong or ours is as agreeable as it is salutary. See for yourself." In fact, the manner in which he was dressed, although new to me, had nothing displeasing about it. His hat no longer had that sad and lugubrious color, nor that embarrassing hornlike brim typical of ours (a). It consisted simply of a skullcap, deep enough to sit well on the head, wrapped in a cloth band. This band, which was rolled gracefully, remained folded over on itself when it wasn't in use, and could retract or advance at the whim of the wearer, to protect against the sun or inclement weather.

His hair was braided neatly and formed a knot at the back of the head (b). A slight suspicion of powder let his natural hair color show through. This simple style was far from our pyramid

(a) If I were to write the history of France, I would pay special attention to the subject of hats. Done correctly, this chapter could be curious and interesting. I would contrast England with France: the first would take up small hats, while the second went for big; then the second would give up its big hats, when the first gave up the small.

(b) If I should take it upon myself to write a treatise on the art of curling hair, how I would astonish my readers by showing them that there are three or four hundred ways to twist a gentleman's hair. Oh! What profundity have our professions! Who can boast of knowing all their minutiae, which lend an air of alarm, or those fixed curls which, far from suggesting a floating mane of hair, have no other merit than that of adding stiffness without either expression or grace!

plastered with pomade and pride. It had no drooping side wings, which give off such an air of gloom, nor motionless curls, which instead of floating like a mane only create an impression of stiffness devoid of grace.

His neck was no longer strangled by a narrow band of muslin (c). It was encircled with a cravat whose warmth varied according to the season. His arms enjoyed a complete freedom in sleeves that were moderately wide, and his body, lightly clothed in a kind of undervest, was covered with a sort of coat-dress, which served equally well in times of rain or cold. A long scarf encircled his loins nobly and assured an even heat. He had none of those garters which cut into the calves and stop the circulation. A long stocking went from his feet to his belt, and a sensible shoe, in the form of a laced boot, encompassed his foot.

He bade me enter a shop, where they proposed an entire change of wardrobe. The chair on which I rested was not anything like those overstuffed chairs that fatigue instead of aiding relaxation. It was a sort of short, sloping sofa covered in matting, which conformed, by pivoting, to the body's movement. I could hardly believe myself to be in the presence of a used-clothing dealer, as there was no talk of honor or conscience, and his shop was very well lighted.

CHAPTER IV

The Porters

My guide was growing more affable with each passing moment. He paid my bill at the second-hand store. It came to a *louis* in our money, which I got out of my pocket. The merchant promised to hold on to it as a collector's item. Everyone paid cash in each shop, and the citizenry, who maintained a scrupulous integrity, no longer acknowledged the word "credit," which disguises all sorts of cheating by both borrower and lender. The

---

(c) I don't at all like the general disapproval of our collars. By staying up late, overeating, and other excesses, we become pale. Our collars, by slightly strangling us, correct that fault and give us back our color.

art of running up debts and not paying them was no longer practiced by members of polite society (a).

As I came out, the crowd surrounded me once more, but the
stares of the multitude were not at all mocking or insulting.
There was only a buzzing on all sides: "There's the man who is
seven hundred years old! How unhappy he must have been in
the early years of his life!"

I was amazed to find so much cleanliness and so little litter in
the streets: it looked like Corpus Christi. The city, however,
appeared to be extremely populous.

In each street there was a guard whose job it was to oversee
public order. He directed the flow of the carriages and of the
porters. He kept a free passageway open, especially, for the
latter, whose burden was always proportionate to their strength.
There were none of those poor miserable creatures, sweating
and panting, with red eyes and bowed heads, who groan under
a load that is fit only for a beast of burden. The rich man did
not oppress humanity by means of a few coins. And the fair sex,
born to carry out happier and gentler tasks, did not assault the
gaze of passers-by with their metamorphosis into porters. In the
public markets, they were no longer to be seen, forcing their
nature with every step and indicting the barbarous insensitivity
of the men who used to watch them labor with perfect equanim-
ity. Women had been restored to the tasks appropriate to their

---

(a) King Charles VII of France, once finding himself at Bourges, ordered a
pair of boots. But as he was trying them on, the intendant entered the shop
and said to the bootmaker: "Take away your merchandise. We couldn't pay
you for these boots for some time. His Majesty can wear his old ones a month
longer." The king applauded the intendant, and he deserved to have such a
man in his service. What, on reading this, would the young fool think who
orders shoes and laughs to himself at having yet again found a poor worker to
trick? He scorns the man who put the shoes on his feet and who he has no
intention of paying, and he rushes off to throw his money away in dens of
crime and debauchery. Isn't the baseness of his soul engraved upon his forehead, on this forehead which doesn't blush at having to duck at every street
corner in order to avoid the gaze of a creditor? If all those whom he owed for
the clothes he was wearing stopped him at an intersection and took back what
belonged to them, what would he have left to cover himself? I wish that every
man on the streets of Paris who was clothed in a suit above his station were
forced, under pain of the most severe punishment, to carry in his pocket a
receipt for the payment of his tailor's bill.

estate. They fulfilled the sole duty imposed upon them by the Creator, that of bearing children and of consoling those around them in the face of life's misfortunes.

CHAPTER V

The Carriages

I remarked that all the people going away from me were on the right, and those advancing were on the left (a). This very simple means of avoiding being run over had only just been invented: so true it is that it is only with time that useful discoveries are made. In this manner, unfortunate accidents were avoided. All exits were easy and safe, and at public events, where there was an outpouring of the multitude, everyone was able to enjoy the spectacle, which they naturally love and which it would be wrong to refuse them. Everyone could then return home, without being either rumpled or suffocated. I no longer saw that ridiculous and revolting spectacle of a thousand carriages jammed together, all immobilized for three hours at a time, while the rich and imbecilic fop, who demands to be carried everywhere, forgetting he has legs, calls out from his carriage door and laments that he cannot advance (b).

The crowd of ordinary people circulated freely, easily, and in an orderly manner. I passed a hundred wheelbarrows filled with foodstuffs or furniture for every carriage I saw, and even this one bore someone who seemed to me to be ailing. "What has become of those wondrous coaches," I asked, "so elegantly gilded, painted and varnished, which filled the streets of Paris in my day? Have you no more financiers or courtesans (c) or

(a) The foreigner is perplexed by the perpetual motion of the French, who rush about the streets from morning till night in an incomprehensible state of agitation, and often without any discernible business to do.

(b) There is nothing more comical than to see, on a bridge, a line of carriages immobilized in traffic. The masters are looking out impatiently; the coachmen are rising from their seats and swearing. This scene comforts the unhappy pedestrians somewhat.

(c) [In eighteenth-century Paris], a superb coach drawn by six horses in magnificent harness passed through the streets. A crowd formed two rows to watch it pass by. The artisans raised their caps—and it was only a whore they had saluted.

dandies? In the past, these three miserable types insulted the public, and seemed to compete among themselves to see who could most terrify the honest burger, who fled as quickly as he could for fear of death beneath the wheels of their carriages. Our noble lords took the sidewalks of Paris for an Olympic battleground, and prided themselves on working their horses to death. In those days everyone had to run for his life."

"Racing of this sort is no long permitted," they assured me. "Wise sumptuary legislation has outlawed this barbarian luxury, which created an excess of lackeys and horses (d). Those whom fortune favors no longer live the soft life, which so revolted the eyes of the poor. Our lords nowadays use their legs; they have more money to spend, and less gout.

"However, you do see some carriages. They belong to old magistrates or other distinguished public servants bowed down under the weight of age. They alone are permitted to travel slowly on the cobblestones, where the simplest citizen is respected. If they had the misfortune to injure someone, they would descend immediately from their coach and help him up into it, and they would maintain a carriage for him, at their own expense, for the rest of his days.

"Such a misfortune never arises. The wealthy lords are estimable men, who see no dishonor in allowing their horses to give way before citizens.

"Our King himself often goes on foot among us. He sometimes even honors our houses with his presence, and almost always, when he is tired of walking, he chooses to rest in the shop of an artisan. He likes to recreate the natural equality which should reign among men. And so he encounters in our gaze only love and gratitude. Our cheers come really from our hearts, and his heart hears and revels in them. He is a second Henri IV. He has the same greatness of soul, the same grit, the same magnificent simplicity, but he is more fortunate. The footprints he leaves on the public pathways are sacred and revered by all. No one would dare to quarrel there; one would blush to commit the smallest disorderly act. 'If the King were

---

(d) These opulent fools who maintain a fleet of footmen have been compared, with reason, to woodlice: they have a great many feet, and they move very slowly.

to pass,' they say. This warning alone would, I think, stop a civil war. How powerful example becomes when it comes from the top! How striking! How inviolate a law! How commanding it is for all men!"

CHAPTER VI

The Embroidered Hats

"Things seem a little changed to me," I said to my guide. "I see that everyone is dressed in a simple and modest manner, and, in the course of our walk, I haven't encountered a single gold-covered suit. I haven't noticed any braid either, or any lace cuffs. In my day, a ruinous and fatuous luxury had deranged everyone's thinking. A mindless body would be encrusted with gilt, and this automaton thereby resembled a man."

"That's exactly what led us to scorn that old-fashioned livery of pride. We see beyond the surface of things. When a man has acquired a reputation for having excelled in his work, he doesn't need a magnificent costume or costly furnishings to trumpet his merit. He has no need of admirers who tout him or protectors to support him: his actions speak for themselves, and each citizen takes an interest in demanding a just recompense for him. Those who share the same career are the first to appeal on his behalf. Each prepares a petition on which are listed, in the full light of day, the services he has rendered to the state.

"The monarch has no hesitation in inviting to his court those who have won public favor. He converses with them for his own edification, for he doesn't feel that wisdom is innate to himself. He derives profit from the illuminating observations of those who have adopted some worthy goal as the object of their meditations. He gives them as a reward a hat with their name embroidered on it, and this distinction is just as sought after as those blue, red, or yellow ribbons which, in the past, bedecked men who were absolutely unknown to their countrymen (a).

(a) For the ancients, human vanity consisted of trying to demonstrate descendance from the gods. One made every effort to be a nephew of Neptune, a grandson of Venus, first cousin of Mars. Others, more modest, were content with being descended from a river, or a nymph or a naiad. Our modern fools have a sadder eccentricity: they want to be born, not of famous ancestors, but of obscure ones from an ancient lineage.

"You can well imagine that someone with a bad name would hesitate to show himself before a public whose reaction would expose him. Anyone who wears one of these honorable hats can pass anywhere; he would have free access anytime to the foot of the throne. This is a fundamental law. By the same token, a prince or a duke who has achieved nothing that would put his name on a hat may enjoy his riches, but will have no badge of honor. He will be regarded in the same manner as the obscure citizen who passes by unnoticed in the crowd.

"There are lands on which it's better not to dig about, and virtues which it's better not to examine too closely. What difference does it make if the motive is not disinterested, if the effect is great and illustrious, and nationwide?

"These eternal critics of first causes are more keen to shrink the circle of virtues than to recognize those that exist, and more eager to justify their own indolence than to make themselves useful to the public.

"Both reason and politics argue for the conferral of this distinction. It is invidious only for those who feel themselves incapable of ever attaining it. Man is not perfect enough to do good only for the honor of having done it. But this nobility, as you might guess, is personal—not hereditary or venal. At twenty-one, the son of one of our illustrious citizens presents himself, and a tribunal decides if he should enjoy the prerogatives of his father. Based on his past conduct, and sometimes on the promise which he shows, we may confirm his honor of belonging to a citizen who is dear to his country. But if the son of an Achilles is a cowardly Thersites, we turn away our eyes to spare him the shame of blushing under our gaze. He sinks into oblivion while his father's name becomes more glorious.

"In your day, they knew how to punish crime, but they gave no reward for virtue. That was a very imperfect legal system. In ours, the courageous man who has saved the life of a citizen in some danger or other (b), who has prevented some public disaster, or done something great or useful, wears the embroidered

---

(b) It is astonishing that no recompense is given to a man who saves the life of his fellow citizen. A police ordinance awards 10 *écus* to a boatman who pulls a drowned man from the river, but the boatman who saves the life of someone in danger receives nothing.

hat, and his respectable name, exposed to the eyes of all, marches before the man who possesses the greatest fortune, be he Midas or Pluto (c)."

"That's very well thought out. In my day, they passed out hats, but they were red [i.e., cardinals' hats]. One went across the ocean to get them, but they signified nothing. They were very much sought after, but I can't rightly tell you how one came to receive them."

CHAPTER VII

The Bridge Whose Name Has Changed

When you're chatting about interesting things, you cover a lot of ground without noticing it. I was so rejuvenated by the prospect of so many new sights that I no longer felt the weight of my years. But what was I seeing! Oh, heavens, what a sight! I found myself beside the Seine. My delighted gaze wandered over everything, taking in the most beautiful monuments. The Louvre was finished! The magnificent space which extended between the Tuileries and the Louvre created an immense square where public ceremonies were put on. A new gallery echoed the old one, where one still admired the hand of Perrault at work. These two august monuments, thus unified, formed the most magnificent palace in all the universe. All the distinguished artists inhabited this palace. They made up a most dignified retinue for the royal sovereign, who boasted to himself only of the arts, which were the basis for the glory and happiness of the empire. I saw a superb mayoral square that could contain a great mass of citizens. The Temple of Justice stood opposite it. Its architecture evoked the dignity of its mission.

"Isn't that the Pont-Neuf?" I cried. "How it's decorated!"

"What are you calling the Pont-Neuf? We've given it another

(c) When an extreme cupidity inspires every heart, the enthusiasm for virtue vanishes, and the government can only award by means of vast sums those whom it used to award with small tokens of honor. Let this be a lesson to all monarchs, who should create some currency which confers honor. This will, however, only be prized insofar as souls feel the noble desire for it.

name. We've changed many others as well to substitute names which are more significant or more appropriate, because nothing has more influence on the spirit of the people than when the names of things are right and proper. Take, for example, the bridge of Henri IV, a means of communication between the two parts of the city: it couldn't have a more respected name. In each of the spaces above the abutments we have placed a statue of one of the great men who, like the King, loved mankind and cared only for the good of the country. We haven't hesitated to put at his side the chancellor L'Hôpital, Sully, Jannin, and Colbert. What a book on morals! What public lecture is as compelling or as eloquent as this line of heroes whose silent but imposing facade cries out to all that it is grand and useful to win the esteem of the public! Your century was never glorious enough to do such a thing."

"Oh, my century had the very greatest difficulties in carrying out the smallest enterprise. People made the most extravagant preparations only to announce, with great pomp, a total failure. A grain of sand stopped the motion of the mightiest machines. We produced the most wonderful speculations, and were always designing things with our pens or tongues. But everything in its time. Ours was a time of innumerable projects; yours is the time of execution. I congratulate you on it. How grateful I am to have lived so long!

* * *

CHAPTER X

The Man in a Mask

"But, if you please, who is that man whom I see passing by with a mask over his face? How quickly he's walking. He seems to be running away from something."

"That's an author who has written a bad book. When I say 'bad,' I'm not talking about defects of style or argument: one can make an excellent work with plain good sense (a). We mean

---

(a) Nothing is truer, and the sermon of a country parson can be more solidly useful than some tome ingeniously filled with verities and sophisms.

only that he has brought to light dangerous principles, which are opposed to healthy morals—to those universal morals which speak to all hearts. In order to atone, he wears a mask so as to hide his shame until he can assuage it by writing things which are more sage and reasonable.

"Every day two virtuous citizens pay him a visit to combat his erroneous opinions by the force of kindness and eloquence. They listen to his objections, answer them, and enjoin him to retract just as soon as he's convinced. Then he will be rehabilitated. He will draw from the admission of his error an even greater glory, for is there anything finer than to abjure one's errors (b) and to embrace a new intellectual world with a noble sincerity!"

"But was his book approved?"

"Who, I ask you, would dare to judge a book before the public sees it? Who can foresee the influence of such and such an argument in such and such circumstances? Each writer stands personally behind what he writes, and never disguises his name. It's the public who cover him with opprobrium if he contradicts the sacred principles that serve as a basis for the conduct and probity of men. It's also the public who support him if he has advanced some new truth useful in the suppression of certain abuses. In fact, the voice of the public is the only judge in these sorts of cases, and everyone heeds it. Every author, who is a public person, is judged by this voice, and not by the caprices of a man who will only rarely have a broad enough and fair enough vision to ascertain what, in the eyes of the nation, will be really worthy of praise or blame.

"It has been shown many times over that freedom of the press is the true measure of civil liberty (c). You cannot attack the one without destroying the other. Thought should be given free rein. To try to curb it or stifle it is a crime against humanity. And what would I have left if my thoughts were no longer mine?"

"But," I replied, "in my time the authorities feared nothing so much as the pen of good writers. Their proud and guilt-rid-

(b) Everything is demonstrable in theory; error itself has its own geometry.
(c) This is the equivalent of a geometrical demonstration.

den souls trembled inwardly when justice threatened to expose their shameless deeds (d). Instead of protecting this public censure, which, if well administered, could have been a powerful deterrent to vice and crime, they condemned all writings to be screened. But the screen was so narrow and so restrictive that the better features of the works were often lost. Bursts of genius were subjected to the cruel scissors of mediocrity, which clipped its wings mercilessly (e)."

Everyone around me began to laugh. "That must have been very funny," they said, "to see men gravely at work dissecting a thought and weighing the syllables. It's amazing that you produced anything of worth at all with such constraints. How could you dance lightly and gracefully under the great weight of your chains?"

"Oh, our best writers quite naturally felt it their duty to shake them. Fear debases the soul, and he who is inspired by a love of humanity must be fearless and proud."

"Here you can write on anything, no matter how shocking," they replied, "for we no longer have screens or scissors or handcuffs. And we publish very little drivel, because that falls of its own weight into the mud which is its element. The government keeps itself well above reproach. It has no fear of enlightened pens; if it feared them, it would indict itself. Its operations are sincere and straightforward. We only have praise for it, and, when the interest of the country is at stake, each man, according to his lights, is an author, without laying claim to the title.

(d) In a drama entitled *Les Noces d'un fils de roi,* a Minister of Justice, who is a vile courtier, says to his valet, speaking of philosophical writers: "My friend, those people are pernicious. You can't allow yourself the smallest injustice without their remarking on it. In vain we wear a clever mask to hide our true face from the most probing looks. These men, as they pass by, seem to say to you: 'I know you.' All you philosophers, I hope to teach you that it is dangerous to know a man like me: I don't want to be known."

(e) Half of the so-called royal censors are people who could not be included in the world of writers, even in the lowest category. One could say of them, literally, that they do not know how to read.

CHAPTER XI

The New Testaments

"What, everyone an author! Heavens, what an idea! Your walls will burst into flames like gunpowder, and everything will explode. Good God! A whole population of authors!"

"Yes, but without gall, without pride or presumption. Every man writes what he thinks in his better moments and, as he grows older, he draws together a collection of the finest reflections of his lifetime. Before his death he compiles a book, which is larger or smaller according to his own way of seeing and expressing himself. This book is the soul of the departed. It is read aloud on the day of his funeral, and this reading alone constitutes his eulogy. Children collect, with great respect, all the thoughts of their forebears and meditate upon them. These are our funeral urns. I think they're preferable to your sumptuous mausoleums or your tombs with their distasteful inscriptions dictated by pride and engraved by vulgarity.

"This is how we fulfill our duty to our descendants to paint a vivid picture of our lives. This honorable souvenir will be the only asset which we will leave behind us on this earth (a). We give it a great deal of thought. These are the immortal lessons which we are leaving for our descendants, and they will love us all the more for them. Portraits and statues portray only the body. Why not picture the soul itself and the virtuous sentiments that have inspired it? They flower as we give them loving expression. The history of our thoughts and actions gives instruction to our families. They learn from the choice and comparison of our ideas to perfect their way of seeing and feeling. Note, however, that the most prominent writers—the geniuses of their age—are always the suns who dominate the universe of ideas and keep it circulating. They set the intellectual world in motion, and, as the love of humanity inspires their generous heart, all hearts respond to that same sublime and victorious voice which has just struck down despotism and supersti-

---

(a) Cicero often asked himself what would be said of him after his death. He who cares nothing for a good reputation will disregard the means of acquiring one.

tion."—"Sirs, permit me, please, to defend my century, at least what was praiseworthy about it. We also had, I believe, virtuous men and men of genius?"—"Yes, but you barbarians! You either failed to recognize them or you persecuted them. We have been obliged to expiate these crimes by making reparations to their spirits. We have put up busts in public squares so they can receive homage from us and from the passing stranger. They stand in the form of statues, with their right foot crushing the face of the tyrant who tormented them. For example, Richelieu's head lies under the heel of Corneille (b). Are you aware that you had remarkable men? We cannot comprehend the stupid, foolhardy rage of their persecutors. Their own baseness was as great as the lofty height at which these eagles flew; but they are now condemned to the opprobrium which should be their lot for eternity."

As he spoke, he was leading me into a square, where the busts of the great men were displayed. I saw Corneille, Molière, La Fontaine, Montesquieu, Rousseau (c), Buffon, Voltaire, Mirabeau, etc. "So all these famous writers are well known here, are they?"—"Their names make up the alphabet for our children. As soon as they have reached the age of reason, we put in their hands your famous *Encyclopédie,* which we have carefully reedited."—"You surprise me! The *Encyclopédie* as a primer! Oh, what a leap you have taken toward the advanced sciences, and how ardently I desire to take instruction with you! Open your treasure chests to me, so that I may, at one fell swoop, enjoy the accumulated works of six centuries of glory!"

*　*　*

(b) I wish that the author had specified upon whose heads Rousseau, Voltaire, and other associated authors would stand. There will certainly be some heads, mitered or not, which will not rest easy, but each must wait his turn. [The remark on Richelieu and Corneille does not appear in the editions published after 1771.]

(c) We speak here of the author of *Emile* [i.e., Jean-Jacques Rousseau], and not of that poet [i.e., Jean-Baptiste Rousseau], devoid of ideas, whose only talent was for rearranging words and sometimes clothing them with a pomposity that served to hide the sterility of his soul and the chill of his spirit.

Chapter XIX

The Temple

We turned the corner, and I discovered, in the middle of a beautiful square, a temple in the form of a rotunda crowned by a magnificent dome. This edifice, which was supported by a row of columns, had four tall doors. On each pediment were inscribed the words "Temple of God." Time had already left a venerable patina on its walls, which only increased their majesty. As I reached the door of the temple, I was greatly astonished to read these four lines engraved in capital letters on a tablet:

Loin de rien décider sur cet Etre suprême,	Far from concluding anything about this Supreme Being,
Gardons, en l'adorant, un silence profond;	Let's keep, as we worship it, a profound silence;
Sa nature est immense et l'esprit s'y confond:	Its nature is immense and the spirit merges with it:
Pour savoir ce qu'il est, il faut être lui-même.	To know what it is, one must be the Being itself.

"Oh!" I said to him in a low voice, "you're not going to try and tell me that this is from your century."—"It's no credit to yours," he replied, "because your theologians should not have presumed to go beyond that point. These words, which seem to come straight from God Himself, remained mixed up with other verses which were generally forgotten. I don't think there are any more beautiful for the sentiments they convey, and I think they're right at home here."

We followed the crowd who, with thoughtful demeanor, was advancing slowly and sedately into the depths of the temple. Each one sat down in his turn on the rows of little backless chairs, the men separate from the women. The altar was in the center; it was devoid of decoration, and everyone had an unimpeded view of the priest, who was lighting incense. His voice, as it pronounced the sacred chants, alternated with the rising notes of the choir. Their sweet singing echoed the respectful sentiments in their hearts. They seemed to be pervaded by a sense of the divine majesty. There were no statues, no allegorical figures, and no paintings (a). The holy name of God a thousand times repeated, written in many languages, could be seen on all the walls. Everything announced the unity of one God. Extraneous ornamentation was scrupulously forbidden: God at last was alone in His temple.

If you raised your gaze to the summit of the temple, you saw the heavens uncovered, because the dome was not enclosed by a stone vaulting but by clear windows. At certain moments a cloudless and serene sky announced the goodness of the Creator; at others thick clouds that poured forth torrents depicted the dark side of life, and suggested that this sad earth is but a land of exile; thunder proclaimed how redoubtable God is when He is offended; and the calm air which followed upon the lightning flashes announced that submission disarms His avenging hand. When the pure air of life wafted in on the spring breeze like a healing current, it suggested a salutary and consoling truth—that the storehouses of divine mercy are inexhaustible. Thus, the elements and the seasons, whose voice is so eloquent for those who know how to listen, spoke to these sensitive men and revealed to them the master of nature in all its aspects (b).

There were no discordant sounds to be heard. Even the voices of the children had been joined together to form a majestic plainsong. No lively or profane music. Simple organ playing (which was not at all loud) accompanied the voice of this

(a) The Protestants are right. All these works of man encourage idolatry in the people. In order to proclaim a God who is invisible yet present, you must have a temple in which only He is present.

(b) A savage wandering in the woods, contemplating nature and the heavens, sensing, so to speak, the only master he acknowledges, is closer to the real religion than a monk buried in his cell, living with the phantoms of his overheated imaginatination.

great congregation and seemed to be the song of the immortals mixing with the prayers of the people. No one entered or left during the invocation. No ungainly verger, no importunate beggar came to interrupt the meditation of the faithful. All those present were imbued with a devout and profound respect; some of them were prostrate on the ground. Amidst this silence, this universal contemplation, I was struck with a holy terror: it seemed that the Divinity had come down into the temple and was filling it with His invisible presence.

There were boxes at the doors for offerings, but they were placed inconspicuously. These people knew how to do good works without the need of being noticed. Finally, in the moments of adoration, silence was so religiously observed that the holiness of the place, joined to the idea of the Supreme Being, left in every heart a deep and salutary impression.

The pastor's sermon to his flock was simple and natural, eloquent in what he said rather than in his style. He spoke of God only to inspire love for Him; of men only to encourage in them humanity, goodness, and patience. He didn't attempt to make his intellect speak; rather, he sought to touch hearts. He was a father conversing with his children on the proper path to take in life. It was all the more striking, as this lesson came from the mouth of a perfect gentleman. I wasn't a bit bored, because the discourse included neither declamations nor vague portraits nor fancy turns of phrase, and, least of all, those chopped-up bits of poetry grafted onto a prose which is ordinarily much the worse for them (c).

"In this way," said my guide, "we have our customary public prayer every morning. This lasts an hour, and the rest of the day the doors of the building remain closed. We have hardly any religious festivals, but we have civil ones, which entertain

(c) What I especially dislike in our preachers is their lack of moral principles that are stable and sure. They take their ideas from their texts and not from their hearts. Today, they may be moderate and reasonable, but go to hear them tomorrow and they will be intolerant and outrageous. These are only words they are uttering. It hardly matters even if they contradict themselves, provided that their three points are made. I have even heard one preacher who pilfered from the *Encyclopédie* while railing against the encyclopedists.

the people without leading them to debauchery. On no day should man remain idle. Like nature, who never abandons her tasks, he should feel guilty for abandoning his. Rest is not idleness. Inaction is an actual injury done to the country, and cessation of work is, at bottom, a kind of sin. The time given to prayer is fixed: it is adequate for lifting one's heart to God. Long services induce boredom and disgust. All secret prayers are less desirable than those which unite publicity with religious fervor.

"Listen to the form of the prayer which we use. Each says it aloud and meditates on the thoughts it contains.

" 'Unique Being, uncreated, intelligent Creator of this vast universe! Because Thy goodness has provided it as a spectacle for man, because so weak a creature has received from Thee the precious gifts of reflection on this grand and beautiful work, do not permit that, like a brute animal, he should pass along the surface of this globe without rendering homage to Thy might and Thy wisdom. We admire Thy noble works. We bless Thy sovereign hand. We adore Thee as master; but we love Thee as the universal father of all creatures. Yes, Thou art good, and Thou art great. Everything tells us this, and above all our hearts. If some fleeting misfortunes afflict us here below, it is no doubt because they are inevitable. Moreover, that it be Thy will is sufficient for us. We obey with confidence, and we hope for Thy infinite mercy. Far from complaining, we give Thee thanks for having created us so that we may know Thee.

" 'Let each honor Thee in his own manner, tenderly or passionately, according to the dictates of his heart. We shall set no limits to his zeal. Thou hast deigned to speak to us only through the resounding voice of nature. All our worship consists of adoring Thee, blessing Thee, crying before Thy throne that we are weak, miserable, shortsighted, and that we have need of Thy helping arm.

" 'If we are mistaken, if some cult, ancient or modern, is more agreeable in Thy eyes than ours, ah! deign to open our eyes and erase the shadows from our minds. Thou wilt find us faithful to Thy commands. But if Thou art satisfied with this feeble homage, which we know is owed to Thy greatness, to Thy fatherly tenderness, give us the constancy to persevere in the respectful sentiments which animate us. Preserver of the human race! Thou, who embraces all things in Thy glance, likewise make charity fire the hearts of all the inhabitants of this globe, so that they will be bound in brotherly love, and will raise to Thee the same song of love and gratitude!

" 'We dare not, in our prayers, limit the duration of our lives. Whether Thou take us from this earth, or leave us on it, we can never be out of Thy sight. We ask of Thee only virtue, for fear of trespassing against Thy impenetrable decrees. But humble, submissive, and attentive to Thy will, deign either that we pass through a gentle death or a painful one; deign to bring us to Thee, eternal source of happiness. Our hearts sigh after Thy presence. Let this mortal raiment fall away, that we may fly to Thy breast. What we see of Thy grandeur makes us desire to see still more. Thou hast given too much to man to have deprived him of boldness in his thoughts: he raises up to Thee such ardent prayers only because Thy creature feels himself born to receive Thy beneficence.' "

"But, my dear Sir," I said to him, "your religion, if you permit me to say it, is very similar to that of the ancient patriarchs who adored God, in spirit and in fact, on the mountain tops."

"Exactly. You have hit the nail on the head. Our religion is the same as that of Enoch, Elijah, and Adam. We go back, at least, to the very beginning. Religion is like the law: the simpler the better. Worship God; respect your neighbor. Listen to your conscience, that judge who is always watchful deep within you: never stifle that celestial and secret voice. All the rest is deception, deceit, lies. Our priests make no claims to be uniquely inspired by God. They consider themselves our equals. They admit that they navigate, like us, in the shadows. They follow the point of light which God has deigned to show us. They point it out to their brothers without tyranny or ostentation. Simple moral teachings and no far-fetched dogma—that's the way to avoid impiety, fanaticism and superstition. We have found this happy medium, and for this we sincerely thank the author of all good."

"You worship a God, but do you admit the immortality of the soul? What is your opinion on this great and impenetrable mystery? All the philosophers have tried to crack it. Wise men and fools have had their say. The most varied philosophical systems, and the most poetic, have arisen around this very question. It has, it seems, particularly inspired the imagination of lawmakers. What is the thinking of your age?"

"You only need to look around you to believe," he answered. "You need only look within yourself to sense there is something in us which lives, which feels, which thinks, which wills, which determines itself. We believe that our soul is independent of matter, that it is by its nature intelligent. We don't theorize much on this point: we prefer to believe in whatever exalts human nature. The system which magnifies it the most is the most sympathetic to us. We don't feel that any ideas which honor God's creatures can ever be false. Opting for the most sublime conception, we don't run the risk of error; instead, we attain our true purpose. Incredulity is only weakness; audacity of thought is an article of faith for an intelligent being. Why should we crawl along toward nothingness when we sense we have wings with which to fly up to God, and that there is no contradictory evidence against this generous boldness? If we were wrong, man would have invented a system more beautiful than that which is. The power of God—I almost said His goodness—would, thus, be finite.

"We believe that all souls are equal in their essence but different in their characteristics. The soul of a man and that of an animal are both immaterial, but one is a step closer than the other to perfectibility. That's where things stand at the moment, but everything, of course, can change.

"We think, furthermore, that the stars and the planets are inhabited, but that all the worlds are different one from another. This limitless grandeur, this infinite chain of different worlds, this radiant circle must be part of the vast plan of creation. Well, these suns, these worlds which are so beautiful, so large, so diverse—we see them all as habitats designed for man. They intersect, they communicate, they have their own hierarchical system. The human soul ascends through these worlds as up a brilliant ladder, which brings it with each step closer to perfection. Throughout his journey, man preserves the memory of all that he has seen and learned. He preserves the storehouse of his knowledge, his most valuable treasure; he carries this everywhere with him. If he propels himself toward some sublime discovery, he bursts forth from the inhabited worlds he leaves behind; he rises on the strength of the knowledge and virtue he has acquired. The soul of Newton soared, on the wings of its own energy, toward all those spheres he had weighed. It would be unjust to think that death could still this mighty genius. Such a destruction would be more unbearable, more inconceivable than that of the material universe. It would be absurd, as well, to assert that his soul would ever exist on a par with that of an ignorant or stupid person. In effect, it would be useless for man to perfect his soul, if it could not elevate itself, either through contemplation or the exercise of virtue. Yet an inner feeling, overcoming all objections, cries out to him: 'Develop all your strength, scorn death; you alone can conquer it and increase life, which is thought.'

"Those debased souls who have crawled through the morass of crime or idleness return to the same point from which they began, or even lower. Long will they remain fixed at the edge of nothingness; long will they reach out toward the material world; long will they make up a vile, animalistic race. While generous souls soar toward the eternal light of heaven, the others sink deeper into the shadows, where a pale gleam of life barely flickers. A monarch might thus, at his death, become a mole, or a minister a venomous snake, inhabiting fetid marshes, while the writer whom he despised—or rather, whom he understood only imperfectly—has obtained a rung of glory among those intellects who love humanity.

"Pythagoras had already noted this equality of souls, he had suggested this transmigration from one body to another, but, for him, these souls orbited in the same world and never left their globe. Our metempsychosis is more rational and superior to the ancients'. For those noble and generous spirits who have chosen to base their conduct upon a love for their fellow man, death opens a brilliant pathway to glory. What do you think of our system?"

"I'm very taken with it. It contradicts neither the power nor the goodness of God. This progression, this ascension into different worlds, all of them the work of His hands, this tour of the creation of the universe—all of it seems to fit the dignity of

322

a monarch who reveals his dominion to those capable of under-standing it."

"Yes, my brother," he replied enthusiastically, "what a fasci-nating image it is: all these suns visited one after the other, all these souls growing richer as they journey along, encountering millions of things undreamed of, growing ever more perfect, becoming more sublime as they approach the sovereign Being, knowing Him more perfectly, loving Him with a more enlight-ened love, plunging into the ocean of His grandeur! Rejoice, O man! You can advance only from marvel to marvel. A spectacle ever new, ever miraculous awaits you. Your hopes are great. You will traverse the immense bosom of nature until at last you lose yourself in the God who is her source."

"But the evildoers," I cried, "who have sinned against natural law, who have hardened their hearts to cries for mercy, who have murdered innocence, who have ruled only for them-selves—what will become of them? Though I'm no lover of hatred and vengeance, I would build with my own hands a hell in which to fling those cruel souls who have made my blood boil at the sight of the evil they have done to the weak and the just."

"It is not up to us—feeble as we are and subject still to so many passions—to pronounce on the manner in which God will punish them, but it is certain that the wrongdoer will feel the weight of His justice. All those who have betrayed others or been cruel or indifferent to their sufferings will be banished from His sight. The souls of Socrates or Marcus Aurelius will never come into contact with Nero's: there will be always an infinite distance separating them. That's all we can be certain of. But it's not up to us to calculate the weights which will be regis-tered on the scales of eternity. We believe that errors which haven't entirely obscured human understanding, the heart which hasn't hardened to complete insensitivity, that kings, even, who didn't think themselves gods—these will be able to purify themselves through self-improvement over a long period of years. They will descend into worlds where physical suffering will predominate. This will be the effective whip which will make them aware of their dependency and their guilt, and will rectify their prestige born of pride. If they bow down under the hand that punishes them, if they follow the lead of reason and submit themselves to its lights, if they realize how far they have fallen from the ideal state, if they make certain efforts to achieve that state, then their pilgrimage will be much abbreviated. They will die in their prime, and they will be mourned. However, though happy at their own deliverance, they will sigh over the fate of those they have left behind on that unhappy planet. Thus, someone who fears death does not know exactly what he fears: his terror is the child of his ignorance, and this ignorance is the first punishment for his sins.

"The guiltiest will, perhaps, also lose their precious sense of liberty. They certainly won't be annihilated, because the idea of nothingness is repugnant to us: there can be no nothingness under a God who is a creator, preserver, and restorer. The evildoer shouldn't look forward to plunging into the void: he will be pursued by the eye of God, which sees all. Persecutors of all kinds will simply vegetate on the lowest rung of existence. They will suffer an endless cycle of destruction, bringing them pain and enslavement. But God alone knows the time it will take to punish or absolve them."

*   *   *

CHAPTER XXIV

The Princely Innkeeper

"You'd like to have dinner," my guide said to me, "because our walk has given you an appetite? Well, let's stop in this inn . . ." I stepped back three paces. "You wouldn't think of such a thing," I said to him. "Look, here's a carriage entrance, coats of arms, escutcheons. A prince must live here."—"Well, in fact, yes! He's a good prince, because he always has three tables set, one for himself and his family, another for strangers, and the third for the needy."—"Are there many such tables in the city?"—"At the homes of all the princes."—"But there must also be lots of idle parasites at them?"—"Not at all, because as soon as someone makes a habit of it, if he isn't a foreigner, then it's remarked on, and the town censors look into his qualifications and assign him a job. But if he seems good for nothing except eating, then they banish him from the city, just as in the republic of bees they chase out of the hive all those who do nothing but devour the common stores."—"Then you have censors?"—"Yes, or rather they should have another name: they are the admonishers who carry everywhere the torch of reason, and who heal intractable or mutinous spirits through their eloquence and sometimes their kindness and skill, too.

"These tables are set up for the old people, the convalescents, pregnant women, orphans, and visitors. They all sit down at them without hesitation and without shame. They're offered here healthy nourishment, light but abundant. This prince, who respects humanity, makes no display of luxury, which would be as revolting as it is lavish. He doesn't have three hundred men working to give dinner to a dozen persons. He doesn't make an opera set of his table. He doesn't take pride in something that is, in fact, shameful, outrageously excessive, ridiculous (a): when he dines, he reflects that he has only one stomach, and that it would be making a god of him if they presented him, as they did the gods of antiquity, with a hundred sorts of dishes which he wouldn't even be able to taste."

As we were conversing, we crossed two courtyards and entered a very long room, the one set aside for foreigners. A single table, on which several places had already been served, ran the whole length of the room. They paid respect to my great age with an armchair. We were served a delicious soup, vegetables, a little game, and some fruit, all of it simply prepared (b).

"This is really admirable," I cried. "Oh, what a good use of his wealth it is to feed the hungry! I find this sort of thinking much nobler and much worthier of their rank. . . ." Everything took place in a very orderly fashion. A proper, though lively, conversation lent further charm to this public table. The prince appeared, giving orders to one side and the other in a noble and

(a) Seeing the engraving of Gargantua, whose mouth, as large as an oven, swallows up in just one meal 1,200 pounds of bread, twenty oxen, a hundred sheep, six hundred chickens, fifteen hundred hares, two thousand quail, twelve hogsheads of wine, six thousand peaches, etc., etc., etc., what man wouldn't say to himself: "This great mouth belongs to a king"?

(b) I once saw a king, entering a prince's palace, cross a large courtyard entirely filled with unfortunates who cried out feebly: "Give us bread!" And having crossed this courtyard without reply, the king and the prince sat down to a feast that cost almost a million.

affable manner. He approached me with a smile on his face; he asked me for news of my century; he insisted that I speak candidly. "Ah!" I said to him, "your forebears weren't so generous as you! They passed their days at hunting (c) and at table. If they killed hares, it was out of idleness, and not to give them to eat to those whose crops had been destroyed by them. They never elevated their souls toward some great and useful purpose. They spent millions on dogs, valets, horses, and sycophants: in short, they were professional courtiers. They abandoned the cause of their country."

Everyone threw up his hands in astonishment. They had a great deal of trouble believing my testimony. "History," they assured me, "never told us all that—on the contrary."—"Ah!" I replied. "The historians have been guiltier than the princes."

* * *

Chapter XXXVIII

Form of Government

"Might I ask you what is the present form of your government? Is it monarchical, democratic or aristocratic?" (a)

(c) Hunting should be regarded as a low and ignoble pastime. One should kill animals only out of necessity, and, of all possible employments, it's certainly the saddest. I always reread with a new degree of attention what Montaigne, Rousseau, and the other philosophers wrote against hunting. I love those good Indians who respect even the blood of animals. A man's nature shows up in the kind of recreation he chooses. What hideous recreation to make a bloodied partridge fall down from the heavens, to trample hares under foot, to follow twenty howling dogs, to see a poor beast torn apart! The animal is weak, he is innocent, he is timidity itself. A free inhabitant of the woods, he succumbs to the cruel bites of his enemies. Man appears and shoots him through the heart with an arrow; the barbarian smiles as he sees his handsome sides red with blood and the useless tears that flow from his eyes. Such a pastime arises from a soul which is by nature hard. The character of hunters is nothing more than indifference mixed with cruelty.

(a) The spirit of a nation is independent of its environment; climate is in no way the physical cause of its greatness or its decadence. All the peoples of the earth have strength and courage, but the causes that set these in motion and sustain them derive from certain circumstances, which can be slow or fast in developing, but which always arrive sooner or later. Those people are fortunate who, out of instinct or enlightenment, seize the moment!

"It is neither monarchical nor democratic nor aristocratic: it is reasonable and adapted to mankind. The monarchy no longer exists. [In later editions this phrase was modified to "Unlimited monarchy no longer exists."] Monarchical states, as you knew—but so ineffectually—always tend to be swallowed up in despotism, just as rivers tend to be lost in the vastness of the sea, and the despotism soon collapses in upon itself (b). All that has happened quite literally: there has never been a more certain prophecy.

It is shameful to think that mankind has been able to measure the distance from the earth to the sun and weigh the solar system—that, having acquired this great knowledge, he has been unable to invent simple and effective laws for governing reason-

(b) Would you like to know what the general principles are which usually hold sway in the council of a bad monarch? Here is a good approximation of what is said there, or rather, what is done. "We must multiply the taxes of every sort, because the prince can never be rich enough, inasmuch as he is obliged to maintain armies, as well as the officers of his household, which must absolutely be the most magnificent. If the overburdened people raise objections, the people will be wrong, and it will be necessary to repress them. This is not injustice toward them because, at bottom, they possess nothing except by the goodwill of the prince, who can call back at his discretion what he has had the kindness to let them have, especially if he needs it for the crown or its splendor. Furthermore, it is well known that a people who are allowed to accumulate wealth become less hardworking and possibly insolent. We must cut back on their happiness to increase their submission. The poverty of his subjects will always be the strongest defense of the monarch; the less wealth individuals will have, the more obedient the nation will be. Once they have accepted their duty, they will follow it out of habit: this is the most certain way of being obeyed. It's not enough just to be submissive; they must believe that the spirit of wisdom resides here in all her majesty, and submit, then, to our infallible decrees, without daring to ask questions."

If a philosopher who had access to the prince advanced to the middle of the council and said to the monarch: "Do not believe these misguided counselors; you are surrounded by enemies of your family. Your security and your greatness are founded less on your absolute power than on the love of your people. If they are miserable, they will ardently long for a revolution, and they will overturn your throne or that of your children. The people are immortal, but you will pass. The majesty of the throne resides more in paternal love than in unlimited power. Such a power is violent and against the nature of things. If you were more moderate, you would be more powerful. Set an example of justice, and be persuaded that the princes who have a morality are stronger and more respected," they would certainly take this philosopher for a visionary, and they wouldn't perhaps deign to punish him for his virtue.

able beings. It is true that pride, avarice, and self-interest presented a thousand obstacles. But what greater triumph than to find the nexus which ties individual passions to the service of the general good? A ship that sails the seas commands the elements at the same time it obeys them: buffeted from all sides, it moves forward in reaction to these forces. Here we have perhaps the most perfect image of the State: borne upon stormy passions, it derives impulsion from them at the same time that it resists their tempestuous energy. *All is in the art of the Captain.* Your political lights were very dim. You stupidly blamed the author of nature, though He had given you the intelligence and the courage to govern yourselves. Just one loud voice was needed to awaken the multitude from their slumber. If oppression thundered over your heads, you had only your own weakness to blame. Liberty and happiness belong to those who know how to seize them. All is revolution in this world: the greatest one of all grew to maturity, and we are harvesting the fruits of it (c).

When we emerged from a state of oppression, we were careful not to commit all the forces and mechanisms of government, all rights and attributes of power, into the hands of one man (d). Having learned from the mistakes of past centuries, we would never have been so imprudent. Even if Socrates or Marcus Aurelius themselves had come back from the dead, we

(c) For some states there is a stage which is unavoidable—a bloody and terrible stage, though it announces freedom to come. I speak of civil war. Here all the great men rise up, some attacking, others defending, liberty. Civil war gives free rein to the most hidden talents. Extraordinary citizens come forth and prove themselves as commanders of men. This is a horrible remedy! But after the long slumber of the state and its inhabitants, it becomes necessary.

(d) A despotic government is only the sovereign in league with a small number of chosen subjects to trick and defraud all the rest. Thus the sovereign, or his representative, overshadows society and divides it; he becomes the central figure, igniting passions as he pleases, and pitting them against one another for his personal benefit. He announces what is just or unjust; his whim becomes law; and his favor becomes the standard of public esteem. Such a system is too violent to endure. But justice is a barrier that protects both subject and prince. Liberty alone can create generous citizens; truth alone can produce men of reason. A king is powerful only when he heads a generous and contented nation. Once the nation is debased, the throne collapses.

wouldn't have entrusted them with absolute power, not out of mistrust, but out of fear of debasing the sacred character of the free man. Isn't law the expression of the General Will? How could we entrust such an important function to one individual? Wouldn't he have moments of weakness? And even if he did not, could men be capable of renouncing liberty, which is their greatest prerogative (e)?

We have experienced how much absolutism is opposed to the true interests of the nation. The art of raising insidious taxes, multiplying them so that their weight becomes constantly more oppressive; our laws in confusion and set one against the other; private property eaten up by squabbling lawyers; cities filled with the tyrants of privilege; the venality of public servants, ministers and intendants, treating the different parts of the kingdom as ripe for conquest; a gradual hardening of the heart approaching inhumanity; royal officers who were not answerable to the people, insulting them rather than deferring to their complaints—these were the results of this vigilant despotism, which brought together enlightened minds only to abuse their power, just as a magnifying glass turns light into fire. You traveled through France, this beautiful kingdom which nature had smiled upon, and what did you see? Cantons desolated by tax gougers, cities become villages, villages become hamlets, their inhabitants haggard, disfigured—beggars, finally, instead of inhabitants. One knew about all these evils, and yet one disregarded established principles in favor of a system of greed (f),

(e) Liberty engenders miracles: it triumphs over nature, it makes crops sprout from rocks, it lends a cheerful air to the saddest regions, it enlightens simple shepherds and renders them more profound than the proud slaves of the most sophisticated courts. Other climates, which are the masterpiece and glory of creation, once they fall into slavery, exhibit only abandoned fields, pale faces, lowered glances which dare not look heavenward. Man! Choose, then, to be happy or miserable, if you are capable of choosing: fear tyranny, detest slavery, take up arms, live free or die.

(f) An intendant, wishing to give the *** [queen], who was passing through Soissons, an impression of the abundance which existed in France, had the fruit trees pulled up from the fields on the outskirts of town, and had them replanted in the streets, where the cobblestones were removed. The trees were intertwined with garlands of gilded paper. This intendant was, *without realizing it,* a very great artist.

whose perfidious shadow covered the general plundering and embezzlement.

"Would you believe it? The revolution came about quite easily, by the heroism of a great man. A philosopher-king, worthy of the throne because he disdained it, more concerned for the happiness of mankind than the appearance of power, concerned for posterity and wary of his own power, offered to restore to the Estates their ancient prerogatives. He sensed that a far-flung kingdom needed to unify its different provinces in order to be governed wisely. As in the human body, where, in addition to the general circulation, each part has its own individual circulation, so each province, while obeying the general laws, adapts its own particular laws to its soil, its geographical position, its commerce, and its various interests. In this way, everything lives, everything flourishes. The provinces no longer exist only to serve the court and ornament the capital (g). A misguided order emanating from the throne no longer arrives to sow trouble in areas where the eye of the sovereign has never penetrated. Each province assures its own security and its own welfare: the principle of its existence is thus never far from the source. It is in its own breast, always ready to reanimate the

---

(g) Error and ignorance are the source of all the ills which afflict humanity. Man is only bad because he mistakes his real self-interest. One can commit errors in theoretical physics, in astronomy, or mathematics with no real negative effects, but politics cannot afford the slightest error. There are administrative mistakes which are more harmful than physical calamities. An error of this sort can depopulate and impoverish a kingdom. The deepest and most rigorous study is necessary, especially in those problem cases where the arguments on both sides of a question are equally balanced. Here nothing is more dangerous than routine: it produces inconceivable hardships, and the state is only aware of them at the moment of its downfall. Thus, no effort should be spared to shed light on the complicated art of government, since the smallest stumble results in an enormous trajectory of error. Heretofore, laws have only been palliatives presented in the form of general remedies; they are (as it has been well said) born out of necessity and not out of philosophy. We must look to the latter to cure what defects they have. But what courage, what zeal, what love for humanity will be needed in the one who would build a proper edifice out of this unformed chaos! Yet what genius could be dearer to the human race? Let him never forget this most important goal, which touches most closely the happiness of mankind and, as a necessary consequence, its morality!

whole, and to remedy any ills which may arise. Caregiving is put into the hands of interested parties, who will not shrink from applying the necessary cure, nor will they rejoice at ills which threaten the country as a whole.

"Absolute monarchy was thus abolished. The leader kept the name of king, but he didn't foolishly undertake to bear the whole burden that had overwhelmed his ancestors. The assembled Estates of the kingdom were the only legislative authority. The administration, political as well as civil, is confided to the Senate, and the monarch, armed with the sword of justice, presides over the execution of the laws. He proposes all sorts of useful establishments. The Senate is responsible to the king, and the king and the Senate are responsible to the Estates, who assemble every two years. Everything is decided by a plurality of votes. New laws, appointments to be filled, grievances to be redressed—these fall within its province. Cases which are individual or exceptional are left to the wisdom of the monarch.

"He is happy (h), and his throne is firmly established on a base which is all the more solid because the liberty of the nation guarantees his crown (i). Men who otherwise would have no distinction derive their virtues from this wellspring of greatness. For the citizen is not at all separate from the state: he is

(h) M. d'Alembert has said that a king who did his duty was the most miserable man in the world, and one who didn't do it was even more pitiful. Why would the king who did his duty be the most miserable of all men? Would it be because of the multiplicity of his tasks? But work well done is a source of real enjoyment. Would he count for nothing this inner satisfaction that comes from the sense of having assured the happiness of mankind? Does he believe that virtue is not its own reward? Universally loved, hated only by the wicked, why would his heart remain hardened to pleasure? Who has not felt the satisfaction of having done good? The king who does not fulfill his duties is the more to be pitied. Nothing could be more just, if, that is, he is capable of feeling remorse and opprobrium; if he isn't, he is even more to be pitied. Nothing is truer than this last proposition.

(i) It is good for all states, even republics, to have a leader, though his power, of course, should be limited.

He is a strawman who frightens the ambitious and nips their schemes in the bud. Royalty, then, is like one of those scarecrows placed in a garden to ward off the sparrows who come to eat the grain.

part of its body (j). Thus we note with what zeal he supports everything that adds to its splendor.

"There is a reason for every law which emanates from the Senate, and the Senate explains concisely its motives and its intentions. We cannot understand how, in your (so-called enlightened) century, your magistrates dared, in their pride, to propose arbitrary laws, like theological decrees, as if the law were not the expression of public reason, and as if the people didn't need to be informed in order to obey more promptly. These gentlemen decked out in judges' bonnets, who called themselves the fathers of the country, were ignorant, then, of the great art of persuasion, that art which acts so effortlessly and so powerfully; or rather, having no fixed point of view, no firm foothold, by turns muddleheaded, seditious, slavish, they flattered and fatigued the throne, sometimes digging in their heels over trivialities, sometimes selling out the people for hard cash.

"You can well imagine that we have got rid of those magistrates who were hardened from years back to dispose cold-heartedly of the life, wealth, and honor of citizens. They were avid in the defense of their slender privileges, but cowardly when it came to the public interest. At the end, it wasn't even worth the trouble to bribe them: they had fallen into a sort of perpetual indolence. Our magistrates are very different. The name 'fathers of the people' with which we honor them is a title which they merit in the full sense of the term.

"Today, the reins of government are confided to wise and firm hands who follow a plan. The laws govern, and no one is above them—which was a dreadful stumbling block in your Gothic governments. The general happiness of the country is based upon the particular security of each subject: he does not fear men; he fears the laws; and the sovereign himself is aware

(j) Those who have said that, in monarchies, the kings were repositories of the will of the nation have spoken foolishness. Is there, in fact, anything more ridiculous than intelligent beings saying to someone else: "Will for us"? The people have always said to their monarchs: "Act for us, in accordance with our wills clearly expressed."

of the laws hanging over him (k). His vigilance makes the senators more attentive to their duties and responsibilities; his confidence in them soothes their pains; and his authority provides the force and vigor necessary for their decisions. Thus, the scepter, whose weight oppressed your kings, seems light in the hands of our monarch. He is no longer a victim pompously arrayed, constantly sacrificed to the needs of the state. He bears only the burden permitted to him by the limited power he has received from nature.

"We possess a prince who is God-fearing, pious and just, who reveres God and country, who fears divine vengeance and the judgement of posterity, and who holds a clear conscience and a spotless reputation to be the highest degree of happiness. It is not great intellectual ability or extensive learning which do the most good, so much as the sincere desire of a pure heart which loves to do good and holds it dear. Oftentimes the much-vaunted brilliance of a monarch, instead of increasing the happiness of a nation, works to the detriment of its liberty.

"We have been able to reconcile two things which seemed almost impossible to bring together, the good of the state with the good of the individual. It has, in fact, been asserted that the public happiness was necessarily distinct from the happiness of

(k) Any government where a single individual is above the law and can violate it with impunity is a sad and iniquitous government. A man of genius [S. H. Linguet] has employed his talents, in vain, to make us appreciate the principles of Asiatic governments: they contradict human nature too outrageously. Imagine a proud ship which defies the elements: one tiny crack could let in foul seawater and bring about its ruin. Likewise, one man who flaunts the law can cause all manner of injustices and iniquities to bear upon the body politic and inevitably hasten its downfall. Does it matter that we perish as a result of one or of many? The misfortune is the same. Does it matter if tyranny has a hundred arms, if only one rules from one end of the country to the other, if it represses all individuals, if it regenerates as soon as it is cut off? Furthermore, it is not despotism itself which is so frightening, but its propagation. The viziers, pashas, etc. imitate their master; they cut throats before their own can be cut. In the governments of Europe, the simultaneous reaction of all the parts—the shock when they come together—affords some moments of equilibrium in which the people breathe freely. The limits of their respective power, which are constantly challenged, provide a kind of substitute for freedom; this phantom, at least, consoles those who cannot attain the reality.

some individuals. We have rejected this primitive political philosophy, based upon ignorance of the true laws or scorn for those who are the poorest and the most useful members of society. There have been abominable and cruel laws which supposed that men were evil, whereas we are disposed to believe they have only become so since the institution of these very laws. Despotism has wearied the human heart, and, in doing so, has hardened and corrupted it.

"To do good, our king has all the power and authority necessary; and, when it comes to doing evil, his hands are tied. He always sees the nation in its most favorable light: its courage is underscored, its fidelity toward its prince, and its horror of foreign domination.

"There are censors who are charged with chasing away from the prince all those who tend to irreligion, libertinage, untruth, and the more harmful art of ridiculing virtue (l). We no longer have that class of men claiming nobility (which, absurd as it was, could be purchased), who rushed to prostrate themselves around the throne; who aspired only to serve in the army or the court; who lived in idleness, fed their pride on faded genealogical documents, and presented the deplorable spectacle of vanity equal to their wretchedness. Your grenadiers went to battle with as much bravery as the noblest among them, and didn't make such a claim for the blood they shed. Moreover, such pretensions in our republic would have offended the other orders of the state. Our citizens are equal: the only distinction between them occurs naturally in the form of virtue, intelligence, and hard work (m).

(l) I am very tempted to believe that the sovereigns are almost always the greatest gentlemen in their courts. Narcissus had an even blacker soul than Nero.

(m) Why couldn't the French some day adopt certain republican forms? Who in this kingdom is unaware of the privileges of the nobility, based upon its origin and confirmed by several centuries of practice? As soon as the Third Estate emerged from its degradation, in the reign of John, it took its place in the national assemblies, and this proud and barbarian nobility accepted it, protesting, as belonging to the orders of the kingdom, even though the times were still rife with prejudices based on the administration of fiefs and the profession of arms. The French sense of honor—which is still a motivating principle and which is greater than our most venerable institutions—could perhaps one day become the soul of a republic, especially when the taste for

There are many precautions taken so that the monarch does not forget his obligations to the poor, should public calamities occur. In addition, he observes each year a solemn fast lasting three days. During this time, our king endures hunger and thirst and sleeps on a hard pallet. This unpleasant but salutary fast fills his heart with a more tender commiseration toward those in need. The truth is that our sovereign has no need of being reminded by means of this physical stimulus, but it is a law of the state, a sacred law, which has been heretofore respected. Following the monarch's example, every minister and all others who hold the reins of government feel themselves personally obliged to experience poverty and its accompanying pain. In this way, they are more disposed to bring comfort to those who are in thrall to the stern law of extreme need (n).

philosophy, the knowledge of political laws, and the experience of so many misfortunes will have destroyed this superficiality and indiscretion which contaminate those brilliant qualities that would make of the French the finest nation in the world, if they but knew how to plan, develop, and sustain their projects.

(n) Facing the cabin of a philosopher stood a high and fertile mountain, blessed by the soft rays of the sun. It was covered with fine pastures, golden stalks of grain, cedars, and aromatic plants. Busy flocks of birds—the most beautiful imaginable, and the most delicious—rent the air with their wings and filled it with their harmonious calling. Bounding deer peopled the woods. Lakes nourished trout, whiting, and pike in their silvery waters. Three hundred families dotted along the back of this mountain shared its prosperity, and lived happily in peace and abundance, and in the bosom of the virtues which these conditions engender. They blessed God with each rising and setting of the sun. But, one day, the indolent, lustful, and dissipated Osman mounted the throne, and the three hundred families were soon ruined, chased from their lands, and forced to wander as vagabonds. The beautiful mountain came under the complete control of Osman's vizier, a noble brigand, who turned the remains of this unhappy people to the profit of his dogs, his concubines, and his sycophants. One day, as Osman was out hunting, he lost his way and came by chance upon the philosopher, whose remote cabin had escaped the wave of destruction that had swallowed up his neighbors. The philosopher recognized the monarch, though the latter was unaware of it. The philosopher did his duty nobly. They spoke of the present: "Alas," said the wise old man, "we were still gay ten years ago; but today the most severe poverty is grinding down the poor and destroying their souls, and the great misery which they must confront courageously every day is slowly dragging them to the grave. Everyone is suffering . . ." The monarch replied: "Tell me, please, what is poverty?" The philosopher sighed, held his tongue, and indicated the way back to the palace.

"But," I said to him, "such changes must have been long and difficult and painful. What efforts you must have had to make!" The wise man smiled sweetly and answered: "Good is not harder to do than evil. Human passions are terrible stumbling blocks, but when intellects are enlightened as to their real interests, they become sound and just. It seems to me that one man alone could govern the world, if all hearts were disposed to tolerance and equity. Despite the general mediocrity of the men of your century, you did make it possible for reason, in the future, to make great strides. The effects of this are now evident, and the happy principles of wise government have been the first fruit of the reform."

Anecdotes sur
Mme la comtesse du Barry

(Anecdotes About Mme la comtesse du Barry)
["London, 1775," probably written by
Mathieu-François Pidansat de Mairobert]

Preface

Although this work is a very complete life of Mme la comtesse du Barry, the author, in order to avoid pretentiousness,
has preferred the more modest title of "Anecdotes." He has
thus freed himself from the necessary structure, the transitions,
and the grave style which a more imposing title would have
demanded. He would otherwise have been obliged to omit, or
to relegate to notes, a multitude of details which would have
sullied the majesty of a history. Though these may appear
meticulous to posterity, they will be extremely spicy for contemporary readers.

Furthermore, it should not be assumed that, in the course of
our extensive information gathering, we have accumulated
willy-nilly an assortment of fables and absurdities concerning
this celebrated courtesan. You will note that throughout our
account, from her birth up to her retirement, we have cited the
sources of our information. We have followed, in this respect,
the scrupulous principles of the historian.

All those who might be tempted by such a title—which often
announces a calumny or a complete fabrication—and who seize
upon the text as if it were a *libelle* intended to foment wickedness and corruption, should recognize their error and reject
this book out of hand. The writer conceived his project during
the most brilliant period of the royal favorite's reign. At that
time he was motivated by neither hope nor fear, and nothing
would have been able to deflect him from his task or to influ-

ence his veracity. When, today, Mme la comtesse du Barry has neither the power nor the credit to counter the public's ill-will, he will not sink so low as to embellish this picture of a life which is already too full of scandal and infamy. His goal was more noble and more useful: to console the simple citizen who, deprived by his obscure birth of access to the court and its glories, might sigh after such things. It was to show him just how these honors are obtained, from which hands they are bestowed, and on whose heads they fall. Happier than many another moralist in the choice of his subject, he found one which combined historical interest with all the pleasures of a novel. His work will delight both the austere philosopher and the frivolous reader, exciting the one to reflection and affording an agreeable pastime to the other. It will, in short, give pleasure to all kinds of readers.

*   *   *

Part One

The origins of Mme la comtesse du Barry are unknown, like certain great rivers which appear insignificant at their source and only draw our attention as they widen and deepen, becoming those majestic waterways that so impress the traveler. And, like the origins of those great families or ancient peoples which were lost in the mists of time, hers also were intermingled with legend and mystery. We do, however, have the account of M. Billard Dumonceau, her godfather, who was very informative during the early days of this lady's rise to power, but who since—out of prudence, perhaps, or by order from above—has become very reserved on her account.

He was, as he tells it, in charge of a provisioning expedition during the war of 1744. His duties took him through Vaucouleurs, a small town in the province of Champagne, which prides itself on being the birthplace of Joan of Arc, and which will doubtless be no less proud to claim Mme la comtesse du Barry. As he bore the rank of matador in the Finance Ministry, he was put up with the local director of tax gathering. During his stay, the wife of an employee in the Tax Farm named Gomart de

338

Vaubernier gave birth. He was one of those minor clerks known as "cellar rats," because they spend a lot of time in cellars inspecting wines and other beverages.

The wife of the director had agreed to be godmother to the child; she asked M. Dumonceau to accompany her in presenting the newborn. This gentleman, who was by nature gallant and playful, accepted the courteous invitation with enthusiasm. The infant was baptized Marie-Jeanne. The ceremony reflected the great wealth of the godfather: for that locale, it appeared magnificent indeed, and terminated, as was customary, with a fête and the general distribution of Jordan almonds and other sweets. The good man then departed, without so much as a worry that the tiny soul whom he had just redeemed for God would soon return to the devil.

Providence, which was watching over the infant more closely than her godfather, gave him the opportunity to rekindle in his breast some sentiments that were more appropriate to the new title he had acquired and more worthy of his Christianity and his humanity.

One morning, several years after his return to Paris, a woman was announced as desiring to speak to him. He summoned her to enter; she was accompanied by a child; he recognized neither of them, and inquired her name. Tearfully, she fell to her knees and informed him that she was that Gomart whose daughter he had presented for baptism. The child standing before him was his goddaughter.

The girl excited his interest. In addition to her sweetness, which is natural to children of her age, she had an unusual grace. He gave her a little kiss and a caress, and inquired of the mother the reason for her visit to Paris.

Mme Gomart explained that she had lost her husband, and that with his death she had found herself in a very sorry state, since his employment had allowed him to accumulate no savings whatsoever. Having thus no means of support in Vaucouleurs, she had come to the capital to look for work and hoped to find a position in service.

The fate of the mother interested M. Dumonceau, but it was the child in particular who excited his benevolence. He gave Mme Gomart 12 francs, telling her to come back at the end of every month and bring her daughter with her; he offered to pay her the same amount again each month for the girl's primary education, that is, to teach her to read and write. Moreover, he promised to help her find a situation. We don't know exactly what became of the mother during these early days, and the memory of M. Dumonceau is not very clear on this point. He recalls only that he continually paid out the aid as promised, and more in addition. It appears that the mother appropriated a good portion of it for herself; certainly the money was not put very advantageously toward the sort of education the godfather had in mind for the girl, because she does not read well and writes very badly. A petition has been discovered, scribbled in Mme la comtesse du Barry's hand in the following manner: "Recommends by Madame the Contested Dubarri."

This oversight, unimportant though it was, did not last long. M. Dumonceau had as his mistress at that time Mlle Frédéric, a very famous courtesan, of whom he was greatly enamored. As the widow Gomart was still without work, he found her a place as a cook for his mistress. He killed two birds with one stone: while doing a favor for this poor woman, he also acquired for himself a spy who could serve his jealous curiosity.

It then became a question of what to do with the girl, who was growing apace and already quite precocious for her age. M. Billard, a relative of M. Dumonceau and a controller in the postal service, who was in the grip of a nascent religious fervor, proposed to send her to Sainte-Aure, a community under the direction of the abbé Grisel, who was also, in a sense, its founder. His zeal was generally praised; his offer was accepted; and he agreed to pay the child's boarding costs in this religious establishment, where she would make her first communion and acquire enough training to be qualified for a job.

We shall lose sight, for a moment, of this precious treasure buried deep in the community of Sainte-Aure, where the young girl was adapting to the exercises of convent life—exercises which, as we know, were not always exclusively spiritual—and we shall give ourselves over to some reflections on this first period of her life.

When we have untangled the chaos of her birth, we have the following results:

(1) She is not a bastard, for she had an ostensible father, and, according to law, *Pater est quem nuptiae demonstrant* [He is the father whom the marriage identifies as such].

(2) She is still less the daughter of a monk. This myth is based upon a joking remark of M. the duc de Choiseul, who, in repeating it, preferred to heap ridicule and scandal upon Mme la comtesse du Barry, whose favor was just beginning, than to speak the truth. For he knew the truth as well as anyone. Once, when the conversation at his table turned to the religious orders, and everyone was heaping blame upon them, "Let's not speak ill of the monks," the Duke said; "they make us beautiful children."

(3) Although her father was not in a brilliant state, she was not, one would have to say, born in the gutter, and she could even, as it has been asserted since her elevation, be descended from an ancient family, either through the Gomarts or the Vauberniers. We leave it to the genealogists to unravel the thread of her parentage, and we return to the next in our series of Anecdotes.

*　　*　　*

Round about 1760, the widow Gomart, who had high hopes for her daughter, gathered together the small amount of money she had been able to put aside, which sum, augmented by her godfather and Madame de . . . , was sufficient to secure a place for Manon in the dress shop of the sieur Labille. This occupation, which is in itself quite respectable, has become so widely criticized that no wise or prudent mother would think of suggesting it to a young, attractive person. To introduce her into such an establishment would be to place her in a very exposed position indeed. In fact, it would be as good as putting her "on the street," so to speak; that is to say, it would invite propositions from men-about-town, from lechers and connoisseurs of fresh flesh. Her mother, who already knew something of Parisian life, presumably had something like that in mind. We do not know if it was in the hope of realizing her plan more easily that she, at this time, changed the name of her daughter. In any case, tradition has it that the latter called herself Lançon at Labille's. And so it is that we shall refer to her henceforth, as we recount this period of her life.

Mlle Lançon was marvelously pleased with her new quarters. A dress shop is a source of infinite delights for a young woman who is just stepping out into the world and who has as yet seen very little of it. It's a veritable temple of coquetry. She is exposed by turns to the richest and most luxurious fabrics, the most elegant and extravagant costumes, frills, flounces, pom-poms, and every sort of ornament which delights a woman, the most exquisite possible products of the needle or the spindle. How could this young nymph resist such temptations? She is like Achilles encountering arms for the first time. Moreover, if such a spectacle must of necessity awaken vanity, as well as a taste for luxury and frivolity, in a young and inexperienced person, the daily tasks of a fashion apprentice, as we shall see, also lead her eventually to succumb, like her peers, to the corruption of her morals. In effect, her job is not only to refashion the various products of French and foreign manufacture, but, even more, to make them serve the passions of her female clients. She has to toil ceaselessly, now swelling the pride of a grande dame, now highlighting a coquette's looks, or fanning the ardor of a lovestruck lady, the tenderness of a sensualist, the rage of a jealous female, or the lasciviousness of a courtesan. Beauty demands the complement of grace; kindness needs some added fire; ugliness wants disguises, tempering, softening. All these women require, in a word, victory, each in her own manner. Even the devout want to appear attractive in the eyes of their directors of conscience.

Furthermore, the sort of flirtatious and frivolous practices which are current in these workplaces tend to turn the heads of the young women who serve there. For instance, a young refugee from a convent is being educated in the art of seduction, so she can ensnare, by her dress and demeanor, the husband who has been chosen for her. Or a recent bride who is to be presented at court, and in whose heart the desire to seduce the King has already begun to form, is making every possible effort to enhance her attractions. Or—most telling of all—an actress or singer or dancer, a shopgirl like themselves from a questionable background, rides about today in a magnificent carriage and receives support from every quarter for the embellishment of her person. And finally a dandy, come to buy presents for his mistress, slips favors, in passing, to these serving maids of Venus. They hear nothing but talk of fêtes and balls, of comedies and love. And if, on occasion, they must minister to the bereaved, their concern is to make them less solemn and to lend them grace. A widow, ordering her mourning, wants to look as though she won't be wearing weeds forever: under her coarse uniform, one senses the metamorphosis of a beauty who will blossom one day more radiant than ever.

In addition to these seductive scenes which assault the senses of a young shopgirl, there are the strenuous efforts of those duennas who are the agents of debauchery. They treat her as a victim to be sacrificed to pleasure, and whisper to her the most flattering propositions, either their own or those of some courtly nobleman whose lustful gaze has happened to light upon the child. From this it will be seen how likely it is that she will succumb to the general immorality about her.

It is not, then, surprising that Mlle Lançon suffered the same fate as the others. Her pretty face caused her to be more in demand than her peers, and her carefree manner only encouraged these advances. Her desire for spending money and her extreme attachment to clothes and trinkets opened an avenue to anyone who wished to tempt her. Moreover, she had no one whose counsel could help to keep her out of danger. Her mother, who should have been watching out for her, while she wasn't so depraved as to put her daughter up for sale, still desired that she should make her fortune by any means whatever, imagining, so we're told, that there would be something in it for her as well. It was in these circumstances that a famous procuress, known as the "Official Superintendant of Pleasures for the Town and Court," learned from her "stalkers" (that is the term in the profession for the lieutenants of such women) about a new arrival in Labille's establishment. This eloquent seductress was a woman named Gourdan. She was a follower in the tradition of The Florences and The Pârises, those names immortalized in the honor roll of Cythera; and, while she had not as yet achieved the same celebrity herself, she was fulfilling with distinction her required functions in the capital. She is still fulfilling them to the complete satisfaction of her customers. She has won the trust of ministers, prelates, solemn magistrates, high financiers, and libertines of all stripes. In fact, there are few gentlemen who would not want to receive a mistress from her hand, for she is renowned for her lessons in the art of voluptuous pleasure giving. She constantly creams off, so to speak, the flower of the Parisian shopgirls. She cleans them up, educates them, gives them style and class, and helps them achieve success in proportion to their looks and talents.

As soon as Mme Gourdan's appraising glance fell upon Mlle Lançon, she knew the candidate was worthy of her efforts. She understood instinctively her potential market value, and quickly set the traps necessary to enlist such a desirable prey. As we have her own version of the details of this episode in the life of Mme la comtesse du Barry, we are going to reproduce here the procuress's own account. We shall leave out only certain improper expressions or overly robust language. In place of depictions which are too strong, we'll give a more tasteful rendering. Mme Gourdan herself is doing the talking.

"I was soon informed by my stalkers that there was a new arrival at Labille's, someone very beautiful, and I set off for there at once on the pretext of needing some new rags. I encountered the loveliest creature a pair of eyes could ever light upon. It must have been sixteen or so but already ravishing: a sprightly yet noble stature; an oval face, drawn as though by a painter's hand; large eyes, very apparent, appraising the world with a sidelong glance which made her all the more seductive; dazzling white skin; a beautiful mouth; tiny feet; and hair so luxuriant that I couldn't have contained it within my two hands. I judged by this exterior what the rest of her might be like: I simply could not miss out on such an acquisition. I approached her quite casually, and slipped into her hand a card bearing my address, together with a coin, and at the same time murmured to her, in such a way as not to be overheard, that she should come to me as soon as she could find a moment, that it was in her own interest to do so.

"I am a woman, and I know how to go about arousing the curiosity of young girls. I was quite sure that my remarks, accompanied by my little gift, would have their desired effect. And the very next day, which was a Sunday, Mlle Lançon came to see me. She told me that she had pretended to be going to

Mass. I made a great fuss over her, gave her something to eat, and inquired if she were happy with her current situation. She replied that she had no complaints, that her present employment suited her better than any other, but that, in general, she wasn't a bit fond of work, that she would prefer a life of continual laughing and playing, and that she envied the life of all those women she saw come into the shop—always so elegantly dressed, handsome cavaliers at their side, always on their way to the ball or the theatre. She was quite right, I said. A pretty girl like herself wasn't made for resting her butt on a chair while she plied a needle in order to earn, at the end of several years' work, maybe twenty or thirty sous a day. This kind of life was fit only for ugly, miserable working girls who could hope for nothing better. I then embraced her warmly and invited her into my apartments. I showed her my boudoirs fitted out for lovemaking where everything bespeaks pleasure and seduction. I urged her to examine the engravings which adorned the walls—nudes, suggestive positions, and all sorts of images for the arousal of sexual desire. I watched my little shopgirl gobbling all this up with her eyes; she was all aflame, but I tore her away, for I had only wanted to verify that my judgment had been correct, that she was right for my purposes.

"I then invited her into a large dressing room, where I opened up several closets for her. I spread out before her fine fabrics, taffetas, laces, silk stockings, fans, diamonds. 'So,' I cried, 'my child, do you want to sign on with me? You'll have all this; you'll live the sort of life you're yearning for; every day you'll go out to the theatre or to some show or other; you'll dine with the biggest and best of the court and the city; and, when night comes, what joy you will have! Oh, what joy! My dear heart, the best expression for this would surely be the joy of Paradise itself! . . . Have you ever experienced that? Just know that true happiness does not exist without it. There is no one who isn't seeking it. Here you'll meet princes, army generals, ministers, magistrates, clerics. They only work in order to be able to come here and relax and enjoy themselves with a juicy morsel like you . . . Come on, now, do you know what I'm talking about?'

"She was smiling at me quite ingenuously, and replied that

she really didn't understand what I meant, that no one before had ever put such a question to her, and that she really was at a loss for what to answer. . . . 'You're right, my love,' I replied, 'it's up to me to have a look.' . . . As I was saying this, I made a pretense of having her try on a gorgeous new dressing gown which happened to be laid out for a girl who was supposed to come for supper there that very evening. I took her in hand and disrobed her completely until she was naked as a worm. I gazed upon a splendid body, and breasts—I've handled plenty of them in my day, but never with such elasticity, such a shape, such an admirable position; a backside to make you swoon; thighs, buttocks. . . . Sculptors wouldn't be able to produce a work more perfect. . . . As for the rest, I know my way around enough to be able to say that her maidenhead was very doubtful indeed but adequate enough to be sold again more than once. . . . That's what I really wanted to find out about. . . .

"Having played this childish little game of dressing up and put on the outfit, which she wanted right away to keep, I explained to her that things couldn't be done like that. As no adventure had as yet been credited to her account, and she was not yet registered with the police, I would run the risk of having her packed off by them and myself with her, if I kept her in my establishment. She would have to return to Labille's until I could find someone to keep her, but she could come surreptitiously to my place and join in the social life, which would earn her a little pocket money. I slipped a six-franc coin into her pocket, and we arranged that I would send a messenger to her when the need arose. This woman would be able to communicate with her without saying a word, using signs agreed upon between us. She fell upon my neck in great happiness and withdrew.

"There was at that time a General Assembly of the Clergy in Paris. A prelate whose name I will not divulge (for, in our line of work, one must have the discretion of a confessor) had been requesting for some time that I find him a novice, someone to whom he could give her earliest instruction in sexual pleasure. I had not yet been able to satisfy him. We are, of course, permitted to employ willing young women who present themselves, but we do not deal in debauchery. Mlle Lançon seemed perfect for this job. I wrote to the monsignor that I had found just the girl for him, that His Eminence should prepare himself: he would be pleased with my selection. He specified a day, and I alerted my virgin in good time. I instructed her in the role she was to play, or rather I told her—without wanting to delve into the secrets of her past or enter into the details of what she knew or didn't know—that she must appear to be absolutely ignorant of everything, even of language. I had her use an astringent lotion which would remove any trace of penetration by a male. I had her perfumed and her hair elaborately dressed. She was elegantly turned out and enchanted with her own brilliant effect. In this state I delivered her to the prelate and received one hundred *louis* for this flower.

"He was clearly enchanted with her, for he wished to keep her, but with the end of the Church Assembly, he was forced to return suddenly to his diocese. And, to tell the truth, this suited me very well: this virgin would have to be deflowered several times over before I would be through with her. Meanwhile, in order to draw her ever closer to me, I made her a gift of a dress and several petticoats. I advised her to lead her girlfriends to believe that she had won the lottery, so as to avoid any suspicion of loose conduct. But I hardly needed to instruct her in this regard: she was as devious as I myself. I had, however, touched her soft spot with my little gifts, which enabled her to become habitually clean and well turned out. She loved me exceptionally well and called me her 'little mother.' She laughed herself silly each time I asked her to play the novice again, but when it came time to assume her role, she put on her little Agnes manner and got away with it among some real experts. Her virginity had been renewed already five or six times. After the Church, the nobility, the magistracy, and high finance had tried it out, it had brought me in more than a thousand *louis*. I was just on the point of turning her over to the bourgeoisie, when an unfortunate occurrence—quite inevitable in establishments such as ours—interfered with my plans and caused me to get rid of Mlle Lançon.

"Dumonceau, one of my former customers, whom I had lost sight of after he took up with Mlle Frédéric, had just lost this mistress of his. And so he came to me again, asking for something new and fresh to cheer him up. He paid good money. My choice fell on Mlle Lançon. My habit is always to keep from my girls the names of the men with whom they're doing business so as not to betray their confidence. And I deal in the same way with the shopgirls who come to my place from time to time, for their own protection and, incidentally, in order to preserve my handling rights. This being the case, nothing could prevent the catastrophe which was about to strike.

"On the appointed day I brought the virgin and the lecher together. At first they didn't seem to recognize one another, but then they looked each other over intently, as though surprised to be meeting. I noted the fire of lust go out of Dumonceau's gaze; he looked angry. Lançon let out a scream and fainted dead away. 'You traitor,' cried Dumonceau, 'could I ever have thought to find you here? Is this the kind of lesson you learned at Sainte-Aure? They were right when they predicted that you would become a loose woman.'

"As he spoke, he advanced upon her as though to strike the miserable girl. I threw myself between them, more dead than alive, being completely in the dark as to the meaning of this tirade. I grabbed hold of the furious individual, called for aid for the young woman, and drew the old rascal away into another room. In the first place, I had feared that this adventure would have some unfortunate consequences for me. I thought Dumonceau must have had some prior contact with the supposed virgin and that his present rage derived from the fact that he had been taken in by us both. But I soon grasped, as a result of the explanation he provided, that their quarrel had nothing to do with me. She was his goddaughter, he explained, along with the rest of the story, which we all now know.

"This emboldened me to undertake the girl's defense. I swore to him that she had only just appeared in my establishment for the first time; that she had been supplied to me by one of my 'stalkers'; that her ingenuousness ought to convince him that she was quite unaccustomed to appearing in such a setting; that she had been brought here without knowing what she was getting into; that she had absolutely no acquaintance with sin. . . .

" 'Oh, yes, indeed, no acquaintance with sin!' the godfather answered, interrupting me with an angry snort. 'Why, she knew it well from her convent days!' I saw that it was dangerous to argue with this man, and so I agreed to everything he wanted, protesting only that I had taught her nothing at all and that she had only this very instant entered my house for the first time. He calmed himself somewhat, and there followed a long discussion of Mlle Lançon and her mother, to whom we attributed all the blame. When I judged that he was sufficiently composed, and after promising him that, because of his special interest in her, this child would never set foot again in my house, I went to look for her with the pretext of making peace between them, but actually so that I could speak to her privately and alert her to the construction I had put upon their meeting. I brought her back with me, but we were greeted with renewed reproaches on the part of the old sinner. She tried to excuse herself innocently with this reply: 'But Godfather, could there be any harm in coming to a place that you frequent yourself?' This sarcastic question wounded Dumonceau in his pride to such a degree that he gave full vent once more to his rage.

"As he vomited forth the most savage imprecations against his goddaughter, her mother, and myself, the young woman sought to flee the terrible rage of her godfather, who was threatening her now with his cane. He pursued her, crying out that he was abandoning her, as well as her rascally mother, to her unhappy fate: he never wanted to hear anything about either of them ever again, and they should never even show themselves on his doorstep. During this time, I had been attempting to restrain the madman, but now he turned on me: 'And you, you abominable procuress, if ever I discover that this shameless hussy comes back here, I'll send you to the hospital, and her, too.' With that he left, brooking no further remark.

"As a result of this scene, his goddaughter received such a terrible fright that she dared not come back to see me at that time, but she continued to feel gratitude, as well as esteem, for me. Later, after becoming his mistress, she occasionally had recourse to my protection. She returned here for one or two secret rendezvous, but nothing very remarkable came of them. I saw her also when she was with du Barry. As he and I sometimes pooled our talent in collaborative ventures, he lent her to me for very grand occasions. I could have set her up as a kept woman a hundred times. She often asked as much of me when she was fed up with this vile man, but then, when it came down to it, she didn't dare leave him. He seemed to have her completely in his power. Besides, he was saving her for a greater destiny, and he was certainly right about that."

Here the account of the Abbess Gourdan ends. She added that the good Dumonceau had stood by his word where she was concerned and never again patronized her establishment. She attributed his apoplectic ravings, which she had described to us so vividly, to his humiliation at encountering his goddaughter in a house of ill repute and at the reprimand he received from her. Perhaps also there was some secret disgruntlement or jealousy, as she was so beautiful and he hadn't reserved for himself, as he could so easily have done, the first enjoyment of her. In short, there were warring passions within him at that moment, for he couldn't satisfy his lust without lapsing from the moral superiority he possessed as her godfather, and yet, if he wished to enjoy the authority of his role, he would have to contain his lewd desires. Whatever the motivations that produced this strange scene, we can draw from Mme Gourdan's account of it some new conclusions in Mme la comtesse du Barry's defense. As for the accusation which, if not defamatory, is at least exaggerated, that she spent her youth in a brothel, we shall have to take her part. For we see that she only went there out of curiosity, and not out of any decided taste for debauchery; nor was she drawn there by any sordid desire for gain, which motivated so many of her comrades, but by that attraction, which is so pardonable in women, for glamour and dressing up.

In short, if she has since become very educated in the art of lovemaking, she took her lessons from her own heart rather than from the conversation of the matrons who are professional in that line of work. Her teacher was the passionate temperament that had tormented her from her most tender age and that real appreciators of women hold to be their finest quality. This false notion of our heroine's background dates back to that remark by the duc de Noailles (then duc d'Ayen), who was more eager to get off a witticism than to tell the truth. When he heard that the King, in the beginning of his relationship with

Mme la comtesse du Barry, was experiencing pleasures that were inexpressible and completely new to him, he explained to the King, "Sire, this is because you have never been to a whorehouse."

* * *

{*After taking up with a clerk in the Naval Ministry and then with a hairdresser, the heroine has to live for a while with her mother. They supplement their meager income by streetwalking, until they run into a monk, who was the former lover of the mother and the natural father of the daughter. He places the girl, now known as Mlle Vaubergnier, in the house of a wealthy widow. After sleeping with the widow's sons and the widow herself, Mlle Vaubergnier seeks some genuine pleasure in the arms of their lackeys. This misbehavior leads to her dismissal. She changes her name to Mlle L'Ange and works as a call girl in a gambling house. There she falls under the spell of her principal lover, an adventurer named Jean du Barry, who calls himself a count and lives by procuring women for the rich and the powerful.*}

In the spring of 1768, the comte du Barry met the sieur Le Bel, one of the King's most trusted valets and the one most deeply involved in His Majesty's secret pleasures. This individual had been put in charge of recruitment for the Parc-aux-Cerfs. In that part of Versailles, Mme de Pompadour had established a kind of depot for those young girls for whom they were constantly on the lookout in Paris and from whose ranks the great lady supplied the bed of her royal lover. She understood the importance of catering to his physical needs with outside help; moreover, by performing this administrative task, she preserved for herself the monarch's affections and all the honor due her as official mistress of the King. One would be hard put to count the number of creatures who passed thus through this sort of menagerie where each one eagerly awaited her turn. For many, in fact, the turn never came at all, or it consisted only of slight familiarities, or it lasted only briefly, either because the monarch lost interest or the directress of the harem grew worried. She was very careful to make sure that those who seemed threatening, whether because of their character or their spirit, or the King's interest in them, should disappear.

But admission to this seraglio carried with it, as one might expect, distinct advantages. These girls were commonly married off with a dowry of 200,000 *livres* and sent to some provincial backwater. By special favor, a few managed to remain in Paris, such as Mme Gianbonne, who married a banker; Mme David, the wife of a highly placed provisioning officer; Mme le Normant, who was the first of all to be taken to bed by His Majesty after he stopped sleeping with Mme de Pompadour (she was known then as Mlle Morfi, and is held today in the very highest esteem, because she has just married her daughter to the nephew of the abbé Terray); Mlle Selin, a serving girl from Brittany, who preferred to retire to a convent and who is known to have had a very distinguished career; and so many others. To name them all would serve no purpose here. From the foregoing, it is easy to imagine just how costly such an establishment would be to maintain, not only because of these young nymphs, who left the harem, on average, at a rate of one per week (representing an outlay of more than 10 million a year), but also, and especially, because of the superiors and subalterns who were charged with finding them, and the costs for cleaning, preparing, and dressing them—getting them into a state, in short, to seduce not only by their innate charm but by the elegance of their exteriors. If we add to these major categories of expenditure the cost of the waste and misappropriation which such an operation naturally entails, we will see that, under the vague and misleading category of "Cash Receipts," it gushed forth funds from the public treasury like a broken tap.

As a consequence of the successive losses he had endured [the deaths of the Dauphin, the Dauphine, and the Queen from 1765 to 1768], the King had decided to close the Parc-aux-Cerfs and give himself up completely to his misery. Advancing age and the ease with which any great prince can satisfy his every desire had served to dull his pleasure in matters sexual. But this need, though diminished, still continued to exist. His courtiers had found it necessary, moreover, to distract him from the long and sad spectacle of the Queen's illness. His doctors assured him that it was dangerous to wean himself too abruptly from a pleasure fundamental to his existence. The monarch must have taken their advice to heart, because, despite the cares of his reign and the loss of his "companion," as he referred to the Queen in his letter to the archbishop informing him of her death, he charged the sieur Le Bel with the task of procurement in this area.

This very zealous servant often did his own field research in the interest of better serving his master. It was in the course of one of these hunting trips, that, fatigued and breathless from his endeavors, he spoke of his problem to the comte du Barry. The latter, who had a good nose in this department, and who moreover was known to the valet as a very useful individual, had no trouble in drawing him out. Le Bel admitted that, to his great regret, his hunting expeditions had turned up no one who was fit for His Majesty. . . . "Is that all that's bothering you?" the impudent Count asked. "I have just the person for you. You know that I'm not short on good taste. Let me handle it. Come to dine with yours truly, and call me a scoundrel if I don't present you with the most beautiful, the freshest, and most seductive woman you've ever seen—a real royal morsel." The royal supplier, heartened at such an encouraging prospect, embraced him and promised to come at the appointed hour. M. du Barry wasted no time in returning home and getting Mlle L'Ange decked out in all her finery. (This was the name by which Mlle Vaubergnier had been known since she had been with him, following the habit of courtesans, who take a *nom de guerre* when they enter society and begin to circulate.) He instructed her in the role she was to play, awakening in her a hope which he could only regard as chimerical, but which has in fact come true. He painted for her a picture of a brilliant destiny. She would not simply appear at Versailles and satisfy *incognito* the royal pleasure: he would make her the King's official mistress, replacing Mme Pompadour. In order to achieve this, she had to pretend in front of the sieur Le Bel, who was on his way there, to be his sister-in-law, as though she had actually married his fat brother, Guillaume du Barry. If she played her role well, making use of all the grace and coquetry at her disposal and leaving the rest to him, everything would turn out well.

Mlle L'Ange, as a sort of joke, had already taken the title of

"Mme la comtesse du Barry" on several occasions. It is rather current usage for kept women to adopt their lovers' title in this manner. And so she had very little trouble in playing this part before the sieur Le Bel, who was delighted with her face, her playfulness, her lustful glances, and her remarks, which matched them. He felt the old man in him becoming younger by the minute, and concluded from his own experience what a happy effect such a talented woman might have upon his master. The dinner was gaiety itself, and the valet would happily have adventured further on his own to see just how thoroughly he might vouch for his new discovery. M. du Barry took advantage of his enthusiasm to point out to the lecher that his sister-in-law must not be presented to the King like the usual sort of *grisette* who was introduced and then sent away quite casually. This, on the contrary, was a woman of breeding who, though honored to share the bed of a prince—an august monarch as well as a coveted lover—desired still more to conquer his heart; and who was not unworthy of such an ambition because of the attachment she felt already for his sacred person, an attachment which could only grow as their intimacy increased.

The simpleton was too lovesick not to see the truth of this argument nor to agree to all the necessary arrangements. It was decided that from this moment on, the supposed Countess would be a sacred piece of flesh. The sieur Le Bel would report his findings to the King and would relay to His Majesty the desire which the lady in question had to please him, the complete devotion of her husband to the royal will, and the happiness which this loyal couple would have in accommodating him. This beauty, however, who flattered herself that she would be able to demonstrate her love over the long term, had the right to expect in return from her princely lover that she would be granted the general exclusion of all other competitors.

Evil-tongued courtiers have suggested that, after this conversation, the ambassador was permitted to take possession of the future mistress in the name of his King. Others pretend that du Barry was more adroit than that, and dangled before him the possibility of such a reward if he succeeded in his mission. Be that as it may, as he was himself very smitten, he put in his account to the King so much heat and passion that he powerfully excited the ardor of the prince. In order to inflame him still further, he proposed that the King should arrange to view the object without her knowledge, so that, before entering into any engagement, he would be able to judge her worth for himself. The valet had a little house set up for this purpose, to which he invited the Countess to supper. There is some suggestion that she had been alerted to the secret witness she was to have. The company was appropriate to the setting, and the meal was so voluptuous that the monarch couldn't contain himself.

That very night he sent for Mlle L'Ange and discovered that she had more charms in secret than her beautiful exterior suggested. Indeed, those who have enjoyed her before the King unanimously agree that she has what it takes to revive the most worn-out partner. For a lover such as the aged King, suffering from a general disgust with women, who heretofore, out of a sense of respect and adoration for his person, had, even in the act of love, failed to make use of all the pleasure-giving resources at his disposal—for such a jaded lover to be suddenly introduced to a new world of sensual pleasures, offering a continuous fount of delights previously unknown to him! What a discovery! What a treasure trove! There had doubtless been women who had come to the prince's bed as knowledgeable as this one, but they had lacked the same unfettered and natural spirit, had not dared to trust their own know-how or ventured to put it to use. Mlle L'Ange, on the other hand, with all her zest, her candor, her freshness, was also the disciple of an expert in the most refined art of debauchery. He anticipated the prodigious effect his lessons might have and their contrast with the cold and inhibited embraces of the King's previous mistresses. Now he had only to stand aside and give his knowing pupil free rein: her initial success encouraged her to deploy her art in all its fullness. If men who are already familiar with the bold and energetic techniques of women of the night still manage to get pleasure from them, what effect mustn't these powerful arts have upon a sensualist who has never before experienced them! For such was the King's situation, according to those courtiers who were the best informed about his private life and amusements.

This daughter of Venus put her talents to such good use that the King could no longer do without her and insisted that she accompany him to Compiègne. During her stay there, which fell within the period of official mourning for the Queen, she maintained the most strict *incognito,* for His Majesty did not wish to flaunt his sexual pleasures before the public. The King, moreover, is very scrupulous where appearances are concerned and careful of the impression he conveys to his countrymen, with an eye to the maintenance of good public morals. But these small obstacles only served to excite his desire and increase it. As a result, Le Bel, we are told, when he observed the decided preference his master was developing for Mlle L'Ange, and saw that things were going much further than he had thought possible, began to regret having joined in the machinations of the Count, and the more so, because he suspected the ruse on which they were based. He felt obliged, therefore, before the royal favorite consolidated her position, to throw himself at the feet of the King and declare exactly in what circumstances this beauty had been discovered; to confess that he had been duped; to explain that she was far from well born and, furthermore, was not even married. . . . "So what?" the King cried, according to the most widely accepted account at court. "So what? Marry her off immediately, so that I can be spared the possibility of some indiscretion." . . . They add that the fool wished to go into greater detail, but that a withering look from the King shut him up. It's said that this zealous servant, who was consumed with regret at having come up with such a creature and fear for the safety of his prince, now prey to such violent passions at the onset of old age, became sick at heart and died. However, others say that, in order to ward off further indiscreet revelations, he was helped along to his demise with poison.

Whatever the case may be, the King's words had a wonderful effect on the spirits of the comte du Barry, known as "the great du Barry," to distinguish him from his brothers. One of the latter, whom we shall call "the fat du Barry," was a sort of old drunkard, a real swine, wallowing night and day in the lowest forms of debauchery. It was decided that he would be the one to receive the hand of Mlle L'Ange. He was informed well in advance, and they had no trouble convincing him to accept, when they explained that his acquiescence would enable him to lead more freely the kind of life he loved and would procure him all the money he could want. Such a prospect would have corrupted much less of a sinner than him. He agreed to the ceremony, and the marriage took place in the parish of Saint-Laurent on the first of September 1768. Le Pot, a notary in Auteuil, approved the contract. He had no notion at that time of the great destiny reserved for the beauty over whose civil affairs he was presiding. But, struck by her charm and grace, he thought to enjoy a privilege that was customary among his colleagues in such circumstances: he stepped forward gallantly to embrace the youthful person. She, however, not expecting it, made the show of resistance which a normal maidenly modesty would dictate, but which she, in the role she had been playing for some time now, had been doubly encouraged to display. On the advice of her prospective brother-in-law, she allowed the public official to brush her cheeks with his lips, while du Barry addressed the notary thus: "Mark this favor well, Monsieur," he said, "for it is the last you will receive from Madame."

The royal lover was delighted to learn that the ceremony had been carried out. He appeared to give himself over with ever greater abandon to the new Countess, and with each passing day his passion, far from lessening with habit, grew stronger, so much so that the du Barrys began to harbor in their hearts the most boundless ambitions. To this end, the royal favorite had to be very well directed; their plan required great care and circumspection.

For such things, the lady herself had no taste, and least of all that sense of intrigue which her position demanded. We have seen, in the course of those adventures which led up to the moment of her elevation, that she was utterly devoid of those ploys which most courtesans have and which are so useful to them when it comes to snaring men. She was motivated by neither ambition nor self-interest, those two passions that are so powerful in the most common souls. Instead, the new Countess brought to her task a quality that is perhaps superior: a sort of good sense which she applied to the advice she received, using it to good effect and profiting by it. In short, she had a wonderful docility where the advice of her brother-in-law was concerned; and his success in their common project only served to reinforce the confidence of his sister-in-law. The sole difficulty, then, was the necessity of hiding from the eyes of the court the secret thread which manipulated the royal favorite. Too much activity by the Count on her behalf might awaken the suspicions of the monarch, as well as arouse the ill-will of the court; but the sudden expulsion of this counselor would leave the favorite too exposed and liable to dangerous errors of judgment.

Here the comte du Barry sketched out a plan of action which can only be considered a masterpiece of its kind in the political realm. He arranged to withdraw from the court entirely, and appeared to abandon his sister-in-law to her brilliant fate. But, meanwhile, he put at her side his sister, Mlle du Barry, whom he judged to be very competent for the task at hand. The latter was, in effect, so ugly that she could awaken no jealousy on the part of the Countess, nor would she be tempted to engage in those amorous intrigues which might distract her from the task at hand. She was very intelligent as well—a real virtuoso, who had exhibited literary talents and even published a letter in the *Mercure*. She was very ingratiating, and—what was most important—quickly gained control of the royal favorite. There was established, thus, a circuit from brother to sister, from the sister to the Countess, and back again from the Countess to Mlle du Barry, and from her to her brother. Young emissaries trained by the Count flew back and forth along the route to Versailles, bearing either verbal or written orders, depending on the circumstances. These messengers could be augmented if necessary, and the favorite was thereby, at any given moment, under his control. She made, on occasion, little trips to Paris, and, as she had no other residence there, she put up at her brother-in-law's house, where she received general instructions, which she applied later on as particular cases demanded.

Despite these numerous precautions, is it not remarkable that a girl of such obscure birth, so poorly educated, who had kept only rather bad company and who lacked any natural aptitude for intrigue, should have been able to survive in court for a period of more than a year, from her first interview with the King until the day of her presentation? During all this time she gave no evidence of misconduct, and avoided any indiscretion or any remark which might make her appear ridiculous.

It was all the more necessary for her to behave with the very greatest circumspection, as she was opposed by the Choiseul cabal, the most formidable at court. At the very name, one is struck dumb with amazement to think of the turns that fate has taken. What revolutions have been wrought by an agent so common and so weak-seeming that she might break like glass under the heel of an all-powerful minister!

Indeed, Richelieu himself may have had no greater power over the mind of Louis XIII than did the duc de Choiseul over that of his master. Ever since the peace [1763], he had carved out for himself an ever greater place in the King's confidence. His artful sense of intrigue persuaded the King that he was a great statesman, and His Majesty's conviction that it was he, by means of his negotiating talents, who kept the nation's natural enemies divided and at bay, made him more increasingly indispensable. The monarch believed that Choiseul alone was capable of preserving the peace which was the sole object of his desires. Moreover, the minister worked in a quick and easy manner, which perfectly suited the natural sloth of his ruler. When he went to report on the weightiest affairs of state, he spoke only of balls and entertainments.

These qualities—his personal charm, his usefulness, or rather, his apparent indispensability—seemed to render the Duke's position unshakable, especially in the service of a prince who, as he aged, would only become more feeble and dependent. Choiseul, moreover, commanded great respect in his own right. He was of noble birth and descended from several different royal houses, in particular that of Lorraine. This carried with it the intimate protection of the Viennese court. His *pacte de famille* [the defensive alliance of the Bourbon powers, principally France and Spain, formed by Choiseul in 1761] had endeared him to the various branches of the house of Bourbon, and the kings of Spain and Portugal favored him especially because of his open war against the Jesuits. Finally, in France itself, he had built up an enormous party of supporters. The administration was filled with his appointees. Half the princes of royal blood were afraid of him, and the other half were bound to him by ties of fellowship or friendship.

The du Barrys, who were initially terrified of such an opponent, sought to win him over to their own side. Choiseul was a great ladies' man and sensualist. It is said that her brother-in-law instructed the Countess to unleash all her charms on him; and if, later, her hatred for Choiseul knew no bounds, it was because he showed only disdain for them. This proud adversary, who thought there was nothing to fear from someone of such vulgar origins, treated her with the very greatest contempt. But the chief cause of the all-out war which broke out between the two cabals was the rivalry with the duchesse de Grammont, the minister's sister. This woman, who was more haughty, more imperious, and more devious than her brother—if that's possible—had got her claws into him and totally subjugated him to her will. Their intimacy was such that it had excited considerable malicious talk in the court; some even pretended that they slept with one another. Be that as it may, she was a real lady of the court in every sense of the term, stubborn, impudent, licentious, and convinced that morals were made only for the common people, not for her. She was no longer young, and her face was far from beautiful. Nevertheless, she saw herself as potentially attractive to the King. By means of her rank and the favor which her brother enjoyed, she was able to gain access to the *petits appartements* and to the bedroom of the monarch. Since the death of Mme de Pompadour, the King had found no one who was her equal at satisfying him. To fill this void, the duchesse de Grammont used her knowledge of his good and easygoing nature, his weakness for the opposite sex, and his tendency to let himself be carried away by the pleasures of the moment, in order to direct his attention to herself.

And so she slipped into His Majesty's bed despite himself—or such is the most widely accepted version of events at Versailles. But their relationship was based merely on convenience, as well as the King's sexual obsession, so that each time they came together she, so to speak, raped the monarch, if one can use this term in relation to a prince who had such extensive experience, and she was, accordingly, soon rejected when a more erotic object appeared to revive his jaded ardor and make his heart beat faster. A woman from the most common background would find it hard to forgive such a slight. Imagine, then, the fury of a high-born woman, consumed with ambition, who suddenly sees herself frustrated in the role she expected to play. Her thirst for revenge overpowered her, and giving no thought to the disastrous results which might come of it, she used her influence over her brother to involve him in her quarrel. Choiseul refused to hear any propositions from the opposing side. This irrational rage was, in fact, the primary cause of their downfall. The du Barrys, having seen that no reconciliation with them was possible—that they must either overthrow them or suffer the same fate themselves—decided on the former course of action, and soon found in the chancellor Maupeou a powerful ally. But we must not get ahead of ourselves in our account of events.

As she planned her revenge, the duchesse de Grammont thought that her best strategy would be to reveal the turpitudes of the new favorite, and even to exaggerate them, making her seem so vile that the monarch would be ashamed to have such depraved taste. She preferred not to launch the attack herself: it might fail completely, or be rejected out of hand as the usual recriminations of a royal mistress who has been abandoned. Her brother was clever enough not to take it upon himself to inform the prince. They both agreed it would be much better if the news reached him, slowly, perhaps, but sooner or later, via the public outcry. Using all the means at the minister's disposal, they circulated rumors about the King's new love affair through every possible channel. They sent emissaries to every social gathering, where it was discussed in detail. They managed to get from the police Mlle L'Ange's life story and embellished it with additional anecdotes, guaranteed to make it more ridiculous and more disgusting; and they managed, finally, to have it repeated, in song, on the streets of Paris and in the provinces.

Here is how it appeared for the first time in the [manuscript] news bulletins that circulated in Paris. These had certainly been seen by M. de Sartine [the lieutenant general, or chief, of the Parisian police], who also joked about them himself:

3 September 1768. . . . There has appeared at Compiègne a certain comtesse du Barry, whose face has excited much talk. It is said that she has been a big success at court, and that the King has been especially welcoming to her. Her beauty and

this sudden celebrity have given rise to a great deal of research. Many people have attempted to trace her origins, and, if we are to believe what has been published about her, she would seem to be of very low birth indeed. She has arrived at her present station by reprehensible means, and her whole life is a tissue of scandals. A certain du Barry, who claims to come from the English Barrymores, and who has married her to his own brother, is the instigator of this new mistress. They say that his taste and experience in matters sexual lead this adventurer to hope that the King will entrust him with the job of sexual procurement, and that he will follow the sr. Le Bel in this post.

One imagines that it would have been difficult to circulate such a bulletin throughout Paris if the gazetteer had not been secretly put up to it by a powerful protector. He added in another, dated 15 October 1768:

... For some time now a song called "La Bourbonnaise" has been making the rounds, and it has spread with a most uncommon rapidity. Although the words are very insipid, and the tune couldn't be sillier, it has reached the very farthest corners of France and is being sung even in villages. One can hardly move anywhere without hearing it. Those in the know claim that it's a satirical vaudeville about a certain little no-account girl who has risen from the most degraded circumstances to play a role, and cut a figure of sorts, at court. What is certain is that one can't help remarking, from the way the story has been spread to all and sundry, the firm intention to blacken the reputation of the woman in question. The anecdote collectors have not been slow to take it up and to fatten their portfolios with it, and with all the commentaries necessary to make sense of it and to render it precious for posterity.

Finally, he published another bulletin in a third edition, of 16 November 1768:

The "Bourbonnaise" is a song that has spread everywhere in France. Behind the rather flat and trivial words of this vaudeville, crafty courtiers can discern an allegory featuring a creature who has crawled up from the very lowest rung of society, out of the slime of debauchery, to be fêted and fussed over by the court and the town. There could be no better way to convey the depths to which Controller General Laverdy has sunken since his fall than by the association with this depraved woman that the public makes by mocking them together in the song.

He then cites some verses which were, in fact, written defaming this minister to the tune of the "Bourbonnaise." Here is the original song, which has given rise to a multitude of others. The approbation of M. Sartine dates from 16 June 1768, the precise moment at which Mlle L'Ange had been surreptitiously introduced to the King.

A New Chanson	Tune: "La Bourbonnaise"
La Bourbonnaise	The young woman from the province of Bourbonnaise
Arrivant à Paris,	Arriving in Paris,
A gagné des louis;	Has made some *louis;*
La Bourbonnaise	The young woman from the province of Bourbonnais
A gagné des louis;	Has made some *louis;*
Chez un Marquis.	At the Marquis's house.
Pour apanage,	Instead of an inherited domain,
Elle avait la beauté,	She had beauty,
Elle avait la beauté,	She had beauty,
Pour apanage;	Instead of an inherited domain;
Mais ce petit trésor	But this little treasure
Lui vaut de l'or.	Was worth gold to her.
Etant servante	Being a servant
Chez un riche Seigneur,	to a rich nobleman,
Elle fit son bonheur	She provided him happiness
Quoique servante;	Although a servant;
Elle fit son bonheur	She provided him happiness
Par son humeur.	With her good humor.
Toujours facile	Always obliging
Aux discours d'un Amant,	To the words of a lover,

Ce Seigneur la voyant	This nobleman seeing her
Toujours facile,	Always obliging,
Prodiguait les présents	Showered presents upon her
De temps en temps.	From time to time.
De bonnes rentes	With good annuities
Il lui fit un contrat,	He made her a contract,
Il lui fit un contrat	He made her a contract,
De bonnes rentes;	With good annuities;
Elle est dans la maison	She is in his house
Sur le bon ton.	Living in style.
De paysanne,	From a peasant,
Elle est dame à présent	She is a lady now,
Elle est dame à présent,	She is a lady now,
Mais grosse dame;	But a grand lady;
Porte les falbalas,	She wears frills and flounces,
Du haut en bas.	From top to bottom.
En équipage,	In a carriage,
Elle roule grand train;	She travels elegantly;
Elle roule grand train	She travels elegantly
En équipage;	In a carriage;
Et préfère Paris	And prefers Paris
à son pays.	To her own village.
Elle est allée	She has gone
Se faire voir en cour;	To appear at court;
Se faire voir en cour	To appear at court
Elle est allée;	She has gone;
On dit qu'elle a, ma foi,	They say she has, my goodness,
Plu même au Roi!	Even attracted the King!
Fille gentille	Nice girl,
Ne désespérez pas:	Do not despair:
Quand on a des appas,	When you have charms,
Qu'on est gentille,	When you're nice,
On trouve tôt ou tard	You'll find sooner or later
Pareil hazard.	The same fate.

How could something so close to the story of our heroine have come about, if this romance had not been specially composed for the purpose? We must admit, however, that the eighth stanza *{"Elle est allée"}*, which best characterizes her, is not to be found in the printed collections, and has probably been composed after the fact. However that may be, other songs were also made up which were not so ambiguous and which, without taking the streets by storm, were very widespread. Here is the most naive and also the raciest:

Another Chanson	Tune: "La Bourbonnaise"
Quelle merveille!	What a marvel!
Une fille de rien;	A worthless girl;
Une fille de rien,	A worthless girl,
Quelle merveille!	What a marvel!
Donne au Roi de l'amour,	Makes love to the King,
Est à la cour!	Is at court!
Elle est gentille,	She is kind,
Elle a les yeux fripons;	She has mischievous eyes;
Elle a les yeux fripons,	She has mischievous eyes,
Elle est gentille;	She is kind;
Elle excite avec art	She excites with art
Un vieux paillard.	An old lecher.
En maison bonne	In a good house
Elle a pris des leçons;	She took some lessons;
Elle a pris des leçons	She took some lessons
En maison bonne,	In a good house,
Chez Gourdan, chez Brisson;	At Gourdan's, at Brisson's;
Elle en sait long.	She knows all about it.
Que de postures!	So many positions!
Elle a lu l'Arétin;	She has read Aretino;
Elle a lu l'Arétin;	She has read Aretino;
Que de postures!	So many positions!
Elle sait en tout sens,	She knows in every way,
Prendre les sens.	How to excite the senses.
Le Roi s'écrie:	The King cries:
L'Ange, le beau talent!	The Angel, what a talent!
L'Ange, le beau talent!	The Angel, what a talent
Le Roi s'écrie;	The King cries;

Encore aurais-je cru,	Could I have dreamed once more,
Faire un cocu.	To make a cuckold.
Viens sur mon trône,	Come on my throne,
Je veux te couronner,	I want to crown you,
Je veux te couronner,	I want to crown you,
Viens sur mon trône:	Come on my throne:
Pour sceptre prends mon V . . {Vit}	As a scepter take my p . . . . [prick]
Il vit, il vit!	It's alive, it's alive!

There were also jokes of all kinds circulating. They said that Mme la comtesse du Barry was the best streetwalker in history, because she only had to make one leap from the Pont-Neuf to the Throne. The Pont-Neuf is a part of Paris where there are lots of prostitutes, and the Throne is a gate some distance away, at the entrance to the Faubourg Saint-Antoine. They said also that Louis XV had the greatest capacity in the kingdom, because he filled a barrel [a pun on *baril* or "barre"l and "du Barry"]. From these banal little jibes, which the dregs of the population bandied about quite publicly, we can deduce just how freely, and with what impunity, opinions were expressed on the new mistress.

*   *   *

{Following Mme la comtesse du Barry's presentation to the court, which gave her official status as the King's maîtresse en titre, *in April 1769, the du Barry faction prepares to take over the government by overthrowing the Choiseulistes.}*

These parries and thrusts were only the prelude to the fight-to-the-death that was to come between the duc de Choiseul and Mme la comtesse du Barry. This lady was beginning imperceptibly to become involved in important matters of state. She made her influence felt for the first time in the affair of the duc d'Aiguillon. This noble, who so loved intrigue, found himself in the middle of a very grave crisis. [As the military commandant in Brittany, he had imprisoned La Chalotais, the attorney general of the Rennes parlement, during a dispute over royal taxation. The parlement retaliated by taking proceedings against d'Aiguillon, who then demanded to be tried by the Parlement of Paris. In June 1770, when that trial threatened to get out of hand, the king quashed it—and a year later made d'Aiguillon Secretary of State for Foreign Affairs.] The King himself had been persuaded to intervene so that his case could be tried in the Parlement of Paris with the princes and peers of the realm in attendance. Hoping at first to be whitewashed and thus put to rest, once and for all, the quarrels which his despotic administration had engendered, the Duke had gladly agreed to appear before this new tribunal. But, when he saw that the animosity of the judges had been excited against him by his secret enemy, the duc de Choiseul, and when he realized that they had so thoroughly investigated his past conduct that they were about to bring further grave charges against him, he feared all was lost. His only recourse was now Mme la comtesse du Barry, who was closely allied at that time with the chancellor [R. N. C. A. de Maupeou]. The latter put himself entirely in her hands, seeing an opportunity to consolidate his position at court, to consummate his plot against the entire judiciary, and to destroy the duc de Choiseul—his original benefactor but now, because of his [Choiseul's] ties to the parlements, his enemy.

Having persuaded the King, in April, to bring d'Aiguillon to trial before the most august body with the very greatest solemnity, so as to clear him and the peers of the crimes imputed to them, in the month of June following, he had the King pronounce that the affair was closed, the peer [d'Aiguillon] absolved, and there was to be no more talk about the whole business. This is not the place to enter into the details of these maneuvers. It will suffice to note the great influence which Mme la comtesse du Barry had at the time—enough to persuade the King, before the princes of the realm, the peerage, the magistrature, all of France and all of Europe, to reverse his position so shamefully. The event was celebrated with a vaudeville song to the tune of the "Déserteur." The duc d'Aiguillon speaks:

Oublions jusqu'à la trace	Let's forget the last trace
De mon procès suspendu:	Of my suspended trial:
Avec des Lettres de grâce,	With letters of clemency,
On ne peut être pendu.	One cannot be hanged.
Je triomphe de l'envie,	I triumph over envy,
Je jouis de la faveur;	I enjoy favor;
Grace aux soins d'une amie!	Thanks to a friend's help!
J'en suis quitte pour l'honneur.	I get off with everything except my honor.

This also occasioned a humorous remark by the maréchal duc de Brissac, who said that Mme la comtesse du Barry had saved the head of the duc d'Aiguillon but had wrung his neck.

The latter did not regard the affair in this light, and was only too happy with the outcome. He felt it all the more crucial to get the trial over with, at any price, as he saw the disgrace of the Choiseuls looming, and he wished to take advantage of it. At this critical juncture, he received another very great mark of favor. During the court's stay at Marly, the King, who had agreed to dine with Mme la comtesse du Barry at her residence at Lucienne, looked with approbation upon the inclusion of the duc d'Aiguillon in the party, and even accorded him a place at the royal table.

A very close relationship developed thereafter between d'Aiguillon and the chancellor, who held their meetings at Mme la comtesse du Barry's. Each for his own reason came together to plot the overthrow of the Choiseuls. They decided that, in order to accelerate their fall, they would stress to the King the intimate relations between Choiseul and the parlements. They would attribute to him the recent protests by the parlements over d'Aiguillon's trial, which, the chancellor had assured the King, could be easily dismissed but which, instead, was creating ever greater turmoil. In this manner, they hoped to turn the opposition's attack against it and to consummate its ruin.

The duchesse de Grammont, meanwhile, had left the court in a fit of jealousy and, under the pretext of taking a cure, had traveled throughout the provinces where parlements are located and had stirred up those parlements with additional evidence of d'Aiguillon's heinous crimes. They let the King know that they had met repeatedly with the Duchess, who had excited them to resistance while assuring them of her brother's protection. Such was the effect of this accusation upon the King that, from that time on, he cooled visibly toward Choiseul. He no longer honored him with his conversation, though he continued to work with him and to admit him to his royal suppers. Choiseul's state of disgrace could not help but be noticed by courtiers, who now generally shunned him.

How could Mme la comtesse du Barry—who was so frank, carefree, playful, and lightheaded—not help but be the dupe of those who sought to flatter her every desire and caprice? The chancellor, during the Compiègne stay, gave a dinner for her, which greatly amused the favorite. The occasion should have covered with ridicule this man, who was the supreme head of the judiciary, but by that time he was no longer susceptible to it.

The favorite then had a little black boy called Zamore. She doted on him, took him everywhere with her, and played with him like a little dog. For his part, the child was very mischievous. Maupeou thought to pay court to the one by amusing the other, for he left no stone unturned in his desire to please Mme la comtesse du Barry. During the sweet course, he had a superb pâté brought to the table. It was only a trick: as soon as a knife was put in it, out flew a swarm of maybugs, which flew all about the room, but principally onto the chancellor's enormous wig. This show greatly amused Zamore, who had doubtless never seen these insects before. He wanted to catch some of them, and came looking for them in the netted hair where they had got stuck. In the end, the boy, wishing to play at his ease with the bugs and showing little respect for the supreme chief of the King's justice, took the minister's wig right off his head. At this Mme la comtesse du Barry gave vent to whoops of laughter, and the chancellor let himself with the best grace in the world be the general sport of his guests. Here is a written description of the incident by a courtier who traveled with the royal party to Compiègne in 1770. The best way to draw a portrait of someone is by recording the contemporary accounts of his peers.

Extract of a letter from Compiègne of 20 August:

You in Paris assume that the chancellor is very taken up with the general uprising by the magistrature and the fact that the various parlements are making life hard for him. He certainly shows no external signs of it: he appears to be enjoying himself with the simplicity and innocence of a child. The story going around the court is that the King recently arrived unannounced at Mme du Barry's and found her—she can be quite naughty—playing blind-man's-buff with some young courtiers. In the middle of all of them was the chancellor, who was pretending to be "it." His Majesty was greatly amused by the sight.

One can only imagine what sport the Choiseuls and their clique made of this indecorous scene; but M. de Maupeou was pursuing his own ends. His party was growing with each passing day. His clever and engaging mind attracted all those whom his rival, the minister, put off with his aloofness. At the same time, a new closeness developed between him and the duc de Richelieu, who had previously attempted to have a foot in both camps.

Richelieu, who was leaving for his post as governor of Guyenne, went to see the duc de Choiseul and, upon taking his leave, mentioned how very flattered he would be if the duchesse de Grammont, who was to pass through the area as she returned from her travels, would consent to honor him by staying as his guest in Bordeaux. He assured her brother that he would do everything possible to provide all the delights and amusements that a lady such as herself merited. The minister did not hide his displeasure. He gave the marshal to understand that he took such an invitation as a mockery; that he knew all about the impertinent talk that had been spread concerning his sister and himself; and that he regarded Richelieu as one of the principal authors. The marshal, upon hearing this, tried to make light of the accusation, but the Duke refused to be placated. He angrily replied that neither Richelieu nor any of his associates should ever darken his door again, and turned his back upon him.

Some time later, Choiseul suffered a humiliation which was very painful to his haughty character. He was obliged to name a du Barry as lieutenant colonel in the Corsican Legion. This was the youngest of the three brothers, who had passed into this corps from the Régiment de Beauce. This was a new stab in the back for Choiseul. He couldn't help but see how the stock of his enemy was rising daily.

Upon his return from Compiègne that year, Mme la comtesse du Barry accompanied the King publicly to Chantilly, and he gave her the right to name the lords and ladies who would come along with them. The duc de Choiseul's, of course, was the first name omitted. It was to Mme la comtesse du Barry that the sovereign confided the worries and cares which were assailing him in this critical period. The tyrannical scene he had had with the parlement on 3 September [after reprimanding the parlement for overstepping its authority, the King had taken d'Aiguillon's case out of its hands] had made a sinister effect upon the population of Paris. He could not help but remark the mournful silence which greeted his entries and exits from his palace: not a single "Long Live the King!" was to be heard.

Afterwards he went to dine at Lucienne, and his hostess was able to draw him out from the depression into which he had sunk. This talent of hers was too precious, too useful, and too beguiling not to give the favorite total control over her lover. As proof of this, the King's intervention with the parlement in favor of the duc d'Aiguillon was often cited. He had stepped in to quash all the judicial proceedings regarding him, which prevented the parlement from pursuing the case further and nipped the whole matter in the bud. D'Aiguillon understood, of course, the enormous importance of the King's gesture, and wanted to show his gratitude with an appropriate gift to his protectress. He had a magnificent carriage made which was all the talk of Paris. It was the most elegant and, at the same time, the most sumptuous that had ever been seen. The carriages of the Dauphine which had been sent to Vienna could not even approach it in taste or exquisiteness of workmanship. A description will reveal the degree to which morals had sunk at court, where the monarch's scandalous love affair was displayed to the eyes of all France in a transparent allegory. In the middle of the four principal panels, on a gold background, were the arms of the du Barrys with the famous battle cry: "Press forward!" On each of the side panels there were a basket of roses, above which two doves kissed lasciviously, and a heart pierced by an arrow, all of which was garnished with quivers, torches, and all the attributes of the god of love. These ingenious emblems were topped by a garland of flowers, the most beautiful thing one could lay eyes on. The rest was very much in keeping: the cover of the coachman's seat, the supports behind for the footmen, the wheels, the steps were details so finely wrought and finished that one never tired of looking at them. The mask of Venus could be seen all over this voluptuous vehicle. Everyone exclaimed that never had the arts been pushed to such a degree of perfection.

As the duc d'Aiguillon has added to the gallantry of the gift by refusing to tell its price, we have never been able to discover it. However, after questioning various workmen, some people have put the cost of this carriage at 52,000 livres. However that may be, to the great disappointment of the duke, Mme la comtesse du Barry never used it once. Different reasons for this have been given. Some have said that she didn't like it; but the more likely explanation is that the King found it too beautiful and decreed that she never set foot in it. It is even said that this was the occasion of a little coolness between the two lovers. What is certain is that the public had been scandalized by such indecent luxury. As a result, they created the following epigram, which takes aim at both donor and recipient:

Pourquoi ce brillant vis-à-vis?	Why this brilliant carriage?
Est-ce le char d'une Déesse?	Is it the chariot of a goddess?
Ou de quelque jeune Princesse,	Or of some young Princess,
S'écriait un badaud surpris?	Cried a surprised onlooker?
Non . . . de la foule curieuse	No . . . from the curious crowd
Lui répond un caustique, non,	A wag answers him, no,
C'est le char de la blanchisseuse	It's the chariot of the washerwoman
	[also: of the woman who whitewashed]
De cet infâme d'Aiguillon.	Of that notorious d'Aiguillon.

The opposing cabal was certainly not slow to fulminate against the insolence of such luxury, but the duc de Choiseul kept himself in check. He didn't shout too loudly, but contented himself with the discreet support of those who did. Their indignation seemed even more justified in view of the sad condition of the kingdom by that time. Bread was very expensive; many Frenchmen were dying of hunger; and it was painfully clear to many that the cost of such a vehicle would have nourished an entire province for several months' time. Another wit disseminated a little piece called "Le Pater." It shows how the general discontent was made manifest in every form. This "Pater" was dedicated to the King, who was addressed thus:

> Our Father, who art in Versailles. Abhorred be Thy name. Thy kingdom is shaken. Thy will is no longer done on earth or in heaven. Give us back this day our daily bread, which Thou hast taken from us. Forgive Thy parlements who have upheld Thy interests, as Thou forgiveth those ministers who have sold them. Be not led into temptation by du Barry. But deliver us from that devil of a chancellor. Amen!

In fact, despite the repeated evidence of their party's decline and the astonishing ascendancy of their adversaries, the Choiseuls still had cause for hope. Their secret weapon, with which they aspired to supplant the favorite, was a new beauty, whose charms, they felt, were likely to seduce the King.

The marquis de Choiseul, son of the late naval officer, who was so well known for his *Vision du Cardinal de Bernis,* had just married a Mlle Raby, a Creole with the most beautiful face in the world, who joined with her natural grace all possible talents. The combination of all these qualities in her person made her one of the most accomplished women at court. She was, moreover, very young and fresh as Hebe, and she seemed certain to produce a strong impression upon the monarch at her presentation, the ceremony necessary for inclusion among the ranks of women of the court. The courtiers awaited with impatience the day when this star would be revealed: all eyes were fixed on the prince, as this prodigy of beauty was announced. Everyone saw, however, that His Majesty seemed to take little notice of her, only enough, in fact, so as not to snub her completely.

When this last resource had failed to bring the desired effect, everyone concluded that the Countess was henceforth invincible, and all bowed before her. The women, up to that point, had tried not to compromise themselves by avoiding any marked hostility. They, likewise, had avoided all overtures, maintaining a sort of prudent reserve. Now they were so frightened by the disgrace of the comtesse de Grammont that they prostrated themselves before the idol of the day. Even the comtesse de Grammont, who had dared to force a confrontation at Choisi by her obvious impertinence to Mme du Barry—behavior which had provoked the King's anger and brought about her exile from the court—could not long endure her solitude and her banishment. She sank so low as to ask to come back. Using the duc de Gontault and the duc de Noailles as intermediaries, she begged forgiveness of the favorite, and it was granted with the proviso that she should no longer appear at court.

It was at Fontainebleau, especially, that Mme la comtesse du Barry triumphed in all her glory and humiliated the duc de Choiseul. The King's Regiment had come to camp near that town in order to pass in review before His Majesty. This ceremony could not take place without the Minister of War [i.e., the duc de Choiseul, who combined the ministries of War and Foreign Affairs]. Mme du Barry was present, accompanied by the duchesse de Valetinois and the marquise de Montmorency. The comte du Châtelet, a lieutenant colonel, that evening gave a supper party in his tent with the ladies in attendance. Mme du Barry was seated beside the King, replacing the Dauphine, who had been announced as coming but who did not in fact appear. It was the first obvious schism between herself and the favorite. The duc de Choiseul, who was beside himself with rage, gave illness as a pretext for his absence and skipped both the review and the dinner.

The King, in even the smallest details, gave evidence of the interest he took in everything pertaining to his charming mistress. During the Fontainebleau stay, he delighted in the marriage of her first chambermaid. We have already mentioned that she had been the mistress of Mme du Barry's brother-in-law and had been cast aside for Mlle L'Ange de Vaubergnier. She had sunk into a miserable state, when Mme du Barry was asked to hire her in the aforementioned capacity. She then so gained the grace and favor of her mistress that the latter agreed to her marriage with a certain Langibeau, to whom she gave a post carrying with it an annuity of 10,000 livres. As his wedding present, His Majesty gave 25,000 livres and some very beautiful diamonds. Mme Langibeau has continued in the service of Mme du Barry, and still carries out confidential errands for her. Although she is the meanest person imaginable, she has acquired such control over her mistress that Mme du Barry is incapable of letting her go—another proof of the favorite's goodness of heart.

All these small marks of affection were only the prelude to the great influence that Mme du Barry would wield in the revolution which was being prepared by the chancellor and the duc d'Aiguillon, each of whom, while acting in concert, was pursuing his own ambitions. Together they employed the Countess as a mouthpiece to convey their ideas to the King. They convinced her that it was in her own interest to support their position: she could not rest easy as long as Choiseul was in power, and he could not be removed unless they managed to awaken the King's suspicions about his contacts with the parlement. Furthermore, they said, the effort to blacken his reputation would be best served by blackening the parlement as well, by representing it to the monarch as an ambitious body ready to trample upon and invade his authority and to usurp the rights of the throne. Choiseul's expulsion would initially benefit d'Aiguillon, his enemy, but also, secondarily but no less importantly, the collection of taxes and, consequently, the King's munificence to herself. So many advantages, presented so convincingly, tended to alienate the favorite from the magistrature. She was soon able to infuse into the heart of the monarch the hatred she had come to feel for the parlement, and to which he was, in any case, strongly disposed. Thus it was that this weak prince, so lacking in a firm purpose, decided finally to stand behind the new law, which was propagated in the famous Edict of December 1770 and registered in the parlement by *lit de justice* on the third of that month. [The edict severely restricted the political activities of all the parlements. It was denounced in a tumultuous session of the Parlement of Paris on December 3, then registered by force in the special ceremony known as a *lit de justice* held in Versailles on December 7, not December 3 as stated here.]

But the chancellor and the duc d'Aiguillon well understood the pusillanimous nature of the monarch, and did not rely upon his apparent firmness. They took advantage of it only to carry forward their plan of action, to make him advance so far that retreat was impossible. Mme du Barry was, from this point of view, admirably suited to their purposes. As the King dined with her almost every evening, they prepared her in advance for what she should say. They gave her orders prepared for the King's signature, and, when her lover—his blood heated from the fine wines she had served and his heart burning from the love inspired by her embraces—begged for her ultimate favors and could refuse her nothing, she extorted the fateful signatures. Thus was the council of ministers circumvented; at least, the other ministers complained loudly that they had had no knowledge of these violent acts against the Parlement of Paris.

It was thus that the *lettre de cachet* against the duc de Choiseul was finally issued on December 24. It had already been signed several times over by the King, in moments of drunken lovemaking, but in each case he had repented the following day. This time he held fast, and it was communicated, at eleven o'clock in the morning, by the duc de la Vrillière to the minister in question, who had only twenty-four hours to take himself to Chanteloup. It was couched in the following terms:

My cousin,
    The displeasure which your service causes me forces me to exile you to Chanteloup, where you must be within twenty-four hours. I would have sent you much further away, were it not for the particular esteem in which I hold Madame the duchesse de Choiseul, about whose health I am particularly concerned. Take care that your conduct does not force me to another course of action. With this, I pray to God, my cousin, that He may keep you in His blessed care.

The presence of the duc de la Vrillière, who delivered the King's orders, was yet another source of mortification for Choiseul, because this minister, an uncle of the duc d'Aiguillon, couldn't help but be secretly pleased with his assignment. Choiseul, therefore, was not fooled by the polite words of condolence offered by his colleague, and he answered him thus: "M. le duc, I am very aware of the great pleasure you have in bringing me such news."

The duc de Praslin [Choiseul's cousin, a secretary of state who directed the Royal Council of Finance], who was in Paris, suffering from gout which had spread to his head, received on the same day a *lettre de cachet* that was much shorter and more scornful, to wit:

> I have no further need of your services, and I exile you to Praslin, where you must be within twenty-four hours.

Once these ministers had left the court, the affair of the parlement could not long continue. On 22 January [1771] the entire body was sent into exile.

As can well be imagined, these events produced a great deal of murmuring, indignation, and protest; and above all they occasioned an outburst of epigrams, songs, and pasquinades. The following are the most remarkable of them. First, there was a little song which, for all its brevity, captured the King's behavior and his incompetence. It also robbed him forever of the precious nickname [Louis the Well-loved], which he should have tried at all costs to keep, though he hardly deserved it in the first place.

Le Bien-aimé de l'Almanach	The Well-loved of the Almanac
N'est pas le Bien-aimé de France;	Is not the Well-loved of France;
Il fait tout ab hoc & ab hac,	He does everything willy-nilly,
Le Bien-aimé de l'Almanach:	The Well-loved of the Almanac:
Il met tout dans le même sac	He puts it all in the same sack
Et la Justice & la Finance:	Both Justice and Finance:
Le Bien-aimé de l'Almanach	The Well-loved of the Almanac
N'est pas le Bien-aimé de France.	Is not the Well-loved of France.

Another vaudeville made the rounds which, though it was quite scandalous and abominable, should be preserved for the historical record as testimony to the contempt the public felt for the supreme head of the magistrature. It was obviously composed during the period of rivalry between the two factions, when it was thought that the chancellor would fall under the efforts of the parlement, supported by the duc de Choiseul.

Le Roi, dans son Conseil dernier	The King, at his last council meeting
Dit à Monsieur le Chancelier:	Says to the Chancellor:
Choiseul fait briller ma couronne	Choiseul makes my crown gleam
De la Baltique à l'Archipel;	From the Baltic to the Archipelago;
C'est-là l'emploi que je lui donne:	This is the job I give to him:
Vous, prenez soin de mon B. . . . . {Bordel}	You, take care of my B. . . . . . . [Bordello]
Le Chancelier lui répondit,	The Chancellor answers him,
Sire, que vous avez d'esprit!	Sire, how clever you are!
D'un pauvre diable qui chancelle	For a poor devil who's wavering
Vous raffermissez le crédit:	You increase his influence:
Que ne puis-je en votre ruelle,	If only I beside your bed,
Raffermir aussi votre V. .! {Vit}	Could firm up your p. . . . [prick]!

The last piece was an amusing caricature [i.e., a print] relating to the parlement's decree of 10 December, in which this body informed the King that they would unanimously offer him their goods, their liberty, and their heads, etc., etc.

In it the King was represented surrounded by the chancellor, the controller general, and Mme la comtesse du Barry. The first president of the parlement was laying at the feet of the King a little basket full of heads, purses, and male organs of the members of parlement. The chancellor was pouncing upon the heads, the controller general upon the purses, and the favorite upon the penises.

It is not known whether or not she was aware of this caricature, but if so, she would certainly have found it amusing. She would have laughed all the more heartily for having rid herself of her enemy.

For his part, Choiseul stood up to the catastrophe with a great deal of backbone: it was almost a victory for him. Although he was forbidden to receive anyone during the rest of his stay in Paris, an enormous crowd of people from all walks of life left written messages at his door. And the duc de Chartres, who was an intimate friend of his, broke through all the barriers and threw himself in his arms, covering him with his tears.

The next day, the day of his departure, those who had not been able to see Choiseul lined the route he would take. The crowd, as he passed by, was so great, they formed a double row of carriages on either side of the road.

Though the King didn't like Choiseul, he was accustomed to him. Though he feared him, he also relied heavily on him in the parlous conjuncture where he found himself, between England and Spain [a dispute over the Falkland Islands; Choiseul favored going to war in support of Spain and the Family Compact]. What convinced the King, it seems, to get rid of this minister was the accusation planted against the minister that he had secretly sought to bring about war, despite the obvious attempts he had made to adapt himself to the increasingly pacifist views of his master.

Having thus blackened his reputation with the King, the victorious group needed to deal with the problem of the public's open sympathy for Choiseul. (The public is always blind, in its sympathies as in its hatreds.) Shortly after his exile, on 23 December, they ostentatiously published a royal edict on the grain trade. It only served to restate the position of the various decrees of the parlement on this issue, all of which had been overturned [by the King in his council]. This regulation, which reaffirmed their wisdom and necessity, was absolutely useless at that moment, for it was quite impossible to export any grain at all. On all the markets, the price of grain was above the level fixed to halt its export; but, more importantly, the rarity of the commodity made it too expensive within France for anyone to dream of sending it abroad. Even the most casual observers of the political scene could sense that this document was designed to heap upon Choiseul the blame for all the monopolies and shortages put together.

Mme du Barry could not be other than overjoyed at the removal of the sole obstacle to her domination. But it was not enough just to banish her enemy; now she had to put her own followers into the government.

The duc d'Aiguillon convinced her that she could find no more loyal servant than himself. Accordingly, she had him named to the Naval Ministry. He had, in fact, already taken it over, but then cooler heads counseled him to bide his time. He was persuaded by these advisers that the moment was not ripe to enter the government. He had just come to the public's attention through the publication of new judicial *mémoires* [lawyers' briefs] in the Brittany Affair; the Provincial Estates of Brittany were still declaiming against him in their closing sessions; and there was such an outpouring of sympathy for the Choiseuls that it was thought he would do better to stay in the background and wait until some misstep by a new minister provoked the public to cry out for a change. The abbé Terray, who was a clever dog [controller general of Finance since December 1769] but quite obscure—without birth or strength of character, and forced to rely entirely on himself—was chosen in the interim [to head the Naval Ministry], with the understanding that he would readily give up the place when asked to do so. His real plan was to keep it; and just as he thought he could run the Finance Ministry, though he had had no experience in that area, he imagined that his genius would serve him equally well in the new department over which he was responsible. He hoped that some favorable development would allow him to keep the latter and abandon the former, which was extremely perilous and becoming more so every day. The duc d'Aiguillon, reasoning from his own self-interest, saw Terray as an excellent custodian. His ignorance of the Marine and his isolation would make him easy to get rid of when the time came.

The Ministry of War was to be given to the comte du Muy, an experienced soldier, but so pious and austere that his refusal to kneel before Mme du Barry cost him the post. The prince de Condé had his own candidate, and Mme du Barry could not help but agree to the nomination of the marquis de Monteynard, the person His Highness felt was most suitable for carrying out his program, details of which we will not go into here. The Ministry of Foreign Affairs remained without a head; and this was another area which the duc d'Aiguillon planned to take over.

All those who had been associated with the Choiseuls shared in their disgrace. The baron de Breteuil had been named Ambassador to Vienna. He had already sent ahead his carriages and was readying himself to take up his mission, when he received an invitation from the duc de la Vrillière to call upon Mme du Barry. His destination, she informed him, had been changed. In effect, this diplomat, our most able negotiator after M. de Vergennes, was forced to go bury his talents at the court of Naples. Because he was a supporter of the exiled Duke, and owed his nomination to him, it was feared that he would exert pressure on the Empress [Maria Theresa in Vienna], urging her to write strongly on Choiseul's behalf. It was essential to their party to have someone of unquestionable loyalty in Vienna, no matter how inept he might be, and this led them to send Prince Louis there. This major political error was, no doubt, the basis for the calamity that befell Poland [the first partition of 1772]. The nation's interests, and those of our allies, were thus sacrificed to particular interests, those of an obscure cabal, and France not only lost her standing abroad but was thrown into internal turmoil.

*　*　*

Mme la comtesse du Barry was unable to procure the *Feuille des Bénéfices* [the office in charge of clerical appointments] for one of her favorites, but she was in a stronger position for securing the post of Secretary of State for the Navy for Bourgeois de Boynes, the right arm of the chancellor. He was just the man to carry out the cornerstone of Maupeou's policy, the creation of a new low court which was to take the place of the parlement. This was in fact promulgated, on 13 April, in a *lit de justice,* which shall never be forgotten. There is no better gauge of the Countess's influence on this occasion—or of the influence she thought she had—than her remark to the duc de Nivernois, one of the peers who protested against the coup. Having crossed paths with this lord and reproached him concerning his conduct in this affair, she added: "M. le duc, we can only hope that you will cease your opposition, because you have marked it well. The King said that he will never change." "Yes, Madame," replied the Duke, "but he was looking at you." He extricated himself thus, with a witty and gallant comeback, from a potentially embarrassing exchange.

A quatrain, which had been reworked and applied to Mme du Barry, suggested even more strongly the degree to which she was held responsible for the country's miseries. It went like this:

France! quel est donc ton destin?	France, what is your fate, then?
D'être soumis à la femelle.	To be ruled by a woman.
Ton salut vint d'une pucelle,	Your salvation came from a virgin, [i.e., Joan of Arc]
Tu périras par la catin.	You will perish by a whore.

It is not known whether she was aware of this savage epigram; but she would have paid little attention to it. She wanted to demonstrate very unambiguously how eager she was to contribute, in any way she could, to the formation of the new parlement. To convey her satisfaction to M. Joly de Fleury, the attorney general of the new tribunal and the only one of the former parlementary magistrates who, thanks to his absence of courage, survived in office, she made his wife, Madame de Fleury, a gift of a hundred thousand francs' worth of diamonds. In fact, there is much reason to believe that her actions were guided by others.

Her brother-in-law, Count Jean, was the brains of the operation, although he very rarely went to court. He resided in Paris, and had many young men in his service who were constantly coming and going, relaying his various instructions, not to his sister-in-law but to his sister, Mlle du Barry, who because of her superior intellect had acquired much influence over the Countess. She rarely left her side. The communication between these three was such that virtually everything the King's mistress said or did had been orchestrated by the Count a day or two before, depending on the circumstances.

Furthermore, these same young emissaries, who were well informed and well educated, were constantly traveling about the kingdom, as well as to foreign courts, though no one knew the reason for their movements. Some thought that M. du Barry, who had always shown a great interest in politics, had studied the interests of monarchs, and was very well versed in what we might call foreign affairs, was occupying this vacant post without the title of minister. He was, presumably, assisting the King in conducting his own foreign affairs—as His Majesty did, following the disgrace of Choiseul, with much distinction. Others suggested, more convincingly, that du Barry could never have dared to aspire to the ministry and was only a subordinate in the service of the duc d'Aiguillon. This latter supposition was proven correct by subsequent events. In June, d'Aiguillon, whose trial had begun a year before and who was still tainted by an outstanding decree of the parlement, entered the king's council and was named Minister of Foreign Affairs.

* * *

Part Two

{*After the destruction of the old parlements and the creation of a new judicial system, power remained concentrated in the hands of the three key ministers, Maupeou, Terray, and d'Aiguillon. While neglecting the interests of France, they quarreled among themselves. D'Aiguillon fortified his position by seducing du Barry and thus, so to speak, cuckolding the King. And the favorite's brother-in-law, comte Jean du Barry, concentrated on squeezing the treasury dry in order to give full vent to his own depravity.*}

The brother-in-law, comte du Barry, was not the lightest burden on the state. His great influence over his sister-in-law led him to think of the royal treasury as his own personal bank account. He suffered enormous losses at the gaming tables. But far from worrying about them, he didn't ever bother to keep them quiet. When, on occasion, a run of ill-luck caused his fellow players to feel sorry for him, he said: "Don't worry on my account, my friends. It's you who will pay for all this." In the spring of the year 1773, he shut himself up in the superb château of Triel, which had been lent to him by the sieur Brizard, a farmer general, to whom it belonged. He had borrowed it in order to have an isolated spot where gamblers like himself could come together and give vent to their common passion. In one session alone, he lost 7,000 *louis;* at that time he boasted of being 5 million in the red. In payment of the aforementioned debt, he handed over a note drawn on the abbé Terray, as was his custom. The latter, remembering the insolent remarks made about himself, refused to cash it. The debtor went after the controller general tooth and claw, but his refusal was backed by the duc d'Aiguillon, who took offense. The latter had informed Mme du Barry, in order to ward off any possible attempt by her brother-in-law to turn her against the abbé. The Count, when he got wind of this maneuver, did not try to hide his displeasure. He spoke openly about it at a supper party, declaring that, if the duc d'Aiguillon forgot how much he owed him, he could easily get him fired—all the more so as he had got him the job in the first place. He had no fear, he added, of saying this openly, and he hoped it would be repeated. The ministers must have trembled at this, for the whole affair was patched up, and the debtor received the necessary funds.

*   *   *

It was time for all this depravity to come to an end. France was heading for inevitable destruction, had not the death of Louis XV intervened to change the face of the kingdom. The most singular thing about this event was the fact that it was brought about by the very people who had the most to lose from it.

For some time His Majesty had been more despondent. The sudden death of the marquis de Chauvelin, one of his favorites and his companion in all his carousings, had sorely affected him. Though he enjoyed excellent health, Chauvelin had succumbed before the King's very eyes in the course of one of their pleasure parties. The King was continually reminded of it. The death of the maréchal d'Armentières, another intimate and very close in age to the monarch, only added to his melancholy. He was, moreover, racked by remorse brought on by a particularly strong sermon preached by the Bishop of Senez on Maundy Thursday. The du Barry group decided that they should redouble their efforts to snap the King out of his sad state, resorting even to orgies, which might give an invigorating shock to his system {*machine*}. Consequently, it was decided to propose an excursion to Trianon [the royal château in the park of Versailles], where he would be able to give himself over more easily to those activities which the liberty of the setting inspired. They noticed that the King had looked lustfully upon the little daughter of a carpenter; they sent for the girl, cleaned her up, perfumed her, and put her into the bed of this distinguished lecher. This morsel would have been very hard indeed for him to digest, if they hadn't come to his aid with some strong stimulants, which gave him, for the moment, sweet relief and more pleasure than is usually the lot of a libertine in his sixties. The child, who unfortunately already felt unwell, had a great deal of trouble accepting what was demanded of her, and only agreed because of their threats and the hope of riches. They didn't know at the time that she was infected with smallpox; the onset of the disease was very swift, and she died soon after.

The germ had been communicated to the King, and the following day His Majesty took sick, though no one yet knew the cause of his malady. Accordingly, they advised Mme du Barry to keep the patient there, where she could remain mistress of his person. But Sieur de la Martinière, his chief surgeon, who took advantage of the King's weakness to assert his authority, insisted that he be immediately transported to Versailles, where the King was diagnosed the next day as suffering from smallpox. There was little doubt that the case would be fatal. At first, however, they didn't want to frighten him; they hid the danger from him. The favorite had taken the precaution of inspiring in her august lover much confidence in Sieur Bordeu, her own doctor. He played the greatest role in the King's care, and, as chief physician, treated him, together with Sieur le Monnier, who fulfilled the duties of *premier médecin*. From the very beginning of his illness, they debated the problem of how to handle the last sacraments of the King. The Archbishop of Paris had gone to Versailles in the hope of ministering to the conscience of the royal penitent, but Dr. Bordeu was strongly opposed to any mention of it, claiming that this prospect alone killed off three quarters of all patients. His motive for speaking in this way was clear to all: it was less a desire to save His Majesty than the attachment he felt to Mme du Barry, who would have had to leave the palace if this ceremony had been carried out at that time. This would have been a stroke of luck for the camp of du Barry's enemies.

She stayed on, then; and the archbishop, whose arrival at that moment displeased the monarch, was sent away by the patient himself. As he was standing at the King's bedside, His Majesty gave as an excuse the presence of too many people in his sick-room, which bothered him, and ordered that everyone except the servants should leave forthwith. M. de Beaumont was forced to return to Paris, thereby arousing the contempt of the clergy. The prelate was at that time suffering from a bladder infection, of which much sport was made. The scoffers said that "Monseigneur pissed blood in Paris, and could only make water in Versailles." After that, Mme du Barry spent the whole day at the King's bedside. She appeared there frequently on other days as well. His Majesty, still ignorant of the gravity of his condition, had her pass her delicate white hands over his festering sores. They maintain that he still caressed her from time to time, and that once he even grasped her breasts and kissed them. But finally they had to come to their inevitable parting.

The King himself, on on the fifth day of his illness, in the night, spoke to those around him: "I have no desire to be forced to replay the scene at Metz. [When he fell gravely ill at Metz in 1744, Louis's confessor forced him to publicly renounce his mistress, Mme de Châteauroux.] Tell Madame la duchesse d'Aiguillon that she would please me by taking away Madame la duchesse du Barry." As a result, the favorite went to Ruel to stay with the Duchess. By all accounts, she bore this expulsion with great fortitude. She wrote her mother immediately to tell her of her move: His Majesty, she explained, had decided that it was unsuitable, in such a critical situation, for him to keep his mistress in the palace, and he had sent a message to reassure her: there was no cause for worry, she would be taken care of. We know, furthermore, that he hadn't acted willingly but in a moment of delirium, for, a short time afterwards, the King forgot that she was absent and asked for her again.

The deed, however, was already done. She had, at this time, occasion to recall the *Almanach de Liège,* which had obsessed her, and whose publication she had suppressed as best she could. One of its predictions for April contained this phrase: "One of the most favored ladies will play her last role." She had modestly attributed this allusion to herself, and often said, "I certainly would like to see this horrid month of April past." But who would have thought it possible? In the sorrowful state in which she found herself at Ruel, her taste for luxury and the soft life never left her for a moment. When she found that the beds at the château of the duc d'Aiguillon were not comfortable enough, she had her couch brought from Lucienne. Certainly, she remained hopeful almost to the last day, even though the King declared, through his Grand Almoner, just before receiving the last rites, "that His Majesty was chagrined to have brought scandal to his subjects, and He only wanted to live henceforth to uphold the faith, religion, and the happiness of his people."

Mme du Barry well knew how much the promises of a dying man are worth once he has come back to health, and the courtiers themselves recalled it to her. Two days before the death of Louis XV, when his condition seemed less grave, there was a continual procession of carriages between Versailles and Ruel, a greater traffic, in fact, than from Paris to Versailles, but it dropped off soon, as the news of his health became more alarming. And when they saw that the King was absolutely at death's door, those who had kept quiet for political reasons now thundered against the mistress and her family. The name "du Barry" was such an anathema that the young marquise du Barry (Mlle de Fumel), who was obliged to remain at court as lady-in-waiting to the comtesse d'Artois, when she saw how much scorn was heaped upon her, decided to take the livery off her servants, in order not to stand out so much. It was well known, in fact, that she had always been repelled by this marriage, which had been forced upon her. This should have spared her from public ridicule, and even elicited sympathy for her; but despite the gravity of the circumstances, there was jeering at her expense. For example, they said, "The barrelmakers were going to have plenty to do, because all the barrels were leaking" [a pun on "du Barry" and *baril* for "barrel"]. In effect, her enemies spread the rumor that the Countess had escaped from Ruel, which was not only false but impossible. She received the fateful news of her royal lover's death there, and the duc de la Vrillière came to serve upon her a *lettre de cachet* exiling her to the Abbaye du Pont-aux-Dames in Brie, near Meaux.

She could not restrain herself at the appearance of this minister, who had been groveling at her feet only a short time before. She heaped bitter reproaches upon him for the role he had played. And, as for the orders from the King, she cried with her customary energy: "What a fucking way to begin a reign—with a *lettre de cachet!*" She was even more furious when she learned the terms of her incarceration: she could have only one chambermaid, could see no one, not even members of her family, and could send no letter unless the Abbess read it first. Such severity struck many as being disrespectful to the memory of the late King, but it was politically necessary in the days following his death. There was no question but that the favorite knew state secrets, and it was essential that such an irresponsible woman be prevented from divulging them. To prevent the softhearted from pitying her for the treatment she received, they spread around an anecdote which was designed to ignite the public's indignation against her and to counterbalance its possible sympathy. They informed the public that she had just ordered one hundred hatbrims from her milliner, which implied one hundred servants in livery—an unbelievable luxury, so the story was calculated to produce a sense of universal joy at being delivered from such a scourge.

Moreover, it was soon discovered that the tone of the *lettre de cachet* was far from harsh: His Majesty, it said, was obliged by reasons of state to order her to a convent; he would never forget how much esteem his ancestor had evidenced for the Countess by his protection; and, at the first meeting of the council, they would see to it that she receive an appropriate pension, if she needed one.

The King's generosity seemed all the greater, for the courtiers knew that Mme du Barry used to say all sorts of indecent things about him. She called him "that big, badly brought-up boy," and traded on her familiarity with the King by referring to Madame the Dauphine as "the redhead." And—what is even more criminal, and really punishable—she had joked: "Sire, you had better take care that this redhead doesn't get herself screwed in some corner." Evidently, the monarch and his consort, like Louis XII, who forgave the insults he had received when he was duc d'Orléans, had forgiven those done to them as Dauphin and the Dauphine. Reasons of state alone were dictating their conduct in respect to Mme du Barry. The same could not be said of comte Jean, her brother-in-law, who was known at court as "the rake." Respectable people wanted to throw the book at him.

They say that when this schemer saw himself in jeopardy, not knowing whom he could trust, he confided, at the moment of the King's death, in the Sieur Goys, a mischievous buffoon with whom he was very close, and asked him for advice on what course of action he should take. "My heavens, my dear Count," the clown answered, after rubbing his forehead, "a moneybox and post horses." The Count, rejecting this advice and indignant at being obliged to run away like a scoundrel, begged his friend to find him some other, more honorable solution. The Sieur Goys rubbed his forehead once again: "Well," he answered, "post horses and a moneybox." Du Barry was only able to follow half of this advice: his sister-in-law didn't trust him enough to put him in a position where he could carry it out completely. He left, in fact, secretly, and thus embarrassed the police, who had an order to have him thoroughly searched. There was no doubt that his escape had been aided by the duc d'Aiguillon, his friend, who was still, at that time, Minister of Foreign Affairs. All the tongues were wagging about him; the most outrageous stories were told. They recounted, for example, among other indecent acts of criminality on his part, how, when he ran out of money, he said, "My kid brother will give us some." He always used this incredible familiarity when speaking of the late King. Probably the last joke that was told about this rake, who exhibited every conceivable vice, was the following. He had hidden, in order to escape, in a basket of mackerel, which were then in season, while singing these familiar words: "Ah! how happy it is to live in the bosom of one's family!"

Notes

GENERAL NOTE:
All material has been translated by the author
unless otherwise indicated.

Introduction

1. Daniel Mornet, "Les Enseignements des bibliothèques privées (1750–1780)," *Revue d'histoire littéraire de la France* XVII (1910), pp. 449–492. See also Mornet's general synthesis, *Les Origines intellectuelles de la Révolution française (1715–1787)* (Paris, 1933), and, as examples of research that continues Mornet's lines of inquiry, François Furet, et al., *Livre et société dans la France du XVIIIe siècle* (Paris and The Hague, 1965 and 1970), 2 vols.; Roger Chartier and Henri-Jean Martin, eds., *Histoire de l'édition française.* Vol. II: *Le livre triomphant 1660–1830* (Paris, 1984); Roger Chartier, *Lectures et lecteurs dans la France d'ancien régime* (Paris, 1987); and Daniel Roche, *Les Républicains des lettres. Gens de culture et Lumières au XVIIIe siècle* (Paris, 1988). For a critical discussion of Mornet's work, see Robert Darnton, *The Literary Underground of the Old Regime* (Cambridge, Mass., 1982), chap. 6, and Roger Chartier, *Les Origines culturelles de la Révolution française* (Paris, 1990). The French phrase, "C'est la faute à Voltaire, c'est la faute à Rousseau" (It's Voltaire's fault, it's Rousseau's fault), conveys the notion that the works of the *philosophes* led directly to the French Revolution.

2. C.-G. de Lamoignon de Malesherbes, *Mémoire sur la liberté de la presse,* written in 1788, published in 1809 (Geneva, 1969, reprint), p. 300.

3. Robert Darnton, *The Business of Enlightenment: A Publishing History of the Encyclopédie, 1775–1800* (Cambridge, Mass., 1968). I have published essays on aspects of this subject in two collections:

The Literary Underground of the Old Regime, and *Gens de lettres, gens du livre* (Paris, 1992). I have also written a preliminary version of the present book in French: *Edition et sédition. L'Univers de la littérature clandestine au XVIIIe siècle* (Paris, 1991). But although *Edition et sédition* covers some of the same material, it concentrates on publishers and booksellers rather than on the books themselves; and it does not include full information about the entire corpus of forbidden works.

Chapter 1

1. The calculation is my own, based on the material on annual condemnations of books in the appendix to Félix Rocquain, *L'Esprit révolutionnaire avant la Révolution, 1715–1789* (Paris, 1878). A large proportion of the condemned works were only topical pamphlets. Instead of being burned, most were merely "suppressed" by an edict of the Conseil d'Etat or the Parlement de Paris, which meant they would be confiscated if seized by the police, and the dealer who sold them might be fined or imprisoned.

2. The fullest list compiled by the officials in charge of the book trade can be found in the Bibliothèque Nationale, ms. fr. 21928–21929, which contains 1,563 titles for all sorts of works, many of which were never printed, from 1696 to 1773. But it is not very accurate and does not represent the literature in circulation during the pre-Revolutionary years. The inspector of the book trade Joseph d'Hémery took notes on all the books that came to his attention. Although his journal is another valuable source of information, it covers only the years 1750–69, and it can be read as testimony to the vastness of the corpus of forbidden books and the inability of the police to bring it under control: Bibliothèque Nationale, ms. fr.22156–22165 and 22038. See Nelly Lhotellier, *Livres prohibés, livres saisis. Recherches sur la diffusion du livre interdit à Paris au XVIIIe siècle,* an unpublished *mémoire de maîtrise* at the University of Paris, I, 1973, and Marlinda Ruth Bruno, *The "Journal d'Hémery," 1750–1751: An Edition* (unpublished doctoral dissertation, Vanderbilt University, 1977).

3. Hans-Christoph Hobohm, "Der Diskurs der Zensur: Über den Wandel der literarischen Zensur zur Zeit der 'proscription des romans' (Paris, 1737)," *Romanistische Zeitschrift für Literaturgeschichte,* vol. X (1986), p. 79.

4. Bibliothèque Nationale, ms. fr. 21933–21934. The earlier registers, mss. 21931–21932, cover the period 1703–71, but they do not usually give the reasons for the confiscations; the later registers give too many reasons. Hence the confusion. But as explained

below, the most illegal and most dangerous books can be win-
nowed out from all the verbiage, and so these manuscripts are a
valuable source for identifying forbidden literature.

5. Jean-François Pion of Pontarlier to the Société typographique de
Neuchâtel, Nov. 21, 1771, with the text of the note from M.
Petit, the "buraliste" at the customs office in Frambourg: papers
of the Société typographique de Neuchâtel (cited henceforth as
STN), Bibliothèque publique et universitaire, Neuchâtel, Swit-
zerland.

6. Poinçot to STN, undated letter received on Sept. 22, 1781, and
Poinçot to STN, June 1, 1781.

7. Veuve Baritel to STN, Sept. 9, 1774, and "Livre de Commissions"
of the STN, entry for Baritel's order of Sept. 9, 1774.

8. On September 24, 1768, the Parlement of Paris condemned Jean-
Baptiste Josserand, a grocery boy, Jean Lécuyer, a dealer in second-hand goods, and Lécuyer's wife, Marie Suisse, for selling *Le
Christianisme dévoilé, L'Homme aux quarante écus, La Chandelle
d'Arras,* and similar works. They were exposed in chains for three
days on the Quai des Augustins, Place des Barnabites, and Place
de la Grève, wearing a sign saying: "Purveyor of impious and
immoral libels." The two men were then branded on the right
shoulder with the letters GAL and sent to the galleys, Lécuyer for
five years, Josserand for nine years followed by perpetual banishment from the kingdom. Mme Lécuyer was sent to prison in the
Maison de force of the Salpêtrière for five years. The punishments
were softened by *lettres de grâce,* but the letters arrived too late:
Bibliothèque Nationale, ms. fr. 22099, folios 213–221.

9. Charpentier, *La Bastille dévoilée, ou recueil de pièces authentiques
pour servir à son histoire* (Paris, 1789), IV, 119.

10. A.-F. Momoro, *Traité élémentaire de l'imprimerie, ou le manuel de
l'imprimeur* (Paris, 1793), pp. 234–235. Momoro specified that
this "term from the Old Regime" covered "libels, works against
the state, morals, religion, the ministers, the king, magistrates,
etc."

11. STN to J. Rondi, Sept. 9, 1773.

12. The quotations, in the order of their appearance in the text, come
from P.-J. Duplain to STN, Oct. 11, 1772; Manoury to STN, Oct.
4, 1775; Le Lièvre to STN, Dec. 31, 1776; Blouet to STN, Aug.
30, 1772; Audéart to STN, April 14, 1776; Billault to STN, Sept.
10, 1776.

13. Patras to STN, June 6, 1777; Rouyer to STN, June 9, 1781;
Regnault le jeune to STN, Sept. 19 and Dec. 28, 1774.

14. Jean-Elie Bertrand of the STN in Neuchâtel to Frédéric-Samuel
Ostervald and Abram Bosset de Luze in Geneva, April 19, 1777.

15. STN to Téron, April 6, 1774; Téron to STN, April 14, 1774; Téron to STN, April 23, 1774; Téron to STN, June 10, 1777.

16. Gabriel Grasset to STN, June 19, 1772, and April 25, 1774.

17. Grasset's catalogue is in his letter to the STN of April 25, 1774; the catalogues of Chappuis and Didier are in their letter of Nov. 1, 1780.

18. The STN's secret catalogues, along with a half dozen copies of its standard legal catalogues, can be found in a dossier labeled "Société typographique de Neuchâtel" in the papers of the STN. The catalogue, confiscated with the Veuve Stockdorf's papers, is in the Bibliothèque Nationale, ms. fr. 22101, folios 242–249. The remark on Wittel appears in Quandet de Lachenal to STN, May 6, 1781. A full account of the intrigues connected with the remark about keeping the catalogue "mum" can be found in the dossier of Noël Gille, Bibliothèque Nationale, ms. fr. 22081, folios 358–366, quotation from folio 364 recto. Poinçot reported on his interview with Martin, the secretary and right-hand man of Le Camus de Néville, the director of the Book Trade Department, in a letter to the STN of July 31, 1783.

19. STN "Copie de lettres," entries from Aug. 12 to Sept. 19, 1776.

20. Laisney to STN, July 26, 1777; Prévost to STN, May 11, 1783; Malassis to STN, June 27, 1775. See also Teinturier of Bar-le-Duc to STN, Sept. 2, 1776, and Guichard of Avignon to STN, April 16, 1773.

21. STN to Bergeret, July 6, 1773; Bergeret to STN, Aug. 7, 1773; and STN to Bergeret, Aug. 17, 1773. See also the similar exchange between the STN and Prévost of Melun: Prévost to STN, April 10, 1777, and STN to Prévost, April 15, 1777.

22. In sending its latest catalogue of philosophical books to Cazin of Reims on Sept. 24, 1775, the STN regretted its inability to set stable prices for such works: "The prices of books in this genre are, as you know, very irregular in general and depend on all kinds of different circumstances."

23. Grasset to STN, April 25, 1774.

24. The catalogues can be found in Décombaz to STN, Jan. 8, 1776; Chappuis et Didier to STN, Nov. 1, 1780; and the papers confiscated in Stockdorf's bookshop in Strasbourg in 1773: Bibliothèque Nationale, ms. fr. 22101, folios 242–249.

25. Malherbe to STN, Aug. 13, 1774.

26. Favarger to STN, Aug. 16, 1776, and Sept. 4, 1776.

27. For example, Barret of Lyon to STN, April 10, 1772; Mossy of Marseilles to STN, March 12, 1777; Gay of Lunéville to STN, May 19, 1772; Audéart of Lunéville to STN, April 8, 1775; and Le Baron of Caen to STN, Dec. 24, 1776.

28. Manoury to STN, June 24, 1783; Desbordes to STN, Jan. 12,

1773; Malassis to STN, Aug. 15, 1775; Baritel to STN, Sept. 19, 1774; Billault to STN, Sept. 29, 1776; Charmet to STN, Oct. 1, 1774; Sombert to STN, Oct. 25, 1776.

29. Bergeret to STN, Feb. 11, 1775; Charmet to STN, Sept. 30, 1775; STN "Livre de Commissions," entry for April 24, 1776, based on an order from Malherbe of Loudun.

30. Regnault to STN, July 6, 1774; Favarger to STN, Nov. 15, 1778, reporting the instructions given by Nubla; Jacquenod to STN, Sept. 1775 (exact date missing); and Bornand to STN, Oct. 16, 1785, reporting the instructions given by Barrois.

31. Blouet to STN, Sept. 10, 1773.

32. Guillon to STN, April 6, 1773, and STN to Guillon, April 19, 1773.

33. François Michaut of Les Verrières to STN, Oct. 30, 1783.

Chapter 2

1. Of course, various agencies tallied up information about activities in France before 1789, but their data were notoriously unreliable. See Emmanuel Le Roy Ladurie, "Les Comptes fantastiques de Gregory King," in Le Roy Ladurie, *Le Territoire de l'historien* (Paris, 1973), pp. 252–270; Jacques Dupâquier, et al., *Histoire de la population française* (Paris, 1988) vol. II, chap. 1; Bernard Lepetit, *Les Villes dans la France moderne (1741–1840),* pp. 445–449; and Christian Labrousse and Jacques Lecaillon, *Statistique descriptive* (Paris, 1970). Systematic data gathering on a national scale is usually traced to the census of 1806 and scientific statistical analysis to the work of Alphonse Quételet.

2. Relatively few of the STN's shipments failed to reach their destination; when they did, the mishaps were mentioned in the booksellers' correspondence and recorded in the account books. The archives of the STN therefore show which books actually reached readers as well as which ones were most in demand. Unfortunately, the archives do not contain systematic information on sales by the retailers themselves, so the last stage of the distribution process remains relatively obscure.

3. "Liste des imprimeurs de Nancy," January 1767, report with notes by inspector Joseph d'Hémery: Bibliothèque Nationale, mss. fr. 22098, piece 81.

4. *Ibid.*

5. Among the hundreds of letters to the STN from dealers in Lorraine, the most important that relate to Matthieu are those of Dalancourt, Babin, and Duvez.

6. See especially Matthieu to STN, Dec. 28, 1779, and, for back-

ground on the book trade in Lorraine, *Almanach de la librairie* (Paris, 1781).

7. Matthieu to STN, April 7, 1772.

8. Matthieu to STN, August 7, 1774, which echoes similar requests in his letters of February 24 and April 7, 1772.

9. Cazin to STN, March 24, 1777. Cazin spent six weeks in the Bastille and claimed that he lost 20,000 livres from the catastrophe. Although he recovered well enough to continue his business, he reduced the scale of his operations and became wary of taking risks. See his letters to the STN of Jan. 1, 1780; Nov. 17, 1783; and July 27, 1784.

10. The quotations, in the order of their appearance in the text, come from Petit's letters to the STN of June 29, 1783; Jan. 20, 1783; and Aug. 31, 1783.

11. Petit to STN, Sept. 9, 1782; April 24, 1782; and Oct. 24, 1783. Petit's main competitor in Reims, Martin-Hubert Cazin, confirmed his view of overproduction and underselling. Cazin to STN, January 1, 1780: "You must be aware, Sir, that it has become very hard to collect bills and that virtually the entire book trade has been ruined by the excessive quantity of books. For several years, forty or fifty peddlers have been flogging their wares throughout France and drawing their stock from Switzerland, Avignon, Rouen, and other places. They entice the suppliers by paying in cash. Then, when they have won their confidence and built up credit, they stop paying. Not a single dealer can boast of having avoided losses at the hands of these people. All of them [the peddlers] end up by in bankruptcy and poison the province by selling off their books at half price. . . . The trade in this city has been completely ruined."

12. Petit to STN, May 31, 1780.

13. For details on Besançon's institutions, see *Almanach historique de Besançon et de la Franche-Comté pour l'année 1784* (Besançon, 1784); and for its development as an administrative center after the Franche-Comté's incorporation in the kingdom (1674), see Claude Fohlen, *Histoire de Besançon* (Paris, 1965).

14. Charmet to STN, April 18, 1777. On the *Encyclopédie* market and other aspects of the book trade in Besançon, see my *Business of Enlightenment*, pp. 287–294.

15. On the important and neglected subject of booksellers' wives, who often played a key role at the *comptoir*, tending accounts, handling correspondence, and selling books, see Geraldine Sheridan, "Women in the Booktrade in Eighteenth-Century France," *British Journal for Eighteenth-Century Studies*, XV (1992), 51–69.

16. An additional consideration in the case of Raynal's *Histoire philo-*

sophique is the fact that the STN produced its own edition of the book. It usually sold more copies of its own editions than of books in its general stock, so the provenance of the books had some effect on their sales record. In order to alert the reader to this factor, the titles of works published by the STN are marked with an asterisk in the general list of best-sellers at Table 2.5 (p. 63–64).

17. Charmet to STN, Oct. 18, 1775.
18. Charmet to STN, Oct. 18, 1775.
19. Charmet to STN, March 7, 1777.
20. Charmet to STN, Sept. 4, 1779.
21. Charmet to STN, April 28, 1780.
22. Mme Charmet to STN, Sept. 6, 1782.
23. Mme Charmet to STN, Nov. 15, 1782.
24. Mme Charmet to STN, Jan. 9, 1783.
25. Mme Charmet to STN, April 13, 1783.
26. Mme Charmet to STN, April 24, 1787.
27. Mme Charmet to STN, Aug. 16, 1784.
28. Charmet to STN, June 20, 1777.
29. Charmet to STN, Sept. 6, 1782.
30. Charmet to STN, Feb. 20, 1778.
31. Whether Nouffer had really committed himself to supply the *Vie privée de Louis XV* to the STN by means of exchange cannot be determined from the documents. For his side of the story, see his letters to the STN of May 10, June 6, and July 6, 1781. For the versions of the STN and of Charmet, see Charmet to STN, May 18, May 30, and July 18, 1781; and STN to Charmet, June 12 and July 22, 1781.
32. In a letter to the STN of June 9, 1781, Charmet advised it against reprinting *Philosophie de la nature* by Delisle de Sales: "I think this work is worn out. The same goes for philosophical books in general, which have rarely been requested for more than a year now." In this case, Charmet used the term "philosophical" in its conventional sense, to designate treatises of philosophy.
33. Charmet to STN, April 17, 1782. In a letter of October 2, 1782, Charmet noted that he expected Mirabeau's attack on arbitrary government to appeal especially to the lawyers and magistrates connected with the parlement of Besançon. On April 18, 1777, he wrote that readers were falling all over themselves in the scramble to get an equally outspoken tract, *Lettre de M. Linguet à M. le comte de Vergennes:* "Some copies have sold for four to five *louis* [96 to 125 livres, an astronomical price]."
34. Charmet to STN, Nov. 8, 1774.
35. Charmet to STN, Sept. 30, 1775. The *Précis* was a pamphlet that was also published with a similar *libelle: La Gazette de Cythère, ou*

aventures galantes et récentes arrivées dans les principales villes de l'Europe, traduite de l'anglais, à la fin de laquelle on a joint le Précis historique de la vie de Mad. la comtesse du Barry (London, 1774).

36. Charmet to STN, Oct. 12, 1781. In this case, Charmet seemed to have got his "espions" mixed up, because *L'Espion anglais,* which ran to ten volumes, was an extended version of the four-volume *L'Observateur anglais, ou correspondance secrète entre Milord All'Eye et Milord All'Ear,* which originally appeared in 1777 under the imprint of London.

37. Charmet to STN, Aug. 28, 1782.

38. On the high literacy rate of the northeast as opposed to the south, see Michel Fleury and Pierre Valmary, "Les Progrès de l'instruction élémentaire de Louis XIV à Napoleon III," *Population,* XII (1957), 71–92, and François Furet and Jacques Ozouf, *Lire et écrire: L'alphabétisation des français de Calvin à Jules Ferry* (Paris, 1977).

39. *Etat et description de la ville de Montpellier, fait en 1768,* an anonymous tract published by J. Berthélé as *Montpellier en 1768 et en 1836 d'après deux manuscrits inédits* (Montpellier, 1909), quotations from pp. 52 and 57.

40. *Ibid.,* pp. 27 and 55.

41. *Manuel de l'auteur et du libraire* (Paris, 1777), p. 67. For background on the book trade in the province, see Madeleine Ventre, *L'Imprimerie et la librairie en Languedoc au dernier siècle de l'ancien régime* (Paris and The Hague, 1958).

42. Jean-François Favarger to STN, Aug. 29, 1778. In 1764, Montpellier had four booksellers and two printers: see Ventre, *L'Imprimerie et la librairie en Languedoc,* pp. 227–228. Faure was the associate of the widow Gontier; and the firms of Rigaud and of Pons had merged under the direction of Isaac-Pierre Rigaud in 1770, although they were listed separately in the *Manuel de l'auteur et du libraire* of 1777, which in general is not a reliable source.

43. An anonymous, undated *requête,* probably from 1754, sent to the director of the book trade: Bibliothèque Nationale, Ms. fr. 22075, fo. 229. On the peddling of illicit books by peasants from the Dauphiné, see *ibid.,* fo. 234, "Mémoire remis à M. de Saint Priest" by Eméric David of Aix.

44. The report, dated July 24, 1754, is in *ibid.,* fo. 355.

45. Ventre, *L'Imprimerie et la librairie en Languedoc,* p. 227.

46. Rigaud to STN, May 23, 1777.

47. Rigaud to STN, Oct. 25, 1771.

48. Rigaud to STN, June 29, 1774. For details on the tariff legislation, see my "Reading, Writing, and Publishing in Eighteenth-Century

France: A Case Study in the Sociology of Literature," *Daedalus* (Winter 1971), 231–238.

49. For example, Rigaud refused to order the original edition of Voltaire's *Questions sur l'Encyclopédie* from Gabriel Cramer of Geneva so that he could save by purchasing a cut-rate, counterfeit edition from the STN, but he found the STN's paper abominable and its delivery far too slow. Rigaud to STN, Nov. 9, 1770: "This is all the more vexatious for us in that a letter that arrived yesterday from M. Cramer in Geneva informs us that he has sent a shipment for one of our colleagues and that he is astonished that we haven't ordered any from him. By going directly to you, we expected to get a better price and quicker service, and we see, to our infinite regret, that we have failed in the last point, which is the crucial one." On August 28, 1771, after his patience gave out, Rigaud wrote to the STN, "We seem to be separated by five or six thousand leagues."

50. Cézary to STN, June 25, 1781.

51. Cézary's financial situation was analyzed for the STN by an attorney in Montpellier named Chiraud in a letter of June 5, 1779. The following account is based on Chiraud's letters as well as those of Vialars, a local merchant who also represented the STN, and those of Cézary himself.

52. Cézary to STN, June 25, 1781.

53. Relatively little is known about the *cabinets littéraires* of the eighteenth century. For some preliminary reconnoitering of the subject, see Jean-Louis Pailhès, "En marge des bibliothèques: l'apparition des cabinets de lecture," in *Histoire des bibliothèques françaises* (Paris, 1988), pp. 415–421; Paul Benhamou, "The Reading Trade in Pre-revolutionary France," *Documentatieblad Werkgroep Achttiende Eeuw,* vol. 23 (1991), 143–150; and my own sketches of two *cabinets* in *Edition et sédition,* pp. pp. 80–86, and "First Steps Toward a History of Reading," *Australian Journal of French Studies,* XXIII (1986), 5–30.

54. Fontanel to STN, May 11, 1773.

55. Fontanel to STN, March 4, 1775.

56. Fontanel to STN, Jan. 18, 1775.

57. Fontanel to STN, Jan. 24, 1781.

58. Fontanel to STN, May 24, 1782.

59. Fontanel to STN, May 18, 1781.

60. Fontanel to STN, March 6, 1781.

61. Vialars to STN, Nov. 3, 1784.

62. Vialars to STN, Aug. 30, 1784.

63. Rigaud to STN, March 23, 1774.

64. Rigaud to STN, April 15, 1774, and June 2, 1780.

65. Rigaud to STN, Sept. 23, 1771.

66. Rigaud to STN, Feb. 8, 1782.

67. Rigaud to STN, Nov. 22, 1779.

68. Rigaud to STN, July 12, 1782.

69. Rigaud to STN, July 27, 1771.

70. Rigaud to STN, July 30, 1783.

71. Rigaud to STN, Aug. 15, 1777. Rigaud was referring to Linguet's *Lettre de M. Linguet à M. le C. de Vergennes, ministre des affaires étrangères en France* (London, 1777), one of the most audacious and popular tracts of the pre-Revolutionary era.

72. Rigaud to STN, July 30, 1783.

73. The crucial measure in the government's campaign against seditious literature was an order by the Foreign Minister, the comte de Vergennes, of June 12, 1783, which required all book imports to pass inspection in the Chambre syndicale of the booksellers' guild in Paris, regardless of their destination. This measure was quite effective, although it has not been noticed by historians, because it did not take the form of a royal edict. See my "Reading, Writing, and Publishing in Prerevolutionary France," 226–238.

74. As I have already published several other case studies, I have chosen not to repeat them here—see chaps. 3–6 of *Edition et sédition.* See also "The World of the Underground Booksellers in the Old Regime," and "Trade in the Taboo: The Life of a Clandestine Book Dealer in Prerevolutionary France," in Paul J. Korshin, ed., *The Widening Circle: Essays on the Circulation of Literature in Eighteenth-Century Europe* (Philadelphia, 1976), pp. 11–83.

75. The above sketches do not include much information on the most marginal characters in the illegal book trade, notably peddlers. For a case study of a peddler and his business, see *Edition et sédition,* chap. 3.

76. André to STN, Aug. 22, 1784.

77. On the history of the archives of the STN and of the publishing house itself, see John Jeanprêtre, "Histoire de la Société typographique de Neuchâtel, 1769–1798," *Musée neuchâtelois* (1949), 70–79, 115–120, and 148–153; and Jacques Rychner, "Les Archives de la Société typographique de Neuchâtel," *Musée neuchâtelois* (1969), 1–24.

78. The emergence of the publisher at the end of the eighteenth century in France has not yet been adequately studied, although there is some information scattered through Chartier and Martin, eds., *Histoire de l'édition française,* vol. II: *Le livre triomphant 1660– 1830.* The best account of this new social type is still to be found in Balzac's *Illusions perdues.* Scholarship in Britain and Germany is more advanced: see the syntheses in Philip Gaskell, *A New Intro-*

duction to Bibliography (New York and Oxford, 1972), pp. 297–311, and Reinhard Wittmann, *Geschichte des deutschen Buchhandels. Ein Überblick* (Munich, 1991), pp. 111–142.

79. Discussions of these and many other ruses can be found throughout the STN papers. See for example the dossiers of Dufour of Maastricht, Machuel of Rouen, and Barret of Lyon.

80. Information on the practice of exchanges is scattered throughout the STN papers. Most of the material on the confederation of sociétés typographiques is grouped in ms. 1235.

81. On the economics of this affaire, see my *Gens de lettres, gens du livre*, pp. 219–244. On the politics, see Charly Guyot, "Imprimeurs et passeurs neuchâtelois: l'affaire du *Système de la nature* (1771)," *Musée neuchâtelois* (1946), 74–81 and 108–116.

82. STN to Mossy of Marseille, July 10, 1773.

83. STN to Astori of Lugano, April 15, 1773.

84. Mossy to STN, Aug. 4, 1777.

85. Matthieu to STN, April 23, 1771.

86. As already explained, the STN did not publish many hard-core forbidden books, but it stocked them and procured them for its customers by means of exchanges with specialists in the genre. The statistics therefore derive from its activities as a wholesaler rather than as a publisher. On the exceptional occasions when it produced its own edition of a *livre philosophique,* that book occupied an unusually important place in its stock and its marketing; and booksellers tended to place orders for it more often than for other works supplied by the STN. Nonetheless, the STN did not reprint such books without carefully sounding the market (one can actually speak of "market research" despite its anachronistic ring): see my "Sounding the Literary Market in Prerevolutionary France," *Eighteenth-Century Studies*, XVII (1984), 477–492. So works published by the STN such as d'Holbach's *Système de la nature* and Raynal's *Histoire philosophique* really were best-sellers, even though they probably do not deserve as high a place as they occupy on the best-seller list.

The STN continued to sell forbidden books in France throughout the 1780s, but it cut back on its trade as a result of severe restrictions on book imports that the French government imposed in June 1783: see my "Reading, Writing, and Publishing," 226–238. Therefore works like Mirabeau's *Des Lettres de cachet et des prisons d'Etat* (1782) and Linguet's *Mémoires sur la Bastille* (1783) probably sold better than appears in the statistics derived from the STN's sales. Finally, there is a possibility of a geographical bias in the STN's sales pattern: the statistics may favor books produced in Switzerland as opposed to those produced in the Low Countries.

Although the STN traded extensively with houses like Gosse of the Hague, Dufour of Maastricht, Plomteux of Liège, and the Société typographique of Neuwied, it exchanged books most actively with other Swiss publishers. Its heavy sales of works by Voltaire might show a Swiss bias on the supply side. However, its sales of works by d'Holbach and his group were equally heavy, and they were published for the most part in Holland, the main exception being the STN's own edition of d'Holbach's *Système de la nature.* Although I have found signs of a strong commercial rivalry between the Dutch and the Swiss, I have not turned up evidence of any basic difference in the kinds of forbidden French books that they published.

87. All these works except *Vie privée de Louis XV* also occupy prominent places in the catalogues of forbidden books.

88. On the publication of the works of d'Holbach and his circle and the problems of attributing authors and publishers to them, see Jeroom Vercruysse, *Bibliographie descriptive des écrits du baron d'Holbach* (Paris, 1971).

89. The booksellers often made remarks that suggested which writers stood out in the public eye. For example, in a letter to the STN of March 30, 1783, Delahaye of Brussels, who had traded heavily in Mercier's *Tableau de Paris,* said he would speculate on two hundred copies of a new book by the same author even though he had not yet seen it, "since you assure us that it is really by the famous M. Mercier and that it is indeed interesting." The writers mentioned most often in the booksellers' letters were Voltaire, Rousseau, Raynal, Mercier, and Linguet. The others at the top of the list never became well known, because they remained shrouded in anonymity.

90. The prodigious success of *La Nouvelle Héloïse* was first demonstrated in the early research of Daniel Mornet: "Le Texte de *La Nouvelle Héloïse* et les éditions du XVIIIe siècle," *Annales de la société J.-J. Rousseau,* V (1909), 1–117. Thanks to the new *Bibliography of the Writings of Jean-Jacques Rousseau to 1800* now being published by the Voltaire Foundation in Oxford under the direction of Jo-Anne McEachern, we will have a more precise idea of all the editions of Rousseau's works. Dr. McEachern has identified nineteen editions of *Emile* published between 1762 and 1770. She has found only eight for the period 1770–90, and of them, six were produced by the same publisher. So the demand for it probably declined as the market became saturated. That hypothesis is confirmed by the feeble number of copies ordered from the STN: only six in all. The *Emile* appears in only one of the six clandestine catalogues and in two of the ten inventories of police raids. How-

ever, it was confiscated twelve times in the Paris Customs, of which seven came from the year 1771 alone. I would like to thank Dr. McEachern for generously showing me the results of her study before its publication as volume 2 in the *Bibliography: Emile, ou de l'éducation* (Oxford, 1989).

91. Barret to STN, Aug. 13, 1779.

92. Pyre, a Parisian bookseller who supplied information and copy for pirating to the STN, reported on March 23, 1776: "I am not sending you any of the separate works of M. Diderot. Aside from the fact that they are very difficult to find, they would cost more than his complete works, which you can get at Lyon at a far cheaper price than here." Of course, some of Diderot's most important works, like *Le Neuveu de Rameau*, were not published during the eighteenth century. His collected works sold fairly well, according to the orders placed with the STN (thirty-three sets ordered on nine occasions), but not as well as those of many other writers, such as Grécourt (fifty-six sets, twelve orders), who are far less famous today.

93. This figure does not include the sales of the eleven-volume collection of Rousseau's *Oeuvres posthumes*, which were marketed as a supplement to earlier editions of his collected works: 107 sets sold in response to 16 orders.

94. In putting these questions in this manner, I do not mean to imply that literary historians should abandon the study of great books, even though greatness itself is a culture-bound category. Nor am I arguing for a revival of positivism. I think it important to discover patterns of literary demand by means of empirical research, but I also consider it crucial to go on to questions about how books were read, taste was formed, and literature was related to other elements in culture and society.

95. Two subcategories in the classification scheme are especially problematic. The first, "Irreligious ribaldry, pornography," could be placed under the general rubric of works that are primarily about religion or the rubric of works that mainly concern sex. In classifying individual books, I have had to make arbitrary decisions about the relative weight of the irreligious as opposed to the pornographic ingredients of their texts—a task that hardly does justice to books meant to be bawdy and anti-clerical at the same time. In order to minimize the danger of distorting their character, I have placed such books—*L'Arrétin*, for example, and *La Pucelle d'Orléans*, and even *Histoire de dom B . . .* in the hybrid subcategory, "Irreligious ribaldry, pornography," and have put it under the general rubric of "Religion." It could go just as well under "Sex." The reader can allow for this bias by shifting the subcate-

gory itself, which would make the entire corpus appear appear somewhat bawdier. The second problematic subcategory, "General social, cultural criticism," includes works like Voltaire's *Lettres philosophiques,* Raynal's *Histoire philosophique,* and Mercier's *Tableau de Paris.* They attacked the orthodox values of the Old Regime on many different fronts, but they also expressed *philosophie* as it was understood, in a broad manner, during the eighteenth century. Therefore, they have been placed in an omnibus subcategory, which itself appears under "Philosophy." Distortions created by arbitrary classifying can be corrected by studying the "Statistics of Demand" in the accompanying volume, which contain information about the best-selling books arranged according to genre, and by reworking the more detailed information after each title in the "Basic Checklist," which also appears in that volume.

96. The catalogues can be found in the STN archives under the names of the publishers. They refer to different editions in different formats, some with and some without illustrations. Most of the prices are wholesale "prix de libraire."

97. Linguet's *Mémoires sur la Bastille* followed in the wake of two pamphletlike appeals to public opinion, which also sold like hot cakes: *Requête au conseil du roi* and *Lettre de M. Linguet à M. le comte de Vergennes.* Mirabeau's *Des Lettres de cachet et des prisons d'Etat* probably sold even better than is indicated by its position on the bestseller list, because it appeared late in 1782, just before the STN began to cut back on its trade in France. Although Mirabeau's rhetoric was just as bombastic as Linguet's, it was somewhat less personal. Mirabeau pretended to write an objective treatise on the abuses of royal power, and he confined most of his remarks on his own experience to the Introduction and the second half of the book. Although it appeared anonymously, and even "posthumously," Mirabeau's authorship was an open secret.

98. The propaganda against Maupeou will be analyzed in detail in a forthcoming book by Shanti Singham. For a recent survey of the crisis as a whole, see Durand Echeverria, *The Maupeou Revolution, a Study in the History of Libertarianism: France, 1770–1774* (Baton Rouge, 1985).

99. Of course the meaning of books and pamphlets depends on the way they were read, a problem that is raised but not resolved in chapter 4. I hope to deal with it more fully in a future book, but meanwhile I can refer the reader to a preliminary attempt to explore the contemporary understanding of the pre-Revolutionary crisis in my doctoral dissertation, "Trends in Radical Propaganda on the Eve of the French Revolution (1782–1788)" (Oxford, 1964).

100. For an encyclopedic overview of information on the eighteenth-century press, see Jean Sgard, ed., *Dictionnaire des journaux 1600–1789* (Oxford, 1991), 2 vols.; the older synthetic survey directed by Claude Bellanger and others, *Histoire générale de la presse française* (Paris, 1969), vol. I; and the very old but very useful work by Eugène Hatin, *Histoire politique et littéraire de la presse en France* (Paris, 1859–61), 8 vols. On the *Gazette de Leyde,* which published nothing on the Maupeou coup but quite a lot on the Diamond Necklace Affair, see Jeremy D. Popkin, *News and Politics in the Age of Revolution. Jean Luzac's Gazette de Leyde* (Ithaca, 1989). And on the *nouvellistes,* see Frantz Funck-Brentano, *Les Nouvellistes* (Paris, 1905).

Chapter 3

1. Nicolas-Edmé Restif de la Bretonne, *Le Pornographe ou Idées d'un honnête homme sur un projet de règlement pour les prostituées* (London, 1769; reprinted in *L'Enfer de la Bibliothèque Nationale* [Paris, 1985], vol. II).

2. For a somewhat overstated argument about the anachronism inherent in the concept of pornography, see Peter Wagner, *Eros Revived: Erotica of the Enlightenment in England and America* (London, 1988). The influence of Aretino in eighteenth-century France is thoroughly explored in Carolin Fischer, *Die Erotik der Aufklärung. Pietro Aretinos Ragionamenti als Hypotext des Libertinen Romans in Frankreich,* a doctoral dissertation at the Freie Universität, Berlin, 1993. In the burgeoning scholarship on early-modern erotic literature, see especially Jean-Pierre Dubost, *Eros und Vernunft. Literatur und Libertinage* (Frankfurt-am-Main, 1988); François Moureau and Alain-Marc Rieu, eds., *Eros philosophe. Discours libertins des Lumières* (Geneva and Paris, 1984); and Lynn Hunt, ed., *The Invention of Pornography. Obscenity and the Origins of Modernity, 1500–1800* (New York, 1993).

3. See Walter Kendrick, *The Secret Museum: Pornography in Modern Culture* (New York, 1987); Jeanne Veyrin-Forrer, "L'Enfer vu d'ici," *Revue de la Bibliothèque Nationale,* 14 (1984), 22–41; and Annie Stora-Lamarre, *L'Enfer de la IIIe République. Censeurs et pornographes (1881–1914)* (Paris, 1990).

4. These terms appear everywhere in the registers of books confiscated in the Paris Customs: Bibliothèque Nationale, mss. fr. 21931–21934. *Galant,* however, sometimes implied obscene.

5. Malesherbes, *Mémoires sur la librairie et sur la liberté de la presse* (Geneva, 1969 reprint), pp. 89–90.

6. Diderot, "Salon de 1765," quoted in Jacques Rustin, "Preface" to

the reprint of *Vénus dans le cloître* in *Oeuvres érotiques du XVIIe siècle. L'Enfer de la Bibliothèque Nationale* (Paris, 1988), VII, 307.

7. *Thérèse philosophe, ou Mémoires pour servir à l'histoire du Père Dirrag et de Mademoiselle Eradice,* reprinted in *L'Enfer de la Bibliothèque Nationale* (Paris, 1986), V, 102.

8. Sade, *Histoire de Juliette* in *Oeuvres complètes* (Paris, 1967), VIII, 443.

9. For the text of the police report and a discussion of the situation in 1749, see "Les Encyclopédistes et la police," in my *Gens de lettres, gens du livre.*

10. J.-F. Barbier, *Journal historique et anecdotique du règne de Louis XV* (Paris, 1851), III, 89–90, entry for July 1749: "They also arrested M. Diderot, a man of letters and a wit, who is suspected of being the author of a tract that appeared under the title of *Thérèse philosophe....* This book, which is charming and very well written, contains some conversations about natural religion, which are extremely forceful and very dangerous."

11. See Jacques Duprilot, "Nachwort," in *Thérèse philosophe. Erotische Küpferstiche aus fünf berühmten Büchern* (Dortmund, 1982), especially pp. 228–232. Although this essay provides the fullest account of the circumstances surrounding the publication of *Thérèse philosophe,* it does not make out a convincing case for Diderot's authorship. For further information about the background of the text, see the introductions to editions of it by Pascal Pia (Paris, 1979), Jacques Duprilot (Geneva, 1980), and Philippe Roger (Paris, 1986).

12. *Thérèse philosophe,* p. 69.

13. *Ibid.,* pp. 58–59.

14. *Ibid.,* p. 54.

15. *Ibid.,* p. 87.

16. *Ibid.,* p. 86.

17. *Ibid.,* p. 95.

18. *Ibid.,* p. 85.

19. *Ibid.,* p. 101.

20. *Ibid.,* p. 41.

21. *Ibid.,* pp. 170 and 175.

22. *Ibid.,* p. 180.

23. *Ibid.,* p. 186.

24. The most important survey of this vast subject is still Ira O. Wade, *The Clandestine Organization and Diffusion of Philosophical Ideas in France from 1700 to 1800* (New York, 1967). As an example of more recent scholarship, see Olivier Bloch, ed., *Le Matérialisme du XVIIIe siècle et la littérature clandestine* (Paris, 1982).

25. *Thérèse philosophe,* pp. 51 and 53.

26. *Ibid.*, p. 59.
27. *Ibid.*, p. 87.
28. *Ibid.*, p. 66.
29. *Ibid.*, p. 54.
30. See Otto Mayr, *Authority, Liberty, and Automatic Machinery in Early Modern Europe* (Baltimore, 1986).
31. See Jean Marie Goulemot, *Ces Livres qu'on ne lit que d'une main. Lecture et lecteurs de livres pornographiques au XVIIIe siècle* (Paris, 1991), p. 48.
32. Mirabeau, *Ma Conversion ou le libertin de qualité* (London, 1783), reprinted in *L'Enfer de la Bibliothèque Nationale*, III, 38.
33. See Simon Henri Tissot, *L'Onanisme, dissertation sur les maladies produites par la masturbation* (Lausanne, 1760), and Goulemot, *Ces Livres qu'on ne lit que d'une main*, pp. 43–55.
34. *Thérèse philosophe*, p. 62.
35. Many of the illustrations have been reprinted in *Thérèse philosophe. Erotische Küpferstiche.*
36. *Thérèse philosophe*, p. 170.
37. *Ibid.*, pp. 186 and 189.
38. *Ibid.*, p. 51.
39. Herbert Dieckmann, *Le Philosophe. Text and Interpretation* (St. Louis, 1948).
40. *Thérèse philosophe*, p. 115.
41. *Ibid.*, pp. 112–113.
42. *Examen de la religion dont on cherche l'éclaircissement de bonne foi. Attribué à M. de St. Evremond. Traduit de l'anglais de Gilbert Burnet* (London, 1761), p. 24. *Thérèse philosophe*, p. 108. In saying "God is everywhere," the author of *Thérèse philosophe* really meant He did not exist, because in other passages it transformed a pantheistic-sounding argument into an all-pervasive materialism. (I quote from the 1761 edition of the *Examen*, because I was unable to find a copy from the edition of 1745.) In an article on the *Examen* in *Les Supercheries littéraires dévoilées* (Paris, 1847), J.-M. Quérard attributes it to a military officer named La Serre and says that it was condemned to be burned by the Parlement of Paris after its publication in 1745. In *The Clandestine Organization and Diffusion of Philosophic Ideas in France from 1700 to 1750*, pp. 141–163, Ira Wade provides a much fuller discussion of the *Examen* and attributes it to César Chesneau du Marsais. The STN was still selling it in the 1770s and 1780s. In comparing the texts, I have found a consistent pattern. *Thérèse philosophe* takes passages from many sections of the *Examen* and frequently modifies the phrasing to make it pithier and more irreligious, so the overall effect is quite different. See, for example, *Examen*, p. 141 and *Thérèse*, p. 112;

and the series of passages in *Examen,* pp. 24–27, and *Thérèse,* pp. 108–110. Of course, it is also possible that both works borrowed from a third text or a series of texts that circulated amongst the philosophical manuscripts.

43. *Examen de la religion,* p. 141; *Thérèse philosophe,* p. 112.
44. *Thérèse philosophe,* pp. 112–113 and 116.
45. *Ibid.,* pp. 85–86.
46. *Ibid.,* p. 94.
47. *Ibid.,* p. 175: "The first principle that one should follow to live happily in this world is to be a gentleman {*honnête homme*} and to observe the laws of society, which are like the ties that bind our mutual needs together."
48. *Ibid.,* p. 190.
49. On the need to rethink the problem of literacy and to revise old estimates of literacy rates upward, at least for urban France, see Daniel Roche, *Le Peuple de Paris. Essai sur la culture populaire au XVIIIe siècle* (Paris, 1981), chap. 7, and Roger Chartier, "Du Livre au lire," in Chartier, ed., *Pratiques de la lecture* (Paris, 1985).
50. We know very little about the readers of erotic books in eighteenth-century France. The correspondence of the STN indicates that they appealed to officers in garrison cities, but nothing more. Iconographic evidence suggests that they were also read for sexual stimulation by women. But do the pictures correspond to actual practice, or are they, too, the products of male fantasies? See Erich Schön, *Der Verlust der Sinnlichkeit oder die Verwandlungen des Lesers. Mentalitätswandel um 1800* (Stuttgart, 1987), pp. 91–93, and Goulemot, *Ces Livres qu'on ne lit que d'une main,* pp. 43–47.
51. See, for example, the discussion of pornography in Catharine A. MacKinnon, *Feminism Unmodified. Discourses on Life and Law* (Cambridge, Mass., 1987), part III.
52. *Thérèse philosophe,* p. 169: "Such is the effect of the sympathy of hearts: it seems that one thinks with the organ of the other."
53. These figures provide only a very rough idea of what was a very complex demographic pattern. See Jacques Dupâquier, et al., *Histoire de la population française* (Paris, 1988), II, especially chaps. 8 to 10.
54. If they ever came upon this argument, demographers would probably laugh it out of court. But they are still searching for an explanation of why the French adopted birth control on a massive scale and at an early date, thereby preventing their population from entering into a "transitional" stage (a low mortality rate and a high birth rate) and exploding, as it did in most European countries. Other erotic French books from this period also contain descrip-

tions of *coitus interruptus,* which in some cases almost read like an instruction manual. See, for example, *Le Triomphe des religieuses ou les nones babillardes* (1748), reprinted in *L'Enfer de la Bibliothèque Nationale,* V, 223–226. The diffusion of a best-seller like *Thérèse philosophe* may even have led indirectly to the spread of information about birth control among the illiterate.

55. *Thérèse philosophe,* p. 58. By contrast, Thérèse fights off a wealthy financier who attempts to rape her: p. 125.
56. *Ibid.,* p. 175.
57. *Ibid.,* p. 176.
58. See Steven Hause and Anne Kenney, *Women's Suffrage and Social Politics in the French Third Republic* (Princeton, 1984).

Chapter 4

1. This interpretation is based on the unprecedented outpouring of letters that Rousseau received from his readers after the publication of *La Nouvelle Héloïse* in 1762: see my *The Great Cat Massacre and Other Episodes in French Cultural History* (New York, 1984), chap. 6, and Claude Labrosse, *Lire au XVIIIe siècle. La Nouvelle Héloïse et ses lecteurs* (Lyon, 1985). The argument also rests on a reading of Rousseau's writings on culture, particularly his *Lettre à d'Alembert sur les spectacles.* For a fuller version of it, see Ernst Cassirer, Jean Starobinski, and Robert Darnton, *Drei Vorschläge Rousseau zu Lesen* (Frankfurt-am-Main), chap. 3, and Darnton, "The Literary Revolution of 1789," *Studies in Eighteenth-Century Culture,* vol. 21 (1991), 3–26.
2. The fullest account of Mercier's pre-revolutionary career is still Léon Béclard, *Mercier, sa vie, son oeuvre, son temps d'après des documents inédits. Avant la Révolution (1740–1789)* (Paris, 1903). On the publishing history of *L'An 2440,* see the excellent study by Everett C. Wilkie, Jr., "Mercier's *L'An 2440:* Its Publishing History During the Author's Lifetime," *Harvard Library Bulletin,* vol. 32 (1984), 5–31 and 348–400.
3. As Wilkie demonstrates in "Mercier's *L'An 2440,*" Mercier produced four main versions of the text: the first edition in one volume, 1771; a slightly revised edition, 1774; a much-expanded edition in three volumes, 1786; and a three-volume reprint with an expanded preface, Year VII (1799). I have studied and compared editions of 1771, 1775 (a reprint of the revised edition of 1774), 1786, and Year VII. For the sake of convenience, I will quote from the 1786 edition, which is available as a Slatkine reprint with a helpful preface by Raymond Trousson: *L'An deux mille quatre cent quarante suivi de L'Homme de fer* (Geneva, 1979),

cited henceforth as *L'An 2440*. But I will quote only passages that were taken over without change from the 1771 edition, which represents the basic text that reached most readers.

4. Among the most helpful works in the large literature on Utopianism are two that discuss *L'An 2440* at length: Bronislaw Baczko, *Lumières de l'utopie* (Paris, 1978), and Frank E. and Fritzie P. Manuel, *Utopian Thought in the Western World* (Cambridge, Mass., 1979).

5. *L'An 2440*, I, 17.

6. The quotations, in the order of their appearance, come from *L'An 2440*, III, 97; I, 133; and I, 273.

7. *Ibid.*, I, 51.

8. *Ibid.*, I, 190. Mercier's diatribe against the Physiocrats occurs in a gigantic footnote running from page 192 to 194.

9. Mercier, Preface to the edition of the Year VII (1799) in *Ibid.*, ii.

10. *Ibid.*, II, 110–112.

11. *Ibid.*, II, 115.

12. *Ibid.*, I, 43.

13. *Ibid.*, I, 129.

14. *Ibid.*, I, 29–30.

15. Mercier scattered his criticism of Louis XIV throughout the original text and concentrated them in a new chapter, "Louis Quatorze," in the edition of 1786. See especially *ibid.*, I, 254–259.

16. Mercier often expressed his admiration for Young and added an essay, "Eclipse de la lune," between chaps. 29 and 30 of *L'An 2440*, even though it had nothing to do with the narrative. It merely provided a dose of lugubrious sentimentality "in the taste of Young": *Ibid.*, I, 299.

17. *Ibid.*, II, 94–95. The text of this chapter, "Throne Room," is the same in all the editions, but Mercier added two long notes in the later editions, which made his debt to Montesquieu clear. I have a general impression that the edition of 1786, in contrast to that of 1771, shows a more thorough understanding of Montesquieu, and that by including so much new material it somewhat blunted the radical message of the first edition. But the message is essentially the same in all the versions of the book.

18. *Ibid.*, II, 105. This key chapter, "Form of Government," is the same in all the editions, except for one small but crucial change. In the edition of 1771, Mercier wrote, "The monarchy is no more." In the later editions, he changed this to, "Unlimited monarchy is no more." However, the Rousseauistic argument about the General Will and the essentially symbolic power of the king remained the same in all the editions. The later editions contain some new notes, but they do not increase the force of Mercier's

attack on despotism, which stands out clearly in both the text and the footnotes of the first edition.

19. *Ibid.,* II, 193–194. The text and the notes are the same in all the editions.

20. *Ibid.,* II, 107. This note exists in all the editions.

21. See, for example, *ibid.,* II, 120.

22. Preface to the edition of the Year VII (1799), in *L'An 2440,* p. i. On the problem of dating Mercier's composition of the text, see Wilkie, "Mercier's *L'An 2440,*" pp. 8–10.

23. *Ibid.,* I, 157.

24. *Ibid.,* I, 169. This and the following passages are the same in all the editions of the book.

25. *Ibid.,* I, 113.

26. *Ibid.,* II, 105.

27. *Ibid.,* II, 118.

28. *Ibid.,* pp. xxix–xxxi.

29. In developing this image, Mercier actually named the police inspector, Receveur, who was notorious for arresting authors and carrying them off to the Bastille: "I imagine *Receveur* arresting *Jeremiah* who would cry out in the streets, 'Woe to thee, Jerusalem.'" *Ibid.,* p. xl.

30. *Ibid.,* p. xxxvii.

31. *Ibid.,* p. xxxviii.

32. As an example of Mercier's many declarations on this subject, see his remarks on perpetual peace: "It is the printing press that produced this great revolution by enlightening mankind." *Ibid.,* I, 283. Of the many studies of the idea of progress, the work by John B. Bury still stands out: *The Idea of Progress: An Inquiry into Its Origin and Growth* (London, 1932).

33. *L'An 2440,* I, 67. The later editions do not include the reference to Corneille and Richelieu.

34. *Ibid.,* I, 37.

35. *Ibid.,* I, 60.

36. *Ibid.,* I, 60.

37. *Ibid.,* I, 66.

38. *Ibid.,* I, 65.

39. *Ibid.,* I, 65.

40. *Ibid.,* I, 175.

41. *Ibid.,* I, 167.

42. *Ibid.,* I, 157 and 164. See also the similar remarks in I, 147.

43. *Ibid.,* I, 61.

44. *Ibid.,* I, 283.

45. *Ibid.,* I, 31.

46. *Ibid.,* II, 192, and I, 203–204.

Chapter 5

1. Whether Bachaumont, who died in 1771, actually wrote any of the *Mémoires secrets pour servir à l'histoire de la république des lettres en France* (London, 1779–89), 36 vols., is not clear; but the basic study of him and his group is still Robert S. Tate, Jr., "Petit de Bachaumont: His Circle and the *Mémoires secrets*," in *Studies on Voltaire and the Eighteenth Century* (1968), vol. 65. See also the article on Mairobert by Tate in Jean Sgard, ed., *Dictionnaire des journalistes (1600–1789)*, pp. 250–253. On the vast subject of news and *nouvellistes,* the scholarship from the *belle-époque* is still the most useful. See especially Eugene Hatin, *Histoire politique et littéraire de la presse en France* (Paris, 1859–61), 8 vols., and Paul Estrée and Franz Funck-Brentano, *Les Nouvellistes* (Paris, 1906). The most recent synthesis is Claude Bellanger, et al., *Histoire générale de la presse française* (Paris, 1969), vol. I.

2. This list indicates roughly which *libelles* and *chroniques scandaleuses* were most in demand between 1769 and 1789, but it should not be read literally. The demand for some works, like *Mémoires de Mme la marquise de Pompadour* (1766), had probably peaked before the STN began doing business, while the demand for others, like *La Chronique scandaleuse* (1783) and *Vie privée, ou apologie du très sérénissime prince Mgr. le duc de Chartres* (1784), probably continued to grow after the STN had reduced its business in France.

3. Of course, there were earlier examples of this kind of writing, notably during the Fronde in 1648–49. For a discussion of the problem of continuity and change in *libelle* writing, see the next chapter.

4. *Anecdotes sur Mme la comtesse du Barry* (London, 1776), p. 19.

5. *Ibid.,* p. 24.

6. The metaphors of hunting and eating dominate our historian's account of this institution: see *ibid.,* pp. 48 and 57.

7. *Ibid.,* p. 57.

8. *Ibid.,* p. 31.

9. As an example of this general interpretation in English, see Alfred Cobban, *History of Modern France* (London, 1961), vol. I, and, in French, the more substantial and nuanced work by Michel Antoine, *Louis XV* (Paris, 1991).

10. *Anecdotes,* p. 34.

11. *Ibid.,* p. 96.

12. *Ibid.,* p. 269.

13. See J. F. Bosher, *French Finances, 1770–1795. From Business to Bureaucracy* (Cambridge, Engl., 1970).

14. An enormous proliferation of journals took place in the eighteenth century, and many of the French-language journals published outside of France covered French affairs in unprecedented detail. But they were vulnerable to censorship or to measures cutting off their distribution system within the kingdom. Even the best of them, *La Gazette de Leyde,* did not carry much information about Maupeou's battles with the parlements in 1771–74.

15. For example, he made a great deal of a song that was all the rage in Paris just before the collapse of the Choiseul government. To the provincial eye, it consisted of nothing but innocent banalities; but in fact, as the narrator's exegesis made clear, it provided a fiercely anti-Choiseuliste commentary on current events, "whose saltiness could only be appreciated by people in the known." *Anecdotes,* pp. 129–130.

16. In the eighteenth century, "la cour et la ville" was a standard way to describe distinct but interconnected milieux. The author made it clear that he envisaged separate information circuits by remarks such as the following: "While this hidden intrigue [an attempt to procure a new mistress for the king in 1772] occupied people in the court, an event in the city [a cousin of du Barry was implicated in the theft of a chicken] produced a great deal of gossip and laughter among the public." *Anecdotes,* pp. 244–245. See also the similar remarks on pp. 108 and 200.

17. *Ibid.,* p. 215. For further uses of the term *le public,* see pp. 72, 152, and 331.

18. I have not compared editions. The text I have studied, which carries the address "chez John Adamsohn," 1771, on its title page, is divided at page 198 into two parts, although the pagination is continuous and there is no apparent reason for a break at that point.

19. *Ibid.,* p. 147. The other anecdotes can be found on pp. 215 and 223.

20. *Ibid.,* p. 284.

21. *Ibid.,* p. 185.

22. *Ibid.,* p. 167.

23. This and the following quotations come from *ibid.,* pp. 71–77.

24. *Ibid.,* p. 87.

25. *Ibid.,* p. 215.

26. The quotations come from *ibid.,* pp. 203, 221, and 300 respectively. See also the similar remarks on pp. 131 and 203.

27. The first two references in the *Anecdotes* to the "manuscript journal" coincide exactly with entries in the *Mémoires secrets,* and a later one varies only slightly in its phrasing: see *Anecdotes,* pp. 71, 72, 203, and *Mémoires secrets,* entries for Oct. 15, 1768; Nov. 30, 1768, and Dec. 26, 1771. (Passages in the *Mémoires secrets* can be

located better by date than by pagination, owing to variations in the editions.) But seven other references do not have counterparts in the *Mémoires secrets*. They occur on pp. 81, 82, 83, 131, 215, 221, and 300 of the *Anecdotes*. Thus it seems likely that both works drew on the same general source of information, although it is impossible to determine what derived from what in the channels of underground journalism.

28. *Ibid.*, p. 82.
29. *Ibid.*, pp. 81–84.
30. *Ibid.*, pp. 75–76.
31. *Ibid.*, p. 160.
32. *Ibid.*, p. 159.
33. *Ibid.*, p. 160.
34. *Ibid.*, p. 76.
35. *Ibid.*, p. 76. I have adapted the text in this case to the question-answer format.
36. *Ibid.*, p. 76.
37. *Ibid.*, p. 325. For other examples of open, partisan declamation, see pp. 151 and 164.
38. *Ibid.*, p. 76.
39. *Ibid.*, p. 259.
40. *Ibid.*, p. 211.
41. *Ibid.*, p. 153.
42. *Remarques sur les Anecdotes de Madame la comtesse du Barry. Par Madame Sara G. . . .* (London, 1777), pp. 106–107.

Chapter 6

1. Chartier, *Les Origines culturelles de la Révolution française;* see especially pp. 25–35.
2. "Bürgerlich" also poses problems of translation, because *Bürger* means "citizen" as well as "bourgeois" in German. But Habermas's debt to an outmoded, Marxist social history is clear throughout his book. Although his argument begins with a general distinction between society and the state, it actually concerns three "spheres": the private sphere, the sphere of public authority, and between them the "authentic 'public sphere'": Jürgen Habermas, *The Structural Transformation of the Public Sphere. An Inquiry into a Category of Bourgeois Society* (Cambridge, Mass., 1989), trans. Thomas Burger, p. 30, and Habermas, *Strukturwandel der Öffentlichkeit. Untersuchungen zu einer Kategorie der bürgerlichen Gesellschaft* (Darmstadt, 1984; 1st edn. 1962), p. 45.
3. Chartier, *Origines culturelles*, pp. 110–111.
4. As examples of this extensive literature, see James Tully, ed.,

Meaning and Context. Quentin Skinner and His Critics (Princeton, 1988); J. G. A. Pocock, *Politics, Language, and Time. Essays on Political Thought and History* (Chicago, 1960); John Dunn, *The Political Thought of John Locke* (Cambridge, Engl., 1969); and Richard Tuck, *Natural Rights Theories: Their Origin and Development* (Cambridge, Engl., 1979).

5. See especially Michel Foucault, *L'Ordre du discours. Leçon inaugurale au Collège de France prononcée le 2 décembre 1970* (Paris, 1971).

6. François Furet and Mona Ozouf, eds., *Dictionnaire critique de la Révolution française* (Paris, 1988), p. 8.

7. Keith Baker, *Inventing the French Revolution. Essays on French Political Culture in the Eighteenth Century* (Cambridge, Engl., 1990), see especially pp. 301–305. I have discussed Baker's argument more extensively in "An Enlightened Revolution?", *The New York Review of Books,* Oct. 24, 1991, pp. 33–36.

8. Marcel Gauchet, "Droits de l'homme," in Furet and Ozouf, eds., *Dictionnaire critique,* quotations from pp. 685, 689, and 694. In developing his notion of a "Rousseauistic category" and a "Rousseauism of functional opportunity," Gauchet scornfully dismisses any consideration of the diffusion of the *Social Contract,* p. 690. For a fuller account of his argument, see Gauchet, *La Révolution des droits de l'homme* (Paris, 1988).

9. François Furet, *Penser la Révolution française* (Paris, 1978), pp. 41, 72–73, and 109.

10. François Furet and Denis Richet, *La Révolution: des Etats Généraux au 9 thermidor* (Paris, 1965).

11. Isser Woloch, "On the Latent Illiberalism of the French Revolution," *The American Historical Review,* vol. 95 (December 1990), 1467.

12. As examples of this sort of *histoire des mentalités* achieved without reference to discourse or semiotics, see Georges Lefebvre, *La Grande Peur de 1789* (Paris, 1932), and Richard Cobb, "The Revolutionary Mentality in France," in Cobb, *A Second Identity. Essays on France and French History* (Oxford, 1969), pp. 122–141.

13. Furet and Ozouf, eds., *Dictionnaire critique,* pp. 8–9 and 12.

14. See Keith Baker, *Inventing the French Revolution. Essays on French Political Culture in the Eighteenth Century* (Cambridge, Engl., 1990), Part II, and Baker's summary of his argument on pp. 24–27.

15. Keith Baker, "Public Opinion as Political Invention," in Baker, *Inventing the French Revolution,* pp. 167–199, and Mona Ozouf, "L'Opinion publique," in Keith Baker, ed., *The Political Culture of the Old Regime* (Oxford, 1987), pp. 419–434.

Chapter 7

1. This is Roger Chartier's formulation of the issue in *Les Origines culturelles de la Révolution française*, p. 86. In quoting it, I do not mean to imply that he takes a simplistic notion of ideology and revolution. On the contrary, I follow him in using the question to challenge a simple view of ideological causation.

2. I have discussed this model more fully in "What Is the History of Books?" in my *The Kiss of Lamourette. Reflections in Cultural History* (New York, 1990), pp. 107–135.

3. I have developed this argument in greater detail in *Edition et sédition*, chaps. 2–6, and *Gens de lettres, gens du livre*, chaps. 10–11.

4. Chartier, *Les Origines culturelles de la Révolution française*, chap. 4; "Intellectual History and the History of *Mentalités:* A Dual Re-evaluation," in Chartier, *Cultural History. Between Practices and Representations* (Cambridge, Engl., 1988), pp. 40–42, and "Du livre au lire," in Chartier, ed., *Pratiques de la lecture*, pp. 62–88.

5. Chartier, "Intellectual History," p. 42, and Michel de Certeau, *L'Invention du quotidien* (Paris, 1980), p. 286.

6. de Certeau, *L'Invention du quotidien*, pp. 279–296.

7. Richard Hoggart, *The Uses of Literacy* (London, 1960; 1st edn. 1957), see especially chaps. 2 and 4. Hoggart stresses the density and "all-pervading" character of an older, working-class culture in the face of the modern mass media (p. 19), whereas de Certeau emphasizes the individual's creativity as a "poacher" in making what he pleases from the media's products (de Certeau, *L'Invention du quotidien*, p. 292). But de Certeau also maintains that consumption does not mean becoming like the products one absorbs but rather making them one's own, i.e., appropriating them. This notion of appropriation has some affinity with Hoggart's insistence that working-class people integrate popular songs and literature into their own culture on their own terms and do not simply allow themselves to be manipulated by the media.

8. Carlo Ginzburg, *The Cheese and the Worms. The Cosmos of a Sixteenth-Century Miller* (Baltimore, 1980), and Robert Darnton, "Readers Respond to Rousseau: the Fabrication of Romantic Sensibility," in *The Great Cat Massacre*, chap. 6. See also Claude Labrosse, *Lire au XVIIIe siècle. La Nouvelle Héloïse et ses lecteurs* (Lyon, 1985); Cathy Davidson, *Revolution and the Word. The Rise of the Novel in America* (New York and Oxford, 1986); Eric Schön, *Der Verlust der Sinnlichkeit oder die Verwandlungen des Lesers. Mentalitätswandel um 1800* (Stuttgart, 1987); and Brigitte Schlieben-Lange, ed., *Lesen-historisch* in *Lili: Zeitschrift für Literaturwissenschaft und Linguistik*, vol. 15, no. 57 / 58 (1985).

9. For a fuller account of some of these arguments, see Nelson Goodman, *Ways of Worldmaking* (Indianapolis, 1978); Erving Goffman, *Frame Analysis. An Essay on the Organization of Experience* (Boston, 1986); and D. F. McKenzie, *Bibliography and the Sociology of Texts* (London, 1986).

10. On the practice of power and the king's secret, see Michel Antoine, *Le Conseil du roi sous le règne de Louis XV* (Geneva, 1970), especially pp. 618–620. Politics and public opinion outside Versailles has been studied most thoroughly by an older school of historians whose work now seems to be ignored, notably Jules Flammermont, Marcel Marion, Félix Rocquain, Eugène Hatin, and Frantz Funck-Brentano. As examples of the best in more recent scholarship, see Dale Van Kley, *The Damiens Affair and the Unraveling of the Ancien Regime, 1750–1770* (Princeton, 1984), and Arlette Farge, *Dire et mal dire. L'opinion publique au XVIIIe siècle* (Paris, 1992).

11. Daniel Roche, "Les Primitifs du rousseauisme. Une analyse sociologique et quantitative de la correspondance de J.-J. Rousseau," *Annales. Economies, sociétés, civilisations* (1971), 151–172; Claude Labrosse, *Lire au XVIIIe siècle;* Darnton, "Readers Respond to Rousseau"; and Agnes Marcetteau-Paul and Dominique Varry, "Les Bibliothèques de quelques acteurs de la Révolution," in Frédéric Barbier, Claude Jolly, and Sabine Juratic, eds., *Mélanges de la Bibliothèque de la Sorbonne,* vol. 9 (1989), 189–207. In their study of library inventories, Marcetteau-Paul and Varry are careful to avoid sweeping conclusions because they could identify only a small proportion of the books in most of the libraries and they do not equate book ownership with reading. Also, they found inventories of only five persons identified with the Counter-Revolution. Those, and the inventories of moderates who sat in the Constituent Assembly, show a fairly strong percentage of religious works—12 percent in each case—as opposed to the inventories of deputies to the Convention, where only 2 percent of the books concerned religion. When studied in detail, the libraries may look more varied than when compared according to general rubrics such as history and belles-lettres. Thus as one might expect, Lafayette's library contained a great many works about America, but it also had an unusually large proportion—17 percent—of religious works.

12. The manuscript "Chansonnier Maurepas" runs to forty-four volumes: Bibliothèque Nationale, Ms. fr. 12616–12659.

13. On the notion of a "political class," see Pierre Goubert, *L'Ancien Régime,* vol. II: *Les Pouvoirs* (Paris, 1973), pp. 49–55.

14. Daniel Roche, *Le Siècle des Lumières en province. Académies et académiciens provinciaux, 1680–1789* (Paris and The Hague, 1978), 2

vols., and Roche, *Les Républicains des lettres. Gens de culture et Lumières au XVIIIe siècle,* especially chap. 3, "Les Lectures de la noblesse dans la France du XVIIIe siècle"; Guy Chaussinand-Nogaret, *La Noblesse au XVIIIe siècle, de la féodalite aux Lumières* (Paris, 1976); Darnton, *The Business of Enlightenment,* chap. 6; and Darnton, "The Literary Revolution of 1789," *Studies in Eighteenth-Century Culture,* 3–26.

15. Alexis de Tocqueville, *The Old Regime and the French Revolution* (Garden City, N.Y., 1955), pp. 80–81.

16. In drafting the legislation on August 5 to 11, the revolutionaries seemed to take back many of the concessions they made at the delirious session of August 4, but I do not hold with those who deny any substance to the "abolition of feudalism" in August 1789. See the documents published in J. M. Roberts, ed., *French Revolution Documents* (Oxford, 1966), pp. 135–155.

Chapter 8

1. Quoted in Claude Bellanger, Jacques Godechot, Pierre Guiral, and Fernand Terrou, eds., *Histoire générale de la presse française* (Paris, 1969), I, 65. On the etymology of *libelle,* see Emil Littré, *Dictionnaire de la langue française* (Paris, 1957) and *Le Grand Robert de la langue française* (Paris, 1986).

2. *Mémoires-Journaux de Pierre de l'Estoile* (Paris, 1888), III, 279, quoted in Denis Pallier, *Recherches sur l'imprimerie à Paris pendant la Ligue (1585–1594)* (Geneva, 1975), p. 56.

3. Quoted in Jeffrey K. Sawyer, *Printed Poison. Pamphlet Propaganda, Faction Politics, and the Public Sphere in Early Seventeenth-Century France* (Berkeley, 1990), p. 16.

4. Quoted in Hubert Carrier, *La Presse de la Fronde (1648–1653): Les Mazarinades. La Conquête de l'opinion* (Geneva, 1989), I, 56.

5. *Ibid.,* pp. 456–457.

6. Marie-Noële Grand-Mesnil, *Mazarin, la Fronde et la presse 1647–1649* (Paris, 1967), pp. 239–252.

7. Henri-Jean Martin, *Livre, pouvoirs et société à Paris au XVIIe siècle (1598–1701)* (Geneva, 1969), II, 678–772 and 884–900, and Bellanger, et al., *Histoire générale de la presse française,* I, 118–119.

8. *Mémoires-journaux de Pierre de l'Estoile,* III, 279.

9. Niccolò Machiavelli, *The Prince* (Mentor Classic, New York, 1952), chap. 19, p. 95. See also the famous remarks on reputation in chap. 15. Of course, Machiavelli addressed *The Prince* to princes, notably Lorenzo de' Medici and Cesare Borgia. But he also applied the notion of reputation—"name and fame," "public voice and fame," "good reputation"—to his analysis of republics.

See Machiavelli, *The Discourses* (Modern Library College Edition, New York, 1950), book III, chap. 34, pp. 509–510.

10. Richelieu, *Testament politique,* quoted in Sawyer, *Political Poison,* p. 16.

11. Machiavelli, *The Prince,* chap. 19, pp. 96–97. Although Machiavelli did not define his notion of "the people," it contained a plebeian element; but he spoke disparagingly of "the populace," *ibid.,* p. 97. The appeal to "public opinion" also had an international dimension: see J. H. Elliott, *Richelieu and Olivares* (Cambridge, Engl., 1984), pp. 128–129, and Peter Burke, *The Fabrication of Louis XIV* (New Haven, 1992), pp. 152–153. As an example of the dramaturgical view of Renaissance politics, see Steven Mullaney, *The Place of the Stage. License, Play, and Power in Renaissance England* (Chicago, 1988).

12. Amongst the many books on these subjects, I have especially relied on Jean-Pierre Seguin, *Nouvelles à sensation. Canards du XIXe siècle* (Paris, 1959); Robert Mandrou, *De la Culture populaire aux 17e et 18e siècles. La Bibliothèque bleue de Troyes* (Paris, 1964); Geneviève Bollème, *La Bibliothèque bleue. Littérature populaire en France du XVIIe au XIXe siècle* (Paris, 1971); Alain Monestier, *Le Fait divers* (Paris, 1982), a catalogue for an exhibition at the Musée national des arts et traditions populaires; and Roger Chartier, *Lectures et lecteurs dans la France d'Ancien Régime.*

13. See Mikhail Bakhtin, *Rabelais and His World* (Cambridge, Mass., 1968); Marc Soriano, *Les Contes de Perrault: Culture savante et traditions populaires* (Paris, 1968); Peter Burke, *Popular Culture in Early Modern Europe* (London and New York, 1978); Natalie Davis, *Society and Culture in Early Modern France* (Stanford, 1975); and Roger Chartier, ed., *Les Usages de l'imprimé* (Paris, 1987).

14. It is almost impossible to form an accurate view of the incidence of pamphlet literature throughout this period. The notion of a pamphlet itself is notoriously unclear, shading off into that of a book at one extreme and a broadside on the other. Many pamphlets did not include any personal slander, so the proportion of *libelles* within the general body of ephemeral literature cannot be determined. And one can produce only vague estimates of that literature by compiling statistics from pamphlets preserved in research libraries. As their name implies, *occasionnels, feuilles volantes, pièces fugitives* were not intended to survive for centuries, and the ones that have survived may, for that very reason, be the ones that were read the least. The following discussion therefore makes no claims to rigor, and it relies on monographic studies of particular periods, especially Denis Pallier, *Recherches sur l'imprimerie à Paris pendant la Ligue (1585–1594)* (Paris, 1975); Jeffrey

K. Sawyer, *Printed Poison. Pamphlet Propaganda, Faction Politics, and the Public Sphere in Early Seventeenth-Century France;* Hubert Carrier, *La Presse de la Fronde (1648–1653): Les Mazarinades* (Geneva, 1989–91), 2 vols.; P. J. W. Van Malssen, *Louis XIV d'après les pamphlets répandus en Hollande* (Amsterdam, 1936); and Joseph Klaits, *Printed Propaganda Under Louis XIV. Absolute Monarchy and Public Opinion* (Princeton, 1976). The best estimates of pamphlet production in the seventeenth century can be found in Hélène Duccini, "Regard sur la littérature pamphlétaire en France au XVIIe siècle," *Revue historique,* CCLIX (1978), 313–340.

15. See, for example, Gilbert Robin, *L'Enigme sexuelle d'Henri III* (Paris, 1964), and, for a more balanced view, Philippe Erlanger, *Henri III* (Paris, 1948), pp. 188–189.

16. Sawyer, *Printed Poison,* p. 40.

17. Paul Scarron, *La Mazarinade,* in Scarron, *Oeuvres* (Geneva, 1970, reprint of 1786 edn), I, 295.

18. Hubert Carrier, ed., *La Fronde. Contestation démocratique et misère paysanne: 52 mazarinades* (Paris, 1982), I, 11–12. See also Carrier's impressive general study, which makes more moderate claims about the extremism of the *mazarinades* but describes two of them as "the only ones that were really revolutionary in the strict sense of the word": *La Presse de la Fronde,* I, 265. The earlier and less thorough monograph by Marie-Noële Grand-Mesnil, *Mazarin, la Fronde et la presse 1647–49,* (Paris, 1967), treats the *mazarinades* as elements in the power struggle among "les grands" rather than as revolutionary manifestoes, but it does not cover the more radical pamphlets of 1652.

19. *Le Guide au chemin de la liberté,* p. 23, reprinted in Carrier, *La Fronde,* I, pamphlet no. 27. For Christian Jouhaud's interpretation, which seems convincing to me, see his *Mazarinades: la Fronde des mots* (Paris, 1985).

20. In arguing with Jouhaud against Carrier on the radicalism of the late *mazarinades,* I do not mean to disparage the superb research of Carrier, which does justice to the complex political context of the pamphleteering. It may be that in his forthcoming volume on the political ideas of the *mazarinades,* Carrier will demonstrate the existence of a more searching and sustained critique of the monarchy than he was able to demonstrate in his first two volumes. For examples of recent tendencies in the historiography of the Fronde, see Roger Duchêne and Pierre Ronzeaud, eds., *La Fronde en questions. Actes du dix-huitième colloque du centre méridional de rencontres sur le XVIIème siècle* (Aix-en-Provence, 1989).

21. For a good synthesis of the enormous literature on Louis XIV's cultural policies, see Peter Burke, *The Fabrication of Louis XIV*

(New Haven, 1992). The best overview of the history of French journalism is still Bellanger, et al., *Histoire générale de la presse française;* but the current work of Jean Sgard, Pierre Rétat, François Moureau, Jeremy Popkin, Jack Censer, and others is transforming the subject. See especially Jean Sgard, ed., *Dictionnaire des journaux 1600–1789* (Paris and Oxford, 1991), 2 vols. Estimates on literacy rates, notoriously unsure for the Old Regime, are now being revised upward, at least for urban France: see Furet and Ozouf, *Reading and Writing. Literacy in France from Calvin to Jules Ferry,* and Roche, *Le Peuple de Paris,* chap. 7.

22. Aside from the work of Van Malssen, Klaits, and Duccini cited above, see C. Ringhoffer, *La Littérature de libelles au début de la Guerre de succession d'Espagne* (Paris, 1881).

23. Anne Sauvy, *Livres saisis à Paris entre 1678 et 1701* (The Hague, 1972), pp. 11–13.

24. For a convenient edition of Bussy-Rabutin's novellas and their best-known sequels, see *Histoire amoureuse des Gaules suivie de La France galante: romans satiriques du XVIIe siècle attribués au comte de Bussy* (Paris, 1930), 2 vols., which has an introduction by Georges Mongrédien. Most of the sequels came out separately during the 1680s and 1690s. They were not published together as *La France galante*—a collection of seventeen novellas, none of them by Bussy-Rabutin—until 1737. See Léonce Janmart de Brouillant, "Description raisonnée de l'édition originale et des réimpressions de l'*Histoire amoureuse des Gaules,*" *Bulletin du bibliophile* (1887), 555–571, and the catalogue of the Bibliothèque Nationale.

25. Henri-Jean Martin, et al., *Livres et lectures à Grenoble. Les Registres du libraire Nicolas (1645–1668)* (Geneva, 1977), 2 vols. Nicolas's accounts provide some rare information on the sale of printed works, including *mazarinades,* in the provinces. Most interpretations of book distribution involve inferences, and a good deal of guesswork, based on the number of copies that have survived in major research libraries. The best study of book diffusion in the seventeenth century is Henri-Jean Martin, *Livre, pouvoirs et société.*

26. I offer this argument tentatively, because the concept of despotism has not received adequate attention from intellectual historians, and also because there is a good deal of terminological slippage in conventional histories of political thought such as George Sabine, *A History of Political Theory* (New York, 1958). "Despot" and "despotic" were common terms before the eighteenth century, but not, I believe, "despotism." Hence a typical sentence in one of the most radical *mazarinades, La Mercuriale* of 1652: "If a sovereign exercises a despotic empire over his subjects, he is no longer a king but a tyrant." Hubert Carrier, *La*

Fronde, pamphlet 26, I, 8. As a point of departure in the study of this subject, I have taken Robert Shackleton, *Montesquieu. A Critical Biography* (Oxford, 1961), chap. 12, and Melvin Richter, "Despotism," in *Dictionary of the History of Ideas* (New York, 1973), II, 1–18.

27. Paul Hazard, *La Crise de la conscience européenne* (Paris, 1935), 2 vols. For a more recent study of this theme, see Lionel Rothkrug, *Opposition to Louis XIV. The Political Origins of the French Enlightenment* (Princeton, 1965).

Chapter 9

1. As examples of programmatic essays, see Henri-Jean Martin, "Pour une histoire de la lecture," in Martin, *Le Livre français sous l'Ancien Régime* (Paris, 1987); Roger Chartier, "Du Livre au lire: les pratiques citadines de l'imprimé, 1660–1780," in Chartier, ed., *Lectures et lecteurs dans la France d'Ancien Régime;* and Robert Darnton, "First Steps Toward a History of Reading," in *The Kiss of Lamourette.*

2. The main arguments for the "reading revolution" were developed by Rolf Engelsing, especially his "Die Perioden der Lesergeschichte in der Neuzeit. Das statistische Ausmass und die soziokulturelle Bedeutung der Lektüre," *Archiv für Geschichte des Buchwesens,* X (1970), 945–1002, and *Der Bürger als Leser. Lesergeschichte in Deutschland 1500–1800* (Stuttgart, 1974). For contrasting views, see Rudolf Schenda, *Volk ohne Buch. Studien zur Sozialgeschichte der populären Lesestoffe 1770–1910* (Frankfurt-am-Main, 1970), and Erich Schön, *Der Verlust der Sinnlichkeit oder Die Verwandlung des Lesers. Mentalitätswandel um 1800,* especially pp. 298–300. The best and most recent survey of the history of books in Germany treats the notion of a "reading revolution" very skeptically: Reinhard Wittmann, *Geschichte des deutschen Buchhandels. Ein Überblick,* chap. 6. A fairly recent account of the "Werther fever" is Georg Jäger, "Die Wertherwirkung. Ein Rezeptionsästhetischer Modelfall," in Walter Müller-Seidel, ed., *Historizität in Sprach-und Literaturwissenschaft* (Munich, 1974), pp. 389–409.

3. Nicolas-Edmé Restif de la Bretonne, *La Vie de mon père* (Ottawa, 1949; 1st edn., 1779), pp. 216–217.

4. François Furet, "La 'librairie' du royaume de France au 18e siècle," in Furet, et al., *Livre et société dans la France du XVIIIe siècle* (Paris, 1965), and Michel Marion, *Recherches sur les bibliothèques privées à Paris au milieu du XVIIIe siècle (1750–1759)* (Paris, 1978).

5. The best overview of these questions is Chartier and Martin, eds.,

Histoire de l'édition française, vol. II: *Le Livre triomphant 1660–1830.*

6. Chartier, *Les Origines culturelles de la Révolution française,* pp. 103–115.

7. Maurice Tourneux, ed., *Correspondance littéraire, philosophique et critique par Grimm, Diderot, Raynal, Meister, etc.* (Paris, 1877–1882), 16 vols. In praising *Le Christianisme dévoilé,* the *Correspondance littéraire* claimed that it had an energizing, liberating effect on the reader: "It sweeps one up. . . . One does not learn anything new from it, yet one feels involved, engaged" (V, 368). It condemned *Thérèse philosophe* as a work "without taste, without decency, without spice, without logic, without style" (I, 256).

8. *Correspondance littéraire,* XII, 482.

9. *Ibid.,* XI, 399.

10. *Ibid.,* XII, 339–340.

11. Barre to STN, Sept. 15, 1781.

12. Barre to STN, Aug. 23, 1782.

13. Godeffroy to STN, June 10, 1771; May 5, 1772; and Feb. 10, 1776.

14. P.-J. Duplain to STN, Oct. 11, 1772.

15. Le Lièvre to STN, Jan. 3, 1777.

16. Malherbe to STN, Sept. 13, 1775.

17. Petit to STN, August 31, 1783; Waroquier to STN, Jan. 7, 1778; Carez to STN, Feb. 23, 1783.

18. A rare exception was Malherbe's comment that some customers objected that the theological articles of the *Encyclopédie* were written "too much in the taste of the Sorbonne, no doubt in order to favor its circulation in France; but those obstacles to the freedom of thought do not please all the readers": Malherbe to STN, Sept. 14, 1778.

19. Quoted in Jean-Marie Goulemot, *Ces Livres qu'on ne lit que d'une main. Lecture et lecteurs de livres pornographiques au XVIIIe siècle* (Aix-en-Provence, 1991), p. 9. This monograph offers an incisive analysis of how erotic texts orient readers.

20. "Projet pour la police de la librairie de Normandie donné par M. Rodolphe, subdélégué de M. l'intendant à Caen," Bibliothèque Nationale, ms. fr. 22123, item 33.

21. Labadie, "Projet d'un mémoire sur la librairie," *ibid.,* item 21.

22. "Mémoire sur le corps des libraires imprimeurs," 1766, unsigned: *ibid.,* item 19.

23. "Mémoire sur la librairie de France fait par le sieur Guy pendant qu'il était à la Bastille," Feb. 8, 1767: *ibid.,* item 22.

24. On the character of Lenoir's manuscript memoirs, see Georges Lefebvre, "Les Papiers de Lenoir," *Annales historiques de la Révolu-*

tion Française IV (1927), 300, and Robert Darnton, "The Memoirs of Lenoir, Lieutenant de Police of Paris, 1774–1785," *English Historical Review,* LXXXV (1970), 532–559.

25. Papers of Lenoir, Bibliothèque municipale d'Orléans, ms. 1422, "Titre sixième: De l'administration de l'ancienne police concernant les libelles, les mauvaises satires et chansons, leurs auteurs coupables, délinquants, complices ou adhérents."

26. *Ibid.*

27. Lenoir Papers, ms 1423, "Résidus."

28. Lenoir Papers, ms. 1422, "Sûreté."

29. Lenoir Papers, ms 1423, untitled note.

30. Vergennes to comte d'Adhémar, May 21, 1783, Ministère des Affaires Etrangères, Correspondance politique, Angleterre, ms 542.

31. Bibliothèque de l'Arsenal, ms 12517, ff. 73–78.

32. This is the position Roger Chartier seems to attribute to those who would argue that forbidden books had a strong effect on the reading public: Chartier, *Les Origines culturelles de la Révolution française,* pp. 104 and 109.

33. Mercier, *Tableau de Paris* (Amsterdam, 1783), VII, 23 and 25. Chartier cites this passage in order to argue that *libelles* had little effect on readers: *Les Origines culturelles de la Révolution française,* pp. 103–104.

34. Mercier, *Tableau de Paris,* VI, 79.

35. *Ibid.,* VI, 268.

36. *Ibid.,* VI, 269.

37. *Ibid.,* I, 176.

38. Jean François de La Harpe, *Correspondance littéraire adressée à son Altesse Impériale Mgr. le Grand-Duc, aujourd'hui Empereur de Russie, et à M. le Comte André Schowalow, Chamberlain de l'Impératrice Cathérine II, depuis 1774 jusqu'à 1789,* 6 vols. (Paris, 1804–1807), III, 202 and 251.

39. *Mémoires secrets pour servir à l'histoire de la République des lettres en France, depuis 1762 jusqu'à nos jours,* attributed to Louis Petit de Bachaumont and others, 36 vols. (London, 1777–89), entries for Aug. 1, 1781; April 20, 1782; and April 23, 1784.

40. Lenoir papers, ms. 1423, "Extraits de divers rapports secrets faits à la police de Paris dans les années 1781 et suivantes, jusques et compris 1785, concernant des personnes de tout état et condition [ayant] donné dans la Révolution."

41. *Tableau de Paris,* IV, 279. The quotation from the review is taken from Mercier's own reprint of it.

42. Throughout the *Tableau de Paris* and in his other works, notably *De la Littérature et des littéraires* and *Mon Bonnet de nuit,* Mercier

Index

Page numbers in *italics* refer to illustrations and charts.